Also by the authors
The Rockefellers: An American Dynasty
The Kennedys: An American Drama
The Fords: An American Epic
The Roosevelts: An American Saga

Peter Collier
David Horowitz

DESTRUCTIVE GENERATION

Second Thoughts About the Sixties

FREE PRESS PAPERBACKS
Published by Simon & Schuster

FREE PRESS PAPERBACKS
A Division of Simon & Schuster Inc.
1230 Avenue of the Americas
New York, NY 10020

First Free Press Paperback Edition 1996
Published by arrangement with David Horowitz and Peter Collier, Inc.

FREE PRESS PAPERBACK and colophon are trademarks
of Simon & Schuster Inc.

Designed by Oonagh O'Toole/Levavi & Levavi

Manufactured in the United States of America

10   9   8   7   6   5   4

Library of Congress Cataloging in Publication Data
Collier, Peter.
    Destructive generation: second thoughts about the sixties/Peter Collier,
David Horowitz.
    p.   cm.
    1. United States—Social conditions—1960–1980.   2. Radicalism—
United States—History—20th century.   3. Subculture.
I. Horowitz, David, date.   II. Title.
HN59.C63   1996
306'.0973'09046—dc20   90-30531
                                                                        CIP

ISBN 0-684-82641-0

Some chapters have appeared in different form in California Magazine,
Commentary, New West, Playboy, The Public Interest, and Rolling Stone.

*"We shall proclaim destruction—why? why?—
well, because the idea is so fascinating! But—
we must get a little exercise. We'll have a few
fires—we'll spread a few legends. . . . And the
whole earth will resound with the cry: 'A new
and righteous law is coming.' "*

—Dostoevsky, The Devils

Contents

Preface

A while back, we were on a radio talk show about former Sixties radicals. At one point, the host asked us what we thought was the "summary moment" of the decade. The question begged a certain kind of answer: Selma, the Free Speech Movement, the March on the Pentagon, Chicago. But we had discussed the issue before and agreed that the interesting truths about that era were to be found in the small moments rather than in the grand ones. We told the interviewer about one such moment that took place in the summer of 1969.

It was that magic instant when the auguries all seemed to point toward revolution. Tom Hayden, a leading Movement figure facing conspiracy charges in Chicago, was calling for the creation of "liberated zones" in American cities. Weatherman, the faction that had seized control of the Students for a Democratic Society, was planning to begin "guerrilla warfare" before the year was out. But most radicals had fixed their attention on the Black Panther Party, which Hayden had called "America's Vietcong."

Others were talking, the Panthers were doing. Their membership had been involved in shootouts with the police which were widely regarded by the radical community as dress rehearsals for the coming Armageddon. Because the Party leadership had been decimated (Huey Newton was in jail for killing a policeman, Eldridge Cleaver in exile, and Bobby Seale under indictment), "Field Marshal" David Hilliard had taken charge of the effort to keep the Party together and build support among whites. Learning that the celebrated French writer Jean Genet was infatuated with the Panthers, Hillard convinced him to come to the Bay Area to speak in behalf of the Party.

One of the stops was an appearance at Stanford University sponsored by the French Department, whose higher-ups had convinced eminent historian Gordon Wright to host a cocktail party before the speech. The Panthers arrived early in the afternoon in their uniforms of black leather jackets and sunglasses, looking like some lost Nazi legion whose skin color had changed during their diaspora. The small Frenchman with bad teeth and shabby clothes spoke through a young woman translator on loan from *Ramparts* magazine. He praised the Panther's *authenticity* (a characteristic he said he also admired in the Marquis de Sade, whom he called "the greatest revolutionary of all, greater even than Marx"). The Panthers milled around in sullen incomprehension as he talked. Discovering that Wright's son, an Army draftee, had brought a black Army friend home with him on leave, Panther Elmer "Geronimo" Pratt confronted the young man in the kitchen, spitting in his face and calling him an "Uncle Tom" and "enemy of the people." When Geronimo reappeared in the living room, the white guests pretended not to notice.

Not long after the cocktail party began, an unexpected guest dropped in. It was Ken Kesey. He had been on the fringes of the Stanford scene since getting his start as a novelist in one of Wallace Stegner's creative writing seminars. Oblivious to the Panthers, Kesey, his eyes cloudy with drugs and an out-of-plumb smile on his face, said that he had come because he had heard that a great French writer was there; since he was a great writer too it seemed a good thing that they should meet.

The guests sensed that a portentous moment was approaching as Sartre's St. Genet, *deracine* homosexual outlaw, and Tom Wolfe's St. Kesey, picaresque hero of the acid test, shook hands. In what seemed an act of semiotics, Kesey flashed a smile which showed that one of his front teeth had a cap in the form of an American flag. Genet, self-conscious because of his own chipped and discolored teeth, was delighted by the desecration and laughed out loud. Kesey pointed down at his feet. "I'm wearing green socks," he said with a beatific look on his face. Genet frowned uncomprehendingly as Kesey kept on talking: "Green socks. Can you dig it? Green socks. They're heavy, man, very heavy." Trying to keep up, the young woman translator rendered the remarks with awkward literalness: "*Les chausettes vertes, elles sont très, très lourdes.*" Genet looked down at Kesey's feet with the beginnings of sympathy. But before he could commiserate with him over the fact that he had somehow been condemned to wear heavy green objects around his ankles, Kesey's attention had lurched off in another direction. Pointing at the Black Panthers, he said to Genet: "You know what? I feel like playing basketball. There's nothing better than playing basketball with Negroes. I could go for a little one-on-one with some of these Negroes right now."

So taken aback by the boyish innocence of Kesey's manner that they momentarily failed to assess the implications of the words, the Panthers stared at him. Then one of them moved forward threateningly. David Hilliard stopped him: "Stay cool, man. This motherfucker is crazy." He repeated the words to everyone else in a louder voice: "This motherfucker is crazy and we're getting the fuck out of here."

The Panthers left, pulling Genet along with them. The diminutive Frenchman turned and glanced at Kesey, shrugging slightly as if to indicate that left to his own devices he would just as soon stay with him and exchange bizarre comments through a translator. Kesey watched him go. "Wonder what's wrong with those Negroes?" he asked, as the entourage moved away. "Don't they like basketball? I thought Negroes *loved* basketball."

In another era this would have been seen simply as an odd moment—two men from different worlds trying to communicate across a vast cultural divide and winding up in a fatuous contretemps. But this brief encounter, widely discussed in Bay Area Movement circles, was regarded as an "epiphany." Self-identified radicals like ourselves were fond of this word during the Sixties because it tended to elevate life's commonplaces and to infuse a sense of portent into situations whose *heaviness*, like that of Ken Kesey's socks, was not otherwise discernible to the inquiring eye.

Epiphanies: they made the world worthy of us. We searched for them like stargazers. This was part of the decade's transcendental conviction that there was something apocalyptic lurking behind the veil of the ordinary, and that just a little more pressure was needed to pierce the last remaining membrane—of civility, bourgeois consciousness, corporate liberalism, sexual uptightness, or whatever else prevented us all from breaking through to the other side.

From its earliest battle cry—"You can't trust anyone over thirty"—until the end of its brief strut on the stage of national attention, the Sixties generation saw itself as a scouting party for a new world. The "cultural revolution" it was staging would free inmates from the prison of linear thought. It was the social horticulturalist whose "greening of America" would allow the post-industrialist age finally to break through the crust of the Puritan past. It was the avenging angel that would destroy the evil empire of "Amerika" and free the captive peoples of the world.

It is hard to believe in epiphanies now, and it is hard not to wince at these homemade hankerings for Armageddon. Yet while the Sixties, that age of wonders, is over in fact, it is still with us in spirit. Nostalgia artists have made it into a holograph that creates beguiling images of the last good time—a prelapsarian age of good sex, good drugs, and good vibes. For unreconstructed leftists, the Sixties is not just an era of good fun but of good politics too—a time of monumental idealism populated by individuals who wanted nothing more than to give peace a chance; a time of commitment and action when dewy-eyed young people in the throes of a moral passion unknown in our own selfish age sought only to remake the world.

There is truth in the nostalgia. It is the *memory* of the era that is false. The vision we see when we look into the glass of Sixties narcissism is distorted. It may have been the best of times, but it was the worst of times as well. And by this we do not simply mean to add snapshots of the race riots at home and war in Vietnam to the sentimental collage of people being free. It was a time when innocence quickly became cynical, when American mischief fermented into American mayhem. It was a time when a gang of ghetto thugs like the Black Panthers might be anointed as political visionaries, when Merry Pranksters of all stripes could credibly set up shop as social evangelists spreading a chemical gospel.

The Sixties might have been a time of tantalizing glimpses of the New Jerusalem. But it was also a time when the "System"—that collection of values that provide guidelines for societies as well as individuals—was assaulted and mauled. As one center of authority after another was discredited under the New Left offensive, we radicals claimed that we murdered to create. But while we wanted a revolution, we didn't have a plan. The decade ended with a big bang that made society into a collection of splinter groups, special interest organizations and newly minted "minorities," whose only common belief was that America was guilty and untrustworthy. This is perhaps the enduring legacy of the Sixties. The political philosopher Michael Walzer expressed this adversarial sensibility when he confessed, in a recent article in *The New Republic,* "It is still true that only when I go to Washington to demonstrate do I feel at home there."

The Sixties are still with us, therefore, as a nostalgic artifact that measures our more somber world and finds it wanting, and also as a goad to radical revival. It has become the decade that would not die, the decade whose long half-life continues to contaminate our own. The Sixties are the green socks around our ankles: heavy, man, very heavy.

This book is about the Sixties and also about that phenomenon—there's really no name for it—that might be termed the Sixties-within-the-Eighties. It is also about the two of us and our understanding of the weight of Kierkegaard's observation that life may be lived forward but can only be understood backward.

By the mid-Seventies, our own path had begun to diverge from the one taken by other New Leftists who wanted to maintain the struggle and keep the faith. For both of us the withdrawal from radicalism involved an interplay between the personal and political which we have tried to describe in detail in the explicitly autobiographical part of this book. Broadly speaking, however, if there was one event that triggered our reevaluations (and those of others who began to have second thoughts about the Leftism of the Sixties), it was the fate of Vietnam. There was no "new morning" as radicals had predicted, no peasant utopia. Instead, there was a bloodbath greater than the one we set out to oppose and a government worse than the one we had wanted to replace.

Coming out of Southeast Asia in bits and pieces (the flow of information impeded by the Left itself), these facts slowed our forward political motion rather than throwing it immediately into reverse. That was accomplished a few years later when the Soviet Union invaded Afghanistan and the reformed Left reacted not by denouncing the genocide but by denouncing tenuous U.S. efforts to impose sanctions on the U.S.S.R. and to help the mujahideen as the beginning of a "new cold war."

By the early Eighties, we felt it was time to try for an honest inventory of our generation's impact. Some of the accomplishments were undeniably positive. There *was* an expansion of consciousness, of social space, of tolerance, of prospects for individual fulfillment. But there was a dark side too. In the inchoate attack against authority, we had weakened our culture's immune system, making it vulnerable to opportunistic diseases. The origins of metaphorical epidemics of crime and drugs could be traced to the Sixties, as could literal ones such as AIDS.

As we began to write episodically about some of the people we had known and events we had experienced, we encountered considerable resistance from our former comrades. They made it clear that for them there were two categories of truth —the "progressive" truths which aided the cause, and subversive truths which were best left unsaid. We watched them pick up the mothballed banners once again and revive the old slogans, these middle-aged activists with gray sideburns and sagging bellies now agitating for a new anti-Americanism despite the change in what we had once called the "objective conditions" of global power. And we began to realize that one of the strongest holds the Sixties had on our generation was its promise of eternal youth, a state of being that would never require a balance sheet of one's prior acts, let alone a profit-and-loss statement. It was as Lionel Trilling had written in his classic novel of ideas *The Middle of the Journey:* "To live the life of promises was to remain children."

The contents of this book, then, mirror our attempt to understand the movement of which we were a part, to understand the lost boys and girls of the Sixties who never grew up, and to understand ourselves as well. Our approach utilizes memoir, documentary reconstruction, commentary, adumbration. But the overall spirit of these pieces is interrogatory— of ourselves and our past, of our old comrades who chose to keep to the revolutionary road. "Pieces," that journalistic codeword for essays, is indeed an appropriate term for the chapters of this book. Not the "picked up pieces" that usually comprise collections of occasional writings but pieces of the past and pieces of the present that past has influenced; pieces of the puzzle of the way we were and the way we have become. Writing this book was an act of discovery for us which is not over yet.

I

The
Dancers
and
the Dance

— • —

chapter 1 —————————

Requiem for a Radical

"People didn't know whether to regard it as an occasion for nostalgia and rededication," one friend said of Fay Stender's funeral, "or whether to accept it as a requiem for a time of vision in their lives that was finished for good." State Supreme Court Chief Justice Rose Bird came. Radical attorney Charles Garry, Fay's onetime mentor, was there too, passing through the crowd and dolorously shaking hands. The Bay Area's left-wing legal community showed up *en masse*. But most of the three hundred or so mourners were more anonymous, an odd miscellany of people—activists and supporters, friends and fellow travelers—Fay had collected in too short a lifetime.

If the mood of the funeral was perplexed, it was largely because her death had been anticlimactic and the very idea of a memorial service something of an afterthought. Most of the people who were close to Fay had already mourned her during the last tortured year of her life. There were few tears inside the Sinai Memorial Chapel. The casket was almost completely hidden by a cloud of white gladiolas: death put at a distance. The speakers didn't summon the great rallying cries of the past or wave the bloody shirt, as they might have had she died a few years earlier, under different circumstances. They merely tried—somewhat awkwardly—to recall the person she had been, as wife, mother, co-worker, and, of course, as advocate for the oppressed and attorney of last resort for desperate men.

Although the eulogies were subdued in their remembrance of the past, few of those present had forgotten that time of radical enthusiasm when Fay stormed the political barricades as the attorney for Black Panthers Huey Newton and George Jackson, and state prison authorities publicly branded her "the most dangerous woman in California" and privately referred to her as "the Dragon Lady." Virtually everyone present could have recalled some story of Fay in action from that period—badgering establishment attorney friends until they agreed to file writs for one or two of the black felons who wrote her hundreds of letters a month; barging into the office of San Quentin warden Louis Nelson to inform him that the prison reform movement whose godmother she had become would soon be taking over his penitentiary; driving herself past exhaustion to try to free her lover, George Jackson, and the other Soledad Brothers. Although less well known than Charles Garry, William Kunstler, and other radical street fighters in the courtroom, she was perhaps more deeply typical of the Movement and closer to being the paradigmatic radical—relentlessly pushing at human limits; driven to a fine rage by perceived injustices; searching for personal authenticity in her revolutionary commitments; and, at the climax of her career, finally losing the distinction between clients and comrades, work and life.

If references to these triumphant days were curiously muted at her memorial, however, there was scarcely a mention of the personal drama of Fay's last years—the withdrawal from her earlier commitments and the attempt to fashion a new identity out of family and feminism; the violent interruption of this rebirth by an ex-prisoner who claimed to be acting in behalf of the abused memory of George Jackson when he fired five bullets into her; and finally the last months of paralysis and pain, and the lonely suicide half a world away from those who had wanted her to struggle as hard in her own behalf as she had for others.

Perhaps the issues of Fay's life and death were too complex. Perhaps her tragedy, almost Greek in the relentless operation of irony and fate, conveyed too daunting a message for people whose commitments had been bruised by the conservative decade that followed. Yet this omission caused a feeling of incompletion to hover over the funeral, as if it were a tale without a moral, a lesson purposely ignored.

After the service was over, the mourners filed outside and stood on the sun-splashed pavement for a moment. The talk was often more of themselves than Fay: distances traveled in the years that had slipped by since the halcyon days of the radical movement; accommodations made and compromises struck, as well as promises kept. At the cemetery, there was a brief graveside ceremony, where those present were invited to bid a last farewell by tossing a handful of dirt onto the coffin. "As this was happening," one of Fay's closest friends said later on, "you could almost hear her muffled voice—the old Fay, the one we wanted to remember. 'Now wait a minute!' she seemed to be saying. 'Hold on, dammit! There was more to it than that!'"

Like others who burst onto the radical scene in the Sixties, Fay acquired a media personality—cool and unyielding, her face squeezed in a perpetual concentration that pinched her features; remote and ironic, a machine fueled solely by logic. The insights of those who knew her well present quite a different picture.

She was a woman at odds with herself, riven by contradictory feelings. She worried about her looks, about the propriety of being so interested in clothes, about the possible hypocrisy of using makeup on a face she felt was plain. In fact, it was a far more arresting face than she imagined—oblong and strong-chinned; eyes close together; a smile that had to bloom through clenched teeth, the vestige perhaps of traumatic childhood orthodontia. She was a middle-sized woman who feared, correctly, that she gave the impression of awkwardness and bulk. Her profound identification with the "locked-upness" of prisoners came, at least partly, from the feeling that she had been sentenced to solitary confinement in a body that failed to express her. The irony was that while she might experience herself as gawky and inept, those who knew her intimately, especially women, regarded her as one of the most forceful persons they had ever met. In any case, during the course of her life, she evolved a strategy of self-presentation that worked: infusing her physical presence with the passionate intensities of her intellect; developing a swooping manner that moved people in paths she considered righteous.

She could be arbitrary, self-aggrandizing, relentless in behalf of the causes she took up, pushing people beyond their limits into angry recalcitrance which then surprised and hurt her greatly. Yet she was capable of tremendous generosity, gifts of self so utterly uncalled for that the recipients felt bound to her for life. In one well-remembered incident, a friend who had been close to her for years confided about a destructive love affair she felt powerless to terminate; unable to believe anyone incapable of forcing her life to yield to her will, Fay called the friend a "loser" and lost her for good. Such insensitivity, something close at times to moral blindness, was counterpointed by an almost pathological worry that people would think ill of her, the nameless people with whom she collided in her workaday life. Fay could be devastated by a garage attendant who criticized her parking.

Her radicalism seemed to come so naturally that everyone assumed she must be a red-diaper baby or at least a New Yorker coming out of an ambience in which left-wing politics was practiced as a sort of close-order drill. In fact, her family was conservative and conventional, middle-class Jews with three generations of roots in California, pious and yet unostentatious in their faith. It was only in oblique ways that her family situation, including its Jewish culture, spawned angers and yearnings that eventually found political expression.

The father, Sam Abraham, was a quiet man with a stern sense of life's opportunities and hazards, who had apparently been saddened when his first child was not a boy. Fay always felt that her younger sister, Lisie, was prettier and more winning. This left conspicuous achievement as her only path. Her mother, Ruby, reinforced this choice in ways that later augmented Fay's rebelliousness. She made her take piano lessons from the age of three and practice long hours; she bound her hands at bedtime to keep her from destroying a possible concert career by sucking her thumbs. She forced Fay to wear hideous orthopedic shoes, not because of any physical disability, but to ensure that she would have beautiful feet later in life; and she made her wear hated braces so that her smile would one day look right. Even after Fay had been shot and was lying in intensive care, she complained of the way that Ruby Abraham smoothed her brow: the touch was too harsh, feeling more like an attempt to train her hair than soothe her hurt.

The family moved from San Francisco to Berkeley in 1942, when Fay was nine years old. She became a "Berkeley person," a term referring more to outlook than to geography. She was affected by the political and cultural liberalism radiating outward into the community from the university, the sentiment that would eventually result in the birth of the New Left. Friends remember her complaining of being "chained to the piano," although in fact she played well enough to have made a debut with the San Francisco Symphony, playing the "Emperor" concerto, at the age of fourteen. She was a loner, restless and impatient with frivolity, anxious to skip the ambiguity of adolescence and attain adult powers and responsibilities. While acquaintances competed for a place in Berkeley High School's exclusive and possibly anti-Semitic sororities, Fay spent weekends with the Quakers, touring hog farms just outside the city limits, foul-smelling places where impoverished families of blacks lived in communities of muddy roads and tar-paper shacks.

She was rebellious, but there seemed to be more to it than the casual anarchy of most teenagers. She sometimes concealed a *Time* magazine in her music book and read cover stories on international affairs while practicing her scales. Sometimes she would take the bus to San Francisco on a Saturday with a girlfriend and spend the entire day going through all the museums in Golden Gate Park—the De Young, Natural History, the Steinhart Aquarium—walking down the halls and opening every door she could find marked "Private." Not long before quitting the piano altogether, she defied her parents by going to the local Congregationalist church to play for Sunday service, although even there she might break into the middle of some solemn Christian hymn with a few bars of a popular song.

She was conscious of her desires and feelings, but it was in a literary rather than analytical way. Wendy Milmore, one of her closest high school friends, remembers envying her ability to "turn out four or five beautifully calligraphed pages on her innermost thoughts while sitting on a bench for fifteen minutes waiting for a bus." When she went to Reed College, an Oregon liberal arts school with a reputation for iconoclasm and reform, Fay planned to major in literature. But between her sophomore and junior years, she went to Mexico on a Quaker project to inoculate peasants against typhoid, an experience that changed her goals. She transferred to Berkeley for her senior year, prelaw now, and roomed with Ying Lee Kelley, a future member of the radical caucus of the Berkeley City Council. Ying was Betty Lee then, the daughter of Chinese immigrant parents. Fay found this fact attractive, and they had lengthy discussions not only about racism but about communism and imperialism too. "Fay dealt in big ideas even then," Ying recalls.

At the University of Chicago, where she went to law school, Fay took courses with Malcolm Sharpe, who had written a book about the Rosenbergs. He invited her to help him with an appeal in behalf of the "third man" in the celebrated atomic spy case, Morton Sobel. When friends from California came to visit her and asked to go sightseeing, she took them on walking tours of Chicago's slums. She was interested in whatever political activism dared take place in the long shadow of McCarthyism. After a meeting of the student chapter of the proscribed National Lawyers Guild (which the attorney general had not long before identified as a "Communist front"), Fay went up to talk to the group's chairman, Marvin Stender, about her experiences on the Quaker project in Mexico. After courting for three months, they got married, a relationship both saw as a joint venture in behalf of the oppressed.

By 1960, Fay was back in Berkeley, where she and Marvin found the political climate favorable to their commitments.

Twenty-eight years old, a lawyer with two young children, a boy, Neal, and a girl, Oriane, named after a character in Proust, she was a dynamo—mercurial, energetic, almost driven, interested in a wide spectrum of liberal and left-wing causes. In addition to working part time for a firm of left-wing lawyers headed by Charles Garry, she joined with her husband and three other lawyers to found the somewhat extravagantly named Council for Justice. A forerunner of later law collectives, the Council was "an umbrella group to do good," which at the time included helping a little-known Tulare County organizer named Cesar Chavez and filing suits on behalf of Negroes discriminated against by Bay Area landlords. She was involved with everything from legal aid to militant motherhood.

Betty Ann Bruno, now a local TV reporter, recalls encountering Fay at this time. Bruno had been having trouble nursing her first child and, after looking vainly to traditional sources for help, came across an organization called Nursing Mothers Anonymous. Attracted by its slogan ("Don't reach for the bottle, reach for the phone"), she called, and Fay answered. "It was her home phone. She was the founder and probably the only member of this organization. She asked me what my problem was and had lots of ideas to help. She just talked to me as often and for as long as I needed, just gave of herself. That was the thing that seemed incredible to me. I was just some strange woman who was having some problems, and there she was." Afterward, they became friends, and Fay enlisted Bruno's lawyer husband to support a suit she had filed on her own against laws barring fathers from the delivery rooms of California hospitals. Eventually their legal brief got the law changed.

Fay seemed to be everywhere at once. Yet there was something unfinished in her personality, a restlessness, a sort of undisciplined searching that suggested desires no ordinary life would satisfy. One friend of that period says: "Given her talents, Fay was one of the least happy people I knew." Another, Rose Linsky, recalls: "She was exceedingly ambitious in a way that neither Marvin nor I understood. I remember the three of us were in their apartment after an evening in which they had gone to some political to-do. She was full of enthusiasm about whom she had met and what the contacts would mean to her. Marvin and I were aghast at the analytic, calculating ambition. We found ourselves looking at each other more than once over this kind of thing in her."

Ann Ginger, Fay's lifelong legal colleague and the head of the Meikeljohn Institute, says: "She was searching for meaning that was greater than the money she could earn, and greater than the legal principles she could establish. She wanted her life to have meaning, so much so that when her clients did not have as much meaning as she wanted them to have, she endowed them with meaning." The writer Gregory Armstrong, who later worked with Fay on the George Jackson defense, agrees: "She was like others on the Left in those days —she was very hungry. She was in pursuit of the great dream you'd do anything for."

The civil rights movement of the early Sixties provided both an arena and a community of support for her quest. From her political base in the Council for Justice, she became the moving spirit behind the Bay Area Friends of SNCC, the Student Nonviolent Coordinating Committee, a radical civil rights organization headed by Stokely Carmichael, which had become impatient with the nonviolent reformism of Martin Luther King, Jr. Fay organized fund-raisers and benefits for SNCC activists. One Passover, like many Jews in the Movement, she organized a "freedom seder" for the local SNCC members. The service related the liberation of the Jews from their slavery in Egypt to the civil rights struggles of American Negroes. "The ritual was there and the tradition," remembers Sanne Kalter DeWitt. "but instead of Rabbi Gamaliel talking about how many plagues there actually were, there would be a quote from Martin Luther King about the civil rights movement." In 1964 and 1965, Fay went south to work on the Mississippi Summer Project and put forth a tremendous effort filing briefs for the Mississippi Democratic Freedom Party's challenge of the Democratic establishment at the presidential convention.

Two years later, when Stokely Carmichael launched the slogan of "Black Power" and extended the principle of self-determination to SNCC itself, telling SNCC's white supporters to leave the organization, Fay defended the decision. "I was furious," remembers Sanne DeWitt, a Holocaust survivor. "I had a big argument with Fay about it, and also about the growing anti-Semitism of the black movement. Fay was understanding of their feelings because of the legacy of white oppression, Jewish landlords, and that sort of thing. I said, 'I absolutely will not tolerate this. I'm not supporting an organization that's anti-Semitic. There's nothing to understand, from my point of view.' " Fay disagreed with equal vigor.

One black organization that was radical and did not reject white support after the emergence of black power was an Oakland-based group called the Black Panther Party. Since its formation out of an Oakland street gang a year earlier, the Party had concentrated its efforts on cases of police brutality in the ghetto. Patrolling the streets in armed squads, which was legal at the time, they observed arrests and informed people of their rights. Unlike SNCC, which had closed its doors to whites, the Panthers called for a black-white coalition. Unlike the reformist Congress for Racial Equality and the Southern Christian Leadership Conference, the Panthers had a Marxist analysis of racism and a clear "revolutionary" program. In the spring of 1967, the Panthers were still an obscure grouping, but in October of that year, an event took place that was to catapult them into the national limelight. Fay, through her connection with the Garry law firm, was thrust by the same event into the center of one of the most important political trials of the decade.

On the night of October 27, Huey Newton, founder and minister of defense of the Black Panther Party, left a gathering celebrating the end of his probation for a knifing incident three years earlier and, just before dawn, was stopped by Oakland policeman John Frey. Ten minutes later, Frey was dead, with five bullet wounds, two of them entering his back from a distance of twelve inches. Newton had been wounded, as had a back-up officer called to Frey's aid. Two eyewitnesses, the back-up officer and a black bus driver who had happened on the scene, identified Newton as the killer. The Panther leader was charged with murder.

The defense argument was that Officer Frey and Newton had both been shot in the chaos of the moment by the officer who arrived as back-up. But the implications of the courtroom rhetoric, reflecting the escalating radical vision of the time, implied that even if Newton *had* done the shooting, the act was justified. In a pioneering version of what would soon become a radical cliché, Garry, with Fay assisting, put the "system" itself on trial. Newton went on the stand and lectured the jury about racism with the disarming earnestness of a young divinity student espousing a muscular Christianity. He told about his past—how as a high school graduate left illiterate by his education he'd taught himself to read out of a dog-eared copy of Plato's *Republic*; how he'd recruited former street criminals for his political movement. He and Garry fashioned for the trial a persona that resembled a contemporary Frederick Douglass. Within months, Newton had become a cult figure, whose poster in black beret and leather jacket sitting on an African rattan throne, with a spear in one hand and a rifle in the other, began decorating college dorms all over America.

The "political defense" Garry and Fay conducted gave perfect expression to the radical viewpoint of the time and became a model for the trials of Angela Davis, the Chicago Seven, and others that followed. The focus was shifted away from the particular events of that October night and toward society. Before the proceedings had even started, Garry had challenged the racial composition of the grand jury and then of the trial jury itself. His brief, which Fay was instrumental in putting together, became a precedent-setting case in the law governing jury selection. Eventually the court, the police, and the victim himself were indicted by the defense as agents of a racist and criminal system that had conspired to oppress Huey Newton because he was a fighter for black liberation, to deprive him of his rights, and now to threaten his life. So tied was the defense presentation to the radical philosophy of the hour that, in the radical community at large, questioning Newton's innocence became tantamount to questioning the fact that American society was racist and that black people were oppressed.

By the time Newton was finally convicted for manslaughter, the nation had undergone a convulsion. The Tet offensive had punctured the illusion that there was light at the end of the Vietnam tunnel. Detroit and other urban black ghettos had erupted in violence. Student rebels had momentarily seized Columbia and other universities. Martin Luther King and Bobby Kennedy had been gunned down by assassins, and lawmen had clashed with demonstrators at the Democratic convention in Chicago, in a scene of uncontrolled mayhem that conjured images of a police state.

The mood of the Left was increasingly apocalyptic. Weatherman, the militant faction of Students for a Democratic Society, had raised the slogan "Bring the War Home." Radical theory projected the metaphor of America's imperial thrust in the Pacific onto the domestic map: white America was the mother country; blacks were a colonized people with a right, indeed a duty, to free themselves from oppression, by armed force if necessary. At an SDS convention, the Panthers were proclaimed the vanguard of the revolution and were adopted in the New Left's imagination as a sort of domestic Vietcong fighting for freedom in the urban jungles.

Fay had handled all the legal motions in the Newton trial, and when the verdict was in, she handled the appeal. It was based on a technical error in the judge's instructions, and two years later it freed Newton. While working on this appeal, Fay went to Garry and told him she was leaving the firm to be a trial lawyer herself. "I told her she was superb at the law," recalls Garry, "but she was not a trial lawyer. Emotionally she could not handle a jury trial. She was rigid and got too involved with her clients." Nonetheless, Fay left Garry to join the Berkeley firm of Stender, Franck, Hendon, Hill & Ziegler, which soon after was restructured to become the first law "collective" in the Bay Area, with no internal status distinctions and with pay according to need rather than work. The firm handled court actions resulting from demonstrations, as well as draft resistance and drug cases.

Caught up in the increasingly stark radical vision of the time, Fay continued to work on Newton's appeal, visiting him regularly at the San Luis Obispo Men's Facility. These visits seemed to provide Fay with a cause that gave coherence to her life. She seemed to friends to be almost in love with Newton. They looked deeply at each other during her visits, sometimes touching when the guards' attention wandered. Newton told her about another young black, who was already a legend in the California prison system, a man to whose fate the Black Panther Party and to a much greater extent Fay herself would become inextricably bound.

Although only twenty-eight, George Jackson had already spent ten years in jail, nearly eight of them in solitary, a year and a half with the door of his cell welded shut. He did a thousand fingertip push-ups a day to keep in shape, exercise that had so bulked the muscles on his forearms that he couldn't reach through the bars of his cell. He was an expert in karate; he taught himself to read and wrote like a poet himself, quoting from memory the works of Mao and Frantz Fanon. He was a divided personality, telling friends, "Marxism is my hustle," while writing "serious dialectics." He was, the other prisoners agreed, the *baddest.*

If Fay had committed her first impressions of Jackson to paper, they might have resembled the description in Gregory Armstrong's memoir, *The Dragon Has Come:*

> He is young and slender. His face is smooth and un-marked, like a boy's. "I'm really pleased to meet you, man. We got a lot to talk about. I got a lot of questions." Everything about him is flashing and shining and glistening and his body seems to ripple like a cat's. As he moves forward to take my hand, I literally feel myself being pulled into the vortex of his energy. There is no way I can look away. He gives me a sudden radiant smile of sheer sensual delight, the kind of smile you save for someone you really love. As we take each other's hands, I have a sense of becoming almost a part of his very physical being.

Meeting Jackson was something like a seduction for Fay too. From the start, the connection she felt to him was powerful, even more than the one with Newton. Not long after their initial meeting, Jackson was writing her: "You are positively my favorite person." And she was telling friends of the "appalling injustice" of Jackson's imprisonment: in jail since the age of seventeen, better than ten years for the crime of stealing seventy dollars. She told friends that it should be made into an American equivalent of the Dreyfus case. She became a frequent visitor at Soledad Prison, wearing high boots and a leather miniskirt, the "uniform" Weather-leader Bernadine Dohrn had made popular in the militant Left.

But the reasons for her visits were not merely social. On January 13, 1970, three black prisoners had been killed by a tower guard during an interracial fight in the prison yard. One of them, W. L. Nolen, was close to Jackson, having worked with him to radicalize Soledad inmates. Three days later, in retribution for these killings, a guard was beaten and thrown off one of the prison tiers to his death. Three black prisoners were charged with the murder: John Cluchette, Fleeta Drumgo, and George Jackson.

Fay saw the case as an opportunity as well as a duty. She threw herself into it completely, enlisting Dr. Benjamin Spock, Linus Pauling, and others for a defense committee, recruiting activists from Berkeley and Santa Cruz, and beginning a fund-raising campaign that would ultimately raise hundreds of thousands of dollars. She rented a house in San Francisco, thinking that those involved in the defense could live there, but there were far too many of them.

The strategy she organized followed and expanded on the model she and Charles Garry had established in the Newton case. The "system" would be put in the dock as the ultimate criminal. "Three young blacks, inmates of Soledad prison may soon be murdered by the state of California," read the literature of the defense committee she had established. Their crime was being militant; they had been singled out solely because they were politically active. And black. In the defense literature, Fay featured a photograph of the three Soledad Brothers in chains that shackled their waists, wrists, and ankles in a way that evoked images of slave-block auctions and lynchings in the South. The picture of Jackson, eyes closed and horn-rim glasses emphasizing his boyish features, was especially poignant.

Her idea was to dramatize Jackson and create an acquittal ambience long before he entered the courtroom. Within a few months, *Soledad Brother: The Prison Letters of George Jackson* appeared, to rave reviews. It was a project engineered by Fay, who selectively edited letters Jackson had written to her and others, and got French playwright Jean Genet to write an introduction, which gave the book automatic intellectual standing. Her idea was to use the book to make Jackson the symbolic political prisoner, the black Daniel uttering prophecies of judgment from the brutal depths of the lions' den. Activists and supporters, as well as journalists from around the world, flocked to the cause.

Jackson told a friend that his abiding impression of Fay, formed at this time, was of someone talking about the trial and "waving her hands like a conductor."

Fay got state legislators to visit Soledad and convinced the Congressional Black Caucus to initiate an investigation of conditions. Using the surveys and field work gathered by teams of sociologists, she obtained a change of venue for the trial and got Jackson transferred to San Quentin, where he would be free from guards' reprisals.

Fanned by the praise of Newton and Jackson, who called her his "small and mighty mouthpiece," her reputation spread like prairie fire among inmates in the prisons of California and other states. Letters postmarked from prison began to arrive in her office, a few at first and soon an avalanche. Using the people she had gathered around the Soledad Brothers Defense Committee, Fay founded the Prison Law Project to deal with the pleas for help and began to address what she saw as the larger issues of the criminal justice system. She began to speak on campuses and at other public forums, denouncing conditions at Soledad: "Every citizen in the country ought to do something about O Wing of Soledad and others like it. The only thing I can say is that it's the Dachau of America. . . ."

Almost incandescent with energy, she pushed herself as remorselessly as she pushed others, working around the clock, sometimes dragging ten-year-old Oriane to meetings and prisons with her. It was a period of terrible urgency, when "revolutionary violence" was being advocated by certain sections of the Movement as a necessary means to deal with the encroaching "police state." White radicals like Tom Hayden were promoting the strategy of "liberated zones." The Panthers appeared locked in a bloody war with the police forces of several cities, a guerrilla combat that had claimed dozens of casualties and caused Eldridge Cleaver to jump bail for a clandestine flight to Algeria. Radicals called the police program "genocide," and when police raids on Panther headquarters were rumored, they would stand outside to bear witness. Fay was always a step further: she would be *inside* the Panthers' barricaded redoubt, sleeping among the automatic weapons that were propped near sandbags.

"My identity is becoming almost anti-professional," she told a student seminar in the summer of 1970, "and in some sort of way that of a political prisoner. In fact, I sometimes wonder whether my effectiveness will ultimately be enhanced or impaired. I don't enjoy cars and clothes anymore. I don't enjoy vacations. I don't live in that world anymore. I've gotten so schizy going back and forth that I really prefer to spend my working time in prison. In the most selfish way, I have a better time when I am talking to a prisoner. I enjoy myself more; I am more human; I feel more love than when I am in the Supreme Court being treated courteously and having the privileges of being a lawyer. . . . I don't use the expression 'my clients' anymore. . . . That expression is going out of my vocabulary and is certainly going out of my thinking. I feel that they are comrades."

Such transcendent thinking involved a great leap forward, a stepping out into a territory that was intellectually undiscovered and, some of her old friends thought, perhaps undiscoverable. John Irwin, a former prisoner at Soledad who had served his time and after his release obtained a degree in sociology and became a leader of the Prisoners Union, was called into the Soledad Brothers case at about this time. Fay wanted him to listen to tape recordings made of the prisoner witnesses who would testify against Jackson and suggest ways of discrediting them. During his time at the Soledad Brothers Defense Committee offices, Irwin was taken aback by the ease with which Fay and her associates accepted a sentimental and, to his way of thinking, benighted view of prisoners simply as victims of social circumstances, and of prisons simply as an early warning system of the fascist state toward which all American social institutions were tending. "I don't think Fay ever understood the commitment to criminality that many of the persons she dealt with had. Fay really had a strong belief that prisoners were going to be in the vanguard of the social revolution." Irwin was disturbed by the romantic acceptance of violent solutions and by what he saw as a kind of sexual romanticism: "It was mostly women who were doing the organizing. They had each picked their favorite Soledad Brother and were kind of oo-ing and ah-ing over them, like teenagers with movie stars. I couldn't believe it."

Eve Pell, recruited by Fay for the Prison Law Project from the activities board of the San Francisco Museum of Art, was one of the women Irwin remembers. While not disagreeing with his conclusions, she explains the deep feelings of guilt and insecurity that led to the need to romanticize prisoners and their society: "I went to San Quentin to see George from such a position of weakness. Here I am this bourgeois housewife from the upper class, the other end of the social scale from George Jackson. When I went to see him, it was the first time I had ever been in a prison. I thought: This man is not going to like me. This man is going to say, 'Go back to your dumb little life and don't bother us revolutionaries.' Well, that didn't happen. We had this amazing conversation. Visiting someone inside the walls of a prison has to be one of the most intense experiences any person could ever have. There you are in this horrible, horrible setting, with guards and officials who don't want you there and are trying to keep you out. And you're talking to some guy, and this guy is focusing on you with a quality of attention that I don't think you'll ever get anywhere again. He has one hour out of six months to make contact, and he does. I think that's half the reason why almost every woman I know in the Project fell in love with some prisoner."

Fay was not invulnerable to these feelings. Through the ingenious contrivances that prisoners devise, she had become sexually involved with Newton in prison, and authorities at Soledad once had to separate her physically from Jackson and drag her out of the visiting area with her clothes half off. (Gregory Armstrong recalls being at Fay's house for dinner the night Angela Davis was caught by federal authorities after fleeing the Bay Area in a hasty incognito; seemingly buoyed by the tribulations of the woman to whom Jackson had addressed some of his most erotic letters, Fay served dinner on family china that had not been used since her wedding.)

But Fay's romanticism was political as well as personal, coloring the case she built, the alliances she forged, and finally the cause into which she poured all the considerable force of her personality. It was a flaw in her own makeup, as she later came to realize, but even more the flaw in the radical world-view: the belief that the facts of experience were inferior to its hidden "truth"—the readiness to reshape reality to make the world correspond to an idea.

The political myth of George Jackson that Fay helped to construct exemplified the radical willingness to tinker with the facts to serve a greater truth. The ten years of servitude for a seventy-dollar robbery, which Fay attempted to make notorious as a miscarriage of justice, was, on close inspection, something different from what she made it seem. The holdup was Jackson's third serious offense, the culmination of a record that dated back to an arrest for assault when he was fifteen. The indeterminate sentence was repeatedly extended, but not because of a cruel caprice on the part of the California Adult Authority. Jackson's path inside prison was far from model. He had organized a prison gang called the Wolf Pack as a black equivalent of the Aryan Brotherhood and the Mexican Mafia. He ran the prison gambling operations and once attempted to cut a Chicano inmate's throat for welshing on a ten-dollar bet, and he boasted to Eve Pell of having killed twelve men in his prison career and of his "revolutionary" plan to poison the water system of his native Chicago if he was ever released. (Jackson had described this plan in one of the prison letters that Fay suppressed in the course of creating his public myth.) While Fay was working to build the illusion of Jackson's sacred victimhood, he was out to create another kind of myth—of a "wild nigger" embodying absolute, almost cosmic vengeance.

Jackson could be articulate, intelligent, and completely charming to those who came to see him during visiting hours, but he was a different person inside the prison world. In *Who Killed George Jackson?*, journalist Jo Durden-Smith quotes a prisoner he interviewed: "He was the meanest mother I ever saw, inside or out. . . . If you didn't get out of his way, or do things the way he wanted 'em done, you better watch your ass. I mean, he was into everything when I was inside. Dope, booze, peddling ass—you name it. Strong arm. Hit man. He was making his way in the joint."

And eventually Jackson began to chafe under Fay's portrayal of him as an innocent. He felt that it diminished the mad dog manhood he had fought so hard to establish. He wanted her to know the version of self he had perfected during all those years in prison. In April 1970, he wrote her: "The family, the nuns, the pigs, I resisted them all. I know my mother likes to tell everyone that I was a good boy, but that isn't true. I've been a brigand all my life." To have taken his hint, however, would have involved a more detailed inventory of her own character (and the Movement's) than Fay was at that time prepared to make. By the fall, the gap between the image she was projecting and what Jackson saw as his true self began to create serious friction between them.

"Fay cut so much material away from [*Soledad Brother*]," he complained in a letter to Eve Pell, "that it turned out more her than me; there were several hundred pages of remedy left out." These "remedies," which Fay had excised, were later printed in the posthumous *Blood in My Eye*, Jackson's last revolutionary will and testament, which explained that "the power of the people lies in its greater potential violence":

> There are thousands of ways to correct individuals. The way is to send one armed expert. I don't mean to outshout him with logic, I mean correct him. Slay him, assassinate him with thugee, by silenced pistol, shotgun, with a high powered rifle shooting from four hundred yards away and behind a rock. Suffocation, strangulation, crucifixion . . .

Jackson reached out to Fay on July 28, 1970, in a letter that attempted to name the chasm that had come to separate them and through which they would both eventually fall to their destruction:

> Dear Fay, Dear Fay,
> The possibility of us, as persons, misunderstanding each other will always rest on the fact that I am an alien.

It will always be my fault. The secret things that I hide from almost everyone, and especially the people who are sweet and gentle and intellectually inhibited from grasping the full range of the ordeal of being fair game, hunted, an alien, precludes *forever* a state of perfect agreement. You dig what I'm saying now you've conceded this much. Keep it always in mind, strain with me. . . .

The letter was a warning. Its crucial sentence came later on: "An intellectual argument to an attacker against the logic of his violence—or one to myself concerning the wisdom of a natural counter-violence—borders on, no, it overleaps the absurd!!" Jackson was trying to warn Fay about his own character, which she refused to understand, and about the ante that was about to be upped. A few days later, seventeen-year-old Jonathan Jackson, laboring to be worthy of his brother, that mythic figure radicals had manufactured, walked into a Marin County courtroom where a trial was in progress, pulled a .38 from the flight bag he was carrying, and took the judge, an assistant district attorney, and three women jurors hostage, with the idea of hijacking a plane to Cuba and ransoming them for the Soledad Brothers. Within minutes, Jonathan, two prisoners, and the judge were dead, and another prisoner and the assistant D.A. were seriously wounded. This was the beginning of the apocalypse that had come to dominate Jackson's life and writings. After his little brother's martyrdom, there was no way that Jackson the "for-real man," as Huey Newton called him, could emerge from prison other than with guns blazing.

Soon a revolutionary "army" was training in the Santa Cruz Mountains, with weapons stolen from the Camp Pendleton armory. Named the August 7th Movement to commemorate the courthouse raid and martyrdom of Jonathan Jackson, it had as its nucleus Black Panthers, together with a few white student radicals who had been calling unsuccessfully for revolution and now saw black prisoners as the only "vanguard" with sufficient desperation to provide the spark for an uprising. "We have two perfectly harmonious fists," Jackson wrote Jimmy Carr, his chief lieutenant, who had recently been paroled from San Luis Obispo, "the left 'front ram' of the Black Panthers' political thrust and the left 'back ram' of the August 7th Movement." The first target for this army was San Quentin itself, focus of Jackson's extravagant plan involving smuggling in guns for an insurrection that would coincide with the short-circuiting of the prison's electricity and the arrival of jeeps to spirit away the prisoners who scaled the walls.

Jackson put pressure on all his supporters to get behind these plans. One woman on the defense committee, who is still too frightened to be named, recalls: "George asked everybody to bring him guns. It was standard. Weapons and sex—what does any prisoner want? I was too scared, so I said no. But others didn't."

Jackson wanted to use funds from the Soledad Brothers Defense Committee to finance his military venture. At first, emissaries like Jimmy Carr were sent to Fay and, according to other committee members, made "extortionist threats." Fay didn't budge. The last thing she wanted was to see Jackson, whom she thought she could free through the courts, get hurt in some wild adventure. "She felt she had won the case in the public relations arena and would win it legally," recalls Marvin Stender. "It was like him saying, 'I don't trust you.' She was personally affronted. Her attitude was, 'I was smart as a lawyer and did these superhuman things to get you out legally, and now you're going to go and blow the whole thing.' "

In late 1970, there was a head-on confrontation between the two of them in the San Quentin Adjustment Center visiting room, an "epic shouting match" in which Jackson attacked her about the Defense Fund and the royalties from *Soledad Brother*. Eventually she relinquished control of all moneys to him. A friend who called her soon after was shocked by her depressed tone of voice. "I'm not very much involved anymore," Fay said. "I'm thinking of leaving the case. I've done all that I can do."

It was a time of terminal crisis for the Left, of paranoia and despair, when the violence rhetorically aimed at the larger society turned inward. Agents had infiltrated the Panthers and Jackson's "army." As well as a training area, the Santa Cruz Mountains had become a killing ground, where the burned corpses of "soldiers" thought to have been informers were hastily buried, leaving shards of bone in full view. Pressured from within by its own revolutionary rhetoric and from without by police surveillance, the radical grouping around the Panthers began to experience something like the erratic cell division caused by metastasis. Eldridge Cleaver's military wing split from the more gradualist Newton-dominated Panthers, leading to the formation of the Black Liberation Army. Jackson sided with Newton, although it was reportedly Newton's last-minute decision to pull Panther "support forces" out of the Marin courthouse raid that had left his brother Jonathan vulnerable. Meanwhile, the white radicals who had connived in this "vanguard operation" were also splitting apart. Members of the Revolutionary Union left to form the more military Venceremos Brigade (later to split again, leading to the formation of the Symbionese Liberation Army, which would kidnap Patty Hearst). It was Venceremos that urged Jackson to make his move.

Like other radicals who operated on an intuitive rather than an ideological basis, Fay was bewildered by the nature of these events as well as by their velocity. An acquaintance who went to see her at home was surprised to find her sitting listlessly in her bathrobe, reading Nero Wolfe stories. It was not only Jackson who had turned his back on her, but Huey Newton as well. He had recently gotten out of prison on the strength of the appeal Fay had drafted. But at a party sometime after his release, he had ignored her in a deliberately cutting way, leaving her to stand alone on the periphery of the event for the entire evening. Charles Garry later took her to a meeting in the $750-a-month apartment Newton had rented overlooking Oakland's Lake Merritt, the "gilded cage" Cleaver's rival faction said symbolized his remoteness from revolutionary reality. "She started criticizing Huey and the way he was living," Garry recalls. "It ended up in a verbal brawl, and she left."

By June, everything seemed to be unraveling. Jackson's confidant Gregory Armstrong wrote at the time: "Without Fay there is no center. Quiet hopelessness has taken possession of everyone. . . . Without Fay it must seem as if reality itself has disappeared—the reality of the intense struggle that Fay, his mighty mouthpiece, had brought to the case, with her uncompromising need to defeat her enemies—some enemy, any enemy—with the sense of motivation she brought with her, the sense of frenzied activity, the sense that she was locked in a mortal combat and wouldn't accept defeat, the endless number of activities she initiated, the breathless battlefield reports. . . ."

Jackson had turned over the royalties from *Soledad Brother* and moneys in the Defense Fund to the Black Panther Party, whose field marshal he had become. In February 1971, Fay left the case and was replaced by a young attorney from her radical law group named Stephen Bingham. A few days after their break, Jackson wrote a mutual friend: "Call Fay right now and simply say, 'George said he loves you no matter what.'"

In spite of that assurance, a new element had entered Fay's life—fear. Because she had opposed Jackson's suicidal plans, it was whispered on the prison movement's paranoid grapevine that she was a "sellout" and possibly even a "police agent." She made her final decision to leave the case when she opened a piece of mail one day and found a razor blade—a chilling enough message even without an accompanying note.

When Jackson asked to see Fay late in June, the person who relayed the message noted that her face was torn with fear. "I'm not going in there alone," Fay said. "I'll take another lawyer with me."

On the morning of August 21, 1971, Stephen Bingham signed the east gate visitors' book at San Quentin and then waited for several hours to see his client. Finally, he went into the meeting, carrying a tape recorder with him. Minutes after Bingham left the visiting room, Jackson was back inside the Adjustment Center, going through the usual post-interview skin search. A clip of bullets hidden in his Afro wig clattered to the floor. Suddenly he was brandishing a 9-millimeter automatic that seemed to have materialized from nowhere. "The Dragon has come," he said to the guards. Then he gestured to the prisoners as he ordered the cell blocks opened: "The Black Dragon has come to free you."

There was a moment of euphoria and then the realization that there was nowhere to go. In the next few minutes, Jackson and his group of supporters released friends and rounded up guards and enemies. The scene quickly careened out of control; within minutes, three guards and two white convicts lay in Jackson's cell choking on their own blood, their throats slit by razor blades embedded in toothbrushes. As authorities moved to isolate the uprising, Jackson realized that the game was up. True to his vision of himself, he yelled to his friends, "It's me they want!" and charged into the prison yard, firing blindly at the guard towers above, where sharpshooters lay on their bellies, waiting for him to come into their sights. The first of the two shots fired back at Jackson splintered his shinbone; the next one caught him in the tenth rib, ricocheted up his spine, and exited the roof of his skull. His body somersaulted limply as he fell dead on the gravel path.

The abortive escape left a thicket of unanswered questions behind. What was the role of Stephen Bingham, who disappeared after the event? Was he aware that his tape recorder contained a gun—the theory of prison officials who reconstructed the event? Had Jackson been set up? If so, was it by the Cleaver faction of the Black Panther Party? Or by Newton, fearful of Jackson's charismatic competition? Or was it a conspiracy of the state intelligence agents acting in concert with prison authorities? Those who have tried to answer these questions have found themselves walking down a hall of mirrors. Jackson's death has become the radical equivalent of the Kennedy assassination, involving hypotheses of intrigue which became ever more bizarre with close examination.

Fay was devastated. "She wasn't surprised," says her husband, Marvin. "It didn't seem like it could end any other way. But it was a very, very personal blow to her." She loved Jackson; she had said to friends that, outside her own family, he and Newton were the only people she had ever been willing to die for. In the middle of her grief, however, she found cause for alarm. The California attorney general's office suspected her of aiding the military escape plan. She was also a subject of suspicion by those who were concerned because her involvement with Jackson's defense had made her privy to truths that could be dangerous. "She was afraid of the authorities," says Marvin. "And she was afraid of the people she'd helped."

While trying to deal with Jackson's death, Fay was also confronted with a rebellion from within her Prison Law Project. In some ways it was similar to conflicts that had destroyed other radical organizations of the day: a polarization pitting collectivism against "elitism," politics against expertise. The other side was led by younger radicals—most of them nearly a generation younger—activists and law students Fay had recruited and transformed largely through her own enthusiasms.

The trauma involving the constellation of issues surrounding Jackson's death was causing Fay to pull back and question her fierce identification with prisoners, but the radicals in the Prison Law Project were eager to go forward in the struggle. They assumed that the Project would defend the San Quentin Six, those prisoners charged with the murders committed in the Adjustment Center during Jackson's escape attempt.

"We wanted to be involved," recalls Eve Pell. "We regarded the Six as righteous political brothers who'd been singled out for persecution by the fascist prison system. Naturally the system wanted to get these black and brown leaders, and we couldn't let that happen. For us, it was an intense emotional identification with them as heroes, as lovers, as comrades." But while fear prevented her from spelling out her reasons, Fay said no. "Fay didn't want to get involved," recalls Eve, "and we couldn't understand why, because it was the most important thing that was happening. She had led us into involvement with the prisoners on a personal and political level, and then held back."

The radicals split from the Prison Law Project, forming the Prison Law Collective. Struggle for control of a thirty-thousand-dollar foundation grant made the parting all the more acrimonious. Fay traveled to New York and persuaded the donors to give all the money to her organization, after which she offered the Collective five thousand dollars. Outraged by the gesture, Collective members went to her office on a Sunday morning and took half the typewriters and other office equipment. Fay circulated a letter of denunciation among the prison movement's funding sources and to National Lawyers Guild members. Collective members characterized the letter as "red-baiting" and regarded her actions as a "stab in the back." Once friends and comrades, the two sides faced each other across invisible barricades. "It was like a divorce," says Eve Pell, who joined the radical Collective. "There was the same kind of bitterness, the same emotions. By the time of the Attica prison uprising in October, which George had inspired, we weren't speaking to each other."

Fay pushed on with her work, although she sought more professional channels, such as the bar association's individual rights section and its subcommittee on prisons. About George Jackson and her decision to leave the case she would say nothing, not even to those closest to her. "Suddenly she was scared to death of those people she'd worked with and defended," recalls one close associate. "It became an operative part of her life after that. She was constantly afraid of somebody doing something to her because of things that went all the way back to the Soledad Brothers Defense Committee."

She no longer courted the attention of desperate men. Soon after Jackson's death and the split in the Prison Law Project, the Stenders received word that an inmate in a southern California prison was planning an escape and intended to visit with them on his way out of the country. At one time this was exactly the sort of intrigue Fay might have jumped to participate in. When the inmate actually did escape, she hid out her family for three weeks, sleeping on the floors of friends' houses to avoid having to deal with him as he passed through.

A cynical strain began to surface in Fay's outlook. On her birthday following the Law Project split, she was given a calligraphed inscription of one of Murphy's Laws: *No Good Deed Goes Unpunished.* "It had become her favorite saying," notes Marvin Stender, "so she put it on the mantelpiece."

Fay could no longer turn a blind eye to the results of her prison work. "She saw the revolving door syndrome," says Marvin. "Time after time she would get somebody paroled or moved from maximum security to the main line, and a month later he would be back." Doron Weinberg, one of Fay's law partners, recalls her negative reaction to an inmate she had once helped. "He was paroled, and within a month he supposedly threw his girlfriend out the window. She knew the man well, and he had hurt the woman badly. She was beginning to feel feminist issues very strongly. She wanted to know that everything was all right with the guy's case, but she didn't want to have anything to do with it. In the end, it didn't turn out well. I defended him, his parole was not revoked, he didn't go back to prison, and he killed someone." Of all the prisoners she had gotten released, Fay once blurted out to her husband in despair, "only *one*, absolutely only one, stayed out."

In 1974, Fay closed the Prison Law Project and shortly afterward stopped taking prison clients. She began a family-law practice, specializing in custody cases and developing an esoteric sideline in representing psychiatrists and family counselors at licensing hearings. She helped to found California Women Lawyers and ran a yearlong project on child custody for the organization. She became increasingly interested in feminist issues and gay rights.

She was still driven, going from one project to the next, and not even stopping to take care of herself at times when her body faltered. Once, when she was about to try a case in Los Angeles, she became so ill that her doctor told her she had to go home immediately and get in bed. Instead of taking his advice, she found another doctor, who would deal with her on her own terms. "I've got a trial in Los Angeles," she told him. "What shall I do, given the fact that I'm going to Los Angeles?" But despite such incidents, she was not as disregardful of her person as she seemed. She had not resolved the childhood ambivalences over her appearance that had dogged her so long. She had a morbid fear of incapacitation and disfigurement. In 1975, she had to have a lump removed from her finger. Before the operation, she asked Marvin to promise that if the lump were diagnosed malignant, he would not give his permission for the finger to be amputated, even if it meant saving her life. Marvin refused. "We had the biggest fight of our whole marriage over my saying 'a finger is not worth your life.' Fay got a friend, who agreed to her condition, to stay in the operating room instead."

Although moving away from prisoners and prisons, she did take a case in 1977 that seemed to promise to rekindle some of the spirit of the Sixties. It involved the claim of Jane Scherr, longtime companion of *Berkeley Barb* founder and publisher Max Scherr. She had lived with him, taken his name, borne him two children, and helped him build the most successful of all underground papers, but when they separated he resisted her claims for a share of the property. Fay immediately saw its political implications (which were similar to the subsequent and celebrated Lee Marvin "palimony" case), but her efforts to build it into a feminist *cause célèbre* were frustrated when Max produced a legal Chicana wife and three children from a marriage preceding his relationship with Jane. A subsequent suit on implied partnership was also frustrated through the efforts of Max Scherr's attorneys Doris Walker and Harry Margolis, old friends and old leftists as well, who Fay felt had conned her into delaying her filing while the *Barb*'s assets were spirited out of the country. "The Left betrayed me," Fay told friends and associates, allowing the confrontation to fester into a bitterness that isolated her even more within the community that had once been her main support.

Barbara Price, a junior member of the Stender law firm, remembers Fay leaving her front office and pounding down the hall, still moving fast although there was nothing now that needed urgent action. She often argued with Marvin because he was too easygoing in billing and never pressed clients for payment. She installed a pump organ in her office to help her ventilate tension at the end of the day. The song she played most often was "The Battle Hymn of the Republic," because she like the mighty chord progressions.

It was the "Me Decade," a time when many radicals were turning their energies to human potential movements and careers. Fay, too, began to look inward. She was in her mid-forties and had never really taken time to deal with her personal dimension, her political commitments having condemned such activity as bourgeois. But radical politics, on which she had staked everything, had failed her, and now she was forced to reassess herself. She was very capable of dealing with others' problems, legal and personal, but seemed not to know quite how to begin to rebuild her own life. She saw that she had let relationships with those closest to her lapse and moved, somewhat clumsily at first, to heal them. Her daughter, Oriane, for instance, had grown up to be a lovely young woman, of whom Fay was both proud and a little envious. "In a way, she compared me to herself as a teenager," says Oriane. "She was sort of jealous of me because I was popular and successful with the whole social scene in a way she never was. We used to have fights over makeup and things. I would say, 'Give me a break. If I want to spend an hour in front of the mirror, I will.' "After months of struggle, the two of them had joined a mothers and daughters group, and Fay found herself talking about issues involving self and expectation as a woman, which she had never allowed herself to consider.

She began to wonder if she wanted to practice law at all. In 1978, she began to write articles for the feminist journal *Chrysalis* and joined the editorial board of the *San Francisco Review*, a new literary magazine. She returned to the piano and began practicing seriously for the first time in nearly thirty years.

She became more and more interested in feminism and was drawn increasingly to a community of colleagues where the issues of personal life and politics seemed to merge—the community of gay women lawyers. She had joined the board of Lesbian Rights and had invited her gay lawyer friends Patti Roberts and Barbara Price to serve on the board of the Child Custody Project. "We were clearly there to be a lesbian voice," says Price. "Fay did not want to raise the questions herself, but by backing us she forced the board to deal with the issues of lesbian custody and came into serious conflict with the traditionalists present." Someone who didn't know Fay might have said that she had merely gotten involved in the next trendy movement, transferring her concern from one "oppressed group," black prisoners, to another, women. But there was more to it than that. The commitment to feminism and gay rights was part of a process of discovery that was forcing her to dig up the layers of self buried under years of political extroversion.

As she socialized more and more in the lesbian legal community and felt herself attracted to other women, Fay began to seriously examine the possibility of such a relationship and the problems it would entail. It would offer a relief from the macho oppressiveness of black male prisoners, but it was a formidable step in other ways, leading to relationships perhaps even more intense than the heterosexual ones she had known, and less easily controlled. "She talked about the social conventions," Price recalls. "She was worried it would hurt her professionally. She was terribly afraid of what her kids would think. She was also worried about the hurt it would cause Marvin."

Fay's marriage had been a powerful source of stability during those years when the radical centrifuge threatened to pull her life apart. She had formed brief liaisons with other men, affairs she didn't hide from her husband. There had been the passionate interludes with George Jackson and Huey Newton. And once, in the years preceding the advent of the Black Panthers, she had moved in for a time with an old college lover, a Communist who wrote abstruse theory for the Marxist journal *Monthly Review*. But she always had an almost subliminal compatibility with Marvin, even when they were on the outs. It was a preternaturally close affinity: the two of them even looked alike, strangers sometimes mistaking them for brother and sister. He was steady while she was volatile; Marvin could be easily satisfied, while she knew her appetites would always cause a rumbling in the pit of her existence. She appreciated him for his soothing predictability, yet she could not help seeing this quality as an expression of an emotional status quo—something against which to rebel.

It was a measure of Fay's unarticulated conflict that even while she was contemplating an involvement that might jeopardize her marriage, she was also pouring deferred energies into their home. She had the entire house repainted, inside and out, the porch redone, and the furniture recovered. As a centerpiece, she had the kitchen completely remodeled, adding a standing fireplace, brick floor, skylight, and greenhouse window—an elegant arena more suited to a wife and mother devoted to keeping the nuclear family together than to a woman embarked on an odyssey that might destroy it.

In 1978, Fay ran as the only woman candidate for the board of governors of the State Bar of California. During the campaign, which she lost by a two-to-one margin, she met Katherine Morse, a young lawyer.* They became lovers, and the affair brought the crises in her life to a head. Fay was forty-seven years old and had to pick a road to travel for the rest of her life. When the election was over, she announced that she was going to Europe for three or four months to take stock and decide what to do.   • • •

---

* A pseudonym.

Fay had arranged to attend a legal seminar in Warsaw on the rights of children and a Year of the Child conference in Sweden, but the trip had a far more personal dimension. It had aspects of a return to roots. She kept a notebook, in which she wrote her feelings about being a Jew in Europe. Wherever she went, she visited local synagogues and temples. She attended High Holiday services in Greece. She made a special pilgrimage to her father's birthplace in Russia. When she filed a report in the *California Women Lawyers News*, she concluded it with an observation about anti-Semitism:

> On the most personal note of all, and yet to my mind vitally significant, the hospitality of the Polish lawyers was extremely cordial, but the anti-Semitism of the Polish society—manifested by a complete denial that Jews had existed, or did exist, by the ignoring of the Warsaw ghetto monument through four days of sight-seeing and tour-busing—reminds us that some lessons are harder to learn than we have yet to face.

Fay went to Geneva and visited Roberta Brooks and Lee Halterman, old friends who worked in the office of Congressman Ron Dellums. The visit was going to be for one night, but, she wound up staying more than a week. "In a way, it was as though she couldn't leave," Brooks remembers. "She kind of just hunkered down with us. It was a difficult period for her. She was ready to make profound changes in her life." The three old friends wandered through the city's marketplaces and shops, trading confidences, exploring ideas and experiences. One day they drove to the east end of Lake Geneva to the Château Chillon and visited the dungeon where Byron's prisoner had languished, inscribing his name on the cold stone walls. How far Fay had come from the prisoners' movement was not discussed, but it was on their minds.

Among the issues Fay talked about with Roberta, none was more pressing than the decision she knew she had to make about her marriage with Marvin. "She was divided between wanting to be with her family, in her house, with her grandmother's china, as she put it, her kids and Marvin," explains

Brooks, "and with the dissatisfaction that gave her. She kept saying, 'Why can't I have my china and my house and all those other things?' and was angry because she couldn't have everything she wanted." She had pushed the issue to its decision point. "If she returned to the States after Geneva, she would go back to Marvin. If she stayed and went to Sweden, it was the end of their marriage."

The exciting, gratifying, and finally lacerating experiences of the past churned inside her. "From our discussions it was clear that her feminism drew in part on the time she'd spent representing men in prison," Brooks says. "They ripped her off on some level, she felt." She was bitter about something that had happened eight years earlier, before Brooks had even known her. "She told me that she and Huey Newton had been very close, and then when she saw him at a party after he was released on the basis of her appeal, he didn't even speak to her. Her attitude was, 'Jesus Christ, I sacrificed all those years. I sacrificed spending weekends with my family to go down there to San Luis Obispo to deal with his case, and then I see him in a room and he doesn't speak to me.' "

But there were certain aspects of her prison work Fay still didn't want to discuss. Only part of this reticence was caution. She had long since become critical of the self-delusion of the Left. Yet she still reserved a special place in her heart for the most romantic revolutionary of all. For a wedding present, she gave two friends a framed letter from George Jackson, urging her to keep up the fight. It was presented as if it were an icon.

Before she left Geneva for Sweden, there was an exchange of letters and a transatlantic phone call with Marvin about the marriage. A decision was reached to separate. Fay went on to Stockholm, where she lived for two months in a little apartment. It was the dead of the arctic winter of 1978, and the dark shadows of night fell at three o'clock in the afternoon. It was the first time she had lived alone.

In her apartment, she read and wrote. She was working on manuscripts about George Jackson and feminism. Never physically active, she now did push-ups daily—as Jackson had done in his solitary confinement—laboring until she could do twenty in a row. She seemed to be growing into her body for the first time, learning to use and appreciate it. She dieted and lost thirty-five pounds. One night, she went to a piano bar and, after a few drinks for self-fortification, sat down to play. The patrons applauded and demanded an encore. She wondered if she could earn money professionally playing jazz piano. She sent her intimate friends a barrage of letters filled with a new kind of self-assessment.

When she got back to Berkeley, the cherry blossoms were in bloom, a false spring that natives know is always followed by sharp winter frosts. "Fay was really in the best shape of all the time I knew her in that period," says her friend Barbara Price. "She seemed very happy, with a strong sense of herself." Marvin had moved out, leaving the house to Fay and the children. Fay and Marvin agreed to dissolve the firm of Stender and Stender. With Price, Fay laid plans to organize a new office for women lawyers. She resumed her lesbian relationship with Katherine. She spent time writing and continued her program of physical exercise. She jogged daily on the Berkeley High School track and did lap swimming and weight lifting at the university gym. Her body grew strong; her spirits rose. One night her old friend Sanne DeWitt saw her at a performance of Brahms's *German Requiem*, and Fay told her, "I feel confident, capable, and happy." It seemed that she had succeeded in her attempt to seal off the past and prevent it from leaking poison into her future.

It was 1:20 A.M. on May 28, 1979, when Fay's son, Neal, then twenty years old, was aroused by a knock at the front door. He had been only half asleep in a second-floor bedroom, having returned late from a party. Fay and Katherine were sleeping in another bedroom, and his sister Oriane was in still another.

Neal pulled on his pants and rimless glasses, then went downstairs. Switching on the porch light from the hall, he looked through the curtained window of the front door and saw a young black woman in a tan coat. Having grown up as Fay's son, he was neither surprised nor alarmed at the appearance of a stranger in the middle of the night. As he turned the dead bolt and opened the door, the woman was pushed aside by a powerful black man in a dark leather jacket and blue watch cap. The young woman melted into the darkness; the man rushed forward, pointing a .38-caliber pistol in Neal's face.

"Does Fay Stender live here?" he demanded.

Neal answered that she did. The man ordered Neal to show him where she was. Starting up the stairs, Neal felt the snout of the pistol on the base of his skull. "Please don't hurt us," he pleaded.

"Get moving," the man snapped, "or I'll blow your fucking head off!"

When Neal knocked, a sleepy voice called out from his mother's bedroom. "What is it?"

He opened the door and entered. "There's a man with a gun who wants to talk to you."

The gunman stepped up and peered at the faces on the pillows. "Who's Fay Stender?"

"I am," Fay said as she sat up. Next to her, Katherine sank deeper into the covers, until she appeared to be only a pale, frightened face nesting in red hair.

"Prove it."

Fay reached into the desk drawer next to the bed and pulled out a MasterCharge card.

"Don't you have anything better?" asked the man with the gun. She shook her head. "Get up," he said, gesturing with the gun. Fay asked if she could get a robe, and when he shrugged she went to the closet and put it on.

"Sit down at the desk," he ordered. "I want you to write something." As she fumbled for her glasses, the small shelty dog Katherine had adopted snarled at the man. Fay warned him about the animal. As if momentarily forgetting the situation, he thanked her.

"Have you ever betrayed anyone?" he asked.

"No!" She looked up anxiously, worried by the menace in his voice, the tense, volcanic temper she remembered from working in prisons.

"Don't you feel you betrayed George Jackson?"

"No," she said, her voice rising.

A look of scorn crossed his face as he ordered her to write what he dictated. "I, Fay Stender, admit I betrayed

George Jackson and the prison movement when they needed me most."

She started to write but then stopped, as if she couldn't make her pen obey. "Now, this isn't true," she said. "And I would like to tell you why. This isn't true. I'm just writing this because you're holding a gun at my head."

He waved the gun impatiently, staring in a way that made her flinch. She wrote out the sentence, and he took the paper and folded it into his pocket. He asked for money. Neal took four dollars out of his wallet. Katherine sat up in bed and told the man that there was money in her purse. He grabbed it from the chair and emptied it but found nothing. Her face flushed, and she quickly explained. "Oh, I'm sorry. The money is in my pants." He pulled six dollars out of her pocket and then ordered Neal to tie her up. Neal looked around helplessly.

"Oh, man, use your belt." The gunman seemed disgusted at the display of honky incompetence. After Neal had tied Katherine's hands, as he was told, the man went over to the wall and pulled out an extension cord. Ordering Neal to lie face down on the bed alongside Katherine, he bound Neal's wrists behind his back.

Fay had tried to distract the man when he was emptying Katherine's purse, telling him that there was more money in the kitchen. He escorted her downstairs. She went to the kitchen counter and opened a drawer. Again she tried to state her case: "I didn't do it. I didn't betray George or anyone."

The man waved the .38 menacingly. "Come on. Come on." She gave him the forty dollars in the drawer, but before she had got all the bills out, he commanded her to walk into the hall.

He passed her and started toward the door. Just as he got there, he wheeled around suddenly, raised the gun, and braced his right wrist with his left hand, crouching into a police-style firing stance. The first bullet hit Fay in the stomach. He fired again and then again—five shots, all at point-blank range.

Upstairs, Neal heard his mother's screams. Rushing through the darkness, his hands still tied behind him, he kicked open the door to Oriane's bedroom and yelled to her to call an ambulance. Then, running toward the sound of Fay's voice, he found her lying on the floor, her nightgown soaked with blood. "I'm dying," she cried.

At Herrick Hospital, doctors worked feverishly to save her. A tube was inserted in her chest to clear the blood pooling in her right lung. An exploratory laparotomy was performed, and a .38 slug was found floating in the abdominal cavity. A hemorrhage in her liver was controlled; one segment of intestine was removed because of multiple perforations. One bullet was removed from her right elbow, and another, which had lodged in the thoracic vertebra, was also removed. The bullets had hollow points designed to enlarge on impact.

She had been shot in the abdomen, chest, and both arms, with a grazing wound on the side of her head. Newspaper accounts the next day pointed out that the gunman seemed to have intended to imitate the pattern of a crucifix.

Fay began the first days of her convalescence amid the grinding pain that would not leave her the rest of her life. The bullet that had struck her vertebra, doctors told her when they thought she could handle the news, had left her with a paralysis from the waist down, which would be permanent. Fay was devastated by the news; she suspected that the numbness and restricted motion in her hands meant she would never play the piano again. A colostomy had been performed, which meant she would always be incontinent. She pressed doctors to tell her if she would be able to function sexually. Reading between the lines of their bedside manner, she knew she would not. "I wish I had died," she said when friends came to try to lift her spirits in those first days, as the enormity of it all began to hit her.

"Fay just couldn't understand," says Sanne DeWitt. "She was baffled that anyone would want to kill her. She was also terrified by the future. She'd always been one of those people who couldn't allow herself to rely on anybody. She would look at me and say, 'Please wipe my mouth.' I saw how painful it was for her just to ask."

The fact that the gunman did not know her, coupled with the betrayal note she had been forced to sign, made police look for suspects in the Black Guerrilla Family (BGF), a prison gang that had been cofounded by Jackson and regarded him as a martyr. The BGF had ties to former prisoners on the outside and, it was reported, used them to carry out missions of vengeance growing out of internecine struggles in the prison movement. Oriane Stender told investigating officers that a few days before the shooting, she had bumped into Fleeta Drumgo (he and the third "Soledad Brother," John Cluchette, had been acquitted after Jackson's death), and he had told her someone was looking for her mother, a piece of news she passed off as hyperbole of the street.

On June 8, eleven days after the shooting, detectives at a narcotics stakeout on a San Francisco street corner identified themselves to three suspects. One of the men jumped back and reached into a vinyl bag for a gun. In the ensuing struggle, the gunman was disarmed. His bag was found to contain disguises, photos of a power station outside Folsom Prison, a list of foreign consulates and prominent business executives, and hollow-point ammunition. He was identified as Edward Glenn Brooks, an ex-con who had served three and a half years before his release from San Quentin. After posting bail, he and his two associates were released, and promptly disappeared.

After being notified of the arrest, the Berkeley homicide squad had begun a check on the three men and found that Brooks had been stopped by Oakland police prior to the Stender shooting. He had been in the company of Fleeta Drumgo and others who had once known Fay. Two days later, San Francisco police ballistic experts reported that bullets fired from the missing Brooks's gun matched those taken from Fay during surgery. Then, on June 14, Brooks was apprehended during a robbery attempt at a Berkeley bank. Later, he was identified by Neal Stender as the man who had shot his mother. Fay confirmed the identification from a videotape shown at her hospital bedside.

The arrest of a black ex-prisoner, who turned out indeed to be a follower of George Jackson, for the shooting of Fay Stender sent shock waves through the radical legal community. People who had spent their professional lives denouncing the criminal justice system as an instrument of racial and class oppression and defending accused criminals as social victims found themselves identifying with the efforts of the police and the district attorney's office. Fay's former law partner Doron

Weinberg remembers sitting with a group of radical attorneys when the news came of the arrest. "From the first reports it seemed like a bad search. Everyone in the room had to grapple with the same questions: Oh, my God, is this guy going to get out on a technicality? Is some civil liberties lawyer going to come along and get him off? Did the cops fuck up again?"

A Pandora's box of doubt and self-recrimination had been opened and would not close. "I was with two radical attorneys after Fay was shot," recalls Barbara Price. "They were talking to each other and saying out loud what I figured they had never said out loud before about their own criminal practice. They each spoke of how they had successfully defended people on assault and murder charges. They had defended them as radicals who felt it was the system that had put them in the position of being criminals. Within a few months of acquittal, their clients had each murdered some person. And now they had to live with that."

Speculation about the ultimate responsibility for the shooting centered on a Nicaraguan maximum-security prisoner named Hugo "Yogi" Pinell. Reputed to be the head of the Black Guerrilla Family, Pinell, one of the San Quentin Six defendants and former prisonmate of Edward Brooks, had been transferred to Folsom after being convicted of slitting a guard's throat during Jackson's abortive uprising. Although Pinell issued a statement from Folsom dissociating himself from the attempt on Fay's life, police were worried about information picked up from the street that Fay had been only one of several persons on a BGF hit list.

At the preliminary hearing for Brooks, the radical community received another jolt to its sense of security and self-identity when one of its hard-core veterans, a former employee of Fay's and member of the radical Prison Law Collective, showed up as part of Brooks's defense team. Linda Castro, a Chicana paralegal worker, was a personal friend of Brooks, but the justification she offered for taking up his cause was political: "I was just seething at the way the white Left reacted to Brooks' arrest. It was racist. They had never taken this attitude when someone was shot in the past. They had said third world people can't get fair treatment from the police and the courts. And yet, when one of their own was shot, they immediately cooperated with the cops and used the same system they said could never treat people of color fairly."

Castro's irrational presence caused a new wave of paranoia among her co-workers and former comrades in the legal Left, especially when it became clear that she had personal links to Yogi Pinell stretching back to the time when she had worked along with the other radicals in Fay's old law collective on the trial of the San Quentin Six. Was there really a "hit list"? What other names were on it? Says one radical lawyer: "We began to think, if Linda's involved, who might not be? You couldn't tell who your friends were anymore, and who your enemies."

An even denser cloud of fear enveloped the hospital room where Fay lay in agony. She was worried about Neal, an eyewitness to the crime; she was terrified for herself. "I can't run now," she said. "I'm just a target." In August, she left the hospital in a wheelchair, her whereabouts shrouded by elaborate security measures. Only a few people knew the name of the rehabilitation center where she went. She adopted an assumed name and identity for use there; friends went through whispered rehearsals with her at her bedside on the details of her new life history.

At first, she tried to force her way through physical therapy as she had through life, demanding that her body yield to her will and become functional again. She sat propped in front of a piano, commanding her hands to work, but finally gave it up because her fingers were too weak to strike the keys and her dead feet could not work the pedals. She was not able to sit up well enough to foresee even a life of limited mobility in a wheelchair, the pain in her back making any position except lying down almost unendurable. She talked about suicide constantly, begging her friends to help her by getting her sleeping pills. They told her that experts said it took a year to begin to cope with the trauma she had been through and that she must wait to see if she could adapt. "It isn't fair," she wept. "It isn't fair that I have to go through the worst part of this to prove to other people I'm of sound enough mind to make this decision for myself."

After her release she did not return to Berkeley. Instead she took an apartment in San Francisco, on the top floor of a building whose location only a select few friends were allowed to know. She had a nurse, a watchdog, and occasionally an armed guard; friends wanting to visit her would be picked up late at night and taken there via a deliberately confusing route. She bought a gun and was issued a permit making her one of the few people in San Francisco allowed to carry it concealed. She was taken to the firing range periodically but worried that if a situation ever arose in which she would have to defend herself, her hands would be too feeble to permit her to use the weapon effectively.

She had told her lover Katherine that she didn't want her to visit. "Part of it," says Barbara Price, "was that Katherine was hovering over her, being protective. Fay didn't like that. But I think Fay also had a lot of concern for her. She knew she wasn't going to walk, wasn't going to be sexually functional, wasn't going to do anything. That's really why she pushed Katherine out. Her logic was obvious to me: As an act of love I need to prevent this woman from dedicating herself to me, or from going through the guilt of worrying about whether or not to leave an invalid. I'll solve it by just pushing her away. It was real hard on Katherine. Fay wouldn't answer her letters."

For a brief time she indulged the fantasy of patching up her relationship with Marvin and reassembling her family. But Marvin was living with another woman and, despite his continuing love, said no. "She felt remorse over this," says Price. "She knew that if she hadn't come back from Sweden and broken things up just six months before, he would have been right there for her, as he always had been, a twenty-five-year relationship of stability and affection. So there she was—no family, no home, nothing. And she couldn't really say she was wholly blameless in what had happened to her."

Fay had protected some of her illusions for a long time, but she now had no intellectual or political armor left to stave off bitterness. "I should never have gotten into prison work," she told a friend. "This is what happens." And even more despairingly: "I would never again make the mistake of doing something for somebody else's benefit." The ironies of her life gnawed at her. "I structured my whole existence around trying to do something about racism," she said. "I moved my family to a neighborhood where my children would have friends of all races. I passed up other opportunities so I could work with prisoners. Now this. It's too much to bear."

From her bed she filed a suit to get the massive costs of her care covered under workmen's compensation insurance—another landmark case of sorts, and her last. Meanwhile, the generosity she had shown friends, even during those times she had been most preoccupied, was now reciprocated. A committee was organized to raise money, a Fay Stender Trust Fund that would help pay the bills and allow her to live during a period of reentry into daily life. It was a form of encouragement for her to keep going. Eventually more than one hundred thousand dollars was raised. Yet even here there were hard lessons. One of the events was a benefit in San Francisco. There were only two or three blacks in an audience of nearly three hundred. Sanne DeWitt remembers Fay saying: "I don't understand it. I've done so many benefits for black causes. Where are the people I tried to help? Where are they now?"

To preserve her sanity, Fay turned her thoughts to the upcoming prosecution of Edward Brooks and what she knew would be her last appearance in a courtroom, this time as witness for the prosecution. "I'm just living for this trial," she told friends. "I want to see him put away." She regarded Brooks as a gun whose trigger had been pulled by others, and she spent hours contriving ingenious strategies to smoke them out. Some of her friends felt she had given in to paranoia. Yet events provided substance for her fears. A week after the shooting, Soledad Brother Fleeta Drumgo, looking disoriented, had appeared in the Garry law offices. He said he was a member of the Black Guerrilla Family, that he had known of the BGF's plans to shoot Fay two weeks before the event, and that he was willing to sell information. He reappeared on several occasions, sometimes wearing a gun in his belt, and named Yogi Pinell, head of the BGF, as the man who had ordered the shooting. To the police, Drumgo's information was just hearsay. But Fay's mother, Ruby, received a death threat in the mail, signed by the BGF, and one month before Brooks's trial was to begin, Drumgo was shot dead on an Oakland street corner, the victim of what police called "a ganglandstyle execution." At the funeral, Angela Davis eulogized Drumgo as "a Communist martyr."

On January 16, 1980, Edward Brooks entered the court-room, moving with what both Neal and Fay described as a "swagger-walk." He strode over to his handful of supporters—virtually the only blacks present—and gave a clenched-fist salute, oddly torqued, like a punch arrested in midflight. Thomas Broome, the lawyer finally appointed to represent him after several of the radical attorneys who usually accepted such cases had declined, did his best, but the verdict was never really in doubt. The only real drama was what would happen during Fay's day in court.

On the morning of her appearance, the courtroom was packed with friends and supporters, many of whom had been present at the famous political trials of the past, of which this one seemed a grotesque parody. "Virtually everybody who was sitting in the room had either been doing criminal defense work or had been aligned with it politically all their lives," says Fay's attorney friend Mary Millman. "And now they were on the other side. There was a very heavy awareness of that." There was also an awareness of what had happened since Huey Newton stood trial in the same building thirteen years earlier, a time that seemed eons away in terms of innocence lost.

The Movement had long since destroyed itself through sectarian ecstasies and cannibalism, with each new year bringing a few pathetic Weathermen in from the cold after unglamorous underground lives waiting tables and watching afternoon soap operas. The other arm of the great black-white revolutionary coalition was equally diminished. The Panthers were implicated in Oakland graft and rackets, having reverted to their origins as a gang. Huey Newton was constantly in court, facing a variety of charges: murdering a prostitute (two hung juries), assault (acquitted), and being an ex-felon in possession of a gun (convicted). Eldridge Cleaver was back in the country after exile, repeatedly born again, most recently into the flock of the Reverend Sun Myung Moon. Bobby Seale, having been incommunicado from his former comrades because of fear for his life, had emerged on the East Coast, promoting a book of his barbecue recipes. And Yogi Pinell, having denied his complicity in the attack, had been offered "political asylum" by the new revolutionary Sandinista regime in Managua.

Shortly before her turn to testify, Fay was wheeled into

the courtroom by four armed guards, so completely disguised in a gray bouffant wig that many of her friends didn't recognize her until she took the stand. Deputy district attorney Howard Janssen led her dispassionately through the events of the fateful night some six months earlier. Their exchange on the shooting itself was emotionally flat, deliberately so, yet, as Mary Millman says, "You got goose bumps listening just because it was so analytical and removed":

Q: Where do you recall feeling the bullets?
A: I felt the first one in the abdomen, or stomach, and I felt a kind of snap, and I thought that it was a spinal cord thing, and I felt two bullets in either arm, one in each elbow, and I felt one in the chest, and I felt one in the head that sort of whizzed by but did touch me behind the ear.

The defendant did not take the stand to testify. The decision was his attorney's. "Brooks has a lot of moxie," Broome later said. "I think he really had some thoughts about wanting to get up on the stand and tell his story. But I don't think it's a story I wanted to hear." Specifically, Broome did not want Brooks to reveal his feelings about George Jackson, "which was something that he was really into and that would have hurt his case."

On January 25, the jury reached its verdict, finding Brooks guilty of attempted murder, burglary, and two counts of robbery. Four weeks later, in court once again before receiving a sentence of seventeen years in prison—Brooks stood up and asked for permission to read a statement. "And so the railroad continues," he began, glaring at the court, "and you have convicted another innocent man." Judge Harold Hove interrupted him and ordered the defense attorney to take over reading the document. But Broome read only a minute longer before the judge said, "I'm not going to sit here and listen to this," and ordered the statement filed.

Brooks's unread document was like a grim travesty of Fay Stender's career, calling attention to the "connection between conspiracies of the state and the so-called criminal justice system" and then proceeding to recite a litany of prison martyrs, including the three men shot in the Soledad yard back in 1970, Jonathan Jackson and those with him in the Marin courthouse raid, and George Jackson. Others not dead were also invoked, including Yogi Pinell, "framed and railroaded a number of times since 1969, including the S.Q. 6 case, by the forces of the state, for the same reasons. All of these strong, beautiful black men have been and are being framed-up, assassinated, and subjected to assassination attempts simply because they stand and fight as men against the racism, injustice and in humanity that is so embedded in this Amerikkkan society."

After the sentence had been read and the judge was leaving the courtroom, Brooks, who had been blowing kisses to female supporters, suddenly sprinted across the room, swinging wildly, and lunged at the astonished prosecutor, Janssen, knocking him down before being subdued by bailiffs and dragged back, bleeding, to the courthouse jail.

After the trial, Fay would still not go out on the streets, but on rare occasions she did accept invitations to dinner or to a small party. She was like someone who had undergone a sea change, who had successfully passed some crisis and was now safely into the next phase. There was a new softness in her face. Neal's girlfriend, Amy, cut Fay's hair short, making her brown eyes seem larger, more liquid—vulnerable. It was as if events had gentled her. Somewhat fatalistically, she asked Katherine to visit her again.

She tried to find the conditions for continuing her life, using a lawyer's logic in a dispassionate consideration of her alternatives. But always she ran into dead ends. People urged her to get back to work. She said that it was possible she would do tax law. When asked about criminal appellate work, which had always been her forte, she replied, "Oh, no. I'd never do that again. I couldn't be that dumb."

Still in pain, unable to foresee any way of adjusting to life as a seriously disabled person, Fay began to order that part of her destiny still remaining in her control. With an intensity reminiscent of the schemes of the prisoners she had worked with, she began to plan an escape. She announced that she was going to take a trip to Hong Kong, telling people who asked why that if she were away from fear of another ambush, things might look different to her. She set a date in March for her departure and began to organize her remaining time. She arranged for the apartment to be closed, for her business to be wound up, for her belongings to be distributed—"loaned out," as she put it.

It was a poignant time of leave-takings and last things. People coming and going in the final month noted that there was always a fire burning in her fireplace. "She put a constant stream of papers in there," says Barbara Price. "She had me bring her files from the office. Books and manuscripts and texts and court testimonies and briefs—all her prison stuff. Everything she had written." These were the pieces of her life. She watched them char, the fire reflecting in her eyes, a slight smile on her lips. One of the things she burned was the manuscript on George Jackson.

Sometimes she talked as if she were going on holiday and might be coming back. She encouraged Oriane and Katherine to make plans to come to Hong Kong to see her later in the spring, after she was settled. For the first time since she had been shot, she seemed almost happy.

"The day she left was her forty-eighth birthday. She was in the best shape I remember," says Price. "She had on shorts, and she was fooling around. She made a little joke. I was there right before Marvin and Katherine came to see her off. She told me that she had decided to form the Jewish Lesbian Nearly Fifty Paraplegic Gun Club."

But another friend, there to see the car pull away for the airport, remembers Fay looking at her for a moment through the window and silently forming these words with her lips: "Remember, I'm not Joan of Arc."

At first there was a stream of letters—the old Fay, hectoring people, mother-henning them. Roberta Brooks, who was now pregnant, got a note telling her to call the person who had Fay's old maternity tops. Neal and Oriane received mail filled with chatter and, occasionally, despair. Sanne DeWitt got a letter suggesting that her husband, a physicist under fire from the government, consult Doron Weinberg, an expert in such matters. This letter concluded:

As for me, I am in a comfortable apartment with the amenities (color TV, English language newspapers, names of friends of friends), and it is nice not to fear I will be shot every minute—one trade-off from being far from home and loving friends. The pain is almost as bad. I spend three-quarters of my time in bed and continue depressed. I don't know what more to say. It will be a year on 5/28, and I don't find myself interested in anything—and I don't see how the passage of time now is going to change anything. Well, enough gloom. I hope things with your kids and jobs and lives keep on being ok and better.

Fondly,
Fay

This letter was dated May 11, 1980. A few days later, Oriane placed a long-distance call to her mother. "I had gotten three really depressing letters in a week, and I just didn't know what to do. I called her to say, 'Why don't I come visit you now?' That's what I wanted to say." But Oriane's call was taken by the woman who attended Fay, who said that her mother was dead from an overdose of pills.

In a series of letters to those closest to her, timed to arrive after her death, Fay said her last goodbyes. In the suicide note to her lover Katherine she wrote:

Know that I tried and at times with you almost thought I might make it, but—I couldn't—every moment of it hurt overwhelmingly—too deep, too pervasive. . . .

It is hardly surprising that no one at her funeral wanted to deal with the questions of Fay's life and death. The issues were too lacerating, too complex. Her tragedy conveyed too daunting a message. And, if one forgot for a moment the particulars, she was too clearly a radical Everyperson.

After the service, Ezra Hendon, her friend and former ally in the Prison Law Project, sat in his living room, trying to sum things up. "Her funeral marked the end of an era in my life, and I think the end of an era, period. Her conviction that you could be committed to a political goal, work for it, and be brilliant in its service—in a clean way—that's over for me. I don't know about the others, but I can't have that belief anymore.

"You don't ever quite believe you're vulnerable that way. I still represent clients who have varying levels of criminality. Many are on death row, and believe me, I have no illusions—these are dangerous, dangerous people. My attitude toward them is strictly professional: I am their lawyer, and I don't make the mistake of thinking I'm anything more than that.

"I guess it would be easy to say that Fay played with fire, and people who play with fire get burned. But it should count for something that she wanted to be a force for good in this world, that she was a brilliant, remarkable woman who dedicated her life to others and to making the world a better place."

As he said the words, Hendon's eyes rimmed with tears. Like others who missed Fay, he was mourning not merely for a lost friend but for a lost cause as well.

chapter 2 ⸻

The Rise and Fall of the Weather Underground

Doing It

Every March 6, a small cluster of people with flowers in their hands gathers in front of a triangular brick structure whose modern lines set it off from the Federal-style town houses that front the rest of the block. Someone with a knack for places and faces, or an antiquarian's knowledge of radical Leftism, might make the connection. This oddly obtrusive building was inserted into the cavity caused by the town house explosion of 1970 that claimed the lives of three members of the Weather Underground. The people who stand in silence for a moment before setting down the flowers and walking off are their former comrades, among them former Weatherman leaders Billy Ayers and Bernadine Dohrn.

More than anyone else, Ayers and Dohrn embody the odd mix of characters and politics that propelled Weatherman onto the center stage of the American scene in the late Sixties, a strange and frightened augury even for those hypertrophied times. They seem oddly unchanged by the intervening years, as if life in the previously undiscovered country of the American underground, where they lived for a decade, kept them from aging. Dressed in bib overalls, with curly blond hair dancing on his shoulders, Ayers still looks like he did when he was the blithe spirit of Weatherman, expressing the organization's worldview in his large appetite for sex, drugs, and violence, as well as in his insouciant nihilism. Bernadine—by sheer force of will she made herself into one of those public figures it seems natural to call by their first names—still has the strong-jawed sensuality and look of sultry defiance that made her into something like a radical pinup during the years she scourged the nation for its racism at home and genocide abroad and warned that she and her comrades were "crazy motherfuckers" dedicated to "scaring the shit out of honky America."

The two of them were on the run for ten years, setting off bombs, issuing "communiqués," and making themselves into legendary figures. When they negotiated their way back aboveground late in 1980, they were unlike some of the others, who freely admitted that their gods of revolution had failed. The names they gave their two sons, Malik (for Malcolm X) Geronimo and Zayd (for fallen Black Liberation Army "soldier" Zayd Shakur) Osceola, testified to their ongoing commitment. When asked about the lessons she'd learned over the decade, Bernadine replies coolly that she knows now that being a revolutionary involves endurance, a willingness to defer gratification. Less guarded, Ayers conveys a touch of the old whimsical arrogance when he draws a cynical moral about the logic of their lives thus far: "Guilty as hell, free as a bird— America is a great country."

They come each year to the site of the town house explosion, as they did even when they were underground, to honor their commitment as much as their fallen dead. As the years pass, there are other events that demonstrate the price of revolutionary zeal. One happened in October 1981, when a group of "freedom fighters" from the Black Liberation Army attacked a Brink's truck in front of Nanuet National Bank, shotgunning one guard to death and wounding two others, and then killed two policemen at a roadblock near Nyack, New York. The next day, the BLA (a tiny splinter of the Black Panther Party) claimed that the "attempted expropriation" of $1.6 million was intended to finance armed struggle that would liberate a black nation from American soil. The irony that made the event special for Billy and Bernadine and kept it from being dismissed as just another squalid heist was the presence of three whites who were former members of the Weather Underground among those arrested.

Nyack was the enactment of the quintessential Weatherman fantasy, just as the town house had been. It could have been a moment to take stock, as Mark Rudd, another former Weather leader, had in New Mexico when his father called immediately after hearing news of the botched holdup and shoot-out and said: "The blood of those policemen is on your hands." But just as Ayers, Dohrn, and the other survivors robbed the town house explosion of significance by making it a radical equivalent of Memorial Day, so it was impossible for them to see themselves in the bloody events of Nyack or to recognize that what happened there was a delayed moral to the story they had helped to write a decade earlier.

"Bernadine and I got an early edition of the *New York Times* right after we heard about Nyack," Ayers said later on. "We kept looking at the picture of one of the women arrested, who was not identified. We looked at it for hours. She seemed familiar, but we couldn't quite figure out who it was. The next day we found out that it was Kathy Boudin. We'd lived with her all those years underground and had seen her often since. But we never really recognized her. It was weird."

If Weatherman ended in the tragedy of Nyack, it began as farce—a reversal of Marx's formulation about the way history repeats itself. After they had begun to achieve improbable success as the most extravagant development of the politics of the Sixties, the Weatherpeople, like all parvenus, spent considerable time working on a genealogy that would connect them with noble forebears: Russian *narodniki* and European anarchists, Cuban *fidelistas* and Vietnamese guerrillas. In truth, however, the organization was also the bastard child of the American mischief that had entered the Movement in mid-decade, and a whoopie cushion had to figure as prominently on its family crest as the clenched fist.

It was early 1968, and a splinter group calling itself the Action Faction had formed within the chapter of Students for a Democratic Society (SDS) at Columbia University after a debate that had less to do with tactics than attitudes. It was about the same time that the Yippies had begun to inject theatrical panache into the Movement, and other campus political groups—such as the one at Ann Arbor that disrupted a speech by Dean Acheson by showing up in Vietcong dress and snapping off rounds from concealed squirt guns—were learning about the value of agitprop actions. Indicating that it found the New Left's love for endless abstruse discussion and perfect rhetorical formulations not only archaic but boring too, the Action Faction began to practice disruption and dirty tricks. Chief among its achievements was terminating a lengthy debate over military recruiting at Columbia by walking up to the U.S. Army colonel presenting the government's case, smooshing a pie in his face, and running away.

By that spring, when Columbia University trustees decided to go ahead with plans to build a gymnasium in nearby Morningside Heights that would displace black residents, the Action Faction made the decision into a metaphor for larger and more sinister forces at work on campus and in society. The group produced a leader, Mark Rudd. The large, twenty-year-old junior was affable, almost ursine, until he stood before a crowd; then he was transformed into a compelling, even charismatic figure. Rudd attacked the plan as a "racist land grab," in speeches that eventually mobilized thousands of students and sent them off to occupy university buildings.

As events at Columbia escalated, Rudd made the cover of *Newsweek* and became an instant celebrity. ("So you're a Communist now," his conservative Jewish mother said to him. "Well, I guess it could be worse. You could be queer.") But the insiders knew it was Rudd's friend John Jacobs who was the crucial figure behind events. Tall and rangy, with hooded good looks and an intentionally menacing manner, Jacobs showed up for meetings of the Action Faction sporting a leather jacket and Levi's, his shirt collar open to show a lion's tooth on a gold chain, and his hair slicked back into a ducktail. His style was street-corner stud, intended to clash with that of the earnest student radical. While Rudd thrived in the spotlight, Jacobs did better in the shadows as *éminence noire*. Most people at Columbia knew him only by his initials, J.J., which, as the conflict at the university deepened, became a legendary *nom de guerre*. "He had brains, vision, and the ability to talk," Rudd later said of his friend. "When he was on, he was brilliant. Nobody else even came close."

By the time events erupted into violence at Columbia, J.J. had already established a legendary persona, and stories about him circulated by friends were like radical parables. One of them had to do with a friend who had an ulcer and kept a store of milk to soothe it in the refrigerator of a collective household. In the middle of the night, J.J. drank it all. When the friend confronted him the next morning, J.J. stared him down, growling "I'm no liberal." While other student activists looked to the gradual building of a mass movement, J.J., feeling the tremors of the new militancy, spouted Lin Piao's thoughts on people's war and invoked Regis Debray's model of a small guerrilla *foco* that could catalyze social upheaval and bring down an empire. He quoted Che's dictum, which the success of his minifaction at Columbia confirmed: what the Movement needed to succeed was "audacity, audacity, and more audacity."

While Rudd influenced the daily flow of events at Columbia and reveled in the limelight as he occupied the desk of university president Grayson Kirk and smoked his cigars during the occupation, J.J. worked behind the scene, explaining how the events fit into a larger pattern of apocalypse that included the Tet offensive, LBJ's decision not to run for reelection, and the "revolutionary protests" in France, which, by May, nearly toppled the de Gaulle government. The corrupt structure of the capitalist world system was teetering, he argued, and all that was needed was a strategically applied push to send it crashing down. When NLF flags were hung out of the windows of Columbia's occupied buildings, when protesters talked of forming "affinity groups" to fight police, and when "Up Against the Wall, Motherfucker," a line from a LeRoi Jones poem glorifying black holdup artists and white victims, became the protesters' slogan, J.J. saw it all as intimations of revolutionary things to come.

When evicted President Kirk finally summoned police to

his campus to quash the rebellion, J.J. saw his prophecies confirmed. "J.J. was rubbing his hands with glee when the cops
came wading in with their night sticks," one student protester
later recalled. "He said it was 'maximizing the contradictions.' "

If some people at Columbia found J.J. a poseur, one who
found him intriguing was Bernadine Dohrn, a striking, twenty-
six-year-old attorney just then making a name for herself in
New York radical circles. She was typical of the group that
later became Weatherman: raised in the heartland of America;
radical antecedents nil. Her mother was a Christian Scientist,
from whom she inherited her icy good looks. Her father, a
Jew, had hoped to become a lawyer but wound up the credit
manager of a furniture store in suburban Whitefish Bay, Wisconsin, where he'd moved the family from Milwaukee. When
they were growing up, he'd told Bernadine and her sister, Jennifer, that he wanted them to learn how to "make it in a man's
world," but he also made it clear that this injunction contained
no critique of the traditional feminine roles.

By the time Bernadine began showing up as a spectator
at Columbia, her life had already become an exercise of self-
creation. She had been something of an ugly duckling in her
first years in high school, thin and nondescript, nicknamed
"Bernie," one of the good students, who yearned for acceptance by the socially successful. Then, in her junior year, she
had suddenly blossomed into a stunningly attractive woman—
bisque skin, brown eyes, a full figure. Boys who had ignored
her now fought for her attention.

At this moment of triumph, her father had decided to
change the family name from Ohrnstein, because people accused him of "Jewing" them out of their money. Bernadine
professed to be upset, but she also adopted the name Dohrn,
braving taunts from her classmates. The lesson she seemed to
extract from the episode had nothing to do with anti-Semitism
or the credit business, but with the fact that you could become
who you said you were. By the time she graduated, there was
something withheld in her—a latency hinted at by the year-
book aphorist who placed this single line beneath her senior
photograph: "a trace of the exotic."

After entering Miami University of Ohio, she attempted

to pledge Tri Delt, one of the most exclusive sororities there, but, she told friends, was blackballed when research by the national office yielded information about the Jewish name her father had changed. In her junior year, she transferred to the University of Chicago because, as she told her sister, she wanted something "more serious." She had missed out on the civil rights movement but got involved in the JOIN (Jobs Or Income Now) project SDS set up to do community organizing among the hillbillies in uptown Chicago. In 1966, while in the university's law school, she worked with Martin Luther King Jr.'s Southern Christian Leadership Conference in its attempt to attack segregation in the northern suburbs.

Bernadine rarely studied; she survived by what classmates saw as an uncanny combination of poise and the ability to say the right thing. A friend remembered seeing her on the back of a boyfriend's motorcycle on commencement day, black gown hiked up to show her fine legs. Sensing that the emerging antiwar movement would be as much of an arena for making it as the business world had been for her father's generation, Bernadine didn't bother with the state bar exam; instead she landed a staff job as the National Lawyers Guild student organizer.

Hitting New York in the fall of 1967, with her tight miniskirt and knee-high Italian leather boots, she created an instant sensation among males in Movement circles. She traveled from campus to campus doing draft counseling, causing potential resisters to come from miles around just to see her. "I'll never forget the first time I saw Bernadine," says Greg Calvert, then SDS president. "She was wearing an orange sweater and a purple skirt, and while everyone else had on 'Stop the War' buttons, hers said: 'Cunnilingus Is Cool, Fellatio Is Fun.' " Yet on the night of Martin Luther King's assassination, she showed up at a friend's house with tears streaking her face, saying that while King's politics may have been passé, she'd admired the man. Later, she excused herself to go home and change into her "riot clothes" so she could join the mayhem on the streets in Times Square.

She had a boyfriend named Hamish Sinclair and traveled the country in his van as an organizer, but like others buoyed by the new air of sexual freedom, she had relationships

with men who interested her. After Columbia, one of them
was J.J., with whom she'd first slept on the living room floor of
a friend who later called it an "animal mating."

In June of 1968, galvanized by the events at Columbia
and the King and Kennedy assassinations—which seemed to
lend weight to J.J.'s view that "the mother was coming down"
—Bernadine decided to run for SDS "Interorganizational Secretary"—one of three coequal top offices. As a political unknown, she faced a grilling by an increasingly militant
membership ready to regard her well-tended good looks as evidence of superficiality. When she appeared at the convention,
one questioner asked skeptically: "Do you consider yourself a
socialist?" Bernadine eyed him evenly for a moment and then
answered: "I consider myself a revolutionary Communist." She
won by a landslide.

That summer of 1968, Chicago was the place to be. Bernadine was far from the action—in Yugoslavia, on an SDS-
sponsored junket to meet with representatives of the National
Liberation Front and work out ways to assist them in their war
against the United States. And Mark Rudd was in Cuba—his
expenses paid for by SDS. But J.J. and everyone else seemed
to be taunting the Democrats and Mayor Daley in Lincoln
Park. The melee that ensued when Chicago police launched
into an unrestrained assault on the demonstrators appeared to
repeat on a megascale the lessons of Columbia: a small vanguard could catalyze a confrontation into a radical object lesson. Radicals had immobilized a city and compelled the whole
world to watch. More than ever, it seemed the United States
was a pitiful, helpless giant waiting for the determined stroke
that would bring it down.

After the convention, tens of thousands of applications
for membership poured into the ramshackle building on the
West Side of Chicago that served as national SDS headquarters. Aware that control of the national office meant leadership
of the Movement, Rudd, J.J., Bernadine, and others went to
the October SDS conference in Boulder, Colorado, to push
their program for a "revolutionary youth movement" that
would focus on the working-class young—the "greasers" J.J.
emulated in dress and talk—who were becoming disaffected

with the system as they faced a draft for which they had no deferments. After this meeting—the first time they thought of making a serious bid for ideological power—the group went up to stay in a mountain cabin. By the smoky light of kerosene lanterns, they threw the I Ching, receiving a message that seemed almost to have been lifted from Mao's Little Red Book, to the effect that a self-conscious group of people with right ideas had the responsibility to take charge of things and bring leadership to the community.

By late fall, Bernadine and J.J. were living in an apartment on Northrup Street in uptown Chicago, with Steve Tappis and Gerry Long, SDSers from New York. They called it the National Collective. "It was very much a learning experience for Bernadine," recalls Tappis. "She'd been elected to a top position, but she was actually a novice in the subtleties of radical politics, and she knew it. She was attracted to J.J.'s tremendous energy, but in addition to that, by getting it on with him she was able to get a crash course in ideology. They were more or less a monogamous couple, except when she was on the road for SDS. Then she was on her own, doing her own thing, which she did *very* well."

The relationship between the two charged the atmosphere with electricity. On one occasion, Bernadine flew to Boston to personally recruit an editor for the SDS paper, *New Left Notes*. She brought him back and moved him into the spare bedroom, where she continued the recruitment on an intimate basis. Not long afterward, members of the collective decided that J.J. should do "mass work" in addition to his nonstop theorizing; so he went out to the Loop to leaflet students at Roosevelt University and came back with a pair of teenage runaway girls, whom he took to bed in retaliation.

But while the sexual gamesmanship worked as an aphrodisiac for the two of them, it was hard on others in the collective. "Bernadine would be arguing political points at the table with blouse open to the navel, sort of leering at J.J.," remembers Tappis. "It wasn't a moral thing, just sort of disconcerting. I couldn't concentrate on the arguments. Finally, I said, 'Bernadine! Would you please button your blouse!' She just pulled out one of her breasts and, in that cold way of hers, said, 'You like this tit? Take it.'" Another time, the collective sought relief from the greasy french fries that became the staple of their daily diet and cooked some meat. The platter eventually reached Peter Clapp, one of what the group referred to as "Bernadine's young men." As Clapp reached for the last piece, J.J. speared it with his fork. Then Clapp jabbed his own fork into it, and suddenly there was a struggle, real and symbolic, and Bernadine was shrieking at them, "Stop it! Stop! This is infantile!" And she stormed from the room.

Members of the National Collective spent the fall listening to rock music and doing drugs—two areas of expertise they felt they would need if they were to organize "the grease." They became a sort of clearinghouse for radicals passing through Chicago. Many of the big names of the Movement showed up at one time or another, some of them people who would later play a role in Weatherman. When the Motherfuckers, a group blending violent politics with countercultural lifestyle, stopped by Chicago on their way to the hideout they had in the mountains of New Mexico, they paid a visit wearing long black leather jackets, under which they concealed their guns. "We all started doing acid," remembers Gerry Long. "J.J. was wandering around saying, 'Whose son am I?' The Motherfuckers were in the kitchen doing karate exercises. Everybody was very conscious of them as heavy. Word of what they were saying in the kitchen was transformed by acid as it traveled through the house. They called one of the guys a 'cunning Jewish mouse,' but by the time it arrived in the back rooms, the phrase was changed. This guy went around all excited, saying, 'Hey, those guys think I'm a cutting Jewish Maoist.' "

One of those who passed through the Northrup Street house was Jim Mellen. At thirty-five, a good decade older than the others, he had been more alienated than they for a longer period. He came from a family of Okies who had chased the American dream to California during the Depression; he'd married young, fathered two kids, and continued the family's upward striving by getting a Ph.D. in political science and taking a teaching job at Drew University in New Jersey. But the war in Vietnam had interrupted all that. Mellen was fired in 1965 for publicly advocating a National Liberation Front victory. He left his family and spent two years wandering around Africa, observing the clash of empire and revolution firsthand. He'd come home because he thought the domestic political situation was ripening. He was convinced that there should be only one item on the American radical agenda: support for wars of national liberation. Making the radical circuit from Cambridge to Berkeley, he found people "getting serious" about revolution. But the only concrete results seemed to be a few hard-core radicals taking jobs in factories so they could organize the proletariat. For Mellen, this was not only a sterile exercise that repeated the mistakes of the feckless and ineffectual Communist party; it was a criminal disregard for the body count that was piling up higher every day in Vietnam.

Of all the people he met, only Bernadine and J.J. seemed clearest on priorities. What struck Mellen about Bernadine was her determination and a politics of the body that was sophisticated in ways that her politics of the mind was not. "She used sex to explore and cement political alliances," Mellen later said. "Sex for her was a form of ideological activity." What struck him about J.J. was his presence—his high energy (accelerated by the "black beauty" amphetamines he popped), his nonstop, almost demonic chatter, his ability to carry listeners with him by the sheer force of the words rather than their depth. Pacing the kitchen of the National Collective, munching on greasy french fries, J.J. articulated what Mellen himself had come to believe: that American blacks and their ghetto insurrections were part of the third world's war on imperialism, the march of the global "countryside" on the U.S. "metropolis." Whites should form *focos* of disruption inside the walls of the imperial capital; American revolutionaries must see themselves not as Bolsheviks or as Maoists on the Long March but as Vandals and Visigoths battering the gates of America from within. The idea was not to create a perfect state operating by the clockwork principles of Marxist law but to promote a chaos that would cripple America and ultimately cast it into a receivership that would be administered by the morally superior third world. Unafraid to pursue his theme to its logical end, J.J. would add that people shouldn't expect the revolution to achieve a Kingdom of Freedom; more likely, it would produce a Dark Ages.

When Mellen went to Ann Arbor late in 1968 to build an organization that would embody these ideas, he teamed up with people who would play a large role in Weatherman in the frenzied months to come. One of them was Billy Ayers. Ayers had the rumpled good looks of a jock and fraternity boy, which he'd been long before the war changed his life and made him a radical. He was, by his own admission, easygoing and hedonistic, yet there was a taste for the apocalypse in his personality too. On the day LBJ announced that he was not running for reelection, Ayers had felt the shakiness of the American enterprise and late that night walked through downtown Detroit alone, heaving stones through windows as if he could hasten the fall single-handedly.

When Mellen met him, Ayers was working at the interracial Children's Community School in Ann Arbor along with his girlfriend, Diana Oughton. The couple came from similar backgrounds: Billy's father was chairman of the board of the giant utility Commonwealth Edison, one of those Chicagoans who was on a first-name basis with Mayor Daley and regarded as a pillar of the community by the press. ("Ma and Pa Power Broker," Billy called his parents around other radicals.) Diana's father owned two thousand acres of prime Illinois farmland worth millions and was a Republican state legislator. But while Billy was carefree and anarchistic, Diana was sober and pensive, with a gentility she never quite succeeded in obliterating. ("She was the most elegant woman I ever knew," Jim Mellen recalls, a sentiment echoed in one form or another by others who were close to her.) She had gone to Guatemala on a Quaker summer project after graduating from Bryn Mawr, working in a small village and insisting on having a standard of living no better than that of the natives. She'd come home wanting to continue working with America's poor but had met Billy and adopted his politics, although not his style. When they went to the Pentagon demonstration in 1967, he ridiculed the national guardsmen, but she approached them directly: "My name is Diana. I'm from Ann Arbor, and I know you can't talk to me. I'm not asking that you say anything. Just listen. I want to tell you why I'm here. . . ." And then she went on to discuss Vietnam in a way that left the soldier she was talking to with tears in his eyes. During the Chicago convention, while Billy had raised hell in the streets, Diana and Bryn Mawr classmate Kathy Boudin had put on fancy gowns and wandered through hotels, scrawling *Stop Murdering Vietnamese* in lipstick on ladies' room mirrors.

In addition to Billy and Diana, there was Terry Robbins, a shy, wiry twenty-year-old with downcast head and hands habitually in his pockets. Intense, driven, a Bob Dylan freak, Terry had grown up in New York, graduated precociously from high school at sixteen, with a scholarship to Kenyon College and, the same year, joined SDS. He so impressed his radical elders with his skills that they asked him to come to Cleveland for more important organizing work. It was there that Billy first met him. Each had immediately seen qualities in the other that he himself lacked. "What I liked about Terry was that he could sit up all night thinking a problem through," Billy remembers. "What he liked about me was that I was easygoing, that I liked people and they liked me." Terry was small, almost frail. "I feel wimpy, weak," he'd say, and Billy would laugh: "Just loosen up and do it!" Then an intellectual issue would arise, and Billy would be at a disadvantage. "You don't take yourself or anything else seriously enough," Terry would lecture him. They began to think of themselves as Butch and Sundance, two halves of a single whole.

One Christmas, Billy brought Terry home. Terry immediately tried to bait Billy's father into a discussion of the ruling class and its responsibility for the war. Later on, Mrs. Ayers took Billy aside and said, "Now I know how you learned to talk like a New York Jew."

Billy and Diana lived in Ann Arbor on Felch Street in a tiny pre–Civil War house with a cellar that had once served as a stop on the underground railroad. A friend who knew them says: "Billy just said 'Be my baby' and Diana said 'Fine.' Ten years earlier or later they might have gotten married and lived happily ever after. But the times were wrong for them." Billy was galvanized by the sexual freedom in the radical *demimonde* and tried to make Diana feel the same energy by encouraging her to bring people home to sleep with, as he often did. But it was hard for her to do, and instead she tried to ignore the other women and make up for his lapses by a more determined fidelity of her own. When Billy and Terry became regional travelers for SDS, Billy's sexual itinerary grew apace. (At one point, he boasted to an SDS colleague that he'd gotten laid one hundred times in three months, and friends watching him insouciantly proposition one woman after another at SDS organizing meetings, inviting them to join him in his Chevy van during coffee breaks, believed that this was no exaggeration.) Sometimes when Billy was gone, Terry would come up from his base in Cleveland to visit Diana. Eventually they wound up in bed. Completing the triangle made each of them feel closer to Billy.

Joining with Mellen and a few others, this untidy group first called itself the Lurleen Wallace Memorial Caucus, after the Alabama governor's recently deceased wife, and functioned as the Action Faction's equivalent on the University of Michigan campus. Shortly afterward, they rechristened themselves the Jesse James Gang and began to try to assume leadership of campus politics by taking over the local SDS chapter. The Marxists in charge denounced them as brownshirts for their confrontationist tactics, claiming to have been physically intimidated by members of the gang. The result of their assumption of power was a dwindling of SDS membership to half of what it had been. But this was fine with Mellen. Citing Lenin's dictum "Better Fewer, But Better," he pointed out that those who remained were self-selected as the committed ones, willing to become what he had come to think of as "tools of necessity."

In the spring of 1969, Bernadine and J.J. moved to a new house on North Winthrop Street in Chicago. The only pieces of furniture were the mattresses on the floor, J.J. having wrecked the tables and chairs during an LSD rampage. The traffic seemed to prove Sartre's theory that "Revolution is seeing each other a lot." Ayers and Robbins stayed there when they were in town. So did Mellen. They were joined by Jeff Jones, a nineteen-year-old newcomer, the son of a Disney studio technician, who amused everyone with his Donald Duck impersonations. A tall, blond southern Californian with a surfer's good looks and a taste for cowboy boots and ten-gallon hats, Jones had been head of the New York regional office of SDS and a member of the Motherfuckers. Like other WASPs, he was attracted to the Jewish drama of the new group and to "struggle sessions" during which Rudd, Robbins, and J.J. histrionically argued their positions. (Typical of the hard style she was developing, Bernadine now called herself an "Oven Jew," explaining that she only identified with her Jewish side through the knowledge that when the inevitable new genocide began, her Jewish blood would mark her as a victim).

After several weeks of cross-pollination and in anticipation of the national SDS convention in June, where a showdown was brewing with the Maoists of the Progressive Labor (PL) Party, they began to organize their thoughts for a programmatic statement of principle. In the end, J.J. worked around the clock at a typewriter, handing the pages to others for editing and additions. The result was a thirty-thousand-word manifesto reflecting an almost mystical vision of a coming political Armageddon. The overriding issue in considering questions about revolution, the document began, was to realize that "the main struggle going on in the world . . . is between U.S. imperialism and the national liberation struggles against it." Its most audacious claim was that the black revolution in America would lead inexorably to a world revolution: "Blacks can do it alone!" was the rally cry later on. For white radicals not to provide black revolutionaries with support—no matter what the odds—was racist. It was the same message J.J. had been pushing in the private sessions of the group when he invoked the example of John Brown, proposing the formula "John Brown, Live Like Him!" with full, ironic awareness of Brown's fate.

There was a big question: what to call the manifesto. J.J. wanted to name it "The Vandal Statement," in honor of his favorite revolutionary group. Nobody else seemed to like the idea. Terry Robbins suggested using a line from a Dylan song for the title: "You Don't Need a Weatherman to Tell Which Way the Wind Blows." The others agreed. Almost immediately after distributing the document to the SDS convention cadres, the group began to be called Weatherman.

They were opposed by the PL Maoists and other SDS factions, who attacked them for daring to bypass the traditional routes of alliance building and acquiring "mass support." ("You don't need a rectal thermometer to know who the assholes are," one irritated opponent sneered.) Battle lines were drawn over PL's insistence that class, not race, was the primary factor in the coming revolution. But the real issue was the new clique's readiness for action, the violence of its rhetoric, the "Custeristic" nature of its revolutionary ideal.

Midway through the SDS convention, it became evident that the hated Progressive Labor Party would have a voting majority. Since patiently building a base within SDS over the next year was contrary to the identity as homegrown existentialists the Weatherpeople were trying to cultivate, they called for a recess. After adjourning to another building and caucusing, they returned. Standing on a stage flanked by Robbins, Rudd, and the others, chanting "Long live people's war," Bernadine audaciously read a statement expelling Progressive Labor from SDS. Then she led her troops out of the convention hall under the watchful cameras of the Chicago police and proceeded to SDS headquarters to seize the organization's office and assets.

They had begun as a handful of rebels in love with the fuss they created inside SDS; now they *were* SDS. It seemed another in a long series of portents.

In the world according to J.J., there always had to be a next step more daunting than the one just achieved. They had pulled the sword of revolution from the stone of the Movement; now they had to prove they could use it. The Weather Bureau, as the signers of the manifesto had become known during the convention, called for a National Action in Chicago in October to coincide with the Chicago Seven conspiracy trial. In the past, radicals attending Movement demonstrations had been kept in check by moderate leaders. This time the radicals were calling the action; they would control things themselves and "bring the war home."

In preparation, they began spreading their gospel. Overnight, Weatherman collectives were set up all over the country. There were perhaps three hundred hard-core members, but they organized themselves into tight affinity groups willing to go all out in a way they believed would ultimately draw thousands into action. While some members of the Weather Bureau flew from one town to another, anointing leaders in the various collectives and setting up training programs, others traveled to Cuba, like members of a provisional government seeking diplomatic recognition.

Gerry Long, Diana Oughton, and others found themselves showered with attention by Havana officials. But Bernadine was the centerpiece. She was interviewed by Cuba's *Tricontinental* magazine and introduced to dignitaries from throughout the revolutionary third world. Then she and the other Weatherpeople sat down to talk with a delegation of Vietnamese headed by Huynh Va Ba of the Provisional Revolutionary Government. What Huynh told them seemed to confirm the step they had taken, saying that his movement, too, had begun as a middle-class group that recruited among young people and later made common cause with other groups beginning to fight. Then he turned serious: "The war is entering its final phase. You must begin to wage armed struggle as soon as possible to become the vanguard and take leadership of the revolution." Bernadine assured him that they would try to be worthy. As if to solemnize the marriage of true minds, the Vietnamese gave the Weathermen rings forged from the metal salvage of downed American fighter planes. One member of the SDS contingent said later: "I didn't realize it at the time, but they really worked us over with guilt. The message they kept driving home was that the war was entering its crucial moments, and how far were we prepared to go for our comrades who were dying in Vietnam?"

During the Havana trip, there had been circumspectly coded phone calls back home. But until their boat docked in Canada they didn't really get the news about what had happened while they were gone. J.J. and Mellen were there to meet them and said that in their absence, Weatherman had not only taken the first steps toward becoming the New Red Army that would fight in October's National Action, but also captured the imagination of radicals across the country with a series of daring maneuvers. One band of Weatherwomen had entered the classrooms of a Michigan college, barricading the door with the teacher's lectern and using karate they'd learned in their collective on several men who tried to leave during the lecture they gave them on the war. Another women's group had occupied a Pittsburgh high school, run through the halls shouting "Jailbreak!" and then fought with police who came to arrest them. Still another collective had seized the stage of a theater showing the Hollywood film *Che* and ranted about the politics left out of the production. In perhaps the most significant action, Detroit's "Motor City SDS" had marched onto the beaches of Lake Superior, planted an NLF flag, and begun passing out radical leaflets to working-class youths, some of them Vietnam vets. There were fights in which the Weatherpeople had held their own and, still in formation, marched off the beach chanting antiwar slogans.

Bernadine and the others found, in short, that their comrades had begun to toughen, to shed some vestiges of their "white skin privilege," and to rid themselves of middle-class hang-ups about violence. Mark Rudd, for instance, had been hospitalized after a fight that erupted when he and others had brought politics to a teenage hangout in Milwaukee. Yet he had come out and kept working, moving in to organize among "the grease" in a North Side Chicago neighborhood, even though his life was threatened by local mobsters annoyed at the law-enforcement attention that followed him wherever he went and reflected onto them.

In the next few weeks, the reunited leadership redoubled its efforts to prepare for the Chicago "Days of Rage"—as the National Action was now being billed. They were still very much aware of the absurdity of privileged American kids like themselves talking about revolution, and some of their humor had a self-deprecating quality. When the editor of the SDS journal *New Left Notes*—now renamed *Fire!*—reprinted an old *Life* photo showing a grinning five-year-old Chicano boy named Marion Delgado, who had derailed a capitalist train with a brick, the Weatherspeak Slogan of the Day became "Marion Delgado, Live Like Him!" One night, when the scholarly Mellen finished lecturing the leadership about Malraux's parable of the overzealous terrorist Ch'en, who'd blown himself up instead of his target, someone immediately piped up, "Terrorist Ch'en, Live Like Him!" And on one memorable plane flight, J.J. sat in his seat, stripped to the waist, openly fondling Bernadine, while relishing the discomfort of his fellow passengers, then loudly demanded a second breakfast from the stewardess. When she said there was no more food, J.J. paraded up and down the aisles, spearing food from other passengers' plates. "They didn't know we were Weathermen," Bernadine said, mythologizing the incident in a later speech. "They just knew we were crazy. That's what we're about—

being crazy motherfuckers and scaring the shit out of honky America."

But while the Weatherpeople had previously been like the Yippies—in love with their own sense of theater, with the art of *seeming*—they now began to worry about the art of being, as they drew closer to an existential edge where political violence met personal rebirth. Once more, J.J. took the lead, saying that the task of a true Communist was to become an "exemplar of the deed," and the only test was whether or not he could *do it* when push came to shove on the streets, as it inevitably would in Chicago. Addressing a spellbound SDS meeting, he declared, "The dialectic is not like a pendulum swinging from left to right; it is a wrecking ball smashing through one wall and then another wall, and then another wall, and then another!" Over the next weeks, he became the organization's apocalyptician in residence, creating rationales for violence whose weight everyone carried as they pushed themselves toward the brink. The Weather anthem became the Doors' "Break on Through (to the Other Side)." Their movie was *The Wild Bunch*, its scenes of gratuitous acts of violence unfolding in exquisite slow motion seeming to speak directly to their future. They decided that they must be like Sam Peckinpah's heroes and took it as an omen that the Weather Bureau's initials, W.B., were the same as those of the Wild Bunch.

They bought and stocked guns and practiced with them in remote areas; they sometimes carried them as well, giving "bodyguards" .38s to conceal under their coats when they flanked Bernadine and other leaders during personal appearances. They ingested huge quantities of speed and acid and held a "trip-in" at Chicago's Museum of Science and Industry, during which time they were followed by anxious members of the city's Red Squad. It was a symbolic challenge to the enemy on his territory.

Trying to push the limits in the sexual domain as well, they initiated a "smash monogamy" campaign to destroy bourgeois sexual hang-ups in the same way that street fighting was meant to "smash" bourgeois prohibitions against violence. "Any notion that people can have responsibility for one person," Billy Ayers argued in a speech defending the campaign, "that they can have that 'out'—we have to destroy that notion in order to build a collective; we have to destroy all 'outs,' to destroy the notion that people can lean on one person and not be responsible to the entire collective." The campaign against monogamy was begun by the women, who had decided that sexual exclusivity led to inequality; in practice, it was the men in the leadership, like Rudd, Ayers, J.J., and Terry, who profited from what, in a typical Weather self-parody, they called "foreskin privilege."

Once monogamy was smashed—couples who in some cases had been together for years were harangued until they admitted their "political errors" and split apart—the next logical step was group sex. The purpose was not pleasure so much as welding together an enforced unity of the body. ("People who fuck together," as Terry put it, "fight together.") The first such experience (later known as the "national orgy") took place at the Columbus, Ohio, collective during a visit from members of the Weather Bureau. "We were doing booze, dope, and dancing," Gerry Long remembers, "and suddenly you could see the wheels turning in people's minds. Will it happen? When? How to get started? We knew it wouldn't happen of its own accord; somebody had to do something about it. We were constantly talking about asserting leadership in ambiguous situations, and here was a case in point. After a while, Jeff Jones went upstairs to the attic, where the mattresses were, with an old girlfriend. J.J. sees them go up and follows, taking off his clothes, too, and lying down beside them. Finally, Billy yells, 'It's time to *do it!*' and takes the hand of the woman he's been dancing with and goes up too. Within a few minutes, there was a whole group of naked people looking down from the head of the stairs and saying, 'Come on up!'

"I took the hand of this girl and exchanged a few pleasantries to give it a slightly personal quality, and then we fucked. And there were people fucking and thrashing around all over. They'd sort of roll over on you, and sometimes you found yourself spread over more than one person. The room was like some weird modern sculpture. There'd be all these humps in a row. You'd see a knee and then buttocks and then three knees and four buttocks. They were all moving up and down, rolling around." The next day, there was a morning-after awkwardness, until one of the women broke the silence: "I'm sure they have to do it this way in Vietnam."

Weather sex was like the developing Weather politics— a search for the "exemplary deed." One of the last taboos was homosexuality, and the Weather command forced itself toward experimentation in this direction, instructing male and female cadres to "make it" with members of the same sex. But this was one taboo that was hard to break. Gerry Long recalls lying beside a woman at one of the orgies, when a man came over and lay down next to them. "We were all fondling one another. Suddenly he came in my hand. He got so embarrassed that he just stood up and walked off."

Whether gay or straight, however, sex was forced and gray—pleasure being one of those dangerous, bourgeois conceits that had to be attacked. The word "fuck," which they cultivated as a mark of authenticity, never quite divorced itself from the negative connotations of "fuck over." Sex was always part of politics, part of an infatuation with competitive and violent selfhood. Terry Robbins summarized it in a comment made to one of his girlfriends during a conversation in which he voiced the concerns he'd always had about the smallness of his penis: "It's not the size of the dog in the fight that counts, but the size of the fight in the dog."

Shrewdly, conscious of the market value of her sexuality, Bernadine held herself aloof from the group activity, always managing to be someplace else when the orgies broke out. Nor did she allow her monogamies to be smashed by the group. When she invited the Weather Bureau to criticize her relationship with J.J., it was not a sign that she was submitting to discipline but rather an indication that she was finished with him. Soon after the critical session, she moved in with Jeff Jones, whose stock as a leader immediately rose. Gerry Long, who had observed her from the time they'd both lived in the National Collective, says: "Bernadine related to men according to their usefulness. It was the way she could get to be who she wanted to be. In a sense, it was inescapable; she had to relate to men that way because she was determined to be a leader and a personality, and there was no way she could have a passive relationship with a man and still be that. When a new relationship came into being, the man she was with—in a subtle, complicated way—became the most powerful man in the leadership."

Mark Rudd, whose star had begun to fade as Weatherman turned away from the mass movement to focus more and more on its own sectarian essence, was piqued by Bernadine's elitist disdain for the non-monogamy code. "Power doesn't flow out of the barrel of a gun," he challenged her at a Weather Bureau meeting. "Power flows out of Bernadine's cunt." He was immediately jumped on for sexism by all present, but they couldn't deny that there was an interface between the political and the sexual. Finally, Terry Robbins proposed a substitute formulation that everyone could live with: "Bernadine's cunt goes to wherever the power is."

All through September they were speaking, writing, and organizing for the confrontation in Chicago, which they believed would be the beginning of the end for the American state. All the leaders were crossing the country, pushing the collective toward a mood of confrontation and self-sacrifice. "We're not urging anybody to bring guns to Chicago," Billy Ayers told one group. "We're not urging anybody to shoot from a crowd. But we're also going to make it clear that when a pig gets iced, that's a good thing, and that everyone who considers himself a revolutionary should be armed, should own a gun, should have a gun in his home."

Bernadine was especially active, driving herself to the point of collapse, aware that she was becoming nationally known and looked to as a Weather spokesperson. "She could never forget the question of what her role was," Gerry Long says. "How was she fulfilling her historic mission? Where was she in relation to where she'd been the day before? These were the questions that preoccupied her." On October 6, when a dynamite blast destroyed the police monument in Chicago's Haymarket Square, signaling the beginning of the Days of Rage, Bernadine stepped to center stage.

Initially, the Weather Bureau predicted 10,000 demonstrators. Midway through the summer, this figure was lowered to 5,000 and finally to 2,500. As D day approached, recruits trickled into the city in small groups. The numbers were so dishearteningly small that many contingents had to stop their vans outside city limits and stage "criticism sessions" to quell collective fear. Once in town, the tiny bands of Weathermen waited for the train to arrive from Detroit, where Mellen had worked so hard, promising thousands of troops for the battle. But when their comrades from Michigan came marching up to the bivouac in Lincoln Park, there were not even hundreds, but dozens. In the end, fewer than 600 altogether showed up for the test on October 8.

By evening they were ready, organized into affinity groups, everyone wearing motorcycle helmets to cushion blows and gloves to throw back tear-gas canisters and carrying steel pipes to use as truncheons. They were nervous, frightened, ready to quit before they got started. Then Bernadine stood up on a makeshift podium, the wind furling Vietnamese flags around her. "Just think," she yelled through a bullhorn, "only this number had the courage to come. You are truly a vanguard. . . ." After she had pumped them up, she led them off, first at a slow gait, then breaking into a run, flying down streets and into the Loop, smashing windows as they went. Sounds of sirens filled the city. The police closed in on them, and they fought furiously, sometimes forming flying wedges to rescue surrounded comrades being dragged to the paddy wagons. They got loose and took off running again, setting cars on fire and trashing the famed Chicago Gold Coast.

Six were wounded by police gunfire that first night and dozens hospitalized for other injuries. Of the sixty-eight jailed, most got themselves bailed out and returned to meetings to criticize those who hadn't been arrested. The next day was the Women's Action. Again there were disappointing numbers, no more than eighty, but again Bernadine roused the troops with a fiery speech and led them off, shrilling like the women in the film *Battle of Algiers*. Observers thought Bernadine was severely hurt after she flew into the police line, swinging and kicking, got beaten down, and was carried off writhing and screaming. Susan Stern, another Weatherwoman arrested in the action, was mesmerized when she saw Dohrn in jail, alone in a languid pose, her face composed into a mask of contempt: "She looked like a fashion model—short black leather jacket, nice slacks, neat purple blouse, the boots—everything just so."

She seemed hardly aware of the other women in the cell, although they were all very much aware of her, all wanting to be in her favor, to be like her. "She possessed a splendor all her own—like a queen . . . a high priestess, a mythological silhouette."

After three days of rioting, the Days of Rage came to an end. Seventy-five policemen had been injured during the action. Some three hundred Weatherpeople had been arrested, many of them more than once, and some of them on charges ranging up to attempted murder. Their bail totaled over $2.6 million. One city official, Richard Elrod, was paralyzed from the neck down when he attempted to tackle a demonstrator and struck his head on a curb. This inspired Ted Gold, who had become the Weatherman songwriter, to write lyrics to be sung to Dylan's "Lay, Lady, Lay":

Lay, Elrod, lay
Lay in the street for a while
Stay, Elrod, stay
Stay in your bed for a while
You thought you could stop the Weatherman
But up-front people put you on your can
Stay, Elrod, stay
Stay in your iron lung
Play, Elrod, play
Play with your toes for a while. . . .

Following the Days of Rage, the Weather Bureau retreated to a cabin in Illinois's Rock Creek State Park for a week's postmortem. Mellen and Rudd argued that something had gone wrong. Chicago had been intended to unite all SDS factions and other radical groups in a new militancy under Weatherman leadership. The militancy had been there but not the troops. Perhaps, they suggested, the time had come to reverse their tracks and seek to reconnect with the Movement they had left behind.

J.J. disagreed. The Days of Rage, he said, had been a victory in disguise, the beginning of real revolutionary action. Sure, they had been outnumbered, but the odds they'd faced were those confronting an NLF battalion every day it went up against the American army in Vietnam. In his argument, J.J. was backed by Terry Robbins, who had changed more than any of the leaders in the past months. Some had wilted in the pressure-cooker atmosphere created by the buildup for Chicago, but Terry had been buoyed by the rampant sexuality, the drugs, and the prospect of violence. It was as if the ambience itself had allowed him to overcome his anxieties about his small stature. His revolutionary fervor inspired the others to feel that the organization was capable of a triumph of the will. Largely because of Robbins's determination, the split between the moderate and radical positions in the bureau hardened until he and J.J., along with Bernadine and Jeff Jones, proclaimed themselves the Foremost Four in the leadership, relegating Rudd, Long, and even Billy Ayers to subordinate positions.

Mellen, the resident intellectual, alone put up a struggle. But he didn't stand a chance: "The argument, as usual, was in personal terms. I didn't have the 'character' to be a revolutionary. I lacked audacity. I couldn't *do it*. When I tried to point out that military action required exactly the kind of discipline that we'd rejected in favor of 'spontaneity' and a technical capacity we'd never bothered to master, J.J. looked at me and said, 'Jim here is from the Six-Months-in-the-Library School of Sabotage.' Everybody laughed, and that was that."

It was Terry Robbins, Mellen's onetime disciple, who put an end to the discussion by giving him a hard look and saying, "We're the leadership because we want it the most." Afterward, Bernadine came up to him and tried to place a velvet glove over the iron fist that Terry had shown: "She made it clear to me that she was with Jones for the same reason she'd been with J.J.: because he was spontaneous and had no inhibitions. She said she liked men when they were being exemplary and taking strong leadership positions, and when I was strong it made her want me too."

After these meetings, there was a subtle passing of the torch from J.J., Weatherman's thinker, to Terry, who had proposed himself as Weatherman's doer. "J.J. had these fantasies," one ex–Weather leader says, "but it was Terry who was prepared to act them out."

Terry's transformation was evident to his girlfriend, Laurie Meisner.* Terry and Billy had picked her up hitchhiking in Cleveland the year before and invited her for a weekend in Detroit. She had arrived at the Felch Street pad and, that evening, had gone to bed in the pantry-sized room reserved for her and Terry. Two hours later, Terry came in, very agitated. "I had been wondering," she said, " 'Where is this guy? He invites me away for a weekend, and then he disappears.' When he finally came in, I said, 'What's the problem?' He said, 'I've just spent two hours talking to Billy about whether or not to sleep with you.' I think I was his first real girlfriend. After that, I left school and lived with him. Then when the 'smash monogamy' line came down, he started to sleep with a lot of people . . . often the heavies in the organization and therefore intimidating to me. And he did it in a way that seemed calculated for me to walk in on it, which I did with great frequency. It was like he could hardly believe it was happening to him. He was three feet off the ground, high on the *power* of it."

There were other indications that Terry's star was rising. Toward the end of 1969, he showed up in New York for a date with Laurie with a flash wad of money, which he made clear was for dangerous goods and clandestine uses, but with which he offered to finance their evening on the town. "He just said, 'Where do you want to go?' It was like, Hey, Big Spender." They spent a night at Terry's sister's house in Queens, and he told her he had gotten into a fight with Billy because Billy wasn't moving fast enough. It was a physical fight, and it depressed him. " 'Maybe Billy and I should sleep together,' he said. That was a typical Terry thing to say. He was always looking for the next thing, the next wall to try to break through, the next taboo to break. If sleeping with all the women you wanted had been done, then maybe it was time to sleep with men."

But it was the growing violence of their relationship that disturbed her the most. Although she told no one, Terry often beat her up, and though he would be contrite afterward, swearing that he loved her, felt sick about it, and would never do it again, she was increasingly scared of him. He could still

* A pseudonym.

be tender and romantic. One snowy evening they went to see the film *Doctor Zhivago*, and when they came out to the falling flakes, he looked at her and said, "Will you marry me sometime?" But on another occasion, they were in bed, and he suddenly sat up and said, "The only thing better than making love to you would be killing the right people."

In the period following the Days of Rage, members of the Weather Bureau flew almost nonstop around the country on scammed airline tickets and stayed in the elegant apartments of left-wing attorneys and others attracted by their radical chic. But life in the collectives was increasingly grim. SDS money dried up as the organization's membership shrank. The cadres were pressured to donate parental support checks—or to steal or beg—to support the organization. (One popular ruse was to get married, then return the expensive wedding gifts from parents and friends to the stores in exchange for cash.) They had to endure foodless days to save money and prepare for the hardships of life underground, which now seemed inevitable. The places they lived in were foul and filthy, another slap at their middle-class origins. And while their days were filled with weapons training and conditioning, their sleepless nights were filled with interminable ideological struggle.

A Detroit collective talked through the night about a sniper loose in the ghetto. They wanted to support him by spray-painting the slogan "All power to the sniper" on walls around town, but they couldn't decide if it would be politically "correct" for them to sign it "SDS" or leave it anonymous, as though it had been done by blacks. The Columbus collective "trashed" a Weatherwoman who, returning exhausted after minor hospital surgery, had lain on a mattress that had been propped to guard a window against police assault. She had put her own comfort before the revolution. There were "gut checks" for those who held back. They were put up against the ideological wall and challenged: "Do you want the revolution? You don't want it enough!"

While there were moments of almost comic self-parody, most of the self-criticism sessions (called Weather Fries) were emotional collisions of calculating brutality meant to substitute a group identity for an individual one. The apparently innocuous formula "Criticism + Self-Criticism = Transformation," which began to appear on the walls of many collectives, covered a multitude of sins. Any piece of private information—up to and including the deepest confidences between friends—was used in these sessions to burrow into the most private reaches of individual character. No aspect of background or dimension of emotional life was immune from the inquisitorial sessions in which everyone in the group swarmed over one victim and then suddenly swerved to attack someone else. Weatherwoman Susan Stern later characterized the ugly zeal in one of these sessions that left one young man in tears: "Only through a total smashing of his defenses could he really see himself and his role in the revolution and begin to change. We were exorcising Devil America out of him. . . . All of us had to change. History had not taught us how. Our parents had failed us; in some cases, they had perverted us. Our education had left us hopelessly enmeshed in endless lies. There was nothing left but total overhaul."

The assaults on individual character through sexual subordination, deprivation of food and sleep, drugs, and attacks on the recesses of personality were as sophisticated as the techniques used by the religious cults of the next decade. Death was kept uppermost in everyone's mind. Mark Rudd and Gerry Long met in New York for what they called a Last Supper. Diana Oughton sent letters and other memorabilia to friends and family, saying that she didn't want these materials to identify and possibly incriminate her after Weatherman had gone into battle. (The gesture would take on a deeper significance later.) Weather humor, which before had a certain existential *brio*, took on a gallows aspect. Ted Gold penned a new set of lyrics for Creedence Clearwater's "Bad Moon Rising":

> Hope you've got your shit together
> Hope you are quite prepared to die
> Looks like we're in for nasty weather
> One eye is taken for an eye.

The atmosphere of dramatic finality created moments of intensity that would never be forgotten. On November 15, during the Mobilization in Washington, Billy Ayers and Diana spent the night together for the first time in weeks. Billy had changed in the last few months, becoming sharper, less carefree; Diana had changed far more, becoming nervous, depressed, thin almost to the point of anorexia.

"We hadn't seen each other in a while," Billy recalls, "and our relationship had been under a lot of pressure and criticism. For some reason, this seemed to empower her to come to me and say: 'Listen, here are the things that have been really wrong between us all these years.' She started slowly enough, but then it accelerated, and what she was talking about was the ways in which I'd held back from committing myself to her. She described incidents that I'd completely forgotten, that had happened years ago, in which I had not been there for her emotionally, or in which I'd made her feel insecure. Each time I tried to object and say I was really trying to do this or that, she was able to turn it aside and go even deeper. The more she talked, the more freaked out I got, until I was feeling that this was all true; it was true and there was nothing I could do about it. Then she said, 'The thing you don't understand, the thing that's so completely crazy, is that all you have to do is admit to yourself that you really love me and want to be with me and are not embarrassed by me. If you would just admit that to yourself and to me, this whole nightmare of what's gone before would be over.' It was beyond all the ideology. It was just the two of us. It was a moment of profound and important discovery. But it didn't go anywhere because we didn't know what the future held."

At the end of December, there was a three-day "War Council" in Flint, Michigan, in which all the psyching up, the apocalypse mongering, and the cultist indoctrination came to a head in a ritual of political diabolism. The four hundred people entering the Giant Ballroom, a black-owned ghetto concert hall the Weather leadership had rented, were frisked for weapons. The front-door panes had been shattered by bullets the night before when a young black had been shot and killed there—his brown bloodstains were still visible on the floor—and the remaining shards were masked with electrical tape. Inside, one entire wall was papered with red-and-black posters of Fred Hampton, the Black Panther leader killed by

Chicago police at the beginning of the month. From the raf-
ters hung a giant cardboard cutout of a tommy gun.

Bernadine mounted the platform wearing a brown mini-
jumpsuit and thigh-high Italian leather boots, causing a stir
among the tie-dyed, blue-jeaned Weather army sitting at her
feet. After a little pep talk, she introduced Chicago Seven defendant Tom Hayden as a guest of honor. Hayden took the
stage for what he called "more serious business" and proceeded
to lead the troops in a workout of karate jabs and kicks. After a
strenuous fifteen minutes, he sat down, breathing hard.
"Thank you, Tom," said Bernadine, whereupon she launched
a scathing attack on Hayden and his white confederates for not
having torn the court apart when Black Panther Chairman
Bobby Seale was manacled and gagged by order of Chicago
Seven judge Julius Hoffman.

"She was really into it," says one Weatherman who
watched her that evening in awe. "She was prancing around
up there like Mick Jagger; boys and girls both were panting.
She was at the height of her power." Though Terry Robbins
was in jail in Ohio for an action he'd led at Kent State, Bernadine spoke his thoughts: "Since October 11 [last of the Days of
Rage] we've been wimpy. . . . A lot of us are still honkies and
we're scared of fighting. We have to get into armed struggle."
She then began to talk about convicted killer Charlie Manson
and those she called the "Tate Eight"—actress Sharon Tate
and the other victims of the bloodthirsty rampages by the Manson Family in the Los Angeles hills: "Dig it. First they killed
those pigs, then they ate dinner in the same room with them,
they even shoved a fork into a victim's stomach! Wild!" She
held up three fingers in a Manson "fork salute."

J.J. followed Bernadine to the stage, laying out the
"White Devil" theory of world history. "We're against everything that's 'good and decent' in honky America," he concluded. "We will loot and burn and destroy. We are the
incubation of your mothers' nightmares!" Then Rudd delivered a speech listeners felt was as good as any he'd given back
in what seemed another age at Columbia. In one line he compared Weatherman to Captain Ahab and America to the White
Whale in a way that left people unsure whether or not he
remembered who had won that struggle. It didn't matter.

After the speeches by J.J. and Rudd, the assemblage broke up into small discussion groups to mull over the logistics of what going underground meant—procuring weapons, making bombs, securing "safe houses." One delegate from each cell was dispatched to score some stale Pepsi and cold hot dogs from two concession stands run by local blacks, for whom this was just another concert gig.

Each evening, high on handfuls of drugs, the Weather Bureau and their ordained went to the nave of a Flint Catholic church for group sex, recharging themselves for the next day's session. After three days of "Wargasm," as they called it, Bernadine led the Weather army into the climactic finale; they locked arms in a satanic bunny hop, chanting, "Explode! Explode! Explode!" On New Year's Eve, after the Wargasm was spent, the Weather Bureau drove to Ann Arbor for one last binge. One participant remembers: "It was this three-story home of a woman with two small kids. People wound up stoned out of their minds, fucking on all three floors. Bernadine and Jeff Jones were on the top floor alone; everybody else was down below as if to validate the hierarchy. The next morning we woke up and found that the kids of the couple whose house it was had been selling looks at all the naked bodies, at a quarter a peep. We had to laugh: petty-bourgeois capitalism rears its ugly head."

When it was over, Bernadine flew to her parent's retirement home in Florida for a short visit and belatedly hung her Christmas stocking on the mantel, as was the family custom. She then returned to Chicago.

During the first days of the new year, the Weather Bureau met in various midwestern cities, holding sessions in which they passed around slips of paper with the names of possible ruling-class kidnap victims and slapped five on one another's palms as the names were read aloud. They were really going to go underground, going to make bombs—going to *get it on* at last; perhaps they were even going to die.

More than ever, it was the foursome of Bernadine and Jeff, J.J. and Terry, who had come out of jail raring to go. Over the first weeks of 1970, they went around the country carrying out what J.J. called the "Consolidation"—paring down the collectives to the few they deemed able to *do it*. Gerry Long, just back from the first Venceremos Brigade to Cuba, was stunned when J.J. told him, "We've just offed the pig!" and then explained that they had closed the national office of SDS. He was equally dismayed by the brusqueness with which so many who'd suffered with the organization since the previous June's convention were dismissed. Long, who'd been there since the beginning, left the organization.

His friend Jim Mellen was also deeply upset. He did not necessarily oppose plans to go underground or even to undertake what was being called military action, but he didn't want the group to be cut off from the rest of the Movement. He told the four self-anointed leaders that they were "tripping out" from political realities. They countered with the old argument that his personal inhibitions were holding him back. In a caustic attack, Terry brought up Mellen's reserve during the group sex and acid trips. When they were alone, Bernadine made the appeal personal: "I don't understand why you want to fail when you're needed most. The sexual and the political are one; you don't seem to be able to get it up for either. Why can't you be spontaneous, like J.J. and Billy? Why can't you *do it?*"

On Super Bowl IV Sunday, the Weather leaders broke from their nonstop discussions to watch the game. Earlier, J.J. had said to no one in particular: "It gets serious now that we're about to go underground. Anyone who tries to leave now we'll have to kill." Mellen thought at the time that it was probably another piece of hyperbole. But at halftime, he decided to take a walk. Two hours later, he called the house. Billy Ayers answered, and Mellen told him he wasn't coming back. Then he left the phone booth and began to think about what he'd do with the rest of his life.

Emulating the Vietnamese, the Central Committee—as the four now called themselves—set up a system of command that divided the consolidated collectives into regional forces, militia, and mobile attack units. Everything was ready, but someone had to take the first step. Terry and J.J. were the logical ones, and by February they had formed a new collective in New York, whose mission was to bring military action against the enemy. It was called the Fork, after Bernadine's homage to Manson, and was temporarily headquartered in a

Greenwich Village town house on Eleventh Street owned by James Platt Wilkerson, a wealthy media magnate then on an extended vacation in the Caribbean. Wilkerson's daughter, Cathy, was a member of the collective, as were Kathy Boudin, daughter of a prominent leftist attorney, and Ted Gold and Diana Oughton. Cathy and Diana were the two women closest to Terry, besides his girlfriend, Laurie.

Laurie had seen less and less of Terry since his release from jail. Anxious to make up for lost time, Terry had thrown himself into preparations, whose exact nature he said he could not reveal to her. She had decided to leave him. Her fears of his increasingly violent nature were heightened by rumors that the collective planned to bomb targets like the May Company department store, and by her memories of the demonic scenes from the War Council. Fresh on her mind was an incident in which Terry had slugged her in a parking lot, knocking her to the ground. Billy was there and ran over to pull Terry off. "It was the only time anyone ever intervened. He came over and grabbed Terry and said, 'You're going to fucking kill her one day.' "

Laurie saw Terry for the last time on a subway ride from his sister's house in Queens. "I'm going away," she told him. But he seemed not to hear. Later, she received a call at her father's house from Kathy Boudin, who wanted to meet her at a restaurant. "I said okay. I told my father I needed five hundred dollars, no questions asked, and I went to the meeting. Kathy and Diana were there. I knew Terry had sent them. I knew he was sleeping with them; that they were under his spell. For two hours, they pressured me to come stay with them in the town house. They laid every guilt trip on me possible. But I refused. I went straight from the meeting to the airport, bought a ticket with the five hundred dollars, and flew to California."

Late in February, Billy visited the town house. He spent time with Diana, who was in bed with a virus, and with his old sidekick, Terry. Things had changed between them since Terry had been drawn into J.J.'s orbit. The days of their easy camaraderie were over. Terry had recently staged a firebombing attack on the home of the judge presiding over the Panther 21 case. This had been a big step for the rest of the collective, but Terry was ready to up the ante by finding targets that would not be merely symbolic but would result in a real body count. "I don't want you to get left behind," Terry had said to Billy. "In this period, the people who are capable of doing, who are really capable of armed struggle, are the ones who are going to get through. The people who aren't are just going to be left behind. I don't want you left behind." Billy was struck by the formulation: the people who *get through* this period. Again it was that hunger to reach the apocalypse just beyond, the essential act that would make them *real* revolutionaries. He thought to himself as he left Terry: "We're getting ready to take a trip into the Land of the Unknown."

Ten days later, Ayers, who was in Ann Arbor consolidating one of the collectives, received a phone call: A big explosion had obliterated the town house. Three people had been killed.

He returned to New York with the rest of the leadership to meet with Cathy Wilkerson and Kathy Boudin, who had somehow survived the blast, fleeing nearly naked from the ruins and reorienting themselves at Kathy Boudin's parents' home about a block away and then hiding out as the police arrived. The story they told was unlike the sanitized version that eventually surfaced in the press. Terry had been building a bomb in the basement of the town house, an antipersonnel bomb he intended to plant at Fort Dix, New Jersey, and explode during an army dance. Diana, although haggard and sick, had been helping him. Like others in the collective, she had suffered serious doubts about the plan but had given way in the face of Terry's fierce certainty that it was right. Exhausted by the long struggle sessions in which Terry had lectured them about their deficits, about the wimpiness of the bomb attack on the judge's house, which had inflicted no casualties, they had driven themselves to complete the preparations. Ted Gold, who was in a fog because of the all-night arguments, had just gone out to the drugstore for cotton to muffle the ticking of the time-bomb clock, but he was so disoriented that he had forgotten what kind to get and had come back to find out. Just as he started to open the basement door, Terry crossed two wires mistakenly; the bomb blew with such shattering force that the brownstone simply collapsed. The beam over the door fell on Gold, crushing his chest. Diana's body was so mangled that she was identified with certainty only when two of her fingers were found in the debris. Terry was torn into such small pieces that no sure identification was made, although a month later his sister came to talk to Laurie Meisner about it. "I'm not going to bother you," she said, conscious of the possible fugitive status of everyone connected with her brother. "But I have to ask you one question. Do you remember if Terry had a mole on his lower left back?" When Laurie said yes, the sister became hysterical, breaking into uncontrollable sobs, and Laurie knew that Terry, too, was dead.

As he listened to the story, Billy could think only of one thing: His best friend had killed himself and the woman he loved. They had found the apocalypse they'd been looking for; they'd finally managed to break on through to the other side; what they found there, however, was not an epiphany of the new revolutionary self but the mundaneness of death.

The town house was their Rubicon, although what they lived over and over again was their not making the crossing. Perhaps if Terry, their man of action, had been successful in staging his attack on Fort Dix, the urge to keep going would have been irresistible and they would have become the dark avengers of their fantasies. But they had been washed in the blood of their own, and this made the town house a taboo they could never really overcome. It was their most authentic revolutionary act, yet because it was directed against themselves they could only feel ambivalence about it. There was no lack of romanticized references to it. Kathy Boudin said: "It's the kind of time that can't be counted on a clock. . . . You have a chance to see your whole life in that moment and also the lives of your friends." And for years after, those who'd known the dead even slightly would gather on the anniversary of the explosion in something like a radical version of an American Legion memorial to unknown martyrs, play Dylan songs, and listen to a ritual reading of the poem "How Does It Feel to Be Inside an Explosion?"

How does it feel
To be inside
An explosion?

Was there time
To flash upon
The way we came?
Diana and Ted and Terry
Dead inside an explosion
No one of us will ever be the same.

But at a more profound level, beneath the rhetoric about self-sacrifice and commitment, there was an awed disbelief at what they had done. Terry's old girlfriend Laurie found herself often walking by the town house and thinking not about the revolution or the Vietnamese but only about a ring she'd once given him, wondering illogically if she might pass by someday and see it glinting in a garden or gutter nearby and thus have a relic of their relationship. Billy Ayers's sister-in-law, Melody, recalls only the tremendous unspoken guilt: "It had always been a question of who would die first. We didn't say it aloud, but we all understood quite well. If we hadn't killed ourselves, we would have killed others. Deep down, we knew that the town house saved us."

Carrying the weighty, if unacknowledged, emotional baggage of the town house with them, the Weather leaders made their way to California to join Jeff Jones and Bernadine. At the end of April, a summit meeting was held in a beautiful rented beach house on the Mendocino coast. Mark Rudd was a day late for the rendezvous. When he arrived, the living room was filled with arguing people, remnants of the Weather Bureau—the three surviving members of the Central Committee (Bernadine, J.J., and Jones), Billy, Howie Machtinger, and the so-called secondary leadership group, which included Cathy Wilkerson and Kathy Boudin. The shimmering blue waters of the Pacific were visible through the picture-window patio doors, providing a dissonant context for the discussion at hand.

As Rudd sat down, he found that the battle lines were already drawn. Jeff and Bernadine were presiding, presenting themselves as the West Coast faction of the Central Committee. They were arguing that J.J. and Terry had shared leadership of the East Coast organization, and therefore J.J. shared responsibility with Terry for the erroneous course that had led to the explosion. J.J. countered that what had happened was an aberration, one of those setbacks that must be expected in a revolution, a technical failure attributable to inexperience, and that the military struggle should still be the cutting edge of what was now the Weather Underground. What was needed was not fewer, but more audacious assaults. He was halfheartedly supported for a while by Kathy Boudin and Cathy Wilkerson, who had gained stature in the organization as a result of surviving the blast. But as the discussion went on and focused more and more on J.J., his individual faults, and the way he and Terry had pushed the others, he became totally isolated.

"J.J. had no advocates," Rudd remembers. "He was a fighter, and he fought back as well as he could. But he was in the impossible situation of having to defend what had happened, to defend his view that we should keep moving ahead in the same direction. They just chewed him up. Not that anyone said the action was terrible. Just as we had gotten in the habit of calling our defeats victories, so now we called our dead 'heroic.' The criticism was kept to a technical level: how we should have concentrated on a lower level of assault because of our inexperience; how we should have gone for symbolic targets; that sort of thing. Finally, J.J. was told that he had to leave the organization. I thought to myself that it was wrong to scapegoat him. We'd all been enthusiastic about the war against the state; we were all guilty of what Jeff Jones was now calling 'the military error.' But, as usual, I was made to see my reservations as personal failings, as a lack of revolutionary will. So I shut up and let it happen. After J.J. left, they told me that I should go join one of the consolidated collectives in San Francisco and try to pull myself together. They said, 'We've defeated militarism and we'll lead you.' I was still ready to be led."

J.J. became one of the lost boys of Weatherman, dropping out of sight altogether. His departure created a vacuum that Bernadine rushed to fill. Although she had become Weatherman's most public figure, inside the organization she had always felt it necessary to operate through the men she made alliances with. Now that they were underground, she came into her own. Hers was the composed voice on the first tape delivered to the counterculture's "underground" press on May 21. (Her sister, Jennifer, and members of the Yippie organization, working out of William Kunstler's office, were the conduit for this message and those to come.) "Hello, this is Bernadine Dohrn," she began. "I'm going to read a Declaration of a State of War. This is the first communication from the Weatherman Underground." She went on to claim that "revolutionary violence is the only way" and to warn that a "symbol or institution of Amerikan injustice" would soon be attacked. Two weeks later, a blast wrecked the second floor of the New York City Police Headquarters, causing seven minor injuries.

The first days underground went by in a heady rush. The Central Committee traveled the country in disguises, sometimes daring even to stand next to policemen in public places. They used the networks set up during the Consolidation: safe houses and a communication system involving mail drops and coded calls between public telephones. On July 26, three days after the indictment of thirteen Weatherpeople in Detroit, they bombed San Francisco's Presidio army base. On October 8, the first anniversary of the Days of Rage, they blew up the police statue in Haymarket Square again, coordinating it with bombings at the criminal courthouse in Long Island City, New York, and the Hall of Justice in Marin County, California, where black activist Jonathan Jackson and three others had been killed. The next day, Bernadine issued a communiqué stating that these acts marked the beginning of a fall offensive: "We did not choose to live in a time of war. We chose only to become guerrillas and to urge our people to prepare for war rather than become accomplices in the genocide of our sisters and brothers. We invite [South Vietnamese Premier] Ky and Nixon and Agnew to travel in this country. Come to the high schools and campuses. But guard your planes, guard your colleges, guard your banks, guard your children. *Guard your doors!*"

In mid-February, Bernadine called Chicago Seven trial veteran Rennie Davis at his apartment in the Washington, D.C., headquarters of the May Day Tribe, where he was coordinating antiwar demonstrations planned for that spring. She informed him that a bomb was going to be planted at the

Capitol to protest the invasion of Laos. Davis pleaded with Bernadine not to, as it might wreck the plans for the demonstration. He thought he had convinced her, but just before dawn on March 1, Bernadine woke him with a phone call to say that she and Kathy Boudin had placed explosives in a women's bathroom in the Senate.

The Capitol bombing was the Weather Underground's greatest media success during its first year. But the most significant act of the Underground's first year, in terms of the organization's future, had come the previous September 12, when LSD prophet Timothy Leary, serving time at San Luis Obispo for possession of marijuana, climbed a tree and dropped down over the fence of the minimum-security prison, jumped into a car the Weather Underground had waiting for him, and drove off, eventually resurfacing in Algeria on a false passport the Underground had provided. (Leary would eventually repay the favor by testifying before a grand jury, reportedly giving a complete account of the rescue, including the names of the commandos who took part in the "military action.") The Weather Underground's participation in the escape showed the new direction its leadership had determined to follow, despite occasional bombings and fervid rhetoric.

The new line was the brainchild of Californian Jeff Jones, with the indispensable backing of Bernadine. During the struggle session at Mendocino, they had compared the "life trip" of the West Coast with the "death trip" of the East, as exemplified by Terry and J.J. They had decided that their future lay in associating themselves with "tribes" of the youth culture that were forming a new nation. This direction was officially embraced early in December 1970 in the position paper "New Morning—Changing Weather," which they drafted while listening to Dylan's new album at a ranch outside San Francisco. Claiming that they were communicating "not as military leaders, but as tribes at council," they dealt publicly with the town house for the first time, admitting that the explosion had "destroyed our belief that armed struggle is the only real revolutionary struggle. . . . It was clear that more had been wrong with our direction than technical inexperience (always install a safety switch so you can turn it off and on and a light to indicate if a short circuit exists). . . . This tendency to consider only bombings or picking up a gun as revolutionary, with the glorification of the heavier the better, we've called the military error." After noting that "a group of outlaws who are isolated from the youth communities . . . cannot develop strategies that grow to include large numbers of people," they said that they planned to build a mass movement of youth into a Weather Nation.

The ironies were obvious. The broad movement they now claimed to want to build had already been there; it was SDS itself, which they'd taken over and ultimately destroyed. The tribal nation they now wanted to create had already been born, at Woodstock, when they were preparing for their Days of Rage, and had died and been buried at Altamont, when they were holding their War Council. They were, as Mark Rudd later said, "a day late and a dollar short."

In its six years as a functioning clandestine organization, the Weather Underground claimed responsibility for about two dozen bombings. Only two of them, the bombs in the bathroom of the Capitol and in the bathroom of the Pentagon (May 19, 1972, after the mining of Haiphong harbor), did more than negligible damage. It was not much of a record for a group supported by a large aboveground apparatus constantly raising money, especially given the fact that the Treasury Department estimated that there were over five thousand bombings across the country from January 1969 through April 1970 alone.

The fact was that from the moment it went underground, Weatherman spent far less time in making revolution than in simply staying alive—and free. In the first blush of success, they overestimated how invisible they would be as fish swimming in the sea of the people, and in December 1970, a group that included Ayers, Bernadine, Jones, Kathy Boudin, and Judy Clark, some of them high on acid, had gone to a film at a theater around the corner from the FBI's Manhattan office on Sixty-ninth Street. A special agent had been assigned to track down each of the most prominent Weather leaders, and the one with Judy Clark's file happened to see them on the subway and followed them. As the lights dimmed, he walked over and said to Clark, "Excuse me, miss, would you please step out into the lobby?" As she bolted toward the front entrance, swallowing pages from her address book, the rest of the group split toward the exits. By the time the FBI agents in the lobby realized their mistake, it was too late. But the Weather Underground had come that close to having its leadership picked off right at the beginning; and they realized that from then on they'd have to pay more attention to basics. They restricted the flamboyance of their life-style and had to adopt the bourgeois respectability and monogamy they had spent so much effort in earlier days trying to root out. "You could always tell a Weatherman," Ayers later said. "He was the only person who paid his bills on time and obeyed the traffic laws."

The obsessive object became obtaining secure identification. The symbolism of this pursuit might have brought up cognate questions: Who were they? Who had they become? What *was* their identity as "revolutionaries"? But they kept it a technical matter. At first they were like underage kids seeking IDs to unlock the adult world. As Ayers remembers: "Someone would learn a method for getting a driver's license and come back to the others and say, 'I did it! I did it!' Then we'd all do it." Establishing rapport with clerks in motor vehicle and passport offices was relatively easy, and they were able to get IDs with a minimum of documentation, often using something as flimsy as a fishing license as their bona fides. They would go to the passport office and claim that a parent had died and they had to fly there quickly, and they would get a passport—another example, they pointed out among themselves afterward, of their "white skin privilege."

But however successful they were in their con jobs, there was always enough danger to make it seem that they were involved in something substantial. In their second year underground, for instance, the Central Committee, living in San Francisco, ran out of money and called a contact in the East for help. Asked how it should be sent, Jeff Jones said via Western Union, failing to consider that its offices were routinely monitored, and gave one of their false identities as the name the funds should be sent in care of. When he and Bernadine went to pick up the money at the telegraph office on Market Street, Jones immediately sensed that something was wrong. Taking the cash, he hurried out, jumped into the waiting car, and told Bernadine to move. As they started off, a car pulled in right behind them. Bernadine suddenly began to weave in and out of the trolley lane bisecting Market, veering into oncoming traffic. Then she slid into a U-turn and sped up Pine Street.

When they got home, they decided to ditch the car under the Bay Bridge. A few hours later, half convinced that the whole thing had been a figment of their paranoia, they sent someone back to look. But the car was swarmed over with police and "shoes" (as they called the FBI because of the brown brogans agents wore). Back at the apartment, they racked their brains for incriminating clues that would connect the car to their other safe houses. Suddenly Jeff Jones remembered: "The car got a parking ticket in front of the house last week." And then their cover began to collapse. The apartment was tied to another ID, and that ID to another car, which in turn was connected to another apartment because of a gas and electric bill left in the glove compartment. By the time they were through figuring everything out, they had no IDs, no houses, no cars. So they ran, making a risky connection with an aboveground friend, who loaded them into his car and drove for twenty-four hours until they reached another city. Jeff Jones called the mishap the Encirclement. After it was over, they started laboriously building false identities all over again.

"For what?" Mark Rudd had begun to wonder by the end of the first year. "What are we accomplishing?" After the summit meeting in Mendocino, he had been assigned to a "tribe" in San Francisco. He worked all week as a longshoreman, turning over his wages to the collective, where there was always much political discussion but little political activity. One night, hearing screams outside the Pine Street house where they lived, he went outside and chased away a rapist who had cornered a Chinese girl. But then he had to hurry away himself, lest he be recognized. It was like being an invisible man. He had been seeing Sue LeGrand, an old girlfriend from Columbia, who had come to Oakland after leaving the Denver collective she'd been assigned to. She worked as a photo processor during the week and came across the bay on weekends to meet him. Chronically short of money, they rented rooms in squalid Tenderloin hotels and spent Saturdays and Sundays in Golden Gate Park if it was not raining. After New Year's, Rudd decided he couldn't take it anymore. He and Sue bought a truck and went to Death Valley to get away from the Underground for a few days. They decided on a whim that they needed a dog for companionship and drove 150 miles to Las Vegas to buy one, but it immediately contracted distemper and died. This seemed to sum up Rudd's life. Trying to break the guilty ties that held him to his old comrades, Rudd left Death Valley, driving in the opposite direction from San Francisco. He and Sue wound up in Santa Fe, where he dyed his hair and beard blond, adopted the pseudonym Tony Goodman, and became a carpenter.

For some, the Weather Underground was the embodiment of radical chic. For a while before the Encirclement, Jeff, Bernadine, and Billy lived on a houseboat in scenic Sausalito. They received support from show-business personalities like Jon Voight and the Jefferson Airplane and sometimes met with their admirers in the elegant surroundings of Big Sur. But for many of the soldiers in the army, the generals led far too privileged an existence. "They never seemed to have jobs." says Billy Ayers's brother, Rick, who had deserted from the U.S. Army to join them. "They lived off radical lawyers and moneyed friends who told them what they wanted to hear—what courageous revolutionaries they were—while all the rest of us did the shit work and went around blowing things up to maintain their reputations. While some of us were dangerously poor, they always ate good food and they always slept between clean sheets."

Jane Alpert, herself a hunted fugitive and an underground legend (along with her lover, the Attica martyr Sam Melville) as a result of several major corporate bombings in New York City, arranged a meeting with Bernadine during a trip to San Francisco in July 1972. Jane expected the same tawdry disguises, furtiveness, and secrecy that made up the new rules of her own diminished life. What she found was something laid-back and very Californian. Bernadine came strolling up to their meeting spot in Golden Gate Park wearing hip-hugging jeans and a low-cut top. Her hair was dyed a flaming copper that caught the eye of every passerby. After exchanging greetings, Bernadine pressed some beads into Alpert's hands—a present, she said, from women of the Weather Underground who admired her. She graciously said that she hoped to learn from Alpert's experiences, then mentioned casually that many in the Underground were working surreptitiously for Democratic candidate George McGovern, hoping that under his presidency they might "go home again." The next day, she took Alpert to the top of Mount Tamalpais, removed her shirt, and sat there in a crocheted bikini top, pouring a health-food blender drink of cantaloupe and eggs from a thermos as they talked about feminism. Alpert left the meeting confused by Bernadine's politics but struck by the forceful way in which she molded her life. The "Great Mother of the Underground" was how she thought of her.

They might have gone on indefinitely as cool hippie bombers if the war, too, had gone on. But in January 1973, the war went into a terminal phase as the cease-fire agreement was signed. In Santa Fe, Mark Rudd, a.k.a. Tony Goodman, cried, thinking at first that it was for joy but realizing afterward that it was for the large part of himself that was now dead. In San Francisco, Billy Ayers wondered, "Is there life after the war?"

It was a moment of existential panic, which threatened to drain their personality away, and it was made worse by the way the Symbionese Liberation Army, which had kidnapped heiress Patty Hearst, had suddenly usurped their place as the FBI's most wanted organization. Their reaction would seem, in retrospect, the most bizarre chapter of their history. It was not to fold the organization but to push it toward Marxist orthodoxy, which, in the early days, had been seen as cerebral death.

It was Ayers's turn to become the leading male. Jeff Jones had been a casualty of the Encirclement—his incompetence in handling security had been the last straw for Bernadine, who remained unattached for a while and then moved into a couple with Billy. (Jeff's new mate was Eleanor Stein, who had been in the secondary leadership and now became one of a five-member revived Central Committee.) Billy asserted himself, declaring that the time had come to put "politics in command." When it was spelled out, this meant that they would become a Communist party in the tried and traditional sense.

The new code name for the organization was "the School." They set up an actual "cadre training school" in southern California, attended by about thirty-five people at a time, some of them aboveground supporters and sympathizers. They listened to lectures by Eleanor's mother, Annie Stein, an unreconstructed Stalinist and a former member of the Communist Party, and by an even more unlikely figure named Clayton Van Lydegraf.

If Stein was a party hack, the short, crew-cut Van Lydegraf was a personified short course in ideological conflict. The brother of a U.S. Army general, he had joined the Communist Party after serving as a pilot in World War II, flying supplies to the Chinese. He left the party as a disillusioned hard-liner in 1956 because of Khrushchev's downgrading of Stalin and helped to form the Progressive Labor Party with other ex-Communists-turned-Maoists. He was expelled from Progressive Labor a few years later for being "ultraleft." He was nearly fifty-three years old, working as a refrigerator repairman in Seattle, when J.J. "discovered" him in 1969. J.J. had been struck by his revolutionary "authenticity" and, according to rumor, had gotten Bernadine personally to smash Van Lydegraf's thirty-year monogamy. Since then, "Van" had been half in the underground and half out, sleeping in collectives with Weatherwomen young enough to be his daughters, smoking dope, and trying to attain an advisory role. "You kids don't understand Marxism or revolutionary violence," went his typical refrain, "but you mean well and you're on the right track." Something of a pest before, he was suddenly elevated to the role of mentor, using as texts Marx's pamphlet "Wages, Price and Profit" and his own "The Object Is to Win," a tract that had led radicals he pressed it on in the Seattle area a few years earlier to pin on him the derisive nickname "Van Mimeograph."

The ascendancy of Stein and Van Lydegraf brought things full circle. The nucleus of what would become the New Left had begun by attacking the Communists for stale and stultifying orthodoxy in 1961; now its remnant was sponsoring a crash course in these same shopworn creeds. Weatherman had started out as a kind of *enfant terrible* of the Left, engaged in what amounted to a large-scale Oedipal revolt; now it had submissively embraced Stein and Van Lydegraf as its symbolic parents. To complete the *déjà vu*, Bernadine adopted—without irony—Stalin's old title of General Secretary.

In their new incarnation, the Weatherman leadership put down the bomb and picked up the book. In the fall of 1973, they began a series of literary projects, chief among them a statement of their new principles, called *Prairie Fire*. With great difficulty—and at considerable cost—they had created their own underground printshop, although the book itself was perfectly legal. In this way, they told themselves, they were making it an "action." Bound in red covers, *Prairie Fire* was a series of short courses on revolution, racism, imperialism, and Vietnam, along with a lengthy history of the American Left written in such a way as to suggest that they were the logical heirs of all its traditions. The dedication page listed, along with others, John Brown and Sirhan Sirhan, the San Quentin Six, and the Symbionese Liberation Army. The message was summed up in the question-begging catchphrase: "Without mass struggle there can be no revolution. Without armed struggle there can be no victory."

Having finished a book, the Weather leaders turned to film. They had been contacted by director Emile De Antonio (noted for his documentaries *Point of Order!* and *Millhouse*), who reached them through a friend who knew Mark Rudd. "When I phoned Jeff Jones to tell him," Rudd recalls, "he could hardly contain himself. It was like they had made it big." Called *Underground*, the documentary was shot by Academy Award–winning cinematographer Haskell Wexler, with the Weather leaders functioning as codirectors and stars. There were some unexpected moments: at one point, Bernadine and Jeff, posing as television reporters, went to the site of a southern California hospital workers' strike and conducted interviews while the cameras rolled. An FBI agent closed in only moments after they had left. Wexler and De Antonio were served with subpoenas ordering them to surrender the film and appear before a Los Angeles grand jury. A blue-ribbon list that included actor Jon Voight, director Robert Wise, and film executive Daniel Melnick was mustered by the Academy Award–winning producer Bert Schneider to appear at a press conference to protest government harassment of the media. The subpoenas were dropped the next day.

The film was actually surprisingly tame, even banal—a rote recital of Weather rhetoric by Billy, Bernadine, and Jeff, along with Cathy Wilkerson and Kathy Boudin (chosen because of the notoriety attached to their escape from the town house). They explained their experiences and their politics to the cameras, which tracked them through the dusky rooms of an anonymous house. "We're five people from the Weather Underground Organization," Jeff Jones intoned. "We're in a house—you can call it a safe house. We're here with a group of filmmakers and together we're going to make a film. We're underground in this country. We've been underground for five years. . . ."

The film was part of a new strategy, the logical culmination of their new politics: to surface, first a few leaders and then the entire organization. The legend they had acquired underground and their Prairie Fire constituencies, they hoped, would catapult them into the leadership of a new mass movement made up of the Marxist working class they had once felt was contemptible. Jeff Jones christened the strategy the Weather Inversion.

Central to the Inversion was the creation of the Prairie Fire Organizing Committee (PFOC), which had grown out of the distribution apparatus for the book, and a Weather periodical, *Osawatomie* (the Indian name for John Brown). PFOC was created as a traditional Communist-front organization; its original steering committee consisted of Bernadine's sister, Jennifer; Annie Stein; Clayton Van Lydegraf, and other nonfugitive sympathizers, whom Bernadine personally recruited. Shortly after its inception, PFOC began to make arrangements for a carefully orchestrated Hard Times Conference in Chicago in January 1976, which would unify the most "conscious" elements of the working class behind the new Weather Underground ideas about the coming economic crisis and the opportunities it represented.

Because they were still fugitives, the Weather leaders were unable to attend the conference, which attracted some two thousand people. Listening to a live broadcast of the proceedings on Pacifica radio, however, they discovered how badly they had miscalculated the consequences of their ideological U-turn. Almost immediately, the conference slipped out of the control of their surrogates in Prairie Fire. Far from ratifying their plans to resurrect traditional Communism, the conference adopted the resolution of a caucus of black delegates that denounced the Weather Underground as racist. Angered by the zigzagging political course that had followed the town house explosion, their accusers zeroed in on the new course, indicting them for slighting the race issue in favor of "economism," abandoning the struggle for a black nation, and, in effect, betraying the revolutionary priorities that once defined their creed.

It was proof of how uncertain and disoriented they had become that the Weather leaders did not fight the charges but instead capitulated to them. Trying to stem the criticism, the Central Committee launched a "rectification" campaign, admitting to a series of "opportunistic" errors, which had begun in the New Morning period and continued through their most recent Communist phase.

To show their sincerity, members of the Central Committee removed themselves temporarily from leadership. But if they had read more deeply in the history of Communist orthodoxies, they would have realized that it was impossible to practice damage control in a situation such as this, and that every admission would only bring on a more violent accusation. A faction coached by their erstwhile tutor Van Lydegraf presented itself as a "Revolutionary Committee" that would judge them. Using as their operating manual the purge of Communist Party leader Earl Browder conducted by William Z. Foster in the late forties, Van Lydegraf and his protégés put Bernadine, Ayers, Jones, and the rest on trial, accusing them of promoting a "white and male chauvinist line" and of committing "crimes against national liberation struggles, women and the anti-imperialist left."

Using his expertise in sectarian Communist practice, Van Lydegraf promulgated the "theory of contagion," which forbade any of their friends and supporters from communicating with the "infected" Weather leaders while they were suspended, being criticized and awaiting determination of their fate. Rick Ayers remembers encountering his brother Billy, who was traumatized by the personal assaults of his criticism session. "He appeared in a state of shock. Gone was the light-hearted, joking Billy I knew. 'You should have heard what everybody said to me, I feel terrible,' he said. He was so depressed."

The long arm of the purge reached to Mark Rudd, who had for years had only minimal ties with the group. "People were not allowed to talk to me," he remembers. "This included some of my best friends, who were too scared to break the command. It was like the Amish practice of shunning. I could handle it better than the others, being so far away. At one point, Jeff Jones was so totally isolated that no one would talk to him, not even Eleanor Stein, who was living with him. He looked so distraught, Sue and I debated whether to let him baby-sit for us. We were worried that he might go off the deep end. Later, I asked him what he thought of the way he had been treated by people who'd been his closest friends. He said, 'If I were them, I'd probably do the same thing.' It was pathetic. I finally understood Stalin and the purge trials. I'd never read *Darkness at Noon*. I didn't have to. I learned about it in the Weather Underground."

Finally, the Central Committee members were brought individually into a room to face their inquisition. Catechized by the Revolutionary Committee, they all confessed to their own misdeeds and betrayed one another. Van Lydegraf's greatest coup was "turning" Bernadine, who admitted her "crimes" in a self-abasing tape: "This is Bernadine Dohrn. I am making this tape to acknowledge, repudiate, and denounce the counterrevolutionary politics and direction of the Weather Underground Organization. . . ." Referring to a communiqué the Central Committee had issued on the occasion of the Vietnamese cease-fire that failed to mention "imperialist attacks" on the Black Liberation Army, she said of the omissions: "These are crimes—they are naked white supremacy, white superiority, and chauvinist arrogance. . . ." Sins against the women's movement followed: "For seven years I have upheld a politics which is male supremacist and opposed to the struggle of women for liberation. . . . I have been a token woman, part of the structure of women's leadership which actually served male supremacy. . . ."

When she tried to offer an explanation for her crimes, Bernadine was at a loss: "Why did we do this? I don't really know. We followed the classic path of so-called revolutionaries who sold out the revolution. For me to understand this requires much more study and struggle. What I do know is that by standing on my anti-imperialist record in a self-satisfied and self-justifying way, by assuming that I was beyond white privilege or allying with male privilege because I understood it, I prepared and led the way for a totally opportunistic direction which infected all our work and betrayed revolutionary principles."

If there was narcissistic extravagance characteristic of the "Me Decade" in her bizarre insistence on claiming guilt for what amounted to nothing more than impure thoughts, this and the other "confessions" embodied deeper yearnings as well —the desire to overcome the paralysis that followed the town house explosion and made them rebels who had lost their cause.

Bernadine concluded her list of sins with the denunciation of the planned Inversion, which would have allowed the Underground to surface. Then Van Lydegraf expelled her and all the rest of them from the movement they had created.

The following year, Van Lydegraf's Revolutionary Committee made a show of picking up the military actions Bernadine and the others had fumbled over the years by bombing the offices of the Immigration and Naturalization Service in San Francisco. Shortly thereafter, in a fitting finale to the burlesque, the group was busted by Van Lydegraf's roommate, a man who they thought was helping them plan the assassination of California state senator John Briggs—author of an amendment to ban gay teachers from California schools—but who was actually an undercover FBI agent.

The Weather leaders were left to dangle slowly in the wind. Coming aboveground would have proved that all the charges laid against them were right, but underground they were pariahs. Ayers later said: "Bernadine and I were lucky to get pregnant at the time. It gave us something to think about besides our fucked-up selves." Like kids with their noses pressed to a window, they watched the remnants of the Prairie Fire Organizing Committee complete their "rectifications" on the race issue by devolving into the May 19th Communist Organization, a support group for the Black Liberation Army. (The BLA had begun as an offshoot of the Black Panther Party. It made its reputation in the early Seventies by the cold-blooded murders of two black-and-white cop teams honored in the communities they served, and a series of unsuccessful assassination attempts on other police officers.) Billy and Bernadine saw their old comrades Kathy Boudin, Judy Clark, and David Gilbert labor to get back into the good graces of the May 19th Communist Organization by "rectifying" themselves and showing they were ready to serve the third world leadership of the BLA. Billy and Bernadine had named their first son Zayd after a BLA "soldier" who'd been killed in a shoot-out with the police. But although they tried to be worthy, they were too contaminated by their charismatic past to be allowed close to the revolutionary alignment taking place, in which the black liberationists would call the tune and the white "anti-imperialists" would do the dance. After their son Zayd's birth, Bernadine got a job as a waitress. Drawing on his talents as a gourmet cook, which had been developed during the long, boring days underground, Billy got a job as a baker.

After making a solemn pact with Kathy Boudin, Jeff Jones, Eleanor Stein, and other of the remaining fugitives never to divulge details of the Underground, the two of them finally resurfaced in 1980. The first thing Billy's father said to him was, "You still need a haircut." Bernadine's mother wondered anxiously if they were married, and when told that they weren't, she thought for a moment and said, "Well, people will think you are."

The following year, Mark Rudd, who had come up in 1977, ran into Bernadine. She asked him what he thought about the whole experience. He told her that he thought of it as seven years of wasted life; that neither he nor they had accomplished anything, and he wished he'd gotten out at the beginning. "She got furious and said: 'But what about the contribution we made to the overall struggle for armed struggle and revolution in America?' I couldn't believe the rhetoric. The same old shit. I just said to myself, 'Oh, later for you, lady,' and took off. Later on, it occurred to me how her ego was still totally involved with all that dead history. How little she had looked at herself all those years. She should have had to confront what she really did to people—manipulated, maneuvered, and isolated them, fucked them up; she should have had to admit how wrong her ideas were, how *meshuga* her self-conception was. A great revolutionary leader! She had no great revolutionary ideas. None of us did. She was just the daughter of a credit manager of a Milwaukee furniture store."

On May 19, 1982, Bernadine and Billy were heading off to work and school with Zayd and their second child, Malik (named for Malcolm X). With them, too, was Kathy Boudin's son, Chesa, whom they had taken into their family after his mother's arrest at the scene of the Brink's holdup and the killings in Nyack. As they put the children in the back seat of their worn Volvo station wagon, an anonymous gray fleet car with FBI written all over it screeched up to block their path.

When former Weather Underground leaders Judy Clark and Boudin were arrested the previous October, FBI officials (hampered by post-Watergate legislation that restricted their ability to surveil subversive groups) had speculated extravagantly about the development of a new interracial terrorist network. But the names that turned up were the ones that had been around since 1969. Jeff Jones and Eleanor Stein—living quietly under pseudonyms—had been arrested while watching the World Series. Then authorities had turned their attention to Billy and especially to Bernadine, shadowing her so assiduously that she and Billy made jokes about how the tables she waited on were filled with FBI agents who left stingy tips. Yet it was not simply harassment. In the trail of clues that led from Nyack like droppings from Hansel and Gretel, law-enforcement officials had discovered that identification used to rent the getaway cars had apparently been stolen from people who shopped at a Manhattan children's boutique during a time when Bernadine, still underground, had worked there as a manager. It was insufficient to connect her to the attempted holdup, but enough to require her appearance before a grand jury investigating the whole Nyack episode, and the two FBI agents who came over to the passenger side of the Volvo that morning had a summons for Bernadine. That night, she and Billy explained to the children that she would be going away for a while, making the family moment into a child-sized parable about the American legal system.

Six days later, Bernadine surrendered, telling reporters that while she had nothing to hide in this particular incident, she was opposed to grand juries on principle and would refuse to talk, staying in jail until the grand jury term expired. Yet while Clark's and Boudin's choice led to robbery and a shootout at Nyack, those of Bernadine led to television. A public figure in a way that the others, no matter what they did, would never be, she spent an hour discussing politics from her jail with Phil Donahue.

After Bernadine was arrested, Billy spent more time with the children. Working all day at an interracial day-care school where the kids were enrolled, he would come home and deal with single parenthood. After the kids were in bed, he got on the phone and tried to drum up support from people "in the community," explaining how Bernadine's case demonstrated a threat to the Bill of Rights posed by federal prosecutors out to destroy dissent, an exercise he wryly admitted was a type of "popular frontism." Like other veterans of the purges of 1976, he was weary of the subject of Weatherman's past. But sometimes it was hard for him not to allow himself a little nostalgia. "The thing that has stayed with me are the demonstrations we organized. Hitting the streets with that sense of anticipation— there's never been anything to equal that. I remember the National Action in Chicago. Terry was hanging close to me then. We didn't know where Diana was. We only knew we were behind enemy lines. Terry was looking to me to get us back. The rush we got on the streets was unlike anything before or since. I can feel the physical sensation of it when I think back. It's like the rush a soldier must get in the middle of a battle zone. I guess it's our version of post-Vietnam syndrome."

For him and for Bernadine, the year was still 1968 and always would be. The revolutionary weather was clear ahead and would never grow cloudy. Vietnam was still happening— a justification for what they were and what they became. If someone had told them that they were like those Japanese soldiers who wandered for years in the jungle, unaware that they had lost the war, it is a comparison they would probably have accepted.

chapter 3 _____

The Criminal and the Cop

Post-Vietnam Syndrome

In his years as a plainclothes narcotics cop, Steve Bosshard had often crossed paths with Iris Southall. "Rocky," as Southall was known on the streets, was one of those pasty-faced blondes with the punched-out look that comes from too many men, too much dope, too many trips to jail. She was thirty-two but looked closer to fifty. Bosshard knew what the actuarial tables promised for such a woman and wasn't surprised or particularly grieved when he heard she had died. But the circumstances did strike him as a little peculiar. She had gone into the hospital for minor surgery on a shoulder abscess, come out of the recovery room in good shape, and then suddenly went into shock and died the next day. Still, his interest wasn't really piqued until an autopsy revealed that her system had been overloaded with amphetamines, and a terminally ill woman in the next bed led hospital officials to believe that a black man had come in and given the victim a drug. When the man was identified as Luther Brock, Bosshard knew he would be hearing from Homicide.

Dressed like the street people he stalks except for the .357 magnum nesting in a shoulder holster beneath his soiled down vest, the blond, bearded officer spent the next few days touching base with the network of snitches that connected him to the underworld of dope sellers and users. He had made thousands of arrests in his years on the force, receiving medals for heroism and letters of commendation from the city fathers. He knew that he was regarded as a good cop by the department and that he had built a formidable reputation among cons and criminals. He also felt the irony in the fact that what finally defined his career was not really his achievements on the force but the way his fate had been entangled for nearly twenty years with that of Luther Brock. White and black, cop and criminal, family man and freewheeler—they were outwardly as different as they could be, but bound together by circumstances Bosshard could only describe as "karma." They seemed still to be caught in the Sixties after all these years. It was as if each of them were a dark mirror in which the other feared he might see his own face.

As Bosshard drove through the Tenderloin district, he made sure that certain key people knew he wanted to get a call: a white woman who had slept with Luther off and on and carried his dope for him, a seventy-two-year-old black ex-con who (in one of the eerie contradictions Bosshard had come to accept as part of his business) was hanging out with the twenty-six-year-old addict daughter of a white San Francisco policeman.

About a week later, he was awakened at his home at three in the morning by someone from the department, who told him that Luther was waiting to hear from him in a pay phone in Long Beach. As Bosshard dialed the number and began to speak, his wife bolted upright, complaining later that his soul talk made her think a black man had climbed into bed with her.

"Hey, Romeo! What's happenin', man? How you doin'?"

"Fine." Luther's voice was flat. "I hear you been askin' around about me."

"Yeah, I got friends in Homicide, man."

"So?"

"So they want you to come in and talk about Rocky's murder."

"Murder?"

"That's what I said."

"Okay, Steve. Let me tell you something. First of all, Rocky wasn't murdered. Second of all, she was my old lady, and you guys up there hated her. Third of all, you evidently don't like me no more. And fourth of all, I don't talk to no police, not even you."

"Listen, man, just come on in and talk." Bosshard waited for a response, then, getting none, went on. "Thing is, if you don't come up and talk, it's going to end bad. We'll both end up over the barrel of a gun."

"Look here, Steve"—Luther elongated his words for emphasis—"when you go to your squad meeting tomorrow morning, you tell them something for me. You tell them that I can bite a police's head off one night and still go to breakfast the next morning plenty hungry."

"Okay, man, if that's the way you want it."

"That's the way I want it."

After hanging up, Bosshard lay there teasing his imagination with a thought that had occurred to him before: given the kind of people they were, he and Luther might easily have wound up walking in each other's shoes.

Luther, too, remembered quite clearly the day they met. It was long before he had bulked himself out in prison weight yards; it was a time when he had processed hair instead of a carefully sculpted Afro; it was a time when life was still all potential, without the blanks having been filled in. It was March 22, 1964, the day after he turned seventeen, and he was signing his enlistment papers for the Marine Corps. Beside him was a skinny young white kid with a birthmark on his neck. It was Bosshard, there because of the alphabetical proximity of their surnames.

"And how you doing?" Luther remembers Steve asking. "You scared?"

Luther said no, although in fact he was.

They finished their paperwork at about the same time, received serial numbers one digit apart, 2095724 and 2095725, and were given chits for a quick lunch at a dive across from the Oakland Army Terminal and then for a plane ride to boot camp.

"We hooked up right quick," Luther recalls. "We had to have somebody to grab on to."

On the way to San Diego, they told each other about their lives. Steve was eighteen, one of two kids, an Air Force brat who had attended nineteen schools before finishing the twelfth grade, an upbringing that taught him to make and relinquish friends quickly. When he was thirteen, his father, a lieutenant colonel, began to die of cancer, shrinking in a few months from 185 pounds to just over 70, becoming so light that Steve, although small for his age, had been able to carry him out of the hospital for the last time. Before his father's death Steve had thought he might become an Episcopal priest, but watching a good man suffer pointlessly ended his belief in a merciful God.

His father always claimed that the perfect way to fight a war was to drop bombs from thirty thousand feet and then come home and sleep between clean sheets, and so after graduating from San Rafael High, Steve took the test for the Air Force Academy. But with his father gone, he lacked the connections to get admitted. Ever since his father's death, he had had a peculiar feeling—that he would die before he was twenty-one. He figured that the Marines was as good a place for it to happen as any other.

Luther said "fate" was a white man's word. He believed in choice. The oldest boy in a family of six kids, he had grown up in San Francisco's Fillmore district. His mother was a beautician, his father one of her five husbands, an alcoholic whose binges lasted two years at a time. At first, Luther had done well in school, skipping the fourth grade. But then he became involved in—"chose" was the word he used to Steve—life on the streets. He had become the leader of a gang called the Egyptian Angels, named for a drawing one of the members had done of a muscular representation of a pharaoh holding knives and dripping blood from on high. Fighting became one focus of his growing up; loving, the other. He fathered two children before he was fifteen, girls named Lucretia and Ramona, and thus acquired the street name Romeo. His mother moved the family to Palo Alto, where he was one of only sixteen blacks at Cubberly High. Rather than submitting to racist innuendo, he fought. In one brawl, he knocked a white student out. The student's parents threatened to sue, and to spare his mother a court appearance, Luther decided to join the Marines. He chose the Marines because it was the best organization there was, he said, and that was what he wanted to be—the best.

When they reached boot camp, Steve and Luther were both assigned to Platoon 225. Luther was chosen platoon leader. Steve followed his lead and stayed close. When a Cajun recruit goaded Luther with racial epithets, Steve gave the guy a whipping. Luther returned the favor later on, warning some blacks who were laying for Steve because of an imagined racial slur that they would have to fight him too. After evening chow, Steve and Luther would sometimes go out on what was called "the grinder," a big asphalt marching field where they drilled for what seemed like days at a time under the hot sun. They would sit there looking up at the airplanes flying overhead. "Wonder if that one's going to San Francisco," one of them would say. The other would detail a menu of the good things to be done in the city.

Bosshard's mother came down for boot camp graduation ceremonies. So did Mrs. Brock and her youngest daughter, Mona Lisa. The families mingled on the field after the speeches and presentation. As Steve and Luther put their arms around each other's shoulders, one of the relatives aimed a camera and captured what at the time seemed an archetypal image: two young men of different races ready to march off and see what life had in store for them. Luther was assigned to the infantry and sent to an air facility in Santa Ana for training as a teletype operator in a helicopter unit. Steve tried to get the same posting, but the vagaries of Marine Corps personnel procedures kept him at boot camp in an electronics program. They promised to stay in touch.

There was a sense of expectancy in the air in the spring of 1965. It had to do not only with noncoms' talk about brush wars in far-off countries but with social tremors at home. During a brief leave, Steve was driving with a girlfriend on an L.A. freeway when his car was struck by rifle fire—a sniper, he later learned, who had spilled over from the Watts riots. Luther and his helicopter unit had shipped out two days earlier aboard the U.S.S. *Princeton*, headed for an unknown destination. He was swimming near Hawaii, diving off the fantail of the ship, when news of Watts came over the radio, and the strange voice of a brother shouted, "Burn, baby, burn!"

Luther soon found out where the *Princeton* was going. "I'm in teletype and have top-secret clearance," he remembers, "and we get a message about a place called Vietnam, where there's fighting. That's no big thing to me. I haven't been to a war—at least not their war."

The *Princeton* anchored in the South China Sea, and Luther's unit was served steak and eggs for breakfast, the traditional last meal before entering battle. He flew into Vietnam in the middle of Operation Starlight, to a place called Chu Lai. It was not the panorama of war that struck him, or even the violence and bloodshed. It was the little things. Shooting the oxen that served as "trucks" for the Vietcong; machine-gunning sharks from helicopters so GIs could swim on the beaches; finding swarms of huge ants under his tent in the monsoons. It was the foreignness of it all. " 'Vietnam!' I said. 'My God, where am I at?' "

Up to this time, his idea of getting high had been to steal a case of Thunderbird and drink with friends, but in Vietnam he discovered marijuana. "One night I was in the village smoking dope with this whore. And then this other girl comes out of her room and says, 'Romeo! The VC!' I came upstairs to look out the window. My whole damn base was lit up—all kinds of hell coming down. Later on, I found that we had been overrun by a suicide squad. The Cong had sent these little son of a bitches in there with dynamite tied to them to explode our helicopters!"

His first kill came in Da Nang. He was out in the field on an operation, and the point man stepped on one of the spring-loaded land mines called a "bouncing Betty." As the man lay there with both legs blown away and his intestines showing, Luther tried to give mouth-to-mouth resuscitation but drew up a mouthful of the dying man's blood and choked on it. When he returned to his position, he saw a Vietcong dart behind a tree. He picked up a machine gun and shot at the base of the tree until it fell. Then he shot the Vietcong to pieces too.

• • •

Steve had arrived in Vietnam shortly after Luther. He, too, was stationed near Da Nang, as a radar technician operating a seismic intrusion detector he had been told would pinpoint enemy infiltration by picking up the vibration of footsteps. But the heat and humidity of the jungle made the sensitive equipment malfunction so often that it was practically useless, and he wound up carrying a rifle.

He went there with ideals extrapolated from John Wayne movies. He made friends with an orphan girl living in a small village near his base and gave her older sister, a prostitute, money for her support. He was considering trying to adopt the child, but then the orphan girl refused to see him anymore. He kept going to the house; finally, her sister told him that the Vietcong punished children who became too friendly with Americans by cutting off their left hands. He had noticed these amputees before but hadn't realized the cause. After this, the war became nothing more than a series of brutal tableaux.

"Once we entered this village and saw a row of GIs' heads that had been cut off and set on pikes. You got used to bodies after a while, but you never got used to bodies that were mutilated—eyes gouged out, mouths cut off, that sort of thing."

Steve saw racial tension developing in the Corps and sometimes wondered what had ever happened to his old friend Luther. Actually, they were within a few miles of each other, and had been for some time. Late in 1966, Steve was in a place just below Hill 327 near Da Nang that the GIs called Dogpatch, a sprawl of native huts, some made of C-ration boxes and Coke cans stamped flat and nailed together. He caught a glimpse of Luther coming out of a whorehouse. There wasn't time for a real talk, only a few words before his unit moved on. Steve was disappointed. He had thought the reunion, when it came, would add up to something more. He was struck by how much Luther had changed—he was harder, more remote, with a weird look in his eyes. Bosshard wasn't sure if it was drugs, the war, or his imagination. He wondered if he had changed in these ways too.

In 1966, Steve extended his tour so that he could stay in Da Nang and confront what he still believed would be his destiny. Then he turned twenty-one and was still alive. The

Corps sent him back to the United States to teach new recruits to use electronic gear that he knew wouldn't work in Vietnam. Still getting used to the idea that he might have a future, he left the Marines in the spring of 1968 and went home to the Bay Area.

His family had started a dry-cleaning business with the insurance money from his father's death, and he went to work for them. He was angry with his brother for not enlisting in the war effort. He hated the dry-cleaning business. "No excitement, the same thing every day, the same clothes, and the same people. None of the challenge of Nam, none of the conquering and surviving." He missed his old buddies and wondered where Luther was—if he was even alive after the Tet offensive. He was upset by antiwar protestors. "When I heard them talking about how great the VC were, it drove me livid. They were talking all this shit, and I was still having these nightmares about the war in which you wake up yelling, all in a sweat and trying to eat the pillow." Looking for an outlet for his anger, he took the test for the San Francisco Police Department.

It was a time when the Department was still shorthanded because of anti-police sentiment generated by the protesters and was having to recruit heavily throughout the western states just to fill vacancies left by attrition. As a cop, Bosshard felt as though he were back on the front line, although it was a new kind of war. His first arrest stands out in his mind. He was being trained by two officers in a black-and-white. A call came from the heart of the Tenderloin, saying that a burglar had been traced to a certain hotel room. When they got there, the other two officers went to the door and told Bosshard to stay on the fire escape in case the burglar ran for it.

"I'm out their practicing what I'll say in case the guy comes my way: 'Freeze, asshole, up against the wall!' I keep repeating it. So sure enough the guy gets away and comes lunging out the fire escape. I put my gun right in his face, and I go, 'B-b-b-breathe, asshole!' "

By early 1970, he had his own patrol car. One day he saw a '64 Chevy turn onto Market Street. Acting on his developing policeman's intuition, he decided that the car might be stolen and pulled it over to check the registration. The car door opened and out stepped Luther, wearing a purple hat with a long string of tassels hanging from the brim. With his distinctive swaggering gait, Luther came over, looked Bosshard up and down, and said, "Hey, Steve, ain't you looking funky!" Hiding his embarrassment, Bosshard eyed his friend and replied, "Well, Luther, man, you're looking a little funky yourself in your doo-dah hat. What game you playing anyhow, Mr. Ghetto Man?" They grinned at each other for a moment and then tried to make contact through small talk. Bosshard finally said he had to go: "Okay, man, you take it easy and drive safely."

As Luther remembers the encounter, he was about to start the car when Steve came back and leaned in the window, saw two white women in the front seat, and said, "What you doing now anyhow, pimping white girls?" Although posed in semi-jest, the question rankled. It was something the person Luther remembered from boot camp never would have said. But he thought to himself: "Oh, well, he is a police now, and things have done changed between us."

After getting out of the Marines, Luther had come home and tried to get a job with an airline as a teletype operator but concluded that only women were wanted for the job. "The other skills I had learned in the service they didn't need in civilian life—air-to-ground communication, machine-gunning, that sort of thing." He started working part-time jobs. Meanwhile, within a month after his discharge, he had discovered the music and dope scene. "First it was marijuana and LSD. Then speed. And that was the thing! We'd stay up for two or three days—later on, a week at a time—and ride around in cars. Speed would bring me to the point where I was almost on the same level as in the war."

One day a friend of Luther's took him to a house in Half Moon Bay. "The people there had just made ten pounds of speed, and when I walked in the house some other people were there to buy it. They had just laid ten thousand dollars cash money on the table. I told myself right then, I'm gonna have me ten thousand dollars sometime."

By the time Bosshard stopped his car on Market Street, Luther had been arrested more than a dozen times. He had been shot twice—once by a pimp on a Fillmore street corner and once by himself as he was pulling a gun on a man who was trying to rob him. He was deeply into the drug culture, a middleman going between kitchen speed factories that had sprung up on the Peninsula and a growing clientele of crystal users in the Haight—gays, bikers, and hippies. His world was dope and women—usually white women, at whose houses he lived.

When he left the Marines and returned home, Luther had been struck by the new racial ferment. Yet he didn't identify with talk about the lives of black people being determined by poverty or color. He was not frustrated by opportunities denied. Rather than wanting a place in the system, Luther wanted to transcend the system altogether; he wanted a life on his own terms. He thrived on the close calls, constant jeopardy, and random violence of the drug world, his personal version of post-Vietnam syndrome. At times he would even retreat into the straight world to prove he was truly free. He enrolled in a computer programming school in San Francisco, for instance, graduating at the top of his class. But the workaday world simply didn't offer the excitement of the high-stakes game on the streets. He made himself into a competent "chemist" and began manufacturing speed as well as selling it. By the early Seventies, he was established as one of the premier amphetamine dealers in San Francisco, making as much as three thousand dollars a day, and spending it so quickly that he often couldn't make bail when he was arrested. He would rationalize the life he had chosen as merely connecting people with their desires. He didn't think of himself as a pusher, because he never tried to persuade anyone to buy. He merely supplied those who came to him with what they already wanted.

At one point, Luther was sharing a San Francisco house with six gays. He felt comfortable with them because, as he later put it, "they never hassle, and their money is always right." One day, while he was out on a drug deal, one of the couples in the house had a lovers' quarrel that led to a vindictive call to the police. When Luther returned, several officers were waiting inside. They searched him and found some Nembutals, made the arrest, and drove him downtown. He knew there was a warrant out on him for grand theft, and planned to give a false name when he was booked and get bailed out quickly before the ruse was discovered. But as he emerged from the elevator into the booking area, he ran smack into Bosshard.

"Romeo! What are you doing here?" Steve asked, thinking back to their contact on the street about a year earlier.

"Oh, man." Luther grinned. "I was at a neighbor's house to borrow some sugar and they break the fucking door down and say it's a dope raid."

Bosshard asked if there was anything he could do to help out.

"Yeah," Luther replied, "could you help me get my phone call as soon as possible? I've got to get ahold of my little sister Mona Lisa so she can come down and bail me out before she goes to work."

Bosshard said it would be no trouble and went over to look through the booking charges.

"I'm going by Walter Williams," Luther whispered when Steve came back and told him he couldn't locate his name.

"Come on, man," Bosshard said, "this trick won't work."

"Are you going to help me or not?"

"Come on, man, you know there's no way I can get in the middle of this process."

As Bosshard left the room, avoiding his glance, Luther thought to himself, "I really don't know this man. I never did."

By this time, Bosshard was no longer a rookie on the force. Others hired at the same time had already burned out, unable to take the constant frustrations of police work. But the job offered Bosshard what Luther had found in his life on the streets—action and excitement—although in Bosshard's case it was sanctioned by the belief that he was holding the line against the forces of chaos. He had gone from uniformed patrol into the tactical squad, becoming part of a special plainclothes crime-prevention unit floating in and out of violent sections such as the Tenderloin and Hunter's Point. Because he was blond, he and his dark-haired partner were inevitably referred to as Starsky and Hutch by the black children in the ghetto areas they patrolled. After watching Bosshard run over rooftops and chase criminals down the street, the kids would sometimes ask for an autograph. Bosshard would sign, "Good luck. Your friend, Starsky."

He had gotten into narcotics in a roundabout way. One night, he and his partner were driving on their beat. They passed the rock palace Winterland and saw dozens of people running down the street, some of them naked and acting bizarrely. They stopped to investigate and found that a neighborhood commune had loaded a fifty-five-gallon drum with Kool-Aid and LSD and taken it to a Grateful Dead concert, passing it out to the crowd as "electric water." Bosshard made nineteen arrests in the next twenty hours and referred countless people with serious hallucinations to Mt. Zion Hospital. The next few days he did the follow-up on the young people who had been raped or involved in car accidents, or who had simply disappeared. Al Nelder, then chief of the San Francisco police, was impressed and ordered him promoted.

Bosshard had married a secretary in the narcotics division, a pretty woman named Jan who was the daughter of a policeman, and moved the family, which soon included three children, to the Sonoma suburbs, an hour's drive from the high-crime areas of the city in which he worked. He thought that Jan's background in police work would keep them from becoming part of the astronomical divorce rate that afflicted members of the force, but it wasn't easy to maintain domestic tranquillity. Jan had to deal with Steve's irregular hours, his tendency to decompress by putting on a "three-bullet heat" at some bar after a tense shift, and with the fact that he often felt bored and restless when he was at home. It didn't help matters when he was assigned a female partner, an attractive black woman named Paula. The team wasn't to endure, however. In a confrontation that might have gotten them both killed, Bosshard felt that his five-foot-one, 105-pound colleague had lost control of a street punk, and he asked for a new partner. "You've got the heart of a lion," he told her, "but I've got a wife and kids who expect me home at night, so we're not going to be able to work together anymore."

By the mid-Seventies, Steve and Luther were veterans of the silent war on the streets, the war that, except for occasional explosions, was carried out just below the surface of daily life. It was a war, like the one in Vietnam, that had no light at the end of the tunnel. It was like that war too in that it changed the way people looked at the world. Bosshard had entered the force with a lingering sense of the injustices of the world. He now believed, along with most other cops, that "the law has no teeth in it" and that criminals have rights and victims do not. But instead of letting this view sour him on law enforcement, he worked harder to even the score.

After the 1973 meeting in the county jail, Steve heard about Luther occasionally, usually from cops who knew of their relationship and kidded him about it. Once, he was on a team that searched a gay's apartment and found a Marine's uniform in the closet. One of his partners swished by and lisped, "Now, is this yours or Luther's?" But since his old friend was not one of the down-and-out users or drug kingpins narcotics officers focus on, Steve eventually lost track of him. Then, late in 1974, he saw a Homicide poster with Luther's picture on it.

It was, as Luther says, "a complex situation," just as Rocky Southall's death would be several years later. He had sold seven hundred dollars' worth of speed to a woman and then taken a motel room for a two-day stint of sex, during which he helped her use it up. Apparently this was not what the woman was supposed to do with the money, or with the drugs, and shortly afterward Luther found himself under attack by two men wielding golf clubs and demanding their seven hundred dollars back. Luther yelled for help, and a "crime partner" of his obliged by shooting one of his assailants and killing him. A murder warrant was issued for Luther, and Homicide began to circulate the Wanted poster that caught Bosshard's eye.

After holing up with one of his girlfriends for nearly a month, Luther went to his partner's house and double-parked, immediately drawing attention from a cruising patrol car. As he stepped out of his car, the officer came to check him out. Luther knew that his younger brother Patrick had no outstanding warrants and gave his brother's name. With convincing authenticity, he recited Patrick's vital statistics: birthday, mother's maiden name, history of arrests. When they radioed to the Portrero station, a run-down place that cops and criminals alike call Dogpatch, Bosshard happened to be there.

"Bring him in," he radioed back, "and I'll tell you if it's Patrick or Luther." Luther entered the station sweating profusely although it was three o'clock in the morning and he was wearing nothing but a thin polyester shirt open to his navel.

"Tell them I'm Patrick!" Luther whispered as he passed Bosshard.

"It's murder, man!"

"You know I'm not into murder. Tell them I'm Patrick."

"Come on, man," Bosshard said, "you're Marine Corps serial number 2095725. I know it by heart."

"Never mind about that, dammit, tell them I'm Patrick."

"I can't, man, they got you down for murder."

An unbridgeable gap had opened between them. It wasn't just that Luther was on the wrong side of the law; the law as an abstraction wasn't that important. The real problem for Bosshard was his feeling that Luther had lost his integrity, even as a criminal, and become someone who wheedles and chisels, never facing his fate in a manly way. "I could see he'd become one of those guys who's always playing the angles, the kind of guy who's always got a girl with him, for instance, using her because she's got a lot of body cavities where she can hide his stash. When they're nabbed, the first thing he'll do is start hollering, 'The bitch has got it! I'm clean, the bitch has got the dope.' " Bosshard told the arresting officers that they had the right man.

"I thought we were tight," Luther said as he was led to a holding cell.

"We are tight, just as tight as we can be," Bosshard called after him. "But facts are facts."

"You snitched me off!"

"From now on when you fuck up, man, you fuck up."

Luther was charged with first-degree murder and waited eight months in county jail for his case to come to trial. The evidence suggested that he was, at most, an accomplice. But Luther refused to testify against his partner. The district attorney finally had to offer a bargain that did not involve giving evidence; Luther pleaded guilty to voluntary manslaughter and got a year's sentence that was commuted to time served. But he still faced a prior charge of being an ex-felon with a gun, which he had been running from at the time of the killing. He was tried on that charge, convicted, and sent to prison at Susanville.

His six months at Susanville were not hard time. His typing skills, computer know-how, and pleasant manner made him an asset to prison authorities. When Luther got out, he immediately went back to the Tenderloin, more deeply committed than ever to his old life-style. He acquired a large collection of guns and began to go for bigger deals. "I knew everybody who shot speed in California, north and south. I was the main man in the state, dealing all the way from San Diego to Eureka. For me it wasn't just the money. It was being good at what I did."

Luther had five children by this time, all by different mothers, two of them born within three days of each other. He had two grandchildren by the daughters he had fathered as a teenager. He was close to all the kids, often having them with him or taking them to live with his mother and sisters. Soon after his release from Susanville, he met a young white woman named Barbara. "She was an Aries too. We just looked at each other and bam! That was it. We just had to be together."

Despite fierce opposition from Barbara's mother, the manager of a seedy residential hotel, the two began living together in the fall of 1976. It didn't last long. "I had just copped this beautiful stuff," Luther recalls, "some of the best speed I ever took. I took Barbara and another girl with me over to Oakland, to one of those adult motels with velvet bedspreads, mirrors all over the walls, that sort of thing. You couldn't go to the swimming pool unless you were naked, dirty movies twenty-four hours a day on TV, a masseuse whenever you wanted. We had a good time, needless to say." When they returned to Luther's house, however, there were eight policemen waiting to question him in the slaying of an addict. Although the police cleared him in the murder case, in their search of the house they uncovered a syringe, which violated his parole. In February 1977, he was returned to prison for nineteen months, this time to Chino, where his time was not quite so pleasant.

While Luther was at Chino, taping old magazines around his chest for armor and making silverware into knives to defend himself in the violent wars between Mexicans and blacks, Bosshard was moving deeper into the drug world his old friend had vacated. The men he worked with regarded him as a "hard-charging cop"—a high compliment. He had received a dozen medals for heroism, and in 1976 the San Francisco Board of Supervisors sent him a letter of commendation for saving the lives of an elderly mother and her daughter in a fire. But his casual attitude toward authority had kept him from making lieutenant.

Narcotics was a detail in which he felt that he was dealing with the "anus of humanity," especially in that dangerous part of the Tenderloin known as the Razor. "They all have their spot," he says, "the whores, the transvestite hookers, the dope dealers. The whores rip off their tricks and bring the goods to the dealers for drugs. Sometimes the dealers rip off the whores. There's a going rate for everything: credit cards, prescription forms, sex, human life itself. It's like a war zone— a lot of hostile fire incoming."

Yet this grotesque world was also fascinating. Although his long hours of overtime gave him an adequate salary, Bosshard took a moonlighting job at San Francisco's Greyhound depot, the "dirty Dog," as it is known to the cops who double there as security officers. Two days a week, he went directly to the Dog after finishing his eight-hour shift, and spent the next six hours rousting vagrants, breaking up fights, and also meeting his snitches to squeeze them for information on who was dealing what, information he would use the next day at the department after going home to catch a few hours' sleep. "If I hadn't become a cop I might have been an addict myself," he admits. "I've got an addictive personality."

It was not only the elemental nature of life on the street that he found attractive but also, perversely, the people. Although he was in charge of controlling them, he formed relations that were almost "like family." He got to know their problems, their relatives and lovers. The peculiar yet profound intimacy was reciprocal. Once, Bosshard was in the middle of what seemed a small fracas, trying to keep an ex-con named Sonny, whom he liked and knew had a dangerously violent temper, from fighting with another black. While trying to calm Sonny, Bosshard turned his back, and the other man sucker-punched him. He fell to the pavement, hitting his head so hard that his eyes flipped white and his breathing stopped momentarily. Sonny quickly dispatched the assailant and screamed for his wife, a former prostitute named Mickey. She ran down to the street and gave Bosshard mouth-to-mouth resuscitation while several pimps who had seen the situation develop ran into a hotel, yelling, "Officer Steve is hurt!" and demanding an ambulance. Bosshard was in a coma for several hours. After he came around, doctors told him that if there had been a delay in getting him to the hospital, he might have died.

In Bosshard's "other life" in the straight world, relationships were more difficult to maintain. He had a falling-out with his brother over distribution of the cleaning-business assets after his mother's death and refused to talk to him for years. And he had to deal with his wife, Jan, who resented taking a back seat to the riffraff he spent most of his time with. For weeks on end, her only contact with him was in the middle of the night, when he came in and fell into bed, asleep almost before he said hello. She spent the long hours he was away from home trying to brainwash their teenage son to choose any profession except police work. "What you ought to be writing about," she told a journalist who talked to her about her husband, "is not policemen but policemen's wives."

When Luther was paroled from Chino in late 1978, he went to southern California and took a job at a Long Beach trucking firm. Over the next year he went from file clerk to an executive position, making more than five hundred dollars a week. He became involved with a white woman named Jean. She got pregnant, and when she was in labor, Luther used the oddments of medical knowledge he had accumulated in Vietnam and in the years since by treating his own wounds to convince the doctor at the hospital to let him deliver the baby himself. But the relationship with Jean became frayed when she tried to keep him from seeing other women. "I told her that I don't want nobody to be setting no limits on my freedom in that regard. I told her that I'd be willing to let her live the same way, of course."

It had been an unusual year for Luther. He had managed to stay clear of the law. His rap sheet, which started in

August 1967, six months after his discharge from the Marine Corps, had expanded to include more than forty-five arrests, averaging out to one bust every two months for the time he was on the street. Yet if life in Long Beach had been good to him, something was nonetheless lacking. In early summer 1980, he and Jean went to San Francisco for a "vacation." When Luther began to see other women, Jean became angry and went east to visit her family. She didn't return. Luther stayed on.

Within a few days of Jean's departure, Luther had taken up with Rocky and the Southall family—four daughters and their mother, Vinnie Mac, who dealt drugs and functioned as sort of a latter day Ma Barker. Luther was surprised that speed, which had cost $300 an ounce when he first began to sell it, was now going for $1,500. He reentered the drug business with a vengeance.

Bosshard had heard about Luther's job in Long Beach via his grapevine and guessed that it had something to do with drugs, especially after police intelligence reported that a motorcycle gang had begun to use a statewide trucking firm as a front for traffic in amphetamines. He learned of Luther's return to San Francisco from his informants, who said that he was now "the man with the bag on the street." Bosshard trailed Luther and Rocky around town, looking for a situation in which he could stage a credible bust. He took a peculiar pleasure in having Luther as a quarry. It was the same pleasure Luther felt after learning via the grapevine that Bosshard was onto him. One night he walked by his old friend in the Greyhound station carrying a pocketful of speed and wasn't recognized.

On August 13, Vinnie Mae Southall died after being shot in obscure circumstances in Clearlake. Three days later, Rocky went into the hospital for removal of the abscess on her shoulder. She died and Luther disappeared.

After having talked to Bosshard from the Long Beach pay phone in early October and denying any part in Rocky's death, Luther heard that a murder warrant was out on him and traveled up to the Bay Area again, thinking to give himself up. But he arrived virtually penniless and went underground, hoping to make and sell enough speed to be able to hire a good attorney and post bail before he came in. As he traveled around the Bay Area heavily armed, he knew that Bosshard would be looking for him.

On November 13, one of Bosshard's informants called to say that Luther was living with his sister Mona Lisa in San Jose. Bosshard jumped into a car and sped down the Bayshore Freeway, calling San Jose police for assistance on the way. When he arrived, several San Jose patrol cars escorted him to Mona Lisa's address. The uniformed police went to the front door. Bosshard had seen a black teenager—one of the lookouts police call Paul Reveres—run inside the two-story building at his approach. Bosshard sprinted through a courtyard to the back of the property. Almost immediately he saw Luther, naked to the waist, kick out a window screen on the upper floor and vault over the railing of a small veranda. As he hit the ground, Bosshard moved forward, extending both hands and aiming his .357 Magnum. "Damn you, Luther," he said. "I told you it was going to end like this. Now turn around and put your hands on the wall or I'll blow your fucking head off."

After Luther was handcuffed, they drove to the San Jose station. The booking cop said he was going to take six pictures. Luther asked why six instead of the customary two, and the cop replied that he wanted the others for his scrapbook. "Like hell," Luther said. The cop stepped forward, saying he'd better cooperate, or he'd get his ass kicked. Luther looked over at Steve. "You going to let the ass-kicking go down with me handcuffed?" he asked. Bosshard shook his head slightly, staring right into the San Jose cop's eyes: "There isn't going to be any ass-kicking." The cop stood back.

On the ride back to San Francisco, Bosshard sat in the back with Luther while another officer drove. For the most part, they looked out the window and listened to police calls coming in on the radio. But as they neared police headquarters, they began to talk, at first about nothing much and then about the guys they had known in boot camp. They filled each other in on who had died in Nam and what had happened to those who made it through the war. They found it surprising, in retrospect, that they had survived the war. It was surprising, too, that both of them had survived so many scrapes afterward.

"I suppose it will be a feather in your cap," Luther said as he was taken off to his cell, "getting ahold of the mad dog killer who took off Rocky."

"Not really," Steve answered. "I'm the same as you. I got this thing I do for a living, and I'm stuck with it."

The trial began in August. Bosshard doubted that Luther had murdered Rocky Southall. He had constructed his own scenario about what had happened at the hospital. Luther had probably seen that Rocky was feeling low when she came out of the operation, and playing Romeo as usual, had decided to give her a little boost with some speed that her overloaded system couldn't handle. Steve expected Luther to plead voluntary manslaughter and come out of the whole affair with a year or so sentence or perhaps even time served. He was surprised and even impressed by Luther's gall when he tried to beat the rap altogether. However, the jury was not impressed by the bikers and other street people who paraded to the stand as Luther's alibis and character witnesses. He was convicted of second-degree murder and sentenced to sixteen years. While Steve knew that Luther had no doubt gotten away with a lot of things over the years and thus there was a rough justice in his conviction for an offense he probably wasn't in the strictest sense guilty of, he also felt a certain sense of loss. After the trial, another cop asked him how he had ever gotten involved with a junkball like Luther. Steve gave him a hard look. "He wasn't always a junkball."

Sitting in the county jail awaiting his prison assignment, Luther unzips his orange jumpsuit now and then to use one of his six gunshot wounds to illustrate a dramatic vignette in his life. He tries to rationalize how Steve could have caught him and discusses what he considers the inadequacies of the case against him: the fact that the eyewitness's testimony was confused and in places contradictory; the inconsistency of the prosecution's experts who suggested, among other things, that Luther injected speed into the soles of Iris Southall's feet when in fact the autopsy showed no such puncture marks. "There's no way this isn't going to be shot down on appeal." He smiles. "No way. I'll be out in a year, year and a half max. If not, I can do the time. I've done it before, I can do it again. One way

or another, I'll be out on the streets someday, and I'll see old
Steve again."

Moving through the Greyhound depot to roust vagrants
and occasionally pat down some suspicious-looking character,
Bosshard laughs at the idea. "Luther said that? Well, he's probably right. We'll probably hook up again. You've got to remember that we like this game, me and Luther. We like the
conquering, chasing, and evading, the challenging and outwit-
ting of the enemy. The surviving in the jungle. People talk
about law and order, crime and punishment, and all that.
That's okay. But me and Luther see it from a different perspective. For us, it's a chance to be tested. To see who we really
are."

chapter 4 ————————————

The Life and
Times of Huey P. Newton

Baddest

T yrone Robinson, dope dealer
and street hoodlum, was three years old when the Black
Panther Party was founded. His experience of Huey Newton
was not of a revolutionary hero preaching black liberation but
of another small-time gangster competing with him on the
mean streets of the West Oakland ghetto. It was firsthand experience: "Double R," as his crime brothers called him, had
been mugged twice before by Newton, who had ripped off
several rocks of crack from him. And so when he shot Huey
three times in the head in the early-morning hours of August
22, 1989, he was looking for a little payback, and for the respect
that comes from having taken out a man with a big reputation.

In fact, Robinson was forgotten almost as soon as the
Oakland police, the Panthers' mortal foes for over twenty
years, picked him up for the killing. It was Huey Newton who
was transfigured. No longer was he the thug who had terror-
ized the Oakland underworld during the Seventies. No longer

was he that pathetic figure who descended into irrelevance and narcosis in the Eighties. He was once again the radical innocent of the Sixties. Huey was free, as mourners chanted at his funeral, free at last; and his old comrades were free to inflate his flaccid myth to epic size once more.

"Huey Newton lived just long enough to have been the unknown idealist, a popular and heroic champion of the oppressed," read his funeral program. He was "a world hero, our king in shining armor," in the words of one of the eulogists who lined up to praise him. These sentiments were echoed by Ron Dellums and other black politicians who had learned to keep their distance from Huey when he was alive. They were echoed by Bobby Seale, co-founder of the Panthers, who had stayed away from Oakland for ten years, only because he feared that Huey would kill him. "All power to the people!" the mourners chanted throughout the service, raising their hands in the clenched-fist salute.

The dead man's failings were mentioned once in passing, and then only as an indictment of America. "If [his critics] will forgive Huey his weaknesses," said Huey's brother Melvin, "then we will forgive the United States for its genocide of the red man, its enslavement of the black man, and the incarceration of the yellow man during World War II." The speakers were the undertakers as well—smoothing out Huey's features in repose, putting a final good face on his life. They even changed the identity of his killer. "It is the culmination of twenty years of assassination attempts by the police," said former Panther leader Elaine Brown, who herself had avoided Oakland for a decade out of fear of Huey. Panther lawyer Charles Garry was more explicit: "The FBI destroyed him just as they destroyed the Black Panther Party." After the funeral was over, black radicals calling themselves Uhuru House and led by somebody who had taken the name Biko Lumumba jogged South African style through the streets of Oakland, chanting this slogan: "Who killed Huey? / Don't tell me no lie / The government, the government / The FBI."

Part of Huey, the part that had helped pioneer the radical mythmaking of the Sixties, would have been pleased at the way things worked out: curious onlookers dipping their handkerchiefs in his blood as he lay dying; old comrades sending him off to a radical heaven in a way that indicted the power structure and thus cheated Tyrone Robinson of his kill. But another part of Huey, a part his supporters in the Left had chosen not to know, had always been interested in the expression of his authentic self, even though it subverted his myth; a self, he increasingly came to feel, that was beyond good and evil. And this part of Huey probably would have felt that his truth had been shortchanged.

The myth whose creation he encouraged and then subverted began around 4:00 A.M. on the morning of October 23, 1967. Then the young and cocky Minister of Defense for the Black Panther Party, Huey was driving home from a party with a friend, when he was pulled over by two Oakland patrolmen. He later claimed that they frisked him in an aggressive way after roughly rousting him from his car and that one of the officers pulled a gun on him. A witness said that it was Huey who took a pistol out of his jacket and began shooting.

Over the next three years, the gap between these two versions would be filled with metaphysical discussions about truth and perception, shadow and act. But some facts could be stipulated: After the brief confrontation was over, Officer John Frey lay dying on the street from two gunshots, while his wounded partner radioed for help as Huey forced a passing motorist to drive him to a hospital for treatment of a bullet wound in the stomach. Someone took a photograph of him shackled to a gurney, the features of his face set in a look of heroic defiance that spoke for the temper of the time.

It was a summary moment for Huey's supporters in the New Left, who had already formed the beginnings of a cult around the Black Panther Party. For them, the shots fired at John Frey marked the opening salvo in the liberation of the ghetto. Nonviolence was out; revolutionary violence was in. They too had been baptized in Huey's act. The Movement had been washed in the blood of the pig.

But for Huey, it was more complex. Already a homemade existentialist, he regarded the shootout with the Oakland cops as another step into the world he had constructed, where the boundaries between violence and good works, crime and politics were shifting and unclear. Always in the process of self-discovery, he was a man, as he himself acknowledged, with a profoundly divided self.

The fault lines of his own character, he said, were visible in his family. His grandfather, a white, had conceived his father in rape. Growing up with "white features," Huey felt that he had the mark of this act upon him and that violence was therefore coded onto his DNA. He claimed to have sympathy for his father's attempt to live a respectable middle-class life but admitted to contempt for him as well, especially for the way he had labored doggedly under the avalanche of bills that arrived each month like bad news from the white world. The one thing his father had done that galvanized Huey's imagination was to defy a group of whites once in an uncharacteristic moment of desperation, to the degree that they called him a "crazy nigger." The Crazy Nigger: it was a persona that became part of Huey's ambition.

Huey's own divisions existed almost programmatically in the difference between his two brothers. Introspective and scholarly, Melvin became a teacher at a local college. But Walter junior, known as "Sonny Man," was a street hustler, who grew into stature as one of those ghetto figures that command respect because (as Huey said later on) "they drove big cars, wore beautiful clothes, and . . . opposed all authority and made no peace with the establishment." Huey was attracted to Melvin's world of ideas. (He would claim later on, when laying the cornerstone of his myth as a latter-day Frederick Douglass, that he had taught himself to read from his brother's dog-eared copy of Plato's *Republic* after being left a functional illiterate by his formal education.) But Sonny Man's world was where the crazy niggers thrived. It was this world that Huey grew up in and kept returning to all his life.

As a boy, he fought in the classrooms with the teachers who tried to subject him to authority and fought on the streets to gain an authority of his own. He fought because of derogatory chants other children made up from the initial of his middle name ("Huey P. goes wee, wee, wee") and because of insults centering around his baby-faced good looks. Tongue-tied, with a high-pitched voice that would accompany him into manhood, he was not good at "capping"—the ghetto ritual of verbal duels. ("Motorcycle, motorcycle, going so fast / You momma's got a pussy like a bulldog's ass.") Violence was the language he grew up feeling most comfortable with. Violence, even before he had discovered the rationalizations of existentialism, became the vocabulary of self-discovery.

As a teenager and into his twenties, Huey worked as a pimp, strong-armed the weak, pulled off armed robberies, and ran short-change scams. He burglarized homes in the Berkeley hills and hung out at the emergency entrances of hospitals, taking the valuables of those who rushed in on desperate errands. Later on, he discovered a rationale for what had come naturally, when, in his desultory reading, he came across a phrase from Proudhon: "Property is theft." The corollary, very much a Sixties construct, followed easily: "I felt that white people were criminals because they plundered the world. . . . To take what the white criminals called theirs gave me a feeling of real freedom."

Sporadically attending Oakland's Merritt College between crime sprees, Huey took a law course to help him become a more efficient thief. (His proudest hour came when he got sixteen counts of burglary dismissed at a single pretrial hearing.) He had inchoate political yearnings and joined the Merritt College Afro-American Association in 1964. He got into an argument at a party with a black named Odell Lee over an issue involving cultural nationalism. When Lee tugged at his arm in what Huey interpreted as a threatening gesture, he snatched a steak knife off a nearby table and stabbed Lee in the head. At his trial, Huey's defense was that Odell Lee had a scar on his face that identified him as a knife fighter for someone, like himself, who had grown up in the ghetto. The fact that the jury did not know this meant that he was not being judged by his peers and that his conviction and sentence to six months in prison was unconstitutional.

When Huey was paroled in 1965, something was happening. It was the Sixties. Malcolm X had been killed, and a ghetto insurrection had occurred in Watts. The Free Speech Movement had erupted at the University of California, and Berkeley's first big demonstration against the war in Vietnam had spilled over into Oakland. It was an increasingly apocalyptic atmosphere, in which a career of crime might just as easily be seen as an apprenticeship for the job of revolutionary hero.

Returning to Merritt College, Huey linked up with Bobby Seale, whom he had met earlier and who was also interested in the prospects for a more doctrinaire black radicalism that took its cue from Malcolm. Not as intelligent or physically brave as Huey, Seale was a gifted mimic and could play the public role of militant in a way that Huey, with his more cerebral style, could not. More important, Seale was also ready to play the role of Sancho Panza as Newton began what seemed at the time a quixotic attempt to establish his own organization.

Huey read Frantz Fanon, Che Guevara, and Chairman Mao. Most influentially, he read a book called *Negroes with Guns*, by Robert Williams, a former president of the NAACP in North Carolina, who had been indicted on kidnapping charges after advocating that blacks arm themselves and had fled the country to continue promoting his ideas from Cuba, China, and Tanzania. Huey was impressed by what he heard about a group in Lowndes County, Mississippi, that called itself the Black Panther Party, and by the Deacons for Defense in Louisiana. In the spring of 1966, he amalgamated the names and started the Black Panther Party for Self Defense.

Drawing on the two halves of his life, Huey put intellectual blacks, like his brother Melvin, on his advisory cabinet. But the "political wing," which formed the core of the organization, was staffed with "street brothers" like Sonny Man, blacks who, as Bobby Seale later said, "had been out there robbing, pimping . . . and peddling dope." A few weeks after the Party had been founded, Huey sat down and in twenty minutes wrote the ten-point program, that would become its covenant with white radicalism. The points holding that all blacks should be exempt from military service, that all in prison were political prisoners and should be freed, that the black ghetto was a colony of America and ought to have elections supervised by the UN all resonated with the radical zeitgeist. But it was point seven that set the stage for the Panthers' emergence as a national cultural phenomenon: "We believe that all Black people should arm themselves for self-defense."

The symbolism of young blacks smartly dressed in black leathers and berets, patrolling the streets of Oakland cradling shotguns and holding copies of the California Penal Code, was irresistible, especially for white New Leftists, who, as Huey realized, had been deprived of a homeland in the civil rights movement when black militants expelled them from SNCC and other organizations. Huey did not offer them membership in his new party, but he did hold out the prospect of a coalition based on mutual commitment to radical action behind the Panther vanguard. Militant, action-oriented, and above all ideological, the Panthers offered something that the rest of the civil rights movement, just then descending into separatism and negritude, did not.

In the spring of 1967, Huey made national news when he provided an armed escort for Betty Shabazz, widow of Malcolm X, during a Bay Area speaking engagement. After picking her up at the airport, he brought her to *Ramparts* magazine, where his prize new recruit, Eldridge Cleaver, was working. The press was there, and so were the police. A melee developed when newsmen tried to get closer to Shabazz than the Panthers would allow. As the cops offered to enforce order with nightsticks, Huey and the other Panthers racked shells into their shotguns. There were a few minutes of standoff in which time seemed suspended, and then both sides backed off. Afterward, Huey was euphoric, saying that the Panthers had "won" and attributing the victory to "superior firepower." After this incident, Huey and the Panthers were suddenly a national phenomenon, having jumped from the pages of *Ramparts* to the *New York Times*.

But all of this was mere scene setting for the confrontation that resulted in the death of Officer John Frey and the subsequent trial, in which Panther attorney Charles Garry, discovering a courtroom strategy that would be applied to other political trials of the Sixties, mounted an attack, rather than a defense, by charging that America's law enforcement was homicidal and its criminal justice system infected with racism, and that a young black like Huey Newton could no more get a fair trial here than his counterparts could in South Africa.

• • •

During the period of his trial, when "Free Huey!" became as characteristic a slogan of the Movement as "Bring the
Troops Home," Newton underwent an apotheosis. He became, in Eldridge Cleaver's phrase, "the baddest motherfucker
who ever set foot inside history." He was the archetypal black
fighter in an era on the edge of race war, and his icon was the
famous poster showing him sitting on a rattan throne with a
menacing scowl on his handsome face, holding a Zulu shield
in one hand and a shotgun in the other. The poster was the
cause: Free Huey! His legend grew as if by metastasis after he
had been convicted of voluntary manslaughter and sent to
prison.

During the better than two years he was incarcerated,
hundreds of new recruits joined the Black Panther Party, many
responding to no deeper political message than the Panthers'
most famous slogan, "Off the Pig." New chapters were established all over the country, many—like those in Chicago and
Los Angeles—the result of ghetto street gangs enrolling en
bloc. Other than understanding intuitively the value of agitprop and guns, Huey had never had to consider what his organization might become. Now it was left to Eldridge Cleaver,
the Party's maximum leader in Huey's absence, to fill in the
blanks. Excessively susceptible to open-ended Sixties rhetoric,
Cleaver decided that the Panthers were something like the
Algerian FLN, an organization that would spark and spearhead
an armed revolution. It was no longer just a matter of displaying weapons; under Cleaver's militarism, it was a matter of
using them. The slogan "Free Huey!" now had a non-negotia-
ble addendum: "Or the Sky's the Limit!"

Later on, radical survivors who applauded each upping
of the ante as it occurred would try to sanitize the Sixties by
claiming that the Panthers were little more than marginal figures who never set foot upon the moral heartland of the decade. In fact, the Black Panther Party was at the epicenter of
the Movement. At its 1969 convention, SDS—the central New
Left organization—declared the Panthers to be "the vanguard
of the black revolution." Tom Hayden, the New Left's Everyman, proclaimed them "America's Vietcong" in what he believed was the coming civil war that would engulf the nation.
Encouraged by the cheering section of white New Leftists, the

Panthers embarked on a course of grim urban warfare with police forces across the country.

As Huey lamented to intimates later, the results were all too predictable, the element of "superior firepower" now belonging wholly to the other side. But radical mythmakers tried to snatch victory out of the jaws of defeat. The Panthers killed in the conflict were not merely dead; they were victims of "genocide." Thus, in 1969, Newton attorney Charles Garry claimed that thirty-one (or twenty-nine or twenty-eight, depending on what day he was being interviewed) Panthers had been "assassinated" by law enforcement authorities in the past two years. The figure was demonstrably fabricated: Something like this number of Panthers had indeed been killed, but as Edward Epstein later showed in an incisive *New Yorker* article, almost all died in the course of criminal activities or in conflicts with other black militants. Of those Panthers who did die at the hands of cops, all had provoked the shootouts. The tenuousness of martyrdom was seen even in the most celebrated claim of innocent victimhood—the death of Chicago Panther Fred Hampton. Garry and the others claimed that Hampton had been wantonly murdered in his sleep as part of a police-FBI conspiracy. It was true that he was killed in a crossfire of bullets while sleeping off a drug binge. But it was also true that when the police knocked on the door of the apartment, which also functioned as an arsenal of Panther weapons, they were greeted by a blast from Panther Mark Clark's shotgun, which initiated the shootout.

Despite the facts, Garry's assertions were given credibility by the establishment press, which by this time had ceased to maintain a critical distance from the radical worldview. Huey and the Panthers took on the doomy élan of Leonidas and his Three Hundred. Their appeal spread from the New Left into the pop culture itself as they gained the support of personalities as various as Marlon Brando, Jean Genet, and Yale president Kingman Brewster, and were invited to fundraisers such as the famous get-together at Leonard Bernstein's Manhattan town house. By the end of the decade, the Panthers were one part model for radical self-sacrifice and one part house pet of radical chic.

• • •

Huey missed most of the excitement. In the spring of 1970, he was released from prison because of an appeals court ruling that the judge in his case had made an error in his instructions to the jury. Huey returned to Oakland, to find the Panther leadership decimated—Cleaver had fled to Cuba and then to Algeria in 1968 to avoid a trial on charges stemming from a shootout with Oakland police; Bobby Seale was under indictment in New Haven for the torture murder of a Panther named Alex Rackley, who was falsely believed to be an informer. Huey discovered something else—that his myth had grown to almost unmanageable proportions during the time he was in jail. He was a sort of demigod, the Poster that had come down off the wall to walk among them. "It was amazing," he later said of those first days back on the streets. "If I had a piece of bubble gum in my mouth and started to blow a bubble, two or three people would come running up and say that it was the biggest bubble they'd ever seen in their lives."

Immediately upon hitting the streets again, Huey made some grandstand gestures to reinforce his reputation as the baddest, such as offering to send a contingent of Panther volunteers to help the North Vietnamese in their struggle. But his attention was more focused on the internecine struggle within his Party itself. Two days after Huey's release, Jonathan Jackson was scheduled to take hostages at a Marin County courthouse in an operation designed to win freedom for his brother, the celebrated prisoner-revolutionary George Jackson. Cleaver had promised Panther assistance for the operation from his command post abroad, but Huey regarded the operation as suicidal and withdrew from it. Jonathan Jackson was killed by law authorities in the abortive courthouse raid, and some radicals blamed Huey.

Not long after, when he denounced "the military option," equating it with "infantile leftism," many who had supported him when he was only the Poster on the Wall wondered if he had been "turned" in prison. Yet for most, it was clear that his "moderation" was primarily a way of regaining control over his party from Cleaver and his henchmen, whose actions had brought down the wrath of the power structure on the organization and forced the Panthers to spend much of the small fortune they had gathered in Huey's absence on bail. But

Huey had also sensed the seismic reverberations that would soon mark the delayed end of the Sixties. He saw that the Movement was on the downward part of its arc and knew that revolution, always more a metaphor than a serious option, was definitely a dead issue.

When he expelled militants like Elmer "Geronimo" Pratt, a Cleaver supporter who ran the Los Angeles chapter of the Panthers, and announced that the Panthers would concentrate on "survival programs" that would remake the Oakland ghetto, Huey touched off a struggle with the Cleaverites that resembled a turf war of the mob. Sam Napier, a Newton loyalist and the publisher of the Black Panther Party paper, was killed in New York, his body doused in gasoline and set on fire. In retribution, Geronimo Pratt's pregnant wife was stabbed and killed in Los Angeles. It was a development that both shocked and thrilled the Left, which self-aggrandizingly compared the bloody conflict to the struggle between Stalin and Trotsky.

A whole literature would later be created by New Left veterans, claiming that such things happened because Huey and the Panthers had been driven mad by the FBI and its COINTELPRO surveillance and dirty tricks. In fact, a mountain of diggings from the Freedom of Information Act files produced a molehill of evidence to sustain the assertion. It was true that the FBI was on the case and attempted to exacerbate the tension between Cleaver's "international" faction and Newton through a series of letters that were inflammatory fabrications. Yet it was also true that these were rather mild and ineffectual gestures given the threat the Panthers represented —348 arrests for murder, armed robbery, rape, and burglary in 1969 alone. When the FBI saw what violent people they were dealing with, saw in particular that the Panthers would kill each other and rival blacks virtually without compunction, they had second thoughts. Division Five of the FBI rejected the idea of putting forged papers of accusation in one Panther's car , for instance, because "It could result in a Panther murder of one of their [own] leaders."

Huey eventually won out in his "rectification campaign." He closed all the chapters of the Party that had sprung up around the country during his imprisonment and called the loyalists back to Oakland. He went to China in 1971 and met Chou En-lai. He came home and told his remaining supporters that it was time to "put away the gun," because the Party had begun its long march.

Huey had prodigious appetites, but his character also had a whiff of puritanism, perhaps because of the religious upbringing he'd had. It was impossible for those who knew him well to imagine Newton reveling in the extravagance of the Sixties as his rival Cleaver did—running for President on the Peace and Freedom ticket, making common cause with Jerry Rubin in a "Pre-Erection Day" ceremony in 1968, threatening to kill San Francisco mayor Alioto's children and then calling California governor Ronald Reagan a "punk," threatening to beat him to death with a marshmallow. Huey always aimed for a dignity appropriate to the Maximum Leader, the high style of someone who had taught himself to read by studying Plato.

Because of his reedy voice and a tendency to meander into ideological abstraction, he did not perform as well as other Sixties figures before mass audiences. But he was unparalleled in a one-on-one setting. Bulked up by exercise yard weights, his sculpted body set off his male model's good looks. His presence was mesmerizing, especially for whites, and he knew it. When supporters visited the elaborate apartment on the shore of Lake Merritt into which Huey had moved (underlings justified the expense by pointing out that the place was secure against assassination attempts by Cleaverites and cops alike), he would immediately strip off his shirt to show rippling muscles as he paced the floor with a rock star's strut. For some like Bert Schneider, producer of *Easy Rider, Five Easy Pieces*, and other films, who had been introduced to Huey by Jane Fonda and soon became one of Huey's most dependable financial supporters and closest advisers, the experience of being near him seemed to have a palpable sexual charge.

Huey mesmerized white supporters intellectually as well as physically. His apartment overlooked the Alameda County jail, where he had been kept during the year of his trial for killing Frey. He had a telescope trained on the exact place where he had been kept in the large white building, which he called Moby Dick. Hearing him talk, it was easy to believe that he was a black Ahab on an impossible quest for social justice.

To perfect that image, he enrolled in the University of California at Santa Cruz to complete the education that had been interrupted ten years earlier by the stabbing incident at Merritt. Lax requirements, part of the "alternative" educational philosophy of the campus, made his passage considerably easier. It was at this time that he was invited to lead a seminar on racism at Yale along with famed psychiatrist Erik Erikson (the proceedings were later published in book form). When his autobiography, *Revolutionary Suicide* (largely written by Santa Cruz sociologist Herman Blake), was published in 1973, a lengthy *New York Times* review by Murray Kempton showed how seriously this serious side of Huey was taken. "Here is the only visible American who has managed to arrive at the Platonic conception of himself," wrote Kempton, who then compared Huey to Gandhi and Luther.

Fueled by new financial contributions such praise made possible, the "survival programs" he established in Oakland began to flourish. There was the Breakfast for Children program and a "George Jackson Free Medical Clinic." But the flagship of the new strategy was the Oakland Community Learning Center. A $150,000 former church complex in the East Oakland ghetto, the center featured a six-grade elementary school, replete with a black headmistress and little black children in uniforms. Some observers were bothered by the regimentation and the propaganda in the teaching. But for most, it was a model of black self-help. Aided by radical educational theorists such as Herbert Kohl, the school credentialed instructors through the UC-affiliated "University Without Walls." It featured a jazz band and an orchestra funded by the United Air Lines Foundation and an assortment of community service programs.

"Each One Teach One" was the new Panther slogan. It seemed that the first stages of the long march had led Huey's people to the promised land. The party no longer seemed to believe now that power grew out of the barrel of a gun but from community organizing, which had been an emphasis of white radicals before an apocalyptic note entered the New Left (at least partly because of Huey himself) in the mid-Sixties. An indication of what the new Panthers were all about was Bobby Seale's run for mayor of Oakland in 1973, a campaign that hit a whole octave of populist notes and promised to enfranchise

the blacks who formed the vast majority of the city's population. Seale lost, but he gave the city's white power structure an
electoral scare and seemed to point the way to a new black
politics that might remake the city.

There were, however, some muffled noises that disturbed those who heard them. They all had to do with an
erratic, almost megalomaniac, quality that had begun to man-
ifest itself in Huey since his release from prison. He had begun
carrying a swagger stick and insisting on being called "Servant," a shortened version of the new title he had taken, "Supreme Servant of the People." He consumed large quantities
of cocaine and drank Courvoisier (which he called "Vas") by
the bottle. He told the architect designing the new building for
the Panther school that he wanted a bunker-like office in the
center, a decision that was comprehensible only in terms of
another agenda. That agenda was also suggested by the fact
that he was surrounding himself with a praetorian guard he
called "the Squad"—individuals such as a taciturn six-foot-
eight-inch, four-hundred-pound former criminal named Robert Heard, who accompanied Huey everywhere, and a black
gunslinger named Larry Henson. At first Huey explained that
the Squad were bodyguards to protect him from the Cleaverites. But people inside the Party knew that these heavy hitters
Huey lured into a close relationship with hand-tailored suits
and other elaborate gifts paid for by money raised for the
school were not only his guards but his gang as well.

The criminal activity began with a boycott of black-
owned liquor stores, which Huey claimed "exploited the people." The boycott had to be enforced, often by force, and it
was only a short step from this to extorting protection money.
And once that money flowed, it was another short step to
strong-arming after-hours clubs and the pimps with their sta-
bles of prostitutes and the dope dealers who worked the ghetto.
During the space of a few months, there were several unsolved
murders that Huey was said to be involved in. The two most
notable were the Ward brothers, reputed to be the most powerful pimps in the Bay Area. Afterward, the Black Panther
Party took over the operation of *Jimmy Ward's Lamppost*, an
Oakland bar and hangout that was owned by a family survivor.

Even while launching the school and survival programs, in other words, Huey was conceiving a parallel strategy to take over the vice in Oakland. "At first he presented this as the 'mass line,'" remembers a Panther who eventually fled because of the criminal activity. "His position was you couldn't really stop evils in the black community, but you could at least control them, make them 'serve the people.' That was the mass line, but there was a bottom line too—he just liked doing it. It was in his nature."

By 1974, the fault lines of the self had begun to open up in jagged fissures. During the day, when he was with the whites who had set up the school, centerpiece of all Panther programs, Huey was all intellectuality—Plato's *Republic* and Hegel and Marx. Later, like some guerrilla Dracula, he took on his after-dark identity, getting into his sleek Mark IV with members of the Squad and hitting the streets of the Oakland ghetto. Dressed in a cape and fedora and twirling a cane, he was ready once again to be the baddest motherfucker who ever set foot inside history. He beat people up, often while his bodyguards held them. He had his henchmen draw their weapons and block the exits of bars while he engaged in Castroite rants about politics or began to chant, "I am the Supreme Servant! I am the Supreme Servant!"

It was bizarre behavior. One of the things it seemed intended to destroy was the myth of revolutionary sanctity that had come to weigh heavily on him. There was a desire to plumb his own depths, not just privately but in front of his supporters. Either this, or a desire to rub their noses in his reality. Huey told one Panther, for instance, that he had indeed killed John Frey. He could not have admitted this to his white supporters, for whom his innocence in the Frey affair was a cornerstone of belief. But even with them he sometimes tried to reveal his hidden surfaces. "You know," he once said to a white radical who was raising money for the school, "I swore to myself that if I couldn't make it as a revolutionary I would make it as a bank robber." The white tried to deny the possibility. "No," Huey answered, "there are things about me you don't know." There was a look in his eye that invited further inquiry, but the radical turned down the invitation.

•   •   •

The irony was that the survival programs could have succeeded. An enormous amount of money was raised for the school. (Huey once estimated that over $7 million had been raised by the Panthers from white liberals and Leftists in the period 1967–1974.) The Oakland power structure had been ready to deal with the Panthers after Bobby Seale's campaign for mayor and to make large city grants to the school. The state was ready as well. But Huey was no longer interested in incremental steps toward the revolution; he was interested only in his other life, in playing the role of Capone in blackface.

By 1974, his behavior was having an effect on the Panther organization. His violence capriciously turned inward, toward enforcing Party "discipline." There were public humiliations and beatings of members whose commitment to the Supreme Servant was suspect. A lot of the rank and file who had been selflessly involved in the school and the self-help programs became frightened by the spectacle and slipped away. Even Bobby Seale was not immune. Jealous of the celebrity Seale had achieved during the mayoralty campaign, Huey began to denigrate him publicly, and then, in one traumatic outburst, he beat him up as members of the Squad stood by. Seale left town in the middle of the night with none of his belongings, so scared he went into hiding and didn't surface for almost a year and then as far from Oakland as he could get on the East Coast.

Huey had now fully inhabited the Crazy Nigger persona that had always fascinated him—beyond logic and freed from moral considerations by what he saw as the sinfulness of the society into which he had been born. He was a seeker of the apocalypse in the self as well as society. One Rockefeller heiress who had made a large donation to the school was invited to his penthouse headquarters, where Huey told her that before dedicating himself to serve the people he had pursued salvation in sex, making love seven times in one day, but had quit, as he said, because "I didn't find salvation, I only skinned my penis." In fact he had resumed the quest, holding alcohol-and-drug-fueled orgies in the inner sanctum of his apartment, compulsively womanizing among party cadres as well as party groupies white and black, despite the evident pain these episodes caused his wife, Gwen. When he was clean and sober he talked to white supporters about the difficulties of "holding it all together." They assumed that he was talking about the enterprise of the organization. But in fact he was talking about the enterprise of the self.

The first public sign of the tensions came on June 30, 1974, when Huey got into an argument with two off-duty plainclothes cops in a bar in Oakland called *The Fox*. Unable to carry a gun because of the conditions of his parole, Huey screamed at the massive Robert Heard, "Shoot the motherfuckers!" Heard started to go for his briefcase, but the cops drew their weapons and took it from him, finding a loaded .38 and one thousand dollars in cash inside.

Six days later, Huey was coked up and cruising the streets of Oakland, when a seventeen-year-old prostitute named Kathleen Smith called out, "Hey, baby," from a street corner. *Baby:* it was the wrong word. Huey had Heard stop the car; he jumped out and pulled a silver pistol from his shirt and shot the girl in the jaw. Then he drove to Marin, stopping on the San Rafael Bridge to drop his pistol into the bay. He hid out briefly at the Zen Center in Marin before going to Bert Schneider's house in Hollywood, where he spent days snorting cocaine, issuing commands for someone to "get me some pussy," and stating with an odd mixture of anguish and bemusement that this was the first nonpolitical murder he had ever committed.

As the young prostitute hovered between life and death in a coma that prevented her from making identifications, Newton came back to Oakland. Not long after the shooting of Kathleen Smith, he summoned his tailor, a middle-aged black named Preston Callins, to the Lakeshore apartment for a fitting. Callins showed Huey some fabric, and Huey, chugging Courvoisier, became abusive. Callins said, "Oh, baby, don't feel that way." As the tailor told police later on, Huey jumped up and said, "Nobody calls me no damn baby," and began pistol-whipping him with a .357 magnum. By the time Callins managed to escape from the apartment, he had four depressed skull fractures requiring neurosurgery.

Ever since getting out of prison in 1970, Huey had been living under a grant of immunity guaranteed by his myth. Two attempts to reprosecute him for the killing of Frey had resulted in hung juries. (Employing a strategy whose shrewdness contrasted with the radical Left's clichés, Huey insisted on trying to get whites rather than blacks on his juries, calculating correctly that they would be impressed by the spectacle of the illiterate black who had taught himself to read with Plato.) But while his predations in the ghetto had gone unreported and unpunished for over a year, his recent rampage saddled him with serious charges, especially after Kathleen Smith finally died, without regaining consciousness.

As everything began to close in on him, Huey took off for Cuba via Mexico, with the help of his Hollywood coterie. Charles Garry, telling a news conference that Newton had fled because some pimps had put out a contract on him, played for confirmation a portion of a phone conversation in which Oakland police chief Charles Gain warned Huey about the plot. It was a revealing alibi, exposing the cynicism of Garry's previous claims that the police had set out systematically to destroy Huey. But the recorded call was even more revealing in what it concealed through editing. Garry's implication was that the pimps wanted to get rid of Huey because he was cleaning up their act; actually it was because he was muscling in on it.

Huey's absence gave the Party breathing space. There was still enough momentum from the survival programs, especially the school, to give the Panthers cachet. Elaine Brown, an attractive young woman who was a graduate of the Philadelphia Conservatory of Music and L.A.'s toughest street gang, became chairman. She was smart, articulate, ruthless, loyal to Huey, and ambitious.

Over the next two and a half years, Brown followed the path suggested by the Seale for Mayor campaign and turned the Panthers into a significant power in Oakland through electoral politics. The organization was instrumental in the campaigns of Lionel Wilson, first black mayor of the city (who went on the board of the Panther school after his election), and John George, first black supervisor of the county. Brown herself ran for city council in 1976 and came close to being elected. Following her defeat, she was appointed to Oakland's Economic Development Council, where she took her seat beside the heads of the city's largest corporations. While continuing to maintain the Panthers' radical credentials by periodically denouncing the "COINTELPRO repression," she joined forces with Jerry Brown's administration in Sacramento, going to the 1976 Democratic convention as a Brown delegate, and used the clout this association gave her to increase the Panther role in local politics.

It all might have worked out if it hadn't been for Huey. But he was never happy in the workers' paradise of Cuba. Trained as a plumber, he was less interested in working than in running the Black Panther Party through almost daily phone calls to Brown. The Squad was still loyal to Huey. The murders continued. In December 1974, a former *Ramparts* bookkeeper named Betty Van Patter, who had been hired to do the books of the school and then of Elaine Brown's city council campaign, disappeared. She was later discovered floating in San Francisco Bay, with her head caved in. (It was assumed by many who knew the party, that Elaine Brown had ordered the killing, but after Huey's death, Ken Kelley, a former white supporter of the Panthers who functioned as Huey's press aide after he returned from Cuba, disclosed that Huey told him he'd ordered it from there.)

In the spring of 1977, Huey decided that it was time to come home. There were Democrats in the governor's mansion and in the White House. Cleaver had returned to the United States from exile and had not been punished. Moreover, the aftershocks of Watergate had put the FBI on the defensive, lending credibility to the steady drumbeat of propaganda emanating from Charles Garry's office, designed to exonerate Huey of his crimes. He arrived home to a hero's welcome and pleaded not guilty to shooting Kathleen Smith.

But instead of dealing with his problems in the courts, Huey tried to settle them in the streets. A little more than a month after his return to Oakland, a Panther hit squad attempted to kill Crystal Gray, a prostitute who had witnessed the murder of Kathleen Smith. It was a botched operation, one Panther gunman dying from a bullet wound in the process, but it was big news in the Bay Area, the first time that a portrait of the Panthers as a gangster operation made a convincing appearance in the papers.

Soon Elaine Brown had left town, having been beaten by Huey after he resolved a conflict between her and bodyguard Larry Henson in the latter's favor. (Like Bobby Seale, she would not return to Oakland until Huey was safely dead.) Huey resumed his career as Crazy Nigger. Late in 1978, a bizarre story surfaced about a thirty-year-old black woman, the mother of three, who had been standing at a street-corner phone booth when a Cadillac pulled up and Huey's immense bodyguard got out and forced her into the backseat of the car at gunpoint. As she told the story, Huey then opened her blouse and began kissing her breasts. When the woman tried to push him away, he grabbed her arm and put out a cigarette on her flesh. Then, after forcing her to fondle him, he pulled down her slacks and performed cunnilingus on her for several minutes. Afterward, he rifled her purse and took her money before telling Heard to pull over and let her out. He threatened to kill the woman if she went to the police, and then drove off.

The veil of mythology that had protected Huey had now finally been pierced. An Oakland *Tribune* series by reporters Pearl Stewart and Lance Williams documented the misappropriation of city grants to the Panther school as living expenses for Huey's bodyguards Heard and Henson. (After the story appeared, Stewart's Datsun was firebombed.) Even more damaging, a white supporter, guilt-ridden over the death of Betty Van Patter, disclosed the existence of the still secret Squad to journalist Kate Coleman, who wrote a devastating feature called "The Party's Over" for the magazine *New Times*. When the story appeared, Coleman went into hiding in Japan, but her revelations helped finish the Panthers' career as a vanguard of the Left.

But they didn't finish Huey himself. Even after all the mayhem had been reported, California's liberal superintendent of education, Wilson Riles, authorized grants to the Panther school totaling $600,000, and radical Berkeley state assemblyman Tom Bates arranged for Huey to receive a Citizen's Award in Sacramento. With the aid of top-drawer legal counsel paid for by Bert Schneider, his two trials for killing the prostitute ended in hung juries before being dropped by the prosecution. He managed to pay off Preston Callins, thus getting the tailor to recant the statement he had given police right after his beating. But he was unable to escape completely.

Right after they were contacted by Callins, police had gone to Huey's apartment to investigate and had found a gun. Being a convicted felon with a weapon was a technicality that would haunt him in a way that the more serious charges had not. After his conviction, he turned to the appeals process in the hope that he could beat it, but even as he did so he began to have the sense—after five trials for murder in which he had to all intents and purposes beaten the rap—that he had become ensnared finally in the network of deceit he had created.

Huey may have failed as a revolutionary, but he could not commit himself entirely to succeeding as a criminal. The approbation of the white world had come to mean too much to him. In an effort to shore up support from that world, he had gone back to the University of California at Santa Cruz as soon as he returned from Cuba. The memories of him from the mid-Seventies, when he got what was widely regarded as a "courtesy" B.A. degree, centered on the way he had shown up for class in a limo, with a white pimp suit and slouch hat, surrounded by women dressed like prostitutes and the omnipresent bodyguards. ("Everyone was overwhelmingly embarrassed when he showed up," one of his professors recalls, "but we were scared too.") It was whispered that he had failed to attend one class altogether, appearing at the end of the quarter with the two papers that had been assigned, one clearly an "A" and the other a "D" and each written by different people, and he had glowered threateningly at the teacher who said he would give him an incomplete.

Now, against the better judgment of some faculty members, Huey was admitted as a doctoral candidate in the History of Consciousness Program created by historian Page Smith, who was well known for his disdain of graduate education and who regarded Huey's presence as an opportunity to prove its irrelevance. Smith was impressed with Huey's primal myth, even though he garbled the details. ("He taught himself to read in prison using Plato as a text," Smith later told a journalist. "That was a kind of marvelous symbolic event, in that Plato marks the transition from a pre-literate to a literate culture, so it almost was as though Newton was picking up on that and that for him had some kind of symbolic significance in terms of breaking out of his illiteracy into literacy.") Smith's rhapsodic vision of Huey captured precisely what Huey and the Panthers had indeed been for the Left in their glory days: noble savages.

Smith encouraged Huey to write a thesis on the FBI's "war" against the Panthers. A Santa Cruz professor who watched the subsequent charade carries the enduring memory of Huey sitting in a lecture class given for him alone, with his wife, Gwen, filing her fingernails and his immense bodyguard, Robert Heard, half asleep.

He got the Ph.D. with a thin thesis and encouraged people to call him "Dr. Newton." (The *New York Times* would use the title in its obituary, prompting a debate in the Oakland hinterlands about whether it was a gesture of sincere respect or of derision.) But the degree didn't solve his problems. The world continued to close in on him. In 1980, Huey hired a new principal for the school, who quickly discovered that Huey was embezzling its funds to pay for his bodyguards. When the principal took his story to the authorities, the machinery of the legal process was cranked up once again. This time prosecutors were sure they could get Huey. There would be no witnesses to intimidate or buy off. But there was a paper trail that he couldn't erase or discredit through Charles Garry's courtroom bullying.

He had become a man without a party. The school, which had been his best fund-raising device, had closed its doors. As his legal troubles consumed more and more of his life, the Party members who had believed in the survival programs disappeared one by one. Even big Bob Heard left after serving six months on a gun charge that Huey had incurred but for which Heard was made to take the fall. Soon there were no Panthers left, just Huey and Gwen and Larry Henson, the last member of the Squad.

Then Gwen left him, taking off without warning and resurfacing in Chicago as the wife of a building contractor. This was the biggest blow of all. She had been a rock of support for him for over a decade, pulling up her roots and following his fugitive course to Cuba, taking the hits with him, bearing his abusive moods, nursing him through the dryouts, and watching the painful crumbling of the edifice he had built. For months after her departure, the physical signs of his devastation were impossible to conceal. Huey began to spend more and more time in the seedy underside of West Oakland, where he had spent his youth. He turned to crack, which would cost him even the ability to plan new schemes.

Bob Trivers, an instructor at Santa Cruz, watched the fall. A sociobiologist, Trivers gave a course based on the theory that mechanisms of self-deception evolve in the service of deceit—that one who is self-deceived is a better deceiver. The idea fascinated Huey, and the two men struck up a friendship based on the pursuit of the subject.

Trivers watched Huey go on drug binges that became longer and more destructive. He watched him go through periods of "cleaning out" from drugs and alcohol that involved self-discipline and fasting for weeks, ordeals that became increasingly difficult for him. It seemed that Huey realized that his life was behind him now. There were times when he seemed struck by remorse. Trivers was with him once when one of the women who were constantly after him showed up late at night at his home and Huey, after slapping her and getting rid of her, remarked reflectively, "You know, I've killed more men than women."

Beneath the flippant comment was an invitation to explore the subject of the prostitute Kathleen Smith. Trivers said something about her. Huey looked at him and noted, "You're like a white lawyer friend of mine. He thinks I did it but forgives me anyhow." They talked delicately about the subject until Huey seemed to rule it out of bounds: "Look, the statute of limitations on murder *never* runs out." But he couldn't really give it up, and after a few moments of silence he cited Stalin's statement that you can't trust a person until they've stopped killing for at least twenty years. "I'm not sure whether he said twenty years or five," Trivers interjected. Huey got a look on his face and replied, "Well, it *ought* to be twenty."

He was the petrified remains of a Sixties hero. People would stop him in the street and ask him to sign copies of the Poster. A heavy cocaine user for a decade, he now went on crack binges that lasted for weeks. "When he was heavy into freebasing," Bob Trivers remembers, "it was impossible to find him. You'd leave a message and he wouldn't get back to you because he'd be in such dreadful shape. He'd dry out, but as soon as he did, he'd head back onto the streets."

In the spring of 1987, he was convicted of the 1974 gun possession charge and sent to Jamestown Prison Camp for a year. When he got out, there were periodic reports that he was "getting it together." He said that he was going to run for mayor of Oakland. He claimed that he was working with Richard Pryor on a film of his life. But the schemes were built to fall through. He was chronically broke. The law was always catching up on some charge, nickeling and diming him to death. He was arrested several times on drunk-driving charges and put on probation. Parole conditions related to the weapons charge allowed the police to search him or his car or his apartment without a warrant. His hired gun, Larry Henson, became more crucial than ever as his violent prosthetic. But when he was finally unable to come up with money, Henson left him too.

Bert Schneider's estate in Hollywood was one of the few remaining places where Huey got to feel important, as he had in the past. Yet even here he seemed out of joint. On one visit in 1988, Schneider's secretary was working in an office on the property when Newton wandered in, stark naked and obviously coked up, his eyes glazed and his face mottled from debauch. Barely acknowledging the startled woman's presence, Huey rambled incoherently for several minutes about life's unfairness. Then he suddenly paused and shook his head, almost as if coming to. "What I keep wondering," he said, looking at the secretary as if for the first time, "is why somebody hasn't put a bullet into my head yet."

The gears of the legal system continued to grind. In 1988, he was finally ordered to face trial on charges of embezzling the moneys earmarked for the school. A month later, on July 12, he was rejailed for six weeks for using drugs and driving under the influence, violations of his parole. Six months later, he was arrested and sent to San Quentin for six months after being found in a sleazy motel with a hooker named Roxanne Raspberry, basing rock cocaine. While in San Quentin, he pleaded no contest on one count of embezzling funds from the school and was ordered to pay restitution.

When he got out, early in 1989, he hit the streets again. Some people pitied him. But he didn't pity himself. He said to one friend, "I'm glad I don't have an organization. I like being a lone entity." He was in his element in the streets: it was a place where everything came down to a man's resourcefulness and daring.

Bob Trivers, who hung out with Huey during this time, remembers an experience that for him was pure fear but for Huey the stuff of life. "We went into a part of Oakland that didn't have paved streets. It was the sort of neighborhood where a white boy like myself wouldn't have lasted thirty seconds. We got to this crack house. Huey got a little bit of stuff, but didn't have any money. The dealer reached behind a washing machine and pulled out a gun and stuck it into his belt. The argument got louder and louder. Huey wasn't scared, but the guy with the gun was, and that scared me."

Chronically out of money, Huey spent his days stalking dope, either cadging it or, when that failed, "jacking" the small-time dealers awed by his reputation. ("Don't you know who I am? I'm Huey P. Newton of the Black Panther Party!") He talked constantly about death, which he called the "Big Boss."

Huey had always said that he would end things on his own terms. But when the Big Boss finally came to collect him on a street in the neighborhood where officer John Frey had been shot over twenty years earlier, Tyrone Robinson was the collection agent. Robinson put not one but three bullets into Huey's head after an argument over drugs, thus terminating his long wait for the end and also providing relief for the remnants of the radical movement he had embarrassed. Now he could be gathered at last into the Garden of Martyrs of the Left, a serene spot where disquieting biographical truth never enters.

As his body was laid to rest amid eulogies by Bobby Seale and Elaine Brown and all the others who had conspired with Huey and learned to fear him, the two thousand or so Bay Area radicals and members of the black community of Oakland who had come to mourn him shouted, "Huey Is Free!" It was a reference to the cry—"Free Huey!"—that had rocked the Sixties. But it had another connotation too: We are free of Huey now, and we can get on with the work of creating utopia.

II

Second Thoughts

— • —

chapter 5 _____

The Fifth-Column Left

Divided Loyalties

Writing in the 120th anniversary issue of *The Nation*, Gore Vidal marked the occasion with characteristic perversity by attacking *Commentary* editor Norman Podhoretz and writer Midge Decter as "fifth column" agents, whose "first loyalty would always be to Israel"—an allegiance that made their politics subversive of America's national interest. As a furor developed over the anti-Semitic implications of his article, the author sat back to enjoy the mischief while the editors of *The Nation* made a show of steering the debate toward a loftier level: "Vidal has given birth to a controversy that . . . could with luck have the virtue of prompting people to debate and thus define the limits of respectable opinion on the matter of America and Israel."

The relationship of America's communities and their lobbies to foreign powers is certainly a legitimate political concern. But unlike, say, the recent involvement of black Americans in the debate over U.S. policy toward South Africa, the relationship of American Jews to Israel has been the subject of almost endless discussion and analysis. Moreover, Israel's consistency as one of America's most dependable allies diminishes somewhat its potential as a cause for concern. But there *is* one community whose divided loyalties are both undeniable and truly disquieting, although *The Nation* would no doubt exempt it from Vidal's injunction. This is the community of the hardcore Left, which is the real fifth column in American political life.

Unlike American Zionists, the openness of whose support of Israel allows others to judge their motives, American Leftists are steeped in a tradition of conspiracy and deceit whose instruments are secretive "vanguards" and "popular fronts," through which basic commitments are regularly concealed and important agendas are always covert at the same time that charges of "red-baiting" and "McCarthyism" are being invoked to shield the underlying allegiances from the scrutiny they deserve.

In the aftermath of the Vidal article, the editors of *The Nation* smugly called for removal of the "taboo" that suppresses discussion of divided loyalties in our political life and prevents exposure of those who work for foreign powers. On this much at least they are right. America's fifth column is a subject whose time has come. The fifth column that threatens this country, however, is not Jews who support America's Israeli ally but a Left that works in behalf of America's totalitarian enemies and whose influence grows unimpeded.

Fifth columnism is a subject with which we, as former 1960s radicals and editors of the New Left magazine *Ramparts*, are intimately acquainted. We both arrived in Berkeley at the end of the 1950s, a time when, in demonstrations against the House Committee on Un-American Activities, McCarthyism was dying and the New Left was being born. What attracted us to this new political atmosphere was the opportunity to be Leftists in a new way: not as the servile agents of a foreign power but as the shapers of an indigenous American radicalism. Along with other early New Leftists, we regarded members of the Old Communist Left as figures of scorn—ideologues who were perpetually (in both meanings of the term) boring from within and hiding their malign intentions. They were intriguers without a chance of success, forever lurking on the fringes of our meetings, trying to find a group, any group, they could infiltrate and subvert.

The New Left saw itself as a movement that would design its own American future, without imitating foreign models —a sort of American studies project of the real world. The phrase "participatory democracy" captured the intention to make the promise of America real. Its first campaign—for civil rights—was based on a belief in this promise. The Vietnam War provided an opportunity for this optimism to ferment and then to sour. The speed with which the New Left became disaffected from the nation and from its own early ideals, and the fact that this happened with so little resistance, suggests that the movement had a split personality from the beginning —one part believing in an American radicalism and the other not believing in anything at all. Ruminating about the instant alienation of the New Left, one of its leading theorists, Paul Goodman, thought that its primary characteristic was a "loss of patriotic feeling." He wrote: "For the first time . . . the mention of country, community, place, has lost its power to animate. Nobody but a scoundrel even tries it."

That loss of feeling led the New Left to declare war on America, matching every escalation in the Vietnam conflict abroad with an escalation in its own conflict at home. Sympathy for America's alleged victims developed into an identification with America's real enemies. By the end of the Sixties, participatory democracy was a language no longer spoken on the Left. Its slogans had changed. In 1968, the Students for a Democratic Society (SDS)—the heart of the New Left—converted to "Marxism-Leninism," and the following year its convention broke into hostile rival factions, chanting the names of Chairman Mao and "Uncle" Ho. In a few short years, the Communist dictators of China and North Vietnam had become the household gods of the New Left.

New Leftists met with the North Vietnamese and the National Liberation Front (NLF) in Havana, Bratislava, and Hanoi, to collaborate in their war effort by providing propaganda advice and orchestrating a political campaign to demoralize U.S. troops in the field and create disorder and disruption

at home. Activists with Old Left politics like Cora Weiss and
guilty ex-liberals like William Sloane Coffin went to Hanoi to
embrace the Communists and second their cause. After visiting American POWs the Communists had tortured, Coffin and
Weiss assured the world that they had been treated well. In
1969, a group of radicals including SDS leader Bernadine
Dohrn and Castro apologist Saul Landau traveled to Cuba to
meet with the Vietnamese and launch the Venceremos Brigades. The ostensible reason for this effort was to provide help
for the Cuban sugar harvest. The real reason was to meet
Cuban and Vietnamese officials in Havana to map out strategies for the war in America, the "other war," which would
ultimately defeat the United States in a way that the battlefield
situation in Vietnam never could have.

As editors of *Ramparts*, we did not share the totalitarian
enthusiasms of people like Weiss, Landau, and Dohrn, or their
willingness to serve the governments of Communist powers.
When confronted by these tendencies in the Left, we argued
against them. One almost amusing struggle session occurred
with members of the North American Congress on Latin
America (NACLA), a church-funded group with pro-Castro
loyalties, which described its purpose as providing an "intelli-
gence-gathering arm" for the Left and which had helped set
up the Venceremos Brigades. A delegation from NACLA came
to our editorial offices with an article they wanted printed. The
piece proposed itself as a report on the progress of "socialist
democracy" in Cuba, focusing on the passage of a recently
enacted "anti-laziness" law as evidence of the "people's rule."
The article claimed that more than three million Cubans—a
third of the population—had actively participated in the making of the law. We asked the obvious question: If the people's
civic involvement was as high as this, why was the law necessary at all? In the confrontation that followed, NACLA members told us that because of our "white skin privileges" we had
"no right to judge" anything that third world revolutionaries
did. In the words of one of the NACLA spokesmen: "Your
revolutionary responsibility is to print the piece and shut up
about it."

But while we rejected the crude propaganda of people
we regarded even then as Castro's agents, we nonetheless pro-

vided a platform for the more sophisticated apologetics of Susan Sontag, who catechized our readers on "The Right Way (for Us) to Love the Cuban Revolution." The issue of *Ramparts* in which this piece appeared accurately captured the ethos that had come to prevail in the New Left by the end of the Sixties. Over the cover photograph of a wholesome six-year-old carrying a Vietcong flag were these words: "Alienation is when your country is at war and you want the other side to win."

Like most of the Movement, we presumed that a Vietcong victory would mean a peasant "liberation" in Southeast Asia. But we were less concerned with the future of Vietnam than with making sure America's forces were defeated. A fundamental tenet of our New Leftism was that America's offenses against Vietnam were only a fraction of its larger imperial sin. We shared with the rest of the Left its most irresponsible and destructive myth: that America had become rich and powerful not through its own efforts but by making the rest of the world impotent and poor.

To force America's global retreat had become for us the highest good, and we were willing to accomplish this end, in one of the odious catchphrases of the day, "by any means necessary." Our most significant opportunity presented itself in the person of a young man who had just quit his job as a cryptanalyst with the National Security Agency because of his disillusionment with the war. At this time, few Americans knew anything about the NSA, a top-secret organization that accounted for 80 percent of U.S. intelligence data. With the help of this "defector," we developed an article for *Ramparts* that described the NSA's operations and also revealed its capabilities for deciphering Soviet codes, one of the most coveted and carefully guarded intelligence secrets.

Although we gave scarcely a second thought to the moral implications of printing the NSA article, we did worry about the legal risks we faced. The defense team in the celebrated "Pentagon Papers" trial provided us with Charles Nesson, a Harvard professor and renowned expert on constitutional law. Nesson advised us that if we printed the article, and in particular the secret code words it contained, we would be in clear violation of the U.S. Espionage Act. But, he added, in order to prosecute us, the government would be forced to reveal far more information about the NSA's secrets than was contained in the article itself. For this reason, and on the basis of precedents in similar cases, he continued, it was unlikely that the government would indict us.

We had been taught the lesson that other Leftists would learn: that the freedoms of America can be used to subvert American freedom. We printed the article. We were not prosecuted. Instead we were rewarded with a front-page story in the *New York Times* about the information we had revealed and with appearances on national TV.

Like the others present at the creation of the New Left, who had begun the Sixties demanding that America improve itself, we had ended the decade by committing acts of no-fault treason.

The government we had sought to undermine might not be able to punish us, but history would not prove so kind. In the years after America's defeat in Vietnam, we were presented with a balance sheet showing the sobering consequences of our politics. New Left orthodoxy had scorned the idea that the war was about North Vietnamese aggression and Soviet expansion, but soon after the American pullout, North Vietnamese armies were in Cambodia and Laos, and the Russians were occupying the bases at Cam Ranh Bay and Da Nang and se-curing exploitation rights to natural resources in Indochina in unmistakably imperial style. What we had dismissed as impos-sible was happening with dizzying speed. Far from being lib-erated, South Vietnam was now occupied by a conquering army from the North. The "bloodbath" our opponents pre-dicted took place in the form of tens of thousands of summary executions, while many of the "indigenous" revolutionaries of the NLF, whom we had supported, disappeared into "reedu-cation" camps or joined the "boat people" exodus to freedom in the West. In Cambodia, two million peasants died at the hands of the Communist Khmer Rouge, protégés of Hanoi and beneficiaries of the New Left's "solidarity" with the revolution-ary cause. It was a daunting lesson: more people had been killed in the first two years of the Communist peace than in the thirteen years of America's war. There were other consequences as well. During the late Seventies—a time when American democracy was trying to heal itself from the traumas of Vietnam and Watergate—the U.S.S.R. was demonstrating that totalitarianism abhors a vacuum by moving into Africa, Central America, Southeast Asia, and, most brutally, Afghanistan.

For some of us, these events were the occasion for a melancholy rethinking, which ultimately led to our retirement from the Left. But for many of our former comrades, there were no second thoughts and there was no turning back. For these diehards, the Communist victory in Indochina provided a perverse opportunity to prove the mettle of their faith, a time to rededicate themselves to the struggle, which they believed had just begun.

Four years after the fall of Saigon, an event occurred that was to mark the passing of the torch from one generation of the Left to another. Appalled by the new oppression in Indochina, Joan Baez, Richard John Neuhaus, James Finn, and other former antiwar activists reentered the political arena with "An Appeal to the Conscience of Vietnam." In criticizing the Communists and calling for an end to the repression, the signers of the "Appeal" challenged the survivors of the New Left to live up to their claims to be partisans of social justice and the rights of the oppressed.

But rejection of this plea was swift and decisive. A public counterappeal appeared in the New York Times, paid for by Cora Weiss, whose inherited fortune had come to function as a bank account for Left causes. Signed by a list of former antiwar notables including Dave Dellinger, William Sloane Coffin, and Richard Barnet, who reaffirmed their solidarity with the Communists, the advertisement said: "The present government of Vietnam should be hailed for its moderation and for its extraordinary effort to achieve reconciliation among all of its peoples." Within the ranks of the Left, the signers of Baez's original appeal were vilified as "stooges" and "CIA agents," and the claim was made (in a letter to one of them) that even "if the Vietnamese had chosen the course of mass executions and plunder, of political prisoners and torture, it would have been our own strategies of terror and brutality which drove them to it."

To outsiders, the appearance of the two public statements might have seemed a prelude to a struggle for the soul of the Left. But as insiders, we recognized that the issue had already been decided. The chastened radicals who signed and supported the Baez "Appeal" were defeated; there was no longer any ground on the Left that they could occupy. Those who affirmed their solidarity with the Communist victors had won by default.

A revealing indication of the character of the new "Solidarity Left" whose birth was announced in the Weiss ad was its campaign to rehabilitate the discredited American Communist Party, whose members had proved themselves in the post-Khrushchev years to be among the most servile of the Kremlin's camp followers in the world. In books such as Vivian Gornick's *The Romance of American Communism*, the old fifth columnists for Stalin were lionized as warriors of "the good fight" who had stayed the course and thus provided, perhaps, a worthier model for political emulation than the New Left, which had burned itself out in histrionics and extremism.

This romanticizing of people we had once regarded as political hacks was counterpointed by the return of Stalinist fronts to the American political scene. By 1979, the World Peace Council, a Soviet front originally created by Stalin in 1949, was once again operating on the American Left. Its American offshoot, the U.S. Peace Council, was holding conferences attended not only by what was left of the Left but also by senators and congressmen. The pro-Soviet sycophancy of the Communist Party kept its numbers small; but the new spirit of acceptance allowed its influence to grow. Communists became stylistically influential, reintroducing the linguistic and organizational deviousness of the Popular Front period of the late 1930s, which made it hard to know what words meant and harder yet to identify the allegiances of those who spoke them.

While the New Left had announced its birth from a university campus, its successor seemed almost to admit intrinsic hypocrisy by reconstituting itself in New York's Riverside Church, which had been built by John D. Rockefeller fifty years earlier as a headquarters of liberal Protestant faith. The chief architects of the declaration with which the post-Vietnam Left was launched were Riverside's new minister, William

Sloane Coffin, and his patron Weiss, a nonobserving Jew who had positioned herself as head of the Church's "Disarmament Program."

Despite his profession as a man of the cloth, Coffin's true faith had for some time been left-wing causes. He was a representative figure in the movement to infuse Christianity with a "liberation theology," which postulated a Marxist God who had enjoined the faithful to establish a Communist heaven on earth through "solidarity" with revolutionary movements, which Coffin defined as the "essence of Christian faith." Defending his own covenant with the dictatorship in Hanoi, for instance, Coffin declared that "Communism is a page torn out of the Bible" and added that "the social justice that's been achieved in . . . North Vietnam [is] an achievement no Christian society on that scale has ever achieved."

Coffin may have articulated the new politics of the post-Vietnam Left, but Cora Weiss was more typical and far more influential than he. Her $25 million family fortune allowed her to support a network of radical institutions like NACLA and the Institute for Policy Studies, whose programs had elicited the sponsorship of as many as fifty members of Congress and whose influence spread from Capitol Hill to the Carter White House itself.

Weiss was typical of the red-diaper babies who remained loyal to the Communist politics they inherited from their parents, even if they did not join the Party itself. The father whose fortune she dispensed was an old-line Stalinist, and she retained the "progressive" commitments that had determined his political course. As head of the Riverside Church Disarmament Program, she led the opposition to American efforts to neutralize the vast Soviet arms buildup that had taken place in the Seventies. Weiss's efforts (and those of the institutions she bankrolled) were focused on exposing what she called the "myth" of the Soviet threat. Richard Barnet, codirector and resident "expert" on strategic affairs for the Institute for Policy Studies, called the idea of such a threat "the big lie of our times." In May 1979, Weiss herself described it as a "hereditary disease transmitted over the past 60 years."

Barely six months after she made this statement, the Soviets assassinated their own puppet ruler in Afghanistan and launched their invasion. Weiss's Disarmament Program responded to the Soviets' aggression with a warning to Americans: "Any form of U.S. intervention, escalation of a military presence or an increase in the defense budget is unnecessary and inappropriate . . . Russia's challenge continues to demand restraint, study and understanding." Instead of focusing their attention on the Soviet action in Afghanistan, she counseled, members of the peace movement should look at what the United States had done to "poison relations between the two superpowers."

For all intents and purposes, the new "peace movement" did indeed ignore the Soviet aggression in Afghanistan, which showed the distance traveled since the Sixties, when the malignity of the Soviet empire was a given. It also showed how far the U.S.S.R. had come in rehabilitating its image since the Khrushchev revelations, which, in shattering its orthodoxy, had destroyed its ability to hold even its own vanguards in line. But the Vietnam era became a time of new opportunities for the Soviets, an extended school in which Fidel Castro, while on their dole, had become their most important political teacher.

Castro saw that the American Left, still wary of the U.S.S.R., could be made to support Soviet aims indirectly because of its ties—affective even more than political—with him and his revolution, ties that would survive his servile support of the Russian invasions of Czechoslovakia in 1968 and Afghanistan a decade later. At the same time he was making Cuba's economy a satellite of Russia's, and Cuba's intelligence services and military forces instruments of the Soviet state, Castro began the creation of what amounted to a new Communist international.

Before Castro's intervention, the anti-Soviet attitudes of the New Left and the isolation of the Communist Party had frustrated the penetration efforts of the Soviet intelligence services. But in 1969, Castro worked with American radicals to create the Venceremos Brigades, placing them under the control of Cuban intelligence operatives, with results that were revealed later on by a high-ranking officer who defected: "The Venceremos Brigades brought the first great quantity of information through American citizens that was obtained in the United States, because up to the moment when the brigades came into existence . . . the amount of information that we had on American citizens came from public sources, and it was confusing."*

A "revolution throughout the hemisphere" had always been Castro's political ambition, but the cautious Soviets had always been wary of what they considered his "reckless adventurism," which they feared might provoke a U.S. response. But with America's defeat in Vietnam, the Soviet attitude changed. The crucial role that American opponents of the war had played in determining its outcome and forcing America's retreat by protests at home had made Castro's adventurism seem prescient rather than reckless. Within months of the fall of Saigon, the Soviets began an unprecedented flow of arms to Cuba. By 1980, the flow of military supplies had become a flood —ten times greater in a single year than the *total* of military aid that had been sent to Cuba *during the entire first decade of the revolution*, the time when it presumably faced its gravest external threat.

This massive arms buildup had only one purpose: to make Cuba the forward base of a new Soviet expansionism. Indeed, the expansion had begun in the year of Saigon's fall, when forty thousand Cuban troops were dispatched to shore up pro-Soviet dictatorships in the Horn of Africa. While Leftists like *Nation* editor Andrew Kopkind were fatuously praising the Soviet Union for "almost always siding with the revolutionists, the liberationists, and the insurgents," Castro's expeditionary forces in Ethiopia were propping up the Marxist government of Mengistu Haile Mariam, whose main accomplishment was a "Red Campaign of Terror" that killed a hundred thousand intractable citizens. The following year, Castro awarded Mengistu the "Bay of Pigs" Medal, Cuba's highest honor. By that time, Mengistu's Marxist economic policies had precipitated a famine.

But if Africa was the first front of the new offensive, Central America was the ultimate objective. Castro had long

* Gerardo Peraza, Testimony before the Senate Subcommittee on Security and Terrorism, February 26, 1982.

been the patron of tiny guerrilla bands in Nicaragua and El Salvador, whose leaders had been trained in Havana and Moscow and at PLO terrorist camps in Lebanon. Because he had survived U.S. animosity so long and studied American weaknesses so carefully, Castro was in a position to understand the new math of the "Vietnam equation." It was not necessary for the Communists to win for there to be revolutionary success; it was necessary only for America to lose. And losing was defined by what went on in the domestic political process in the United States rather than on the battlefields of the third world.

In January 1977, when the Carter administration took office in Washington, there were crucial questions for Castro and his American supporters to consider. How much weight could be given to the new President's expressions of regret for the interventions of the past and to his determination to avoid "another" Vietnam? How vigorously would he pursue his new "human rights" policy with dictators like Somoza, who relied on U.S. support for survival? Factoring the answers into the Vietnam equation would determine revolutionary options and risks.

No one who was considering these options, including Fidel Castro, could know for certain what the answers would be. But there was no Communist leader in the world who had better intelligence for arriving at an answer than he did. In the changed political atmosphere that followed Vietnam, the networks that his American loyalists had created now permeated the American political process.

As Jimmy Carter took office, Castro's Nicaraguan disciple, Humberto Ortega, unveiled a new political strategy from his guerrilla headquarters in Costa Rica, which bore a distinctive Castro imprint. The Marxist revolution would be deferred in favor of a broad coalition with non-Marxist democrats, united by the goal of toppling the Somoza dictatorship and creating a pluralistic democratic regime. Until that moment, the Marxist Sandinistas had been a minuscule sectarian force, split into three factions, with barely two hundred members in all. But now, as part of a democratic coalition, they could ride a majority movement to power.

By early 1979, it was apparent that the end was near for

Somoza. Castro began to prepare the next stage of the struggle. The Marxist guerrillas, still feuding among themselves, were summoned to Havana. There, Castro created a nine-member "*comandante* directorate," with each of the three factions represented, unifying their command. There, too, he made arrangements to provide them with the tons of arms and military support that would allow them to defeat Somoza and —just as important—would also make them the dominant force of the new Nicaragua.

But as the Vietnam equation had shown, organizing guerrilla forces was only a part, a necessary but insufficient part, of what was required to attack America. Even more essential for success was assembling what Trotsky had once described as the "frontier guards" of the revolution—the vital fifth column, which would make the equation work. Even as Castro was preparing to unify the Sandinista command, his American allies were setting up the guerrillas' support system in the United States, using the "peace movement" as a base. As soon as it was founded in 1979, the Communist Party's U.S. Peace Council front joined forces with NACLA to stage a National Conference on Nicaragua in Washington to mobilize opposition against a potential U.S. "intervention" in Nicaragua, although the only notable military interventions since the Vietnam War had been those of the Communist powers— Russia, Cuba, and Vietnam itself. While the Communist organizers of the Nicaragua Conference claimed that they wanted to prevent "another Vietnam," their real purpose was exactly the opposite—to *achieve* another Vietnam, by preventing any U.S. effort to counter the massive Cuban intervention that had already begun, with the aim of making Nicaragua a Communist state.

The Nicaragua Conference proved to be the first step in a long-range plan: to create a shield of organizations in the United States behind which the Communist revolution in the hemisphere could advance. The conference was a sort of coming-out party to put the stamp of respectability on an organization called the Network in Solidarity with the People of Nicaragua. Started on U.S. college campuses by two Nicaraguan nationals acting for the Sandinistas, the Nicaragua Network soon became a national organization, with chapters in hundreds of American cities and on campuses across the country. Its "Pledge of Resistance" was signed by seventy thousand Americans, who declared themselves ready to undertake illegal actions to oppose U.S. intervention in Nicaragua. The crucial importance the Nicaraguan Communists attached to such activities was underlined by Tomas Borge, one of the most important members of the *comandante* directorate and head of internal security: "The battle for Nicaragua is not being waged in Nicaragua. It is being fought in the United States."

The Sandinista partisans in America mounted their offensive by defining the issues in terms calculated to have a certain domestic appeal—"human rights" and "another Vietnam." This sleight of stance was made possible by the Stalinist traditions of the organizational front they had revived. The Nicaragua Network was only one of a far-ranging array of organizations from which the friends of violent revolutions and repressive dictatorships could speak to other Americans in the language of pacifist and humanitarian concern.

One of the most potent "human rights" groups in the campaign against the *contras* (and a prominent participant in the Nicaragua Conference) was the Washington Office on Latin America (WOLA). Supported by church groups, WOLA had been created by Christian liberationists after the Chilean coup against Salvador Allende. WOLA's director, Joe Eldridge, had been active in Chile before the coup as an Allende partisan, and WOLA's concern about human rights abuses was aimed squarely at the post-Allende regime.

In 1977, when Fidel and his Sandinista protégés began launching their new strategy, WOLA also shifted its attention to Nicaragua, sponsoring bridge-building tours to the United States by the Sandinista *padres* Cardenal and D'Escoto, who mobilized support for the "hemispheric revolution" at the same time they crusaded to Marxize Christ. Led by its Nicaragua coordinator, Kay Stubbs, WOLA also began a campaign against human rights abuses by the Somoza regime and lobbied the Carter administration to withdraw its support. After the Sandinista victory, Stubbs (who all the time had belonged to a clandestine Sandinista cell in Washington and was secretly married to a Sandinista *comandante*) left WOLA to join Nicaragua's Marxist regime.

With the *comandantes* in power, WOLA's interest in human rights abuses in Nicaragua all but disappeared. The reports it now began to feature were focused on El Salvador, where WOLA's investigations were directed by Heather Foote, an American radical with strong ties to the FPL faction of the guerrilla forces. Needless to say, WOLA investigations all but ignored the bloody activities of the Leftist guerrillas in El Salvador.

WOLA's emphasis on human rights had shifted elsewhere, but its solidarity with the new Marxist rulers of Nicaragua remained as strong as ever. In Washington, a new U.S. President had asked Congress for funds to support the anti-Communist *contras* fighting the Sandinista regime. Charges that human rights abuses had been committed by the *contra* guerrillas became a central issue in the congressional debate. A major factor deciding the April 1985 vote of Congress against the *contras* was a report entitled "Human Rights Violations by the Contras," which WOLA had circulated. What was concealed was the fact that WOLA had used its reputation as an independent human rights organization to provide cover for what amounted to a Sandinista covert activity. The report had been initiated by the registered "foreign agent" of the Sandinista regime, attorney Paul Reichler, who selected a fellow Leftist lawyer, Reed Brody, to do the investigation. Brody's housing and transportation were supplied by the Sandinistas while he was in Nicaragua, and his "witnesses" were supplied by the Sandinista security police. Before he departed with his report for the U.S., he was even provided with a photo opportunity, which resulted in a snapshot that showed him hugging Daniel Ortega.

As soon as his protégés were firmly established in Managua, Castro too turned his attention to El Salvador. Six months after the Sandinista victory, a new summons brought five Salvadoran guerrilla factions to Havana, where Castro persuaded them to form a unified command. The new force that Castro created was named the Farabundo Marti Liberation Front (FMLN), after an agent of Stalin's old Comintern whom the Nicaraguan revolutionary Sandino had expelled from his movement on account of his obedience to Moscow's line.

Until this time, the Salvadoran guerrillas had been too isolated and weak to open a revolutionary front, their sporadic actions amounting to little more than radical symbolism. But with Castro (and therefore the Soviets) behind them, the FMLN laid plans for a full-scale guerrilla war. In July 1980, Salvadoran Communist Party chairman Shafik Handal embarked on a journey to Moscow and from there to Vietnam and other way stations in the Communist bloc, where he arranged for shipments of two hundred tons of arms to be sent through Nicaragua and Cuba to the guerrilla forces in El Salvador for a "final offensive."*

While Shafik Handal was gathering arms from the East, his brother Farid was sent on a political mission to America. His mission was to organize a political front in the United States that would support the guerrilla offensive; to create (as he later wrote) "the International Committee in Solidarity with the People of El Salvador." CISPES, as its American branch would be called, was to be modeled on the Nicaragua Network and would have direct links with the Salvadoran guerrilla forces and with the "solidarity committees" the Soviet-controlled World Peace Council had sponsored in sixteen countries around the world.

After touching base at the Cuban U.N. Mission and with the Communist Party's "solidarity coordinator" in New York, Farid Handal went to Washington. The guerrillas' emissary met supporters at the Institute for Policy Studies and WOLA, and then Communist Party members put him in touch with Congressman Ron Dellums's office. Dellums turned over his congressional office space to Handal and arranged a meeting with the Congressional Black Caucus.

Recording these events in the journal he kept (it was

* Details of these efforts were revealed in captured documents belonging to Shafik Handal's brother Farid (U.S. State Department, "Report of Farid Handal's Trip to the United States"). The creation of the solidarity network has been documented in Allan C. Brownfield and J. Michael Waller, The Revolution Lobby, 1985, and J. Michael Waller, Consolidating the Revolution, 1986, both published by the Council for Inter-American Security, Washington, D.C.

later retrieved by authorities in Salvador from a captured guerrilla safe house), Handal wrote: "Monday morning the offices of Congressman Dellums were turned into our offices. Everything was done there. The meeting with the Black Caucus took place in the liver of the monster itself, nothing less than in the meeting room of the House Foreign Affairs Committee." Understanding that the opportunities laid before him would vanish if he spoke in the blunt political language of his brother Shafik and his guerrilla comrades back home, Farid reminded himself to present his cause "with its human features, without political language, and, most importantly, without a political label."

After Farid Handal had left the country, CISPES was formally created by his American supporters. One of the organization's first acts was to disseminate a "dissent paper" it claimed had been drafted by disgruntled members of the National Security Council and the State Department, who allegedly believed that further military aid to El Salvador would eventually force the U.S. to intervene there and who also favored U.S. recognition of the Democratic Revolutionary Front, the political arm of the FMLN guerrillas. Although the State Department immediately denied its authenticity, the CISPES document was accepted as legitimate by several journalists, among them Anthony Lewis, who wrote about it in the *New York Times*. Eventually the FBI established that the "dissent paper" was a KGB forgery, one of many Soviet "active measures" to influence the political process in the U.S., but CISPES continued to distribute the document, and Anthony Lewis and the others who had been duped printed no *mea culpas*.

CISPES opposed not only military aid to the Duarte government but food supplies, medical shipments, and agricultural assistance as well. But when it was not lobbying against aid to the Duarte government, CISPES was raising money to send to the FMLN guerrilla forces.

Despite its thinly veiled hypocrisies and tainted origins, CISPES has been endorsed by Democratic members of Congress and has had fund-raising letters written on its behalf by Representatives Dellums, Mervyn Dymally, and Pat Schroeder. Combining street protests with door-to-door canvassing, it has become a powerful lobby, with chapters among church and civic groups across the country and on hundreds of college campuses. Its agenda has never varied: support for the FMLN guerrillas, however brutal their campaign might become.

In the spring of 1985, a CISPES lobbying effort enabled friendly congressmen on the Subcommittee on Western Hemisphere Affairs to schedule hearings on the "air war" in El Salvador. The object of the hearings was to determine whether the strikes against the guerrillas were strikes against the civilian population, violating the congressional certification conditions for aid to the Duarte government.

Eyewitness testimony was indeed presented for the claim that the Salvadoran air force had wantonly violated Salvadoran human rights by conducting a war against the population itself. It was provided by Gus Newport, mayor of Berkeley and vice-chairman of the World Peace Council. (He once silenced a questioner who asked about Communist control of a Berkeley City Council event by snapping, "I have no problem with Communists; my problem is with Democrats and Republicans.") Newport's partisan impressions of the Salvadoran air war were supported in a written report by Ron Dellums's chief aide, Carlottia Scott. Both Scott and Newport got their air war experience, without notable injury, during a visit they made to Berkeley's "sister city" located in the guerrilla zone.

CISPES became the representative organization of the post-Vietnam Left, a Left built on solidarities with Communist power. A "Vietnam/El Salvador Rally," held by CISPES in the Washington Square Methodist Church in New York, was the occasion for a symbolic assembling of the solidarity chain. A spokesman for the regime in Hanoi was followed by a spokesman for the Salvador guerrillas. Behind these came the "committees in solidarity" with the revolutions in both regions.

The real agenda of CISPES is reflected in one of its internal documents: "to challenge U.S. policy; to disrupt the war effort, to polarize opinion, to inspire people to refuse to cooperate; to create divisions within Congress and every other institution . . . Each escalation of the war must bring a response more costly than the one before, precisely the Vietnam war phenomenon the Administration is trying to avoid." The slogan of the CISPES rally expressed the same intention: *"Vietnam Has Won, El Salvador Will Win."*

We find it hard not to be ashamed of some of the things we did in the 1960s. But New Left radicals had a certain candor in those days, reveling in their outlaw status and not trying to seem something politically that they were not. This is not true today. While the Sixties Left established its political battleground "in the streets," where its commitments could be examined, the Fifth Column Left focuses on the political process and the vulnerabilities of the two-party system. With the cry of "McCarthyism," they preempt scrutiny of their divided loyalties and covert agendas. Enemies of America's democracy, they infiltrate its political mainstream by posing as liberals who only want to make sure there are no more Vietnams.

And they are accepted as such. "Liberal" is in fact the way the establishment media, for example, invariably describe the coterie of Left-wing congressmen whose commitment to American security is not apparent and who consistently support Communist advances in the third world. Perhaps the most representative among them is Ron Dellums, Democrat of Berkeley, whom we helped elect as a radical congressman in 1970, at the outset of his career. When Dellums's bill prescribing sanctions against South Africa was recently adopted by the House, a profile in the Washington *Post* described him as a "liberal" and noted that a colleague had called him a "moral force for reordering priorities."

Dellums has changed his political style since the days when he stood beside Huey Newton and Eldridge Cleaver and harangued Black Panther audiences with revolutionary rhetoric. In those days when he was attacked as a radical, Dellums did not shrink from the charge. "I am not going to back away from being a radical," he said. "My politics are to bring the walls down." But in the Eighties, Dellums changed the words if not the tune. ("If you carry controversial ideas in a controversial personality," he says, "how can you ever get anything done?") When he now supports U.S. adversaries, it is always in the name of "peace" and "democratic values." He finds himself on the side of the Soviets as regularly as he finds occasions to criticize the United States. He is an ever-present ambassador of goodwill for the Soviets' Peace Council events; at home, he is the Armed Services Committee's resident unilateralist, with ready proposals to scrap all of his country's "offensive" weapons. When Jimmy Carter tried to raise the defense budget after the Soviets invaded Afghanistan, Dellums was alarmed by the specter of American "militarism." As for the Soviets, Dellums explained, "they only want a stable neighbor." He opposed a presidential proposal to reinstitute the draft as a counter to the Soviet threat. Addressing a thousand students at a University of California "Stop the War" rally in Berkeley a few weeks after the Soviet invasion, Dellums declared: "From my vantage point, as your Representative, [I believe] we are at an incredibly dangerous moment. Washington D.C. is a very evil place. . . . While Mr. Zignu Breszinski [sic] professes to see the arc of crises in Southwest Asia as the Balkan tinderbox of World War III, well Ron Dellums sees the only arc of crises being the one that runs between the basement of the west wing of the White House and the war room of the Pentagon."

In his role as a ranking member of the House Armed Services Committee, which is entrusted with America's defenses, Dellums is a passionate opponent of military force. But when he travels among the Marxist-Leninists of Latin America, he is an open admirer of their military dictatorships and the revolutions they have instituted by force. In a letter to Grenadian dictator Maurice Bishop before his death, Dellums's administrative assistant Carlottia Scott described the congressman's attitude as follows: "Ron has become truly committed to Grenada, and has some positive political thinking to share with you. . . . He just has to get all his thoughts in order as to how your interests can be best served. . . . He's really hooked on you and Grenada and doesn't want anything to happen to building the Revolution and making it strong. He really admires you as a person and even more so as a leader with courage and foresight, principles and integrity. Believe me, he doesn't make that kind of statement often about anyone. The only other person that I know of that he expresses such admiration for is Fidel."

When the Reagan administration became concerned by the presence of large numbers of "advisers" from the Soviet bloc in Grenada and by the apparent military dimensions of the new airport the Cubans were constructing there, Dellums went off to Grenada on his own fact-finding tour. Upon his return, he defended Grenada before the House Subcommittee on Inter-American Affairs: "President Reagan characterized [Grenada] as a totalitarian left government and . . . stated that Grenada 'now bears the Soviet and Cuban trademark which means it will attempt to spread the virus among its neighbors.' Based on my personal observations, discussion and analysis of the new international airport under construction in Grenada, it is my conclusion that this project is specifically now and has always been for the purpose of economic development and is not for military use. . . . [I]t is my thought that it is absurd, patronizing and totally unwarranted for the United States Government to charge that this airport poses a military threat to the United States' national security."

When American troops landed in Grenada the year after Dellums made this statement, they discovered among the cache of official documents from the Marxist regime the minutes of a Grenadian Politburo meeting that took place after Dellums had made his "fact-finding" trip but before he had submitted his report to Congress. The minutes of this meeting state: "Barbara Lee [a Dellums aide] is here presently and has brought with her a report on the international airport that was done by Ron Dellums. They have requested that we look at the document and suggest any changes we deem necessary. They will be willing to make the changes."

Another document retrieved after Grenada's liberation provided the postscript. In a diary entry dated March 22, 1980, Grenadian Defense Minister Liam James had written: "The Revo[lution] has been able to crush counter revolution internationally. Airport will be used for Cuban and Soviet military."*

Revelations concerning his affection for Maurice Bishop and Fidel Castro have not diminished Dellums's influence. In the 1988 presidential campaign, he appeared as one of Jesse Jackson's chief advisers on defense. And during the primary

---

* *Grenada Documents: An Overview and Selection*, released by the U.S. Department of State and the U.S. Department of Defense, Washington, D.C., 1984.

campaign, the candidate himself picked up some of Dellums's rhetoric, arguing that Nicaragua's resistance couldn't prevail because "15,000 contras can't defeat 3 million Sandinistas," thus equating the Communist dictators of Nicaragua with the entire Nicaraguan people.

In 1914, Lenin created the Communist International by defining a true revolutionary as one who is willing to betray his country for the revolutionary cause. This definition has survived as a revolutionary creed for seventy-five years. Wherever the "world revolution" establishes a beachhead—Stalin's Russia, Castro's Cuba, Ortega's Nicaragua—its defense is always the first loyalty of the international Left. In the Stalinist past, the Communist Party and its fellow travelers displayed this loyalty with reprehensible dedication and catastrophic result. Today, it is the neo-Communists and neo-fellow travelers of America's Fifth-Column Left—people who continue to see the future in Marxist-Leninist regimes even though it is a future that has never worked.

The hard-core Left typically resolves the moral problems raised by its treachery through the belief that it lives, as Farid Handal put it, in the liver of the monster—that it is helping cripple an American empire that oppresses the rest of mankind. This fifth column is effective because of its deceitful layering of the apparatus through which it works and also because of the lack of vigilance of the media in questioning its dissimulation and disinformation.

The Sandinistas' lies about their intentions may be obvious enough when studied in retrospect, but their fifth-column network in the United States has been remarkably effective in promoting these lies in the nation's political forums and thereby affecting the course of the dialogue on Central America. The aims of the revolution that has seized political control in Managua are not Nicaraguan in origin; the power that guides it lies in Havana and Moscow. The revolutionary ambition in Central America is not nationalist but imperialist. The goal of the destruction of the hemispheric system is shared by a minority who edit *The Nation*, who work in organizations like CISPES or WOLA, and, more ominously, who sit in Congress. They may use the language of American democracy, but democracy is not the end they seek. For them, democratic politics is only a means to achieve their revolutionary goal; Vietnam has taught them that the neutralization of American power and the victory of Communist revolution constitute a single symbiotic act.

chapter 6 _____

The Last Refuge of the Left

McCarthy's Ghost

What is necessary is to rectify names. If names be not correct, language is not in accordance with the truth of things. If language be not in accordance with the truth of things, affairs cannot be carried on to success. When affairs cannot be carried on to success, proprieties . . . will not flourish. When proprieties . . . do not flourish, punishments will not be properly awarded. When punishments are not properly awarded, the people do not know how to move hand and foot.

Confucius, *Analects*, Book XIII

Joe McCarthy made a career of finding reds under every bed. Today, the culture that so despises him finds traces of the man himself everywhere. Thus a spokesman for the Tobacco Institute attacks the "McCarthyism" of antismoking activists, while a *Playboy* editor condemns the Meese Commission on Pornography for its "sexual McCarthyism." The author of a recent book on AIDS says that the disease has created "the public health version of McCarthyism," and the editor of the *Journal of American Medicine* claims that urine tests for drug use are "chemical McCarthyism." And in a twist that must have the senator from Wisconsin turning in his grave, a university professor in California has even charged that complaints about the easy access Soviet propagandist Vladimir Posner has to American television are "part of the lingering slime of McCarthyism."

Thirty years after Joe McCarthy's death, "McCarthyism" has become an omnibus synonym for sinister authority and political repression, a word to describe the hate that dare not speak its name. Individuals and parties compete to brand each other with the scarlet *M*, using the term as the moral trump which automatically terminates arguments. Thus liberals sanctimoniously charged former White House communications director Pat Buchanan with McCarthyism when he drew the plausible—if arguable—conclusion that a vote against the *contras* was a vote for Daniel Ortega; and later on, some conservatives who otherwise may harbor a secret fondness for old Joe charged the Senate committee investigating the Iran-contra affair with McCarthyism in its treatment of Oliver North.

In some sense, the term can be dismissed as just another weapon in the language of combat, used equally by all sides of the political debate and often with willful ignorance of its origins. But "McCarthyism" also has a more specific function in our political culture, as a pair of recent events suggests.

The first concerns the furor in the fall of 1987 surrounding a leaked Republican campaign memo about Ohio Senator Howard Metzenbaum's youthful connection with organizations such as the National Lawyers Guild (a Communist front) and the Ohio School of Social Sciences (a Marxist training center, of which he was an incorporator, along with Hyman Lumer, National Education Director of the Communist Party). Although not writing for publication, the Republican authors of the report had a bad case of the jitters, discussing with timorous circumlocution Metzenbaum's past involvement in organizations controlled by Communists (". . . Opponents should cautiously use the material to expose the fact that Metzenbaum's background shows evidence of significant concern for issues of interest to Communist organizations"). They warned Ohio Republicans that if the material got into unfriendly hands, they might be attacked as "McCarthyistic," which is of course exactly what happened when it was leaked to the Cleveland *Plain Dealer*. The authors of the report were blackguarded; Metzenbaum came out of the controversy looking like a martyr.

A similar event with an entirely different outcome had occurred a few months earlier, when George Crockett, three-term black Democrat from Detroit, was named chairman of the House Subcommittee on Western Hemisphere Affairs. Going public with their qualms, a coalition of conservative groups held a press conference in Washington to express alarm, not only about Crockett's enthusiasm for the Sandinistas and his support for American radical groups sending aid to Marxist guerrillas throughout Central America, but even more about his forty-year record of involvement in Communist causes, stretching back to 1947, when Walter Reuther drove him out of the CIO during his purge of Communists from the union. After being purged, Crockett and his law partner founded a firm whose principal clients were the Communist Party and its fellow travelers, the conservatives pointed out. They noted that he had become a regular sponsor of CP front organizations and in 1949 served as one of the counsels for the Party's American politburo who had been indicted under the Smith Act, eventually getting a four-month jail sentence, along with the rest of the Party's defense team, for attempting to disrupt the proceedings. The pattern of forty years earlier was, moreover, still visible in Crockett's record once he arrived in Congress. In 1983, when the Soviets shot down KAL 007 and the House voted 416–0 to condemn this act of murder, Crockett alone abstained; in 1985, when the Soviets shot down U.S. Major Arthur Nicholson in East Germany and denied him medical aid for forty-five minutes while he bled to death, Crockett voted against a House resolution of condemnation.

When the conservative spokesman concluded his summary of Crockett's record, there was a moment of uncomfortable silence, and then a reporter from *Newsweek* spoke up, with a question that had obviously crossed the minds of other journalists in the room: "Isn't this sort of McCarthyism?" The mere mention of this term in effect terminated the press conference. Unlike the case of Metzenbaum, where a report cautiously alluding to some facts in a political figure's background was decried as "McCarthyism" and splashed over the front pages of papers all over the country, here the publicly documented case, dismissed as "McCarthyism," wasn't reported at all.

We may not as yet have returned to a naïveté that would claim Communism is twentieth-century Americanism, but mentioning the distant party affiliations of someone like Senator Metzenbaum or questioning the more profound ties of someone like Congressman Crockett is to provoke a sort of guilty embarrassment for the perpetrator and a protective sympathy for the victim. (This reflex is so pervasive that it has been reified in the nation's political code: The Communist Party is uniquely exempted from election law requirements that campaign donors be identified, on the assumption that they might be subjected to "McCarthyite" harassment.) Political subversion and divided loyalties are now taboo subjects in America's political culture. "Communist" and "fellow traveler" are epithets that seem antique, almost comic. As they have gradually lost their sting, only one term from the 1950s retains the dark power of a political curse: "McCarthyism."

In life, McCarthy was part of the Right. In death, he has been possessed by body snatchers on the Left. The apprehensions aroused by charges of "McCarthyism" are based on the Left's assertion that there is a powerful and destructive impulse lurking just under the surface of our political life: a native fascism easily ignited and ready to rage dangerously out of control. It is an assumption not often questioned, although the evidence suggests that the opposite is true. Arthur Miller's efforts in *The Crucible* to portray it as a peculiarly American atavism notwithstanding, the history of McCarthyism actually shows how alien the witch-hunt mentality is to the American spirit and how superficial its hold on the American psyche. Appearing in the extraordinary circumstances of the postwar period, McCarthyism was brief in its moment and limited in its consequences. And it was complete in the way it was purged from the body politic. The Wisconsin senator's strut on the stage ended in a crushing repudiation by his colleagues in the

Senate and an enduring obloquy in the rogues' gallery of American history, a position close to that of Benedict Arnold and a handful of other villains. His enemies survived to be rehabilitated as martyrs and heroes of an American political "nightmare," while he himself is the only figure from that haunted era to suffer irreparable damnation. The extent to which he has been associated with a social pathology can be seen in a passage from onetime British intelligence officer Peter Wright's *Spycatcher*, in which Wright recalls interrogating Anthony Blunt, the "fourth man" in the Philby spy ring, about yet another spy he had failed to mention in previous debriefings: " 'You said there were no more, Anthony [Wright said]. You said you were telling the truth.' After a pause Blunt replied, 'I could never be another Whittaker Chambers . . . . It's so McCarthyite, naming names, informing, witch hunts.' " Blunt was willing that history judge him as a traitor but not as a McCarthyite.

Why do we hear so much about McCarthyism in the contemporary political debate? Is there a basis for the fear that we will return to the spirit of that brief moment in the 1950s when this bizarre figure dominated our politics? Is there legitimate worry that we will once again be victimized by a pathology that Harry Truman defined in 1951 when he went on television to defend himself against the charge that he had knowingly protected Harry Dexter White (an official in his administration who had been named as a Soviet agent), a pathology that Truman identified as the big lie and the reckless smear; corruption of truth, indiscriminate use of guilt by association, and disregard for due process?

If there is such a danger, it comes not from Joseph McCarthy's followers on the Right, but from the Left, which professes to hate McCarthy's memory. *The Nation* and other left-wing journals regularly smear James LeMoyne, Robert Leiken, Ronald Radosh, and other Central American experts who deny that the Sandinistas are building a utopia as being *contra* hirelings or CIA agents. For his dissent on affirmative action programs, black economist Thomas Sowell was labeled "an enemy of his people" by Roger Wilkins in the same radical journal. There was also the reaction on the liberal left to the appointment of John H. Koehler as Reagan's White House communications director, replacing Pat Buchanan. Once it was discovered that Koehler as a child of ten in his native Germany had belonged briefly to a Nazi youth group, there was a tremendous liberal outcry, although the head of the Jewish Anti-Defamation League observed that it was "ludicrous to judge a 56 year old person by his associations as a 10 year old." After the White House was forced to withdraw the nomination of Koehler under pressure from the Left, it was clear that "Are you now or have you ever been"—even for a month when you were ten years old—is a question that is out of bounds in the political debate only if what you are or were or might have been was a Communist.

It is obviously not the political *methods* of McCarthyism that arouse the indignation of those who invoke its specter today, but the political *ideas* with which McCarthy was associated, specifically his anti-Communism. This is admitted with disarming frankness by New Left professor Ellen Schrecker in *No Ivory Tower*, a tendentious book about the effects of McCarthyism on the university: "After all, what made McCarthy a McCarthyite was not his bluster but his anti-Communist mission. . . ." To dismiss the senator's real malevolence as mere "bluster" may seem fatuous to those familiar with the history of the Fifties, but there is a reason for the use of this term. What Schrecker and others on the Left who have integrated McCarthy into their ideology are saying is that the problem was not the man's methods but what he believed; not his demagogic lack of scruples, nor the psychological demons that sent him careening out of control, but the objectives of his perverse crusade. For them, just as much as for the tiny band of zealots who gather every year at his grave on the anniversary of his death, Joseph McCarthy is a representative American. Yet they summon his ghost not to underscore the importance of civil liberties in a democracy but as part of a morality play about the dangers of anti-Communism. To accuse someone of being a McCarthyite, therefore, has become a way of embargoing ideas that the Left dislikes and invoking cloture on debates that it doesn't want to have.

From the perspective of the Left, McCarthyism preexisted McCarthy. It was the monstrous offspring of the Truman Doctrine, which proclaimed America's opposition to Soviet expansionism. Because of internal security measures and congressional investigations into subversion begun during his presidency, Truman was, in effect, a premature McCarthyite. He made McCarthy possible, according to Left orthodoxy. Thus the revisionist fable: Once upon a time, American liberals indiscreetly embraced a cold war philosophy and an anti-Communist strategy; the result was the surfacing of an indigenous strain of American fascism previously buried beneath the surface of our politics—McCarthyism. Because of the constant repetition of this fable, the present liberal generation directs its vigilance away from the pregnant silences surrounding the commitments of a George Crockett and toward those who are suspicious of what these silences conceal.

Anti-Communism begets McCarthy fascism: It is, after all, a logic that was developed by the Communist Party itself following events of the postwar era. As soon as anti-Communism became the policy of the Truman administration, the Communists marched out of the Democratic Party, where they had camped after the breakup of the Hitler-Stalin pact, and into the new Progressive Party. Appealing to their former liberal allies, they warned that the new anti-Communist policies of the Democrats would lead inexorably to war abroad and fascism at home; if liberals were skeptical, they had only to look at what had happened in Hitler's Germany for a preview of what was in store. One Communist Party publication was entitled "The Deadly Parallel." Disseminated at the time of the 1949 trial of the Party's leaders, it featured photographs of Nazis rounding up first Communists and then Jews and shipping them to Auschwitz, juxtaposed with recent shots of U.S. marshals escorting American Communists to their Smith Act trial and a picture of a detention facility in Allenwood, Arizona, identified as a newly built "concentration camp." The message was simple and clear: The cold war that Truman had launched to oppose the Communists' global advance had put America on the road to a Nazi state. First Communists and then everyone else would fall under the iron boot.

It was one of the few occasions when the Communists believed their own propaganda. After the Smith Act trial resulted in a guilty verdict, the Party interpreted it as the beginning of America's long totalitarian night and sent its leadership into the "underground" so that it would be ready to direct the struggle against the new Nazi order. The rank and file stayed put, denouncing Truman's initiation of security programs as the "internal" cold war required by his cold war abroad. When Joseph McCarthy burst onto center stage following his famous Wheeling speech, the theory seemed confirmed.

McCarthyism preexisted McCarthy: The alleged connection between Truman and the senator from Wisconsin became the thesis for revisionist historians to come. During the Sixties, in fact, it became the dominant thesis about the postwar era. McCarthyism became the brush with which the Fifties was tarred—a "scoundrel time," in Lillian Hellman's phrase, of witch hunts in search of "reds under the beds," of subversives and security risks who didn't exist.

In fact, the historical record shows something quite different. It was only after the Soviets had blockaded Berlin and exploded their first atom bomb, and after Communist armies had invaded South Korea three years later, that an atmosphere was created that a McCarthy could adroitly exploit. The testimony of former Communists and KGB intelligence defectors, as well as evidence revealed under the Freedom of Information Act, shows that the American Communist Party was indeed financed and directed by Moscow, devious in its political agendas and duplicitous in its public face, conspiratorial in its organizational form and treasonous in its ideological heart. Members of the Party like Judith Coplon and Julius Rosenberg *did* spy for their Kremlin masters. Underground Communist cells connected to Soviet intelligence and composed of figures like Alger Hiss and Harry Dexter White *did* attain positions of high influence in areas of policy crucial to the Soviets' interest, while sympathizers like Owen Lattimore and John Stewart Service—later canonized as innocent martyrs burned at the stake of McCarthyism—*did* use their positions to aid the Communists they secretly admired.

The Communist witnesses who eventually invoked the Fifth Amendment before congressional committees and claimed to be progressives concerned about American democracy and the Bill of Rights were in fact members of an international conspiracy whose goal was to exploit democratic institutions in order to serve the Soviet Union. In this sense,

Max Eastman, former Trotskyist, was right when he said that
" 'Red-baiting'—in the sense of a reasoned, documented exposure of Communist and pro-Communist infiltration of government departments and private agencies of information and
communication is obviously necessary . . . [because] we are
not dealing with fanatics of a new idea, willing to give testimony for their faith straightforwardly regardless of cost. We
are dealing with conspirators who try to sneak in their Moscow-
inspired propaganda by stealth and doubletalk."

As a result of Truman's internal security programs,
many Party members did lose their jobs in institutions considered vital to the nation's defense and survival—in government, in the media, and in education. But with extraordinarily
few exceptions, they were not fired from government agencies
and other institutions for holding "unpopular ideas," as the
Communists themselves maintained and as the mythology that
has grown up around the McCarthy period still holds. They
were fired for being members of (or for refusing to cooperate
with inquiries into their membership in) an organization that
was subservient to a hostile foreign power and whose purposes
were inimical to American democracy. Thus Columbia University justified its policy of excluding Communists from its
faculty in the following statement (of which Lionel Trilling,
spokesman for American liberalism, was one of the authors):
"Membership in Communist organizations almost certainly
implies a submission to an intellectual control which is entirely
at variance with the principles of academic competence as we
understand them."

This is not to say, of course, that McCarthy's response
to Communism was not destructive. In his hands, the struggle
against this fifth column was perverted first into a weapon
aimed at the Democrats and ultimately into a scattergun aimed
at his own party, at America, and finally at himself. His reckless
demagoguery did damage to innocent people, and the atmosphere created by his success cast a pall over the political
arena. It imperiled the democratic process, and it destroyed
the credibility of anti-Communism itself. Robert Lamphere,
the head of the FBI counterintelligence team that caught the
Rosenbergs, has since said, "Senator McCarthy's crusade,
which was to last for the next several years, was always anath-
ema to me. McCarthy's approach and tactics hurt the anti-

Communist cause and turned many liberals against legitimate efforts to curtail Communist activities in the United States." Whittaker Chambers saw the problem with McCarthy at the time the problem was unfolding: "All of us, to one degree or another, have come to question his judgement and to fear acutely that his flair for the sensational, his inaccuracies and distortions . . . will lead him and us into trouble. In fact, it is no exaggeration to say that we live in terror that Senator McCarthy will one day make some blunder which will play directly into the hands of our common enemy and discredit the whole anti-Communist effort for a long while to come."

It is easy to see how novelist Richard Condon conceived the premise of *The Manchurian Candidate*.

What is missing from the revisionist mythology about the postwar era, in fact, is the active role of the Communists themselves in creating the tragedy in which Joseph McCarthy starred. Why was the most notorious question of the era asked in the first place: "Are you now or have you ever been . . . ?" Because the Communists concealed who and what they were; because they presented themselves as progressives and patriots even as their covert actions were revealing wholly different values and intentions.

It was they who hid their antidemocratic and anti-American agendas behind "liberal" fronts and facades. If there was an interest in ferreting Communists out of liberal institutions, it was not because the fascist genie had escaped from the unstoppered bottle of American paranoia but because Communists had infiltrated these institutions with their hidden agendas in the first place. If the difference between liberalism and Communism was sometimes difficult to detect, it was not because there was any real identity of purpose or philosophy but because the Communists cynically used liberalism as protective coloration for treasonous activities for the better part of a decade. If the Communists had been forthright about their politics, if Alger Hiss, the Rosenbergs, and other Communist agents had admitted their guilt, could there have been a Joseph McCarthy?

The experience of the radical Sixties certainly suggests that there wouldn't. During the whole of this era, "McCarthyism" was a term that was seldom heard. This was not because

the pathology itself didn't exist. It did—on the Left. In a review
of Schrecker's *No Ivory Tower*, the historian C. Vann Wood-
ward compared the assault on academic freedom from the
Right in the Fifties with the attack on academic freedom from
the Left a decade later:

> The right had used with powerful effect the laws, the
> courts, the subpoena, and the hearings before congres-
> sional committees. Without these instruments at their dis-
> posal, the left employed coercions of a more elemental
> sort. These included mass demonstrations, sit-ins, occu-
> pation and pillaging of presidents' offices and other build-
> ings, picketing and disruption of classes, "trashing" of
> library stacks and catalogs, and on some campuses even
> arson and explosives against laboratories suspected of mil-
> itary connection. The simple expedient of disruption took
> care of speakers with objectionable or nonconformist
> views. . . . As in the earlier era, bitter divisions split ad-
> ministrations, faculties, departments, and colleagues,
> even family members. Several suicides at Cornell have
> been attributed directly or indirectly to the tragic struggle
> on that campus. . . . As in the McCarthy period, there is
> no reckoning the number of books not written, research
> not done, and the standards, values, and ideals be-
> smirched or trashed.

The disappearance of the term "McCarthyism" in the
Sixties cannot be ascribed, either, to a lack of "subversive"
activity, which in fact exceeded anything like it in the past.
Nor can it be attributed to the absence of an anti-Communist
Right, which was in fact gathering momentum through the
Goldwater wing of the Republican Party. The absence of a
"McCarthyist" threat from the Right in the Sixties lies in the
temporarily changed nature of the political Left.

By a coincidence of fate, in 1957, the same year that Joe
McCarthy died in disgrace, the Old Left disintegrated under
the pressure of Khrushchev's revelations concerning the
crimes of Stalin and the Soviets' brutal invasion of Hungary. A
New Left, impressed by the debacle and anxious not to be
involved in its repetition, soon appeared. This New Left had
many faults, but lack of candor was not one of them. Where

Old Leftists had pretended to be progressives and liberals and patriotic Americans, New Leftists insisted on being recognized as Marxists and revolutionaries, pro-Fidel and pro-Vietcong, up against the wall and tear the mother down. It would have caused terminal embarrassment to Sixties Leftists to be accused of concealing their radical agendas inside liberalism or, even worse, to be mistaken for liberals themselves.

The New Left did not want to patiently infiltrate institutions in the American mainstream with whose purposes they were openly at war and whose ends they intended to subvert; they wanted to create their own institutions and to make "a revolution in the streets." It was redundant, as government agencies soon discovered, to interrogate New Left radicals about who they were, because they made no effort to dissemble. Whereas Old Leftists had donned the cloak of the liberal martyr who takes the Fifth only to protect the Constitution, and who is ruefully silent before his inquisitors out of shame for the offense they commit against liberty itself, New Leftists dragged those who threatened to investigate them into their own theater of the absurd. Thus Jerry Rubin's appearance in knee breeches and tricornered hat—American Revolutionary drag—before the decrepit and obsolete HUAC. When asked about his subversive agenda, he said he was a revolutionary and proud of it. And that was that. When the witch says he's a witch, there is no hunt. Thus the "inquisition" of the Fifties ended in the Sixties not as tragedy but as farce.

When the revolution in the streets that the New Left yearned for failed to happen, most of its members disappeared —into health foods, jogging, business school, entrepreneurship, and yuppiedom. The hard core that remained was suddenly overcome by an irresistible nostalgia for the Old Left they had once scorned as politically devious and ideologically ossified. Their own movement had burned itself out in mythomania and histrionics, and in narcissistic fantasies of revolutionary violence. The Communists of the Thirties now seemed admirable for exactly the quality that had once seemed so despicable—their obstinate endurance and their ruthless loyalty to the Party. Whereas during the Sixties they had been scorned as hacks always trying to infiltrate New Left organizations, whose violent spontaneity they then attempted to moderate,

Communists were now seen in a new light—as dogged foot soldiers of "progressivism" who had fought the good fight; who had experienced defeat, disappointment, and even betrayal, but who had also stayed the course and learned a survivorship that might make them good models for what was left of the Left envisioned as the long march ahead.

By themselves, a small and already defeated group of radicals trying to engineer a new attitude toward Communists would not have rippled the national consciousness if they had not been joined by liberals, mired in a self-lacerating post-Vietnam *tristesse*. Indeed, this war had come to seem to them a fulfillment of the old Communist philosophy that the anti-Communist crusade begun by Harry Truman would ultimately cause a defeat abroad and an unraveling at home. If it had not brought fascism, the war had indirectly unveiled, in the Watergate debacle, a crisis that made such possibilities seem less fanciful. If this was America in the Seventies, perhaps those who had rejected it in the Fifties had been right all along.

Out of these feelings was born the public rehabilitation of the discredited Stalinists in mainstream films such as *The Front* (written by one of McCarthy's Communist "victims") and *The Way We Were* and documentaries such as *The Good Fight*. Here, all the old agitprop moralities were again on display as part of a "reassessment" of the Communist experience, which restored integrity and honor and even legitimacy to Stalin's loyal rank and filers. The Communists were presented as they had presented themselves in the postwar era—as martyred defenders of American democracy, hapless scapegoats of American fascism. The villains in this melodrama were not only the troglodytes of the Right, but the treacherous liberals who had tried to protect their own movement from Communist infiltration. Already on the verge of extinction as a result of the war in Vietnam and the takeover of the Democratic Party by the McGovern movement in 1972, these battered anti-Communist liberals were now subjected to a furious attack.

In 1949, Arthur Schlesinger, Jr., had written: "All forms of baiting are okay for the 'anti-anti-Communist' except red baiting. Some of the 'anti-anti-Communists' are not substantively pro-Stalinist. They just seem to have a feeling that a Communist is a rather noble fellow who deserves special consideration in a harsh and reactionary world." In *Naming Names*, his polemic on the blacklist era, *Nation* editor Victor Navasky dismisses Schlesinger's argument as giving in to the malaise that is the root of American evil: "As it turned out, there was only a short distance between denouncing anti-anti-Communists and endorsing the act of informers." It was not just McCarthy who was to blame; it was also the entire liberal tradition which formed the center of gravity for this nation's postwar world view.

But reconstructing the past in a way that made Communist hacks seem heroic and their liberal opponents seem cowards and worse required also resurrecting the Evil One who had been at the center of the Fifties morality play. Thus the exhumation of McCarthy's ghost in the Seventies, which accompanied the rehabilitation of American Communism. The Bible of this new morality was Lillian Hellman's *Scoundrel Time*.

Hellman was canonized by the resurgent progressives as a martyr to the cause, one who had stood up and said no in thunder during the dark time of McCarthy's rule. "I cannot and will not cut my conscience to fit this year's fashions": the sentence would be much quoted by admiring reviewers, who either ignored or were ignorant of the fact that for many years Hellman had willingly cut her conscience to fit the brutal style of Stalin's fashions. She postured in retrospect as an innocent and a naïf, someone who might have been in Moscow during the worst moments of the purge trials but knew nothing about them. But she was not so ill-informed that she couldn't sign an ad in the Communist Party's *New Masses* defending Stalin's atrocities shortly after her return from the U.S.S.R. The ad appeared a few days after the Hitler-Stalin pact and denounced the Congress of Cultural Freedom for spreading the "fantastic falsehood" that the U.S.S.R. was no different from other totalitarian states.*

The problem with this revisionism is that it ignores the

---

* The extent to which Hellman has come to function as an icon and symbol is shown in the way that others intent on rehabilitating American Communism protect her from herself. Thus Navasky in *Naming Names* quotes one of her slips in *Scoundrel Time*—"I do not like subversion or disloyalty in any form . . . "—and seeks to redeem her from this deviation by noting, "She probably meant 'espionage,' not 'subversion.' "

central fact about Hellman and other self-styled "progressives" —that if they had not earlier served Stalinism or maintained a disgraceful silence about its homicidal and subversive nature, there would not have been a field on which a McCarthy could have played. In the current effusion of Leftist nostalgia and propaganda, this is never acknowledged. The realities of the Fifties are not only ignored but purposely mislaid, chief among them the fact that practically all those called before the Mc-Carthy committees *were* Communists—and hence members of a fifth column directed by Moscow—and that, as *Partisan Review* founder William Phillips has noted, "what one was being asked to do was to defend their right to lie about it."

Nonetheless, in the orgy of self-recrimination following the defeat in Vietnam and the Watergate debacle, the specter of "McCarthyism" was embraced as a metaphor for a guilty past to which America must never return. The exhumation of McCarthy's ghost was, for people like Hellman, not an aspect of writing history but a strategy for changing attitudes toward the past and therefore posthumously triumphing over it. It was also a way of rendering the political culture unable to criticize the renaissance of "progressive" politics looming on the horizon, unable to challenge the crucial involvement of the Communists and elements of the hard-core Left in the nuclear freeze movement and in the effort to protect Communist gains in El Salvador and Nicaragua. Joe McCarthy, as it turned out, was a man for all seasons.

From any other vantage, the resuscitation of the McCarthy specter at this historical moment would have seemed to be a matter of strange timing. Exhausted by war and internal division in the late Seventies, the American reality was as far from a "new McCarthyism" as one could imagine. Even with the inauguration of Ronald Reagan, no anti-Communist vigilantes were visible in the political landscape, no retribution was being demanded for a war that had been lost at home far more than on the battlefield abroad. The reality was rather that of a nation overwhelmed to the point of paralysis by feelings of futility and guilt; a nation disarmed by self-doubt, its very tolerance making it vulnerable to strange creeds.

The "lessons" of Vietnam and Watergate that the Left promoted held that America had no real enemies in the outside world or at home. It was threatened only by the phantoms of its cold war paranoia and the hyperactive reflex of its own "national security state." Political institutions responded to this fantasy. Reacting as if America were teetering on the brink of a totalitarian fate, the Congress moved to truncate the nation's external and internal security apparatuses, the CIA and the FBI.

On the face of it, there did not appear to be the kind of evidence of an FBI careening out of control that would warrant the draconian measures the Left was calling for. The most notorious abuse of the Bureau's power cited by critics was its Counter Intelligence Program (COINTELPRO), which had been launched in 1956 as an aggressive campaign against the Communist Party and reactivated in the Sixties against New Left targets like the Black Panther Party and SDS. But it was also true that by the end of the decade, these organizations had begun to reshape themselves as terrorist sects. The Black Panthers had mounted several armed attacks on local police, and in 1969, after a "War Council" in Flint, Michigan, the leadership of SDS had launched an underground "military front" and for five years conducted sporadic bombings and acts of sabotage while successfully eluding the clutches of the allegedly overdeveloped FBI.

In 1971, yielding to a pressure campaign initiated by Left organizations, which called for an investigation of the FBI, J. Edgar Hoover folded the COINTELPRO operation. New restrictive guidelines for the Bureau were authorized by Congress. Under these guidelines, the FBI was barred from surveillance of all political groups, even those whose agendas indicated intentions to engage in illegal and violent acts, like Weatherman before it went underground. Consequently, the Black Panther Party was able to carry out a series of murders in its East Oakland home base, for which no arrests were ever made. And the Weather Underground was able to resurface in 1975 in the form of a rump group that wanted to continue the "armed struggle." Flying new colors as the May 19th Communist Organization, this rump renewed the "war of liberation" against "racist Amerika." Without hindrance from FBI snoopers, these diehard fanatics were able to carry out a string of successful armed robberies to finance their revolutionary fantasy, and to murder innocent people in an abortive robbery attempt on a Brink's armored car in upstate New York.

When Ronald Reagan took office in January 1981, he was presented with a report by intelligence advisers who concluded that "the threat to the internal security of the Republic is greater today than at any time since World War II." The report was no doubt overheated, yet the effort to raise the issue of national security that took place over the next four years served to dramatize how formidable the power of Joe McCarthy's ghost had become in the hands of the Left.

When the new Congress began in 1981, freshman senator Jeremiah Denton announced his intention to head a new Subcommittee on Security and Terrorism. Aware that he would be compared with McCarthy, Denton was careful to separate himself from the abuses of the past, indicating that he had no intention of conducting public investigations of unfriendly witnesses that would turn into show trials.

The response was swift and unequivocal. In a lengthy article, the Washington *Post* warned that the Denton subcommittee was the prelude to a new witch-hunt. The *Post* quoted one authority to the effect that the subcommittee would have the "capability and support to move the country back to the dark ages of McCarthyism." Ironically, this charge was made by the misnamed Center for Constitutional Rights, a new form of the rejuvenated Left, whose architects (William Kunstler, Arthur Kinoy, and Peter Weiss) had long histories of public support for Communist causes and who, in representing such paramilitary groups as the Baader-Meinhof gang and the Black Liberation Army, had attempted to justify terrorist acts and criminal violence by indicting America and its democratic allies as partners in a system of economic oppression and social injustice.

In a previous era, the Center for Constitutional Rights might have been recognized by liberal institutions such as the Washington *Post* as a subversive front for people with covert agendas hostile to the purposes and survival of American democracy. The *Post* might have recognized its own responsibility to expose the radical hypocrisy hidden by the mask of liberal concern for the survival of the Constitution. But the specter of the witch hunt had been raised with such compelling urgency that the newspaper refused to probe behind deceptive surfaces. To do so would be McCarthyism.

Needless to say, the formation of a Subcommittee on Security and Terrorism did not signal America's return to the political Dark Ages. During the five years it was in business, the subcommittee focused its attention almost exclusively on terrorist activities abroad. In 1987, when the Democrats regained control of the Senate, the Subcommittee on Security and Terrorism was quietly put out of business.

During those same years, the global offensive that the Communists had launched after America's defeat in Vietnam had swept fourteen nations into the Soviet orbit on three continents, continuing its advance even to the Central American landmass. About the time that Pat Buchanan was being roundly condemned in Washington as a McCarthyite for his statement that a vote against the *contras* was a vote for Communist expansion, a political rally was held on the West Coast. The occasion for the rally was a "Marxist Scholars Conference" in Seattle, organized by the Communist Party. It was addressed by Herbert Aptheker, a "historian" who for over half a century had proved himself one of the most abject and servile of the Kremlin's loyalists. Aptheker, now a professor of law at the University of California's prestigious Boalt Law School, urged the Marxist professors to return to their campuses and become involved in "imaginative action . . . interfering with the armed forces, interfering with maneuvers, doing everything possible" to oppose the efforts of the U.S. government to stop the Communist advance in Latin America. About Aptheker's incitement to sedition and possible treason, let alone his long-standing commitment to Soviet Communism, the press had no apparent concern. To have commented would have been to commit a McCarthyism.

The "lessons" of McCarthyism in today's political culture come from as partisan a curriculum as the "lessons" of Vietnam. The net result is that today it is improper to regard American Communists as subversive agents of Soviet policy, let alone to pursue the implications of this fact. It is improper to question the divided loyalties of radicals who advance the causes of totalitarian movements such as the Sandinista Leninists and the Salvadoran guerrillas, while simultaneously presenting themselves as liberal critics of government policy. To raise this question would be to bring about another political Dark Ages. We might turn around and find ourselves face to face with McCarthy's ghost.

The term "McCarthyism" as it is used today is thus not a reality recalled but a political blunt instrument to beat critics of Leftism into silence, an aggressive metaphor intended forcibly to deform our worldview. McCarthyism is no longer a term that means character assassination and reckless disregard for due process. McCarthyism means anti-Communism itself. The historical irony is now complete; it means exactly what the Communists claimed it meant back in the Fifties—not an abusive political method but an abusive political objective. The rejuvenation of "anti-McCarthy" vigilance that we see all around us purports to preserve liberal values but ultimately undermines them.

The specter of McCarthyism has cast a spell on American political discourse. It is a spell that creates the self-censorship that prevents us from scrutinizing the records of those in whom we put our political trust. It is a spell that seeks to convince America that the cold war is only a figment of political paranoia, that the only real enemy is our own malignant self. It is a spell, therefore, that indicts and then disarms us, exactly as its creators intended it to do.

There is an antidote for this kind of thinking. It is necessary only to consider the contrast between the era when McCarthy's exaggerations of the security problem permanently removed it from the national agenda and today. Then the Communist expansion was in Eastern Europe and Asia; now it is on the American landmass itself. Then the Communists were stigmatized as fifth-column conspirators, confined to the fringes of political life; now they are tolerated as a party of eccentric hard workers and accepted as equals in the ranks of the solidarity Left. Then the progressives who furthered Communist agendas were isolated in a rump outside the two-party system; now they are inside the Democratic Party and at the center of the system itself. Then McCarthy was an enemy of Communism; now McCarthy is Communism's best friend.

chapter 7 —————————

A Tale of Socialism in One City

SLOUCHING
TOWARDS
BERKELEY

"But I don't want to go among mad people," Alice remarked.

"Oh, you can't help that," said the Cat. "We're all mad here. I'm mad. You're mad."

"How do you know I'm mad?" said Alice.

"You must be," said the Cat, "or you wouldn't have come here."

—Carroll, *Alice in Wonderland*

Even for Berkeley, where municipal politics often attains the status of performance art, the City Council meeting that coincided with the beginning of the 1988 riots on the West Bank was an unusual happening. Five hundred people showed up at the Berkeley Community Theater, all of them first having run a paper gauntlet of handouts from Revolutionary Books, the Israel Action Committee, and Jews Opposed to the Occupation, as well as one anonymous publisher who was giving out typewritten recipes for making Molotov cocktails. Inside the theater, small groups of Jews in yarmulkes were shouting and jabbing fingers at each other, while women wearing *hadas*, the black-and-white Palestinian shawls, were looking on. Of the more than one hundred people who asked to speak, the Council chose nine. One of them was a man who stood up and shouted, "Why are we here? Why do we need to make a statement? Because working in behalf of the oppressed is what Berkeley is *all about!*"

The issue at hand was a recommendation from the city's Commission on Peace and Justice that Council members adopt a Gaza town called Jabalia as a sister city. Ordinarily this would have been no problem. Sister cities are an important part of the iconography of radical politics in Berkeley, which already has a virtual sorority of them: León in revolutionary Nicaragua, San Antonio Los Ranchos in the "zone of popular control" in El Salvador, and Oukasie, a black township in South Africa. But the proposal to adopt Jabalia mobilized a large number of Jews, some of them part of the city's radical *nomenklatura*, who nonetheless drew the line at a measure they regarded as anti-Israel. The resolution lost 6–3, after a bitter debate before the Council and an even nastier one in the audience.

The measure lost in part because passage would have caused deep divisions in the radical community. But in addition to this sudden outburst of pragmatism, a quality not usually associated with Berkeley politics, there was something else at work, a feeling almost of embarrassment at the city's well-known delusions of grandeur. When one of the radicals on the Council mused wearily in the middle of the debate, "In Berkeley we have this sense of megalomania . . .", it was a perception shared by others in the audience. One of the biggest cheers of the evening came for the black minister of the Liberty Baptist Church, who waved aside the soaring rhetoric about the Palestinians and international morality to remind the Council that it had promised long ago to put a stoplight in front of his church and hadn't yet done it. There was also a ripple of assent when one man from among a contingent from

Berkeley's militant homeless yelled out, "Handle your own city first! Adopt the homeless!"

When the meeting had ended and people were filing out, some of them talking in a melancholy way about how the vote suggested that Berkeley seemed to have turned its back on its radical heritage, a reporter paused to ask an elderly woman who had sat through the meeting what she thought. "Oh, I don't know. It is bad what is happening over there. But the West Bank is so far away And we do have other things to worry about, like"—and here she got a look of guilty perplexity on her face—"like potholes. People are suffering around the world, but the potholes on our streets are just terrible. I just don't know. What's a city supposed to be about, anyway?"

What is a city supposed to be about? This is exactly the question that has been agitating Berkeley for two decades now. The answer used to be clear and relatively simple: It was about being a busy and prosperous small town surrounding but not subservient to the campus of the University of California, the semi-independent big city that had grown up in its midst. But somewhere along the line, Berkeley—almost as if adopting the theories of its namesake, the Anglican bishop whose philosophy of subjectivism Dr. Johnson tried to refute by kicking a stone—became a state of mind as much as a place on the map. It became "Berserkeley," the once and future protest town and living museum of insurrection, where the good old days of rage are memorialized in folk murals on the walls of buildings on Telegraph Avenue. It became the "People's Republic of Berkeley," an evil empire of radicalism from the Reagan administration's point of view, but a sister city of the soul for Havana and Managua; a place where the municipal lexicon has been so conscientiously neutered that many of the socially advanced maintain that the plates in the middle of streets must be referred to as "personhole covers"; a place where people commonly talk in the chic Leftspeak that led one self-styled activist recently to address a pressing urban problem in these terms: "Everybody in the country has to deal with cockroaches, but we in Berkeley should take the lead with an environmentally correct, politically progressive solution."

For the radical elite that controls city politics, the question of what Berkeley is supposed to be all about is settled. It is about the symbolism of sister cities and foreign policy "positions"—a mix of third world romance and anti-Americanism recycled from the Sixties; and, more significantly, it is about power—how to seize and redistribute it, how to create new relationships to it among the populace, and how to use it to further the radical vision. For this elite, Berkeley is a radical demonstration project—a "beacon," to use a favorite term of the local Left, for the rest of the country. And, indeed, the Berkeley experiment has become an inspiring example for Madison, Santa Monica, Burlington, and other would-be "socialist" towns across the country. It has been lauded as a bastion of progressivism by socialist leaders around the world. In Berkeley itself, however, there is murmuring in the congregation. Many residents, it seems, who are otherwise quite progressive don't want to live inside a metaphor. There is a bitter self-realization in the graffito that recently appeared on one of the city's walls: "Berkeley—too small to be a nation-state; too big to be an insane asylum."

Radicals have built a formidable political machine in Berkeley, but in the process they have also caused disillusionment on the part of citizens who believe that the new machine has no soul. The opponents are not only members of the Republican old guard, a long-vanquished minority, but also many who once embraced the experiment in municipal Leftism. People like Bill McKay, for instance, a veteran of Berkeley's thirty-year war—the HUAC demonstrations, the Free Speech Movement, the Vietnam protest, People's Park, and eventually the radical seizure of city hall. "It's okay to joke about socialism in one city," he says, "but it's also necessary to get serious about what the radicals have done during their years in power here. They've divided this city right down the middle, that's what they've done. They've set whites against blacks, landlords against tenants, students against long-term residents, people with kids against people without, and so on. The Berkeley of the past, the place we set out to take over and make over? They've destroyed *that* city, and replaced it with something vastly inferior. And in the process they've also done something I thought nobody could *ever* do—they made me into a conservative."

. . .

It may have elements of civic farce, political soap opera, and urban tragedy, but, as Bill McKay's comments suggest, the story of Berkeley is also the story of paradise lost. As late as the early Sixties, it was still the dream city of the 1920s, a time when it was widely regarded as a "California Athens." Backed up into the hills of Tilden Park and looking down onto the Bay, it had the feeling of an elegant small town—confident of itself and smartly turned out as a result of the work of architects such as John Thomas Hudson, Julia Morgan, and above all Bernard Maybeck, whose redwood and brown shingled homes were acknowledged as the exemplary Berkeley habitat.

Republican "downtown" interests controlled city hall in the early Sixties, but municipal politics still had a progressive feel. In 1923, for instance, Berkeley was one of the first places in California to set up a city-manager form of government to eliminate machine politics. The city's police department was widely regarded as a model by municipalities across the country, as was its commitment to parks and open space.

Berkeley demographics changed during the depression, as the city absorbed a large number of blacks fleeing the Jim Crow South in search of jobs. They moved into south and west Berkeley, close to the Bay, in what became known as the Flatlands, buying homes there that were advertised as the "workingman's bungalow." These modest single-family dwellings appreciated in value over the years as the black flatlands developed into a network of stable neighborhoods a world away from the angry ghettos of Oakland, Richmond, and other nearby cities.

At the same time the racial composition of the city was changing, so was the university, as veterans returning from the war swelled the enrollment from 12,000 in 1945 to 25,000 two years later. The federal government pumped money into research, and the state government acknowledged the position of the Berkeley campus as the jewel in its crown of statewide universities. Emerging suddenly as one of the half-dozen best schools in the country, UC was on the way to becoming the "multiversity," a term coined by its president Clark Kerr to describe its profound and reciprocal connections to business, industry, and government.

It was in the Fifties that the university also acquired its distinctive identity as a place involved with left-wing causes, largely as a result of the loyalty-oath controversy that rocked the Berkeley campus in 1952. It was an event that opened wounds which had still not healed a decade later. Fraternity row might be the scene of panty raids and the college high jinks that occurred in other parts of the country, but on Telegraph Avenue there was a political and cultural ferment at odds with the Eisenhower years. By the end of the decade, auguries of a New Left could be seen in the demonstrations against HUAC, the protest against the Caryl Chessman execution, and the emergence of SLATE, a radical student party. The conservative establishment of the Bay Area, whose most palpable symbol was Oakland *Tribune* publisher William Knowland, grumbled about the way that the "little red schoolhouse" had allowed itself to become a staging ground for political mischief and demanded that the administration enforce discipline.

The city of Berkeley, too, was feeling the clash between past and future, in an electoral struggle that broke out between the Republican old guard and a new group of liberals—"hill liberals," as they became known, because of the redoubt of noblesse oblige above the flatlands where they lived. These liberal Democrats had been galvanized by Adlai Stevenson's first presidential campaign in 1952. By the middle of the decade, they had gotten organized and were beginning to elect candidates to the City Council; by the end of the decade, they were ready to make a serious bid for power.

There was a liberal renaissance all over the state, as the growing influence of the California Democratic Council and similar organizations showed. But the liberal movement in Berkeley was *sui generis*, resting on a distinctive coalition between whites of the hills and flatlands blacks, who, because of neighborhood stability and other factors, had a sense of connectedness and upward mobility not seen in other minority communities in the Bay Area. Perceiving the local Democratic Party as a vehicle for advancement, blacks joined whites to form the Berkeley Democratic Caucus. They took white candidates for the City Council around in the flatlands, and whites did the same for their candidates in the hills. White liberals soon became an active minority on the Council, and by the early Sixties, blacks, too, were getting elected. In 1961, when black lawyer Wilmont Sweeney joined the Council, the liberals finally had their majority in Berkeley city government.

Coming after a long political struggle, the liberal era seemed as if it would last forever. There was an ambitious agenda. Integration, fair housing, rational development, affirmative action: all these issues were raised in Berkeley before they became national causes. But if there was one issue that summarized the liberal dream of progress more than any other, it was school integration, the issue Berkeley liberals had grappled with by developing a visionary yet hardheaded plan for the citywide busing of all public school children. Unprecedented in scope and magnitude, the plan called not only for the city's black children to be bused to schools in the hills but for white kids to be taken to the flatlands. The integration plan provoked a bitter response from the city's old guard, but school board president Carol Sibley and the liberal establishment stood fast, triumphing over a recall attempt. The Berkeley School Plan stood out as something unique in an era pinioned between awakening minority aspiration and racial backlash. A commitment to do voluntarily what the rest of the nation would do later on only under sullen coercion, school integration defined the kind of city Berkeley was.

In the mid-Sixties, in fact, Berkeley should have been that shining city on the hill, as liberal leader Carol Sibley later said. It was firmly committed to the liberal vision of a decent and compassionate society. Its politics was dominated by a painstakingly assembled coalition of black and white, and by a worldview that assumed all social problems could be solved. In that regard, Berkeley was the quintessential city of a can-do era; not surprisingly, it was also wounded by the Sixties as no other American city was.

The event that opened a fault line between the city's past and its future was the Free Speech Movement of 1964. The first major student uprising in decades, the FSM was supported by much of the Berkeley political community. At first, it seemed yet another example, albeit a somewhat raucous one, of Berkeley exceptionalism. Some of the euphoria receded in the aftermath of the protest, however, when the city became a radical mecca attracting left-wing pilgrims from all over the country, people who wanted to be present for the fire next time.

In 1967, after the Be-In across the Bay, Berkeley began to sprout communes and collectives; it gained a subpopulation of "street people." Almost overnight, the city had become a theater at which there were not enough seats to go around. Telegraph Avenue was now one of the most famous promenades in the country, and young people came from all over the country to put in an appearance, arriving without money and with only vague expectations, like the Gold Rush immigrants one hundred years earlier. Berkeleyans set up institutions like the Free Church and the Free Clinic, and gave away clothes and food. But there was no putting off the reckoning. A new sort of person had come to town: a person who was in Berkeley because of its presumed radicalism and who wanted the city to live up to its reputation for action.

After the Free Speech Movement, the question had always been what would come next. The answer soon appeared: Vietnam. In the spring of 1965, the University was the site of one of·the first major college teach-ins on the war. That fall marked the beginning of a series of marches and protests, which quickly escalated in size and radical content. The liberal city government reacted sympathetically. But good intentions had become grounds for suspicion rather than understanding. Events of the next few years would be discerned through the haze of tear gas.

With heavy doubts, many Berkeley liberals had backed LBJ at the beginning of the war. As one escalation followed another, many of them simply retired from liberalism. Those who didn't were left dangling as the Johnson administration dissolved into dissonance and incoherence. Once forced to retreat, they became inviting targets for an evolving radical movement whose philosophy was based chiefly on one tenet: that liberals—cold war liberals, corporate liberals, and, in Berkeley, especially the *hill liberals*—were responsible for all the woes of the world.

Until 1968, the attention of Berkeley radicals had been focused on national symbols of the war, such as the Oakland

Army Induction Center. But that summer, a few weeks before the riots at Chicago, Berkeley's Young Socialist Alliance decided that it was time to shut down Telegraph Avenue. The announced purpose of the demonstration was a show of solidarity with the French students then fighting in the streets of Paris, but there was also a restlessness among radicals who believed that Berkeley liberals had got a free ride during the post-FSM, era. As YSA leader Peter Camejo said, "There has been no action in Berkeley for a long time, and we have to create something."

What ensued was a full-fledged riot, in which police battled demonstrators for the first time and in which they were physically assaulted for the first time by radicals using steel bars, chunks of concrete, and Molotov cocktails. "We set barricades on fire," one of the rioters wrote euphorically later on in an underground newspaper, "and someone even had the balls to set a cop on fire."

Over the next year, the City Council, most of whose members also opposed the war, found itself in the classic liberal bind: to show its good faith, it allowed the radicals more and more freedom; but a situation had evolved in which more, by definition, could never be enough. The city fell under the rule of quotidian violence and ritualized confrontation. A summary moment occurred in the spring of 1969, in the struggle over a city block of land just off Telegraph Avenue owned by the university, which planned to make it into a field for student athletics. Hippies and street people had congregated there, planting it and, under the influence of the nascent ecology movement, claiming it as their own "People's Park." After an unsuccessful attempt to compromise, the university fenced the area and brought in police to protect it. Soon a coalition of students and nonstudent lumpen decided to "take the park." In the riot that followed, law-enforcement units from all over the area arrived to back up the beleaguered Berkeley police. Officers were stabbed and assaulted; one demonstrator was killed by a shotgun blast and another was blinded by birdshot. Afterward, there was random violence throughout the city, and a mass arrest of nearly five hundred demonstrators before Governor Reagan called out the National Guard. Some thirty thousand people attended a peaceful march a few days later that institutionalized People's Park as a symbol of post-revolutionary Berkeley, which was now a "liberated zone," in Tom Hayden's phrase, within the deathscape of Amerika.

If the FSM had marked the beginning of an era in Berkeley, People's Park marked the end. The war was starting to wind down, and the New Left was about to implode in the dada of hippiedom and in fantasies of armed struggle and "revolutionary violence." Was there life after Vietnam? In Berkeley, some radicals had already decided that there was, although it was a life involving diminished left-wing expectations. They would have to settle for taking over the city instead of taking over the country. The beginnings of an agenda already existed, albeit somewhat crudely phrased, in the Berkeley Liberation Program, which Hayden and his collaborators had put together during People's Park. "The people of Berkeley must arm themselves and learn the basic skills and tactics of self defense and street fighting," they had written. And then: "We will expand and protect our drug culture. . . . We will break the power of the landlords and provide beautiful living for everyone. . . . We will create a soulful Socialism in Berkeley."

Radicals had shown a passing interest in city government a few years earlier, in 1967, when a slate headed by Robert Avakian (future maximal leader of the Revolutionary Communist Movement) ran for City Council, and Jerry Rubin ran for mayor. But in keeping with the temper of the times, the campaign had been primarily "educational" in nature, an attempt to do consciousness raising on the municipal level, and the radical candidates had all lost by significant margins. After People's Park, however, the focus was on Berkeley—the municipality rather than the state of mind—in a way that it hadn't been before. Radicals got a taste of power when they elected local black community organizer Ronald Dellums to the Berkeley City Council in 1970 and, the following year, to Congress. They formed an ad hoc organization called the April Coalition to decide on a slate of candidates to run for city office in 1971.

The April Coalition first had to deal with an internal conflict between the "ideologues," who were suspicious of electoral politics and especially of the Democratic Party and wanted primarily to attack and destroy the local "power structure," and the "pragmatists," who believed that it was worth working inside the Democratic Party to gain power and make radical social changes in the city. The pragmatists won out and decided to support two candidates for the four seats being contested in 1971—a self-described "radical housewife" named Loni Hancock and a UC student named Rick Brown. Worried by the fact that they had few blacks in the organization, members of the Coalition gave the other two endorsements to a pair of young, well-educated black radicals named D'Army Bailey and Ira Simmons, who had shown up in town on the political make.

In the general election, three of the Coalition-backed candidates won—Hancock, Bailey, and Simmons. In addition, Warren Widener, an incumbent black councilman running with the backing of the Coalition, was elected mayor. The radicals were still a minority on the Council, and would remain one for many years; but from this moment onward, they called the tune and the city of Berkeley did the dance.

The temper of the time was expressed as much in the initiatives that the radicals sponsored as in their candidates. A Black Panther Party–backed measure on the 1971 ballot for "Community Control of the Police" (it would have split the department into districts, forced officers to live in the district where they worked, and put them under the control of neighborhood councils) failed, but it cleared the way for other anti-police measures and for the final triumph of the paranoid view of law enforcement and the romantic view of criminality. In 1973, for instance, after his men had seized better than $1 million worth of narcotics during the previous few months, Berkeley's chief of police appeared before the City Council to ask for permission to apply to the state for money to help in the fight against dealers. Instead he was grilled by the radicals, Councilwoman Hancock accusing him of wanting to set up an "undercover surveillance mechanism." The Berkeley police department, at this point still regarded as one of the most efficient and progressive in California despite the city's "troubles," was decimated by resignations, losing almost half its officers between 1971 and 1973.

Despite its successes in altering the nature of civic discourse, however, the April Coalition was unable to mount a final challenge to the liberal majority on the Council. Part of the reason had to do with the disorder of its own house. D'Army Bailey had proved to be a loose cannon on the radicals' deck, more interested in his own version of a cultural nationalist agenda than in their program. He disrupted City Council meetings with obscenities and diatribes, and attacked members of the Coalition freely, including Loni Hancock, whom he called, "the spokesperson for the white ruling class." When he was subjected to a recall election, radicals sat it out, allowing him to be removed from office.

But it was not just a matter of personalities. Radicals saw that they had to change their approach if they were to be more than a sideshow in Berkeley politics. By 1975, two decisions had been hammered out. The first was that radicals would henceforth refer to themselves as "progressives." The reason for this move, as one member of the Coalition said, was that Berkeley was overwhelmingly "liberal," and thus "class identification" was confusing; it was necessary, therefore, "to accommodate to a wide range of supporters with similar populist and radical goals." The other decision was to replace the April Coalition with a more permanent membership organization, which would function roughly as a vanguard party in the effort to build socialism in one city.

This idea was partially that of Congressman Dellums, who needed to keep the peace among fractious radicals at home so he could devote his attention to Washington, where he was part of a small group trying to steer the Congressional Black Caucus toward an ultra-Left identity. But radicals also had their own reasons for wanting a membership organization that would be a year-round presence in Berkeley politics. Such an organization would instill discipline, and when the radicals finally took over, it would provide coherence in program and personnel. It was decided that Berkeley Citizens' Action, as they christened the new organization, would have a twelve-person steering committee made up of one-half "third world" and women, along with two students, one gay, one senior, and one disabled. To ensure the radical character of the organization, prospective candidates asking for endorsement would have to submit a detailed inventory of their stands on issues ranging from abortion to America's Mideast policy. As one cynic said later on, "This is where we ask things like, 'Do you masturbate?' And, 'Do you read Karl Marx while you're doing it?' "

The appearance of Berkeley Citizens' Action showed that radicals now understood that power in municipal politics grew out of the barrel of organization. There had to be structure; there also had to be long-range objectives. The organization's philosophy was influenced by *The Cities' Wealth*, a document by some local "urban theorists," which appeared at about the same time that BCA was formed.

Much of *The Cities' Wealth* was radical boilerplate, clichés about the "power structure" that had been in the air since C. Wright Mills. What was original in this document was the notion that the appropriate objective for a radical movement was seizure of the resources of a city—its money, property, and influence—which it could then use to entrench itself in power while changing the basic structures of civic life. *The Cities' Wealth* showed how rent control, for instance, might become the key to power in a place like Berkeley. And what the authors envisioned was something more far-reaching than simply capping rent increases or regulating capricious eviction policies. "By enacting rent control legislation and thereby restricting investors in future rentals," they wrote, "a city may actively reduce the present value of a property. This is essentially community expropriation in favor of tenants."

Members of Berkeley Citizens' Action saw that they could take power if they were able to use this sort of thinking to exploit the divisions that already existed in the city and to forge a constituency of former Sixties politicos, environmentalists, street people, and neighborhood activists. To these the late Seventies added the most important group of all, UC students—transient, without roots or responsibilities in the community—who were especially susceptible to intoxicating rhetoric and idealistic appeals. It took time for them to realize it, but the radicals had been given their victory when eighteen-year-olds were given the vote: this was the key to a majority coalition that would support the vision of expropriated wealth and slow-motion class warfare articulated in *The Cities' Wealth*.

• • •

Throughout the mid-Seventies, people in the hills talked
in hushed tones about the struggle for Berkeley's soul. But it
was not clear to them exactly what they could do. Traditional
liberals did form the All Berkeley Coalition (ABC, in the evolving alphabet soup of city political groups). But unlike the BCA,
it was not a party; the ABC was only an endorsing and a fund-
raising group, an attempt to counterpunch and hold the line.
In fact, liberalism, Berkeley's *ancien régime*, faced a crisis of
identity. Even though they were the same people who had
broken the Republicans' control of city hall back in the early
Sixties, those who formed the ABC were now regarded as the
"false" Democrats. The "true" Democrats were now those who
belonged to the party of Ron Dellums. "Liberalism" had become a bad noun in Berkeley unless it was preceded by the
adjective "left" and unless it was committed to the popular
frontism of "progressive" politics.

In fact, the major obstacle standing in the way of the
radicals was not the liberals but the residents of Berkeley's
flatlands. There was only a handful of blacks in Berkeley Citizens' Action, most of them regarded as opportunists who had
seen that the organization's preferential option for ethnicity
guaranteed them almost immediate leadership positions. But
the BCA had no base in Berkeley's black community, which in
fact was deeply suspicious of the radicals and resented what it
regarded as their manipulation of racial and ethnic issues.
Blacks knew that they had realized real gains as a result of the
coalition they had built with white liberals in the Fifties and
were wary of seeing these gains jeopardized. As Wilmont Sweeney, one of the chief spokesmen for the black community, said:
"The radicals make a mistake. They fail to realize that politically a lot of black people are conservative. Its been tough for
them to accumulate capital or property and they're not interested, like radicals, in doing things with one roll of the dice."

For BCA radicals, however, such remarks were "objectively racist," and Sweeney and others like him were simply
"bourgeois." They made it clear that their organization would
continue to search for its own "authentic" blacks as an antidote
for such conservatism. They found one in Eugene "Gus" Newport, who showed up at the 1979 BCA nominating convention
looking to become Berkeley's mayor.

The logical nominee that year was John Denton, an eighteen-year Berkeley resident, BCA stalwart, and Council member, with strong local credentials as an environmentalist as a result of the Neighborhood Protection Ordinance he had helped draft. But Denton was middle-aged and middle-class, and worst of all, he was a white male. Dellums operatives at the nominating convention let it be known that the BCA would not be regarded as "progressive" if outgoing black mayor Warren Widener, whom they hated, was replaced by a white man, even one who was in their camp. They browbeat and harangued the convention into accepting Newport, a newcomer to Berkeley, who claimed to have been a manpower resource consultant in the East and a onetime aide to Malcolm X. After six bruising ballots, Denton lost out.

During the ensuing campaign, Newport succeeded in calming voters' doubts by saying that he was no ideologue but rather a "bureaucrat who analyzes the feasibility of new programs." Once he was elected, however, it was clear that Newport was serious only about one thing: establishing a foreign policy for Berkeley. The kind of foreign policy it would be was indicated by his first trip as mayor—to Cuba for the "nonaligned" countries conference manipulated by Fidel Castro. Soon after, Newport was globe-trotting for the World Peace Council, a front created by Stalin in 1949, which had resurfaced in the late Seventies as part of the Soviet propaganda effort to mobilize opinion against the installation of U.S. missiles in Europe. As Newport showed up repeatedly at WPC events in Czechoslovakia, Sweden, Finland, Spain, and elsewhere, there were jokes about "Galloping Gus" and about the advent of the "People's Republic of Berkeley." But some BCA insiders were not amused; in fact, they feared that a significant transition had been made in the organization. "Everything was different," BCA organizer Clifford Fred later said. "There were no longer open discussions inside the organization, no free flow of ideas. You had a sense that someone had forced focus away from local issues toward some kind of party line on 'World Peace.' "

As Newport became ascendant, Loni Hancock and other old hands of the BCA faded into semiretirement. But most of Berkeley's activists approved of the new course and of the slogan that now began to be heard in BCA circles: "Think Globally, Act Locally." After all, this was why they had seized control of the city in the first place: to make Berkeley a beacon. Nor was there much concern when Newport began to fill key roles in city hall with members of the local Communist Party. Only a few former New Leftists with a strong historical sense were bothered. "It was ironic," one of them says. "Back in the Sixties, we had always had scorn for the Communists. They were party hacks, zombies repeating everything the Russians said. We laughed at them. Now here they were in the Eighties at the center of things in Berkeley. You didn't know why, and you couldn't say a goddamned thing about it, because if you did you'd be accused of 'McCarthyism' or 'red-baiting.' We were prisoners of our own rhetoric."

Eldridge Cleaver, darling of Berkeley radicals twenty years earlier, when efforts to block his lectures at the University had caused large demonstrations, but now their *bête noir* as a result of his reincarnation as a Moonie, said: "Ron Dellums is a tool of Moscow and Havana, and Gus Newport is a tool of Dellums." The comment was widely disregarded as more of Cleaver's reactionary raving, but it was true that Newport took his cues from Dellums and that both hovered near the Soviet Line. Like the congressman, Newport trumpeted the virtues of Fidel Castro; like Dellums, he was rabidly supportive of the new regime in Grenada, setting up a U.S.-Grenada Friendship Society in Berkeley and sponsoring a visit by New Jewel Movement ambassador Dessima Williams. After the U.S. invasion, in fact, Newport led a large Berkeley street protest, which featured a burning of the American flag. ("Tonight we have seen some of the greatest demonstrations since Vietnam," he said. "I'm very proud of the students and citizens of this town.") He almost got a resolution through the City Council condemning the Reagan administration for "the death of Maurice Bishop . . . and all the others who lost their lives as a result of the invasion," until another Council member noted dryly that the dictator had actually been killed by his fellow Grenadian Communists, not by Ronald Reagan.

Refocusing on Central America as the Euromissile issue became old news, Newport traveled to El Salvador to visit San Antonio Los Ranchos, Berkeley's sister city in the "zone of popular control." Claiming he had come under fire there by government forces, he returned to testify before Congress about the "U.S. Air War," part of a concentrated effort on the part of Leftists to get Congress to cut off aid to the Duarte government. (Later, it would be revealed that San Antonio Los Ranchos, in whose behalf the pro-guerrilla Berkeley support group New El Salvador Today had collected several thousand dollars from city residents, had actually ceased to exist some time earlier, its inhabitants having abandoned it because of the civil war.) Newport also went to Nicaragua, where he met with Daniel Ortega and established another sister city for Berkeley in León.

Some Leftists were disturbed by the fog of "solidarity" politics that had descended on the city, but other than a random potshot now and then ("Why don't we get some priorities a little closer to home," black BCA member Jerome Wiggins once asked, "like maybe a sister city in the South Bronx?"), few spoke out openly against it. There was little opposition elsewhere. Republicans had long since become a vanished breed, moving out of politics if not out of town. And the liberal Democrats who might have provided a center of gravity that would have counterbalanced Newport's programmatic anti-Americanism were so traumatized by events of the Sixties and intimidated by the Left's liberal-bashing that they did not dare claim center ground. "We had no choice but to say, in effect, me too," one of these liberals noted later on. "Gus would raise the issue of U.S. 'imperialism' in Central America. It's clear how we should have responded—'That's garbage.' But if we'd said this, we would have been ripped as 'reactionaries' and seen even the diminishing influence we had in city politics disappear. So all we could say was, 'Yes, we, too, believe more or less what Gus believes, except we're not quite so radical about it.' Obviously, this wasn't a position that did much for us or the city."

During this period, someone compared going to City Council meetings with having Elmer's Glue injected into your veins. But people not only went but stayed on into the early-morning hours, in large part because hidden agendas had a habit of appearing round about midnight. Many of the meetings wound up being about "racism," which, as one observer noted, functioned as an omnibus charge for radicals the way "communism" had for McCarthy. Although there were few blacks in the organization, the BCA continued to use black people as the rationale for its policies, a fact that never ceased to rankle. ("Always they say, 'We're doing this for poor people and black people,' " black activist Pam Sanford says. "My question is who asked them to? Black people in this city were doing just fine before these folks took over.")

One particularly lacerating issue was the radicals' decision to change the name of Grove Street to Martin Luther King Way. Many of the older blacks in South Berkeley were upset, not only because Grove Street had a long and important past, but also because many of those now pushing the name change had dismissed King in the Sixties as a sellout and a "Tom." One of those who spoke before the City Council against changing the name was an elderly black woman named Tara Hall Pittman, longtime vice-president of the local NAACP; she was joined by Carol Sibley, now in her eighties and almost blind. One disaffectd BCAer, Merrilee Mitchell, was sickened by the ensuing scene. "The crowd booed and hissed and shouted 'racist' at these women. It was disgusting: all these CP types packing the meeting with a bunch of black high school students and inciting them to this kind of disrespectful behavior."

In the end, the black community went along with the move to rename Grove, gratuitous though it seemed, because of the powerful symbolism of King's name. But it remained suspicious of white radicals who had destroyed the old and, from their point of view, productive liberal consensus. Onetime Carter administration appointee Janet Roche, who grew up in the Berkeley flatlands, said: "The BCA people feel that if you're not for them, you're against them. Often those blacks they view as against them are people with long-standing involvement in Berkeley politics and real concerns about the livability of their neighborhoods." Her sentiments were echoed by Carroll Williams, a former Yale professor, who served as chairman of the Berkeley school board: "We black people are used by Berkeley's white radicals. It's in the interest of these whites to cite the condition of blacks as the motivating factor in their agenda. But it doesn't mean that blacks fare better under their regime. We're talking about white radicals who want to be the new elite. I don't think they necessarily mean us any harm; it's just that we're irrelevant to them—invisible, you might say."

Despite the deepening polarization of the city, however, Berkeley exceptionalism was shown once again in 1984, when, in the middle of the Reagan landslide, the student-heavy electorate supported the Left overwhelmingly, electing Newport to another term and giving the BCA an eight-to-one majority on the City Council. It seemed as though the BCA could now have its way with Berkeley, and that the half-joking slogan "socialism in one city" would become a reality. But as one of the few admitted conservatives in town cheerfully observed later on, "They didn't know it, but Thermidor had arrived."

If it was still not safe to criticize the BCA's foreign policy, Berkeley residents could and did point out that some domestic matters were getting neglected, notably the city's much-discussed streets, which were cratered with potholes, and its sewer system, which was decaying rapidly. Also, crime had risen astronomically—some thought because of radical revisionist views on criminals and the criminal justice system. (According to a 1988 report by the federal government, Berkeley was now the fifth most dangerous city in the United States, joining such urban heavyweights as Detroit.) Disturbing echoes of the 1969 Berkeley Liberation Program's insistence on support for "the people's right to drugs" could be heard in the open bartering for narcotics that took place on the streets of South Berkeley.

Radical governance had also involved an appalling waste of money. Some $2 million had been spent on the recycling of solid waste during the ascendancy of the BCA, for instance, money that was supposed to result in a recycling rate of 50 percent, but had achieved only about a quarter of that amount —about the same rate as in neighboring communities that spent only a fraction of what Berkeley did on recycling.

Newport himself was also fair game now, because the city, for two decades a theater, had become under his administration a theater of the absurd. Early in his administration, for instance, he had invited a company that manufactured electric cars to relocate in Berkeley as an example of the enterprise that could flourish in a place that had seceded from American greed; then it was discovered that the head of this new-age business had a record as a white-collar criminal. Newport ran up large bills on the city's credit card; he failed to report payments given to him by various Leftist and Communist organizations before which he appeared. He might be taken seriously as Mayor Newport in revolutionary councils around the world, but at home he was just plain Gus, a phlegmatic, almost comic figure when not tearing a passion to tatters over some international *cause célèbre*.

There was also a growing disillusionment over the fact that the BCA, for all its talk about morality, acted like any other political machine once in power, a sort of radical Tammany packing a proliferating array of city boards and commissions with its time-servers, who played an increasingly important, although largely invisible, policy-making role. The recycling companies that got city contracts were large BCA contributors. BCA Council members voted themselves large expense accounts and then used the money to make contributions to Dellums and the radical causes he favored.

When the BCA took over the administration of some federally funded low-cost housing units on an attractive South Berkeley site called Savo Island, applicants had to fill out lengthy questionnaires, which asked, among other things, for a list of the local organizations in which they had worked, a veiled invitation to show how "progressive" their politics were. To no one's surprise, BCA rank and filers like Florence MacDonald, former BCA city auditor and mother of the singer Country Joe, often got these choice units, while poor people whose politics happened to annoy BCA functionaries got evicted.

If the BCA knew how to reward its friends, it also didn't hesitate to punish its enemies, especially those it turned up within its own ranks. One of them was Myron Moskowitz, a lawyer who had not only worked with Cesar Chavez in the Sixties and the Seventies but also drafted Berkeley's rent control law and fought it successfully on appeal up to the California State Supreme Court. Moskowitz's mistake was to tell a newspaper reporter that he thought a BCA plan to extend rent control to commercial properties on Telegraph Avenue would only reward economic inefficiency. He immediately received a call from a BCA functionary upset over his comments. Moskowitz noted that the organization, with its huge majority on the City Council, could scarcely be hurt by a little opposition. "You don't understand," he was told. "We don't want any opposition *at all.*" Soon after this conversation, an agenda item honoring Moskowitz for his fight in behalf of residential rent control was dropped from a City Council meeting, and when it came time for the city rent control law to be argued before the U.S. Supreme Court, Moskowitz found that he had been excluded from the legal team.

Episodes like this led some to whisper that the BCA was Stalinist, although the stigma against "red-baiting" made "arrogant" the only term acceptable in public discussion. By 1986, however, questions were being raised not only about the style of the organization but about the radical program as well.

Not even rent control, which had until this time enjoyed status as a sacred cow, was exempt from the new scrutiny. Rent control laws had become ever more strict in the decade they had been in effect in Berkeley, narrowing the definitions of who and what were covered, eliminating the loopholes through which some landlords tried to avoid registering their properties, and increasing the penalties for those who took advantage of tenants. Berkeley prided itself on always being a step ahead on this issue. When the state legislature passed a bill allowing evictions if a landlord sold his house, for instance, the Berkeley City Council immediately responded with an ordinance mandating six-months notice, a relocation fee of $4,500, and other mitigating measures in behalf of the tenant.

Landlords and libertarians had always been critical of rent control, of course, claiming that it fomented conflict while also diminishing the incentive to build new units and creating a bloated and self-serving bureaucracy. (Receipts from obligatory registration fees, which had risen from twelve dollars a unit in 1980 to eighty dollars seven years later, had given the Berkeley Rent Board a budget of more than $1 million by 1988.) Yet now rent control was suddenly under attack from the Left as well as the Right, in a study entitled "Who Benefits from Rent Control?" published by the Center for Community Change, an Oakland-based advocacy group for the poor.

The study showed that if the intended beneficiaries of

rent control were middle-aged and middle-class whites, then Berkeley's law was a considerable success, but it was a resounding failure if it was supposed to help low-income people. Author Richard Devine marshaled an impressive array of statistics in demonstrating that Berkeleyans spent an unusually large percentage of their income on luxuries such as stereos and jewelry. They also ate out far more frequently than the norm, a fact that had probably led to the success of the city's "gourmet ghetto" spreading outward from Alice Waters's celebrated Chez Panisse, the restaurant that had made California cuisine internationally famous. Radicals who in other contexts readily admitted that eating well was the best revenge rushed to deny this implication of Devine's work, until someone pointed out a statement made in 1985 by Marty Schiffenbauer, one of the architects of Berkeley rent control: "This city has had enormous success for the last five or ten years based on the gourmet food business and I think rent control has a lot to do with it."

The study also noted that there had been a disastrous decline of housing during the era of rent control, with rental assets being taken off the market and an average of less than five privately financed units a year being built in what had previously been one of the best rental markets in California. As a result, there was housing chaos for the nearly 30,000 students in the city, and Berkeley's homeless population, like that of other rent-controlled cities across the country, had mushroomed. ("The policy has had the perverse effect of exacerbating, rather than alleviating, tenants' problems, because it has discouraged for-profit housing developers from investing . . . and has stimulated the conversion of rental units to owner occupancy.") The final conclusion of *Who Benefits from Rent Control?* was devastating: "Passed by a majority of middle class voters who clearly promoted their self-interest, but under the fabrication that they were responding to a 'housing crisis' . . . this policy has had the perverse effect of institutionalizing the problem it is supposed to solve."

BCA radicals could rationalize the bad news about rent control. However negative its impact on the poor, it did benefit their cadre and constituents, and it did fit into their *jihad* against the local ruling class. (One candidate for the BCA endorsement for rent control board said in 1986, "I'm for what is fair for tenants and landlords. The tenants deserve a decent and affordable place to live and the landlords—well, the landlords aren't even human as far as I'm concerned.") But a far more serious indictment of the BCA regime came from Berkeley parents, who now charged that the organization was destroying a school system that had until a few years earlier been regarded as one of California's finest.

Berkeley's commitment to an integrated quality education had been compromised even before the BCA took power at the school board. In 1971, bowing to pressure from radicals under the sway of black power, school administrators had obtained a windfall of grants totaling some $7 million for a series of experimental minischools whose emphasis would be on ethnicity. Favored by radicals who thought integration was lacking in chic, these minischools—places where blacks would study blackness and Hispanics *chicanismo*—upset parents, who worried that the school district would be racially and intellectually balkanized. These fears were dismissed at the time as reactionary, but by the mid-Seventies, test scores and other evaluations showed that the program, which had monopolized the attention of the school district and caused considerable conflict among students, was indeed an academic fiasco. The two most important minischools, Black House and *Casa de la Raza*, were both shut down by the federal government—ironically, because they promoted segregation. The experiment had wasted millions of dollars; the assumptions about "cultural nationalism" on which it was based had had a demoralizing effect on the school system as a whole. Louise Stoll, the "radical" member of the Berkeley school board at that time, now says that the problem was knee-jerk acceptance of the radical-chic black power ideology: "Nobody even thought about the impact all this would have on a district which a year and a half earlier had embarked on the most important experiment in education in America—the voluntary desegregation of an entire system."

By the early 1980s, a sense of incoherence had gripped a school district that before had had an unusually strong sense of purpose. A community that in the early Sixties had voluntarily raised its taxes and transported students all over the city to achieve integration was now witnessing the massive defec-

tion of children from the public school system. The number
of private schools had risen from six in 1970 to twenty-three by
1985; some 22 percent of Berkeley students were being educated privately, better than twice the state average. Nor was it
only white children who were deserting the Berkeley schools;
high-achieving children of all ethnic backgrounds were leaving
Berkeley schools, their parents voting no with their feet and
their pocketbooks. Black parents who kept their children in the
district were dismayed by test scores showing that their children began kindergarten equal with whites and well above the
national average but, by the ninth grade, slipped far back to
the lowest 23rd percentile at the same time white students
continued to move forward.

The Berkeley schools faced a fiscal crisis as well as an
educational one. Berkeley got better than $500 a year more per
student than comparable districts, and its teachers were among
the lowest paid in the state, yet the district was in chronic
financial difficulty. In 1983, the BCA, which now had a majority on the school board, unveiled a plan to solve the district's
money problems by closing schools. The superintendent's office claimed that $1 million could be saved this way. Non-BCA
school board members were dubious, especially after the figure
was quickly revised downward under sharp scrutiny to less than
$300,000. Financial analysts invited to testify at board meetings
said that savings would be further decreased because of losses
in state revenue that would undoubtedly occur when another
group of parents became alienated and pulled their children
out of the schools. Pediatricians testified that the decrease in
the birth rate Berkeley had experienced—another reason advanced to justify the closings—was a transient phenomenon,
and that by the end of the Eighties the city would find itself in
the middle of a mini baby boom requiring more school space,
not less. The question of economy was further muddied by
revelations that the school board was already leasing surplus
property at rates well below the market value to BCA political
allies like Dellums and State Assemblyman Tom Bates, and to
"politically correct" organizations like New El Salvador Today
and CISPES.

But what raised the ire of parents was the suspicion that
saving money was not the only or even the most important

reason for BCA support of school closings. As the debate over schools sharpened, many of them became convinced that the radicals were using the financial crisis as an excuse to continue their homegrown version of the class struggle by other means —especially to inflict further punishment on the despised hill liberals.

Such an interpretation became compelling when two of the schools the superintendent of schools recommended for closing, which happened to be in BCA electoral strongholds, were spared and BCA school board members substituted schools in the hills. One of them, John Muir School, was a Berkeley landmark, which the school district had recently earthquake-proofed at a cost of nearly $2 million. Because of its physical beauty and good staff, but most of all because of an active parent group, John Muir had been judged worth the expense. It was, in fact, generally acknowledged to be the model school in the Berkeley system. Parents from the primarily white hill neighborhood volunteered at the rate of two per classroom each day. More important, in an era of declining school budgets, they had raised some $30,000 in donations to rebuild the school playground and were providing over $15,000 a year for a variety of art and science enrichment activities.

"Virtually no black parents were for closing Muir," says Carroll Williams, black school board president and an opponent of the BCA majority at the time of the furor over closings. "Half the students were black, bused up there under the integration plan. The parents of these children realized what benefits their kids were getting from schools where white parents pitched in with all this extra participation and enrichment."

Parents formed protest groups and launched lawsuits to preserve John Muir. It soon became clear, however, that for the BCA the issue had less to do with education than with ideology. Like other issues, the schools were part of the political allegory of radicalism and "class struggle." When Carroll Williams, who had moved to Berkeley so that his children could take advantage of a quality integrated system, opposed the radicals who made up the board's majority, he was derided as "objectively racist." When Erica Boyd, a BCA loyalist for years, went to the organization's steering committee to plead with them to rethink the policy on school closings, one BCA leader heard her out with ill-concealed impatience and then sneered, "You come here now, but where were you during the El Salvador demonstrations?"

The BCA school board members withstood a recall, but the controversy continued, heating up when the next—and, many Berkeleyans came to feel, always the ultimate—step in the BCA plan was revealed: to put low-cost housing on the sites of the closed schools. The advantages to the BCA were clear: housing was power, part of the city's wealth. Low-cost units would become part of their patronage—a way, in the words of disaffected radical Peter Tannenbaum, "to build little condos they can fill with their cronies." Using school sites for low-cost units would also, BCA strategists quixotically believed, allow them to help redress the fact that nearly a quarter of Berkeley's black population had left the city in the radical decade 1970–80, many of them cashing in on homes bought forty years earlier and now worth many times what they had originally cost because of the gentrification of South and West Berkeley by whites unable to afford a home in the hills. The departure of blacks had caused BCAers a metaphysical lurch: a city without blacks would be a city without anyone to "help." As Barbara Lubin, a BCA school board member, said with unwitting candor: "The thought of living with 100,000 white people who eat at Chez Panisse every night horrifies me."

The idea of schools being not only closed but razed for low-cost housing sent the debate over education in Berkeley to a new level of bitterness. In the middle of the furor, resistance to the BCA began to form in the "neighborhoods"—areas in the city with strong common bonds and a history of unified political action over issues such as the installation of traffic diverters and the initiation of permit parking. Many of the activists in the neighborhoods, always before a part of the BCA machinery, had become disturbed by the organization's assault on the schools, which were seen as communal neighborhood assets, and also by the fact that the BCA seemed to be turning a blind eye toward commercial developers. (During a debate over whether or not to allow Burger King to open a branch in the center of town, for instance, one BCA functionary charged that neighborhood opponents of the move "don't want there to be a place in this city where working class people can come to have lunch.") But the principal grievance of the neighborhood people was subjective: the sense that the BCA inner circle had its own agenda and, despite what seemed elaborate mechanisms for consultation, was not interested in the community.

The BCA leaders responded to criticism by attacking the neighborhood people for practicing "sandbox politics"—that is, for thinking locally instead of globally. At the height of the conflict, Barry Wofsy, one of the leaders of the neighborhood movement, observed: "The BCA are masters at manipulating symbols and language. No matter what side of an issue you're on, you're a 'racist' if you're not with them. Newport and the rest of them don't care what happens on a local level. It's the Big March of History that they care about, the Great Social Transformation. Our real sin as far as they're concerned is to see Berkeley as a place to live in rather than as a 'model for socialism.' They're progressives everywhere but Berkeley. Here they're reactionaries."

In the spring of 1986, a large coalition of irate parents and neighborhood activists fought back against the BCA by qualifying an initiative for the ballot that mandated the election of Council members by district, thus attempting to break the hold slate politics had given the BCA over city government. Although the measure originated in the black community, the BCA fought against it, Dellums going so far as to recruit Jesse Jackson to denounce it in a series of radio advertisements. But voters regarded the measure as an antidote to the grandiosity of the BCA, and it passed.

In the general election that fall, the BCA ceded the school board to a group of independent candidates representing a coalition of concerned parents. Instead the organization concentrated on the City Council and on a candidate to replace Gus Newport, who realized that he had worn out his welcome in Berkeley and was preparing to go back to Massachusetts. They settled on Loni Hancock, who had worked as a low-ranking official in ACTION in the years since her semiretirement from Berkeley city politics. Drafting her was an attempt by the BCA to relocate the halcyon days of radical city politics, a time when the people in the BCA were still the good guys in Berkeley. It was also an attempt to find someone whose politics were as "progressive" as Newport's, but whose personal

style was more reassuring. "She's not that much different from
Gus in foreign policy," one observer said after hearing that
Hancock had been selected as the BCA candidate for mayor.
"But she's different in temperament. She's got manners. Gus
was a commie. Loni's a white-glove commie. In the current
situation, however, I guess you'd have to consider that a step
forward."

Narrowly elected in November of 1986, Loni Hancock
was presiding over a City Council meeting a few weeks later
at which homelessness was on the agenda and a large contingent of Berkeley's homeless were present. The new mayor had
indicated soon after taking office that unlike her confrontation-oriented predecessor, she liked "win-win" solutions—a
bureaucratic view of the world that, as one observer noted
maliciously, made for "yawn-yawn" City Council meetings.
This particular meeting, however, had quickly slipped out of
Hancock's control. She tried to calm the volatile situation by
reminding the homeless of Berkeley's reputation for compassion and by uttering homilies about how the "heartlessness" of
the Reagan administration was responsible for the national
housing problem. But the homeless kept interrupting and hectoring her about their problem as if she were just another official and not the head of a radical administration. Becoming
more and more rattled, Hancock finally blurted out, "Look, if
we can't have order here, we'll just end the meeting and go
home." One of the homeless shouted, "How can we do that?
We don't have a home!"

This moment, immediately acknowledged as a classic by
connoisseurs of the looking-glass world of Berkeley politics,
showed the extent to which the city had become what Walter
Lippmann had in mind when he talked about the development
of the "pseudo environment"—a place governed by a fictionalized version of reality. In the case of Berkeley, this reality is
dominated by radical schemes and schemers, creating a surreal
context in which events such as the mayor ordering the homeless to go home are the order of the day. In the pseudo environment, international issues dominate, while the problems of
daily life are ignored. In the pseudo environment, it is necessary to have a large bureaucracy to administer the radical vi-

sion, and an imperial mayor who has five full-time aides, four more than the Berkeley mayor had when the radicals became a power.

Berkeley has always been a place with immense human resources, a place distinguished by inventiveness and iconoclasm. But in the pseudo environment, these qualities have been submerged. After two decades of radicalism, the city seems to be rich only in left-wing rhetoric and sister cities. "Of course the BCA has established a foreign policy for Berkeley," one disgusted resident says. "It's part of the bread and circuses. Otherwise it delivers very little, much less than smaller cities without all the hot air and high taxes." Even radicals impatient with fiscal matters are beginning to find it significant that Berkeley's budget of over $140 million is about twice as much as that of Hayward, a neighboring town of comparable size, which appears to deliver more of the services supposedly the responsibility of municipal authority.

The contest between those who want Berkeley to remain a pseudo environment and those who want to turn it back toward reality is a fierce one. Reformers found this out after they recently captured control of the school board. They have to deal not only with a system so battered financially that its budget is overseen by a state-appointed trustee, but also with one whose intellectual atmosphere continues to be contaminated. The new board members—self-identified liberals who were disenchanted by BCA policies—are regularly charged with "racism" by BCA *turbas*, who attend school board meetings to defend the Revolution. They must deal with sideshows such as the furor caused when a black nationalist, invited by radicals to speak at a compulsory Berkeley High School history assembly, attacked Western culture (including the philosophy of "that faggot Aristotle") as a set of ideas and values "stolen" from Africans. Leftist clichés have infected learning from the very first grade, where the peace curriculum has made the tale of Little Red Riding Hood into an occasion for teaching "conflict resolution." Could the Wolf and Little Red Riding Hood have settled their differences amicably? Could Little Red Riding Hood have talked the Wolf out of violence? Was she guilty of stereotyping?

The pseudo environment is strong because it is buttressed by a constant supply of new plans and proposals designed to exhaust and finally overwhelm the proponents of reality. Defeated on the plan to make Jabilia a sister city, for instance, the city's Peace and Justice Commission came right back with a new recommendation, which would prevent Berkeley from keeping U.S. Treasury bonds in its portfolio because of a scholastic interpretation of an ordinance passed in 1986 that made the city a nuclear-free zone prohibited from doing business with companies manufacturing nuclear weapons. Meanwhile, Mayor Hancock and other BCAers, trying to identify the BCA in the public mind as technocratic rather than ideological, began to push a redevelopment scheme that would declare South and West Berkeley flatlands "blighted," thus enabling the city to get millions of federal dollars with which to remake Berkeley demographics through BCA housing schemes. As with other radical plans, this one has increased the civic polarization, causing more neighborhood defense committees to be formed and more citizens to band together out of fear that if they do not, the circumstances of their daily existence—where and how they will live—will be affected by the radicals' plans. As one resident wearily gearing up for the redevelopment fight says, "We never just live here in Berkeley. We are always in some sort of struggle, making sure that some scheme hatched down in the smoke-filled coffee shops isn't going to affect us disastrously. Really we only need one thing in this city—a let-us-alone law."

Indeed, a large part of Berkeley's problem appears to be that so many people are so deeply involved in city government. All those not permanently alienated, it is tempting to say, are involved—but involved in a febrile, almost obsessive way. The involvement encouraged by the radicals has led to cynicism rather than citizenship, to a pervasive sense of civic exhaustion rather than a sense of the rewards of creative civic participation. It is an involvement based on anger and animosity, and it has produced few benefits and many casualties, chief among them the painstakingly evolved techniques for handling conflict that, along with its native imagination and tolerance, once made Berkeley not only a great city but a unique one as well. What has replaced that, as UC professor and Berkeleyologist Joseph Lyford has pointed out, is an atmosphere that is moralistic rather than moral, coercive rather than persuasive. The most salient accomplishment of radical governance in Berkeley has been to polarize instead of reconcile; to transform common political ground into a barren no-man's-land of unremitting combat.

One can document the civic decline caused by the radical assault on Berkeley by meticulous study of the archives of the last quarter century, which record the divisive initiatives, the feuding slates, the petty conspiracies and constant struggle. Or one can simply take a stroll through People's Park, a place that has always symbolized the radical dream. A great many fatuous statements have been made about this place, both at the time when it caused a municipal apocalypse and since. (In a recent book, Berkeley activist Todd Gitlin called it a little piece of "anarchist heaven on earth . . . the one tantalizing trace of the good society.") Yet to visit People's Park now is to see the radical dream revealed for what it is: a place ruled by the desperate and the derelict—not just the beaten and disoriented homeless but an underclass of predators who appear especially after nightfall.

The Berkeley police department must periodically issue warnings urging students to be careful when going near this place, because of the threat of muggings and rape. The fittest who have survived here over the years are not hippie horticulturalists planting peace, love, and good vibes, but drug dealers taking care of business. Followed around People's Park recently for an hour or so by a reporter from the San Francisco *Chronicle*, Berkeley officer Robert Seib, one of the park patrolmen, pulled a wad of color photographs out of his pocket, looked at the groups of men drifting aimlessly around the area, and said, "These are mug shots of dealers. And they're all people who are dealing out here." Seib pointed out a row of young men lounging in the sun, near the sidewalk. "Those are the runners," he said. "They take the buyers to the dealers, who are over there, near the trees. . . ."

In the face of such developments, it is little wonder that many Berkeley residents, even some who cannot bring themselves to publicly give up the commitments of their youth, feel chastened by the experience of socialism in one city and have become more modest in their expectations. Their reaction is expressed not so much in dissidence as in a species of dark humor recalling the celebrated scene in Kundera's *Book of Laughter and Forgetting* where a character passing by someone vomiting in a Prague gutter murmurs, "I know exactly what you mean," and continues on his way.

A few miles away from People's Park is another piece of green, much smaller, named Ohlone Park but usually referred to as the "Dog Park" because it has been set aside as a place where the city's leash law does not obtain. Not long after the fight over making Jabalia a sister city was finished, but before the fight on redevelopment got going, Pam Ferguson, one of those most responsible for the creation of Ohlone, stood in a corner watching the dogs serpentining through the park with lolling tongues and what seemed to be smiles on their muzzles. She talked about how, when the park first opened, there was the usual Berkeley rhetoric, including Xerox handouts about how the animals would "exist harmoniously once separated from their owners' ethic of possessiveness." But high expectations here too were undercut by reality.

"Some people were sure that the dogs would prove to be egalitarians," Ferguson says. "But they aren't. They come here and immediately join the pack, which is a strict hierarchy controlled by the top dog. The upshot is that they have a great time in the pack, but they aren't really very progressive. It was a hard lesson for some of the radical pet owners around town to swallow. Not only have we failed to create the New Man in Berkeley. We haven't even created the New Dog."

chapter 8 _____

Radical Innocence,
Radical Guilt

We worshipped the revolution like romantic lovers. But a shameless brute came along and violated our beloved.

—Gorky

As the Eighties recede, we find ourselves caught in the riptide of a Sixties revival. There are films, histories, and memoirs of what has been made to seem a sort of golden age—an age not only of energy and excitement but also of commitment and belief. This revival can be recognized as a sentimental moment: a generation fondly recollecting a turbulent youth in the tranquillity of its middle years. But the nostalgia is also a political phenomenon. The growing interest in the Sixties coincides with a renaissance of the radicalism that was the decade's dominant trait and is now being used to jump-start the Next Left.

The conventional wisdom tells us that if Leftism has reappeared on the American scene, it is because of the cyclical nature of politics. Just as Eisenhower's holding action in the Fifties led to JFK's New Frontier liberalism in the Sixties, we are informed, so the clamped-down Reaganism of the Eighties has precipitated the current radical resurgence. The most popular, if tendentious, expression of the pendulum theory comes from Arthur Schlesinger, Jr., who applies it to contemporary political culture just as his father, also a historian, did half a century ago.

It is not merely an academic quibble to say that the Left revival now upon us should be seen as intentional rather than inertial. It is not just the weight of history pushing the pendulum but a political movement shoving it ahead for its own reasons. Like the slowly metamorphosing monster of a horror film, the Left has actually been recreating itself during its apparent dormancy since the end of the Sixties, succeeding so well that now it has reappeared stronger than ever. If there is a cyclical dynamic at work in this rebirth, it has less to do with the laws of history than with the laws of Leftism, which since 1917 has alternated between styles of militant extremism and "popular front" moderation. The current revival will not bring a revolutionary army into the streets, as in the Sixties. It will involve an offensive of "progressivism" whose targets are the Democratic Party, the church, the universities, and various liberal institutions.

The Left today is as hostile to American power as it was two decades ago; it still believes that what is wrong with America is systemic. It has understood, however, that to be taken seriously, it must submit to a make-over. The change required is not simply cosmetic: there must also be a reassertion of the innocence radicalism lost as a result of its excesses during its previous incarnation. This recovery is being achieved by a mock admission of guilt, which is actually self-exculpation in disguise. If American radicals did wrong in the Sixties, explains former revolutionary and current Democratic Party politician Tom Hayden in his autobiographical memoir, it was not because they were radicals but because they were Americans and unable to rise above this vice: "We ourselves became infected with many of the diseases of the society we wished to erase. Thinking we could build a new world, we self-destructed in a decade. Claiming love as our motivation, we could not subdue hate."*

Spending the early Reagan years in the wilderness, radicals like Hayden cemented the marriage of their old politics to the popular culture, making the good old days seem so exciting, so heroic even, that every starlet in Hollywood now wants to experience the heady morality of Leftism for herself. Chic in a way that it wasn't even in the days of radical chic, the Left has reemerged from its brief demise purified of past misdeeds and born again. Old radicals are ready to preach anew. Thus Hayden writes, "Despite outer repression and inner absurdity, we of the sixties accomplished more than most generations in American history. . . . I hope that the ideals of the sixties, tempered by harsh experience, can have a second coming in our lifetime."

One almost has to admire the brazenness of such self-congratulations by this Everyman of the Movement, an individual who seems to have experienced almost everything and learned practically nothing. "We created the most massive resistance to a war in the nation's history," he boasts. Yet the corollary never occurs to him: that this resistance, which caused the defeat of America, resulted in a monster regime that, more than a decade after the end of the war, still torments its own people, driving them deeper into poverty and diminishing their freedoms through Marxist repression and imperial conquest.

The manufacture of innocence out of guilt: it is the eternal work of the Left. The true genius of radicalism is constant self-recreation and reappearance in new guises. Never mind that the sloughed-off skins it leaves behind are fossilized remains of the death and destruction caused by its past commitments. For Leftists, there are only tomorrows. They never talk about the evil they have done, except superficially, to imply (as Hayden does) that it has increased their moral sensitivity. But they are always anxious to discuss the utopia to come. The future perfect is the only tense in their political grammar. Thus they are willing to criticize every revolution but the one currently unfolding—the one in which there is still a choice. Their opponents' misdeeds must never be forgotten, but their

* Tom Hayden, *Reunion: A Memoir* (New York, 1988).

own can never really be recalled. While Central America is alleged by Leftists to be "another Vietnam," Nicaragua is never another Cuba.

How does the Left maintain its belief against the crushing weight of its failures in the past? By recycling its innocence, which allows it to be born again in its utopian faith. The utopianism of the Left is a secular religion (as the vogue of "liberation theology" attests), its promise an earthly kingdom of heaven. However sordid Leftist practice may be, defending Leftist ideals is, for the true believer, tantamount to defending the ideals of humanity itself. To protect the faith is the highest calling of the radical creed. The more the evidence weighs against the belief, the more noble the act of believing becomes. In this sense, Tertullian is the true father of the radical church. "*Credo quia impossibile*": "I believe *because* it is impossible."

In the Stalin era, an English Quaker, returning from a visit to Bolshevik Russia, reported to his flock:

> The Communist view of human nature seems to me far more inspired by Faith, Hope and Charity than our own. . . . The simple unostentatious life of Russia's rulers represents a notable advance in *real* civilization—real because based on a more enlightened interpretation of human nature, both of its needs and capacities; an interpretation which incidentally is also a more Christian one.

Almost forty years later, in the mid-Sixties, the Reverend William Sloane Coffin declared that "Communism is a page torn out of the Bible" and that "the social justice that's been achieved in . . . North Vietnam [is] an achievement no Christian society on that scale has ever achieved." Today, softheaded Witness for Peaceniks come home from Managua saying much the same thing. It is understandable that they should have found a heaven on earth there, for the Sandinistas have consecrated the marriage of the religious and the revolutionary by combining the offices of *comandante* and priest. "For me, the four Gospels are all equally Communist," declared the Marxist *padre* Ernesto Cardenal. So committed is he to the infallibility of his spiritual and temporal leader that after returning from a trip to Havana to kiss Castro's ring, Cardenal reported that Cuba's homosexuals "were actually happier in the concentration camps [that Castro had built for them], a place like that where they were all together must have been almost like paradise for them."

It is often observed that a symmetry exists between the extreme ends of the political spectrum, that the fanatics of the Right are mirror images of the zealots on the Left. But once we leave the extremes, there is this tangible difference: the Right seeks to conserve (and the Left to undermine) workaday democracy; the Left seeks to defend (and the Right to defeat) the destructive fantasy of a heaven on earth. This is why American Leftists in their "innocence" embrace political evil in a way that American conservatives in their realism do not. A Bill Buckley might defend a Pinochet in Chile on pragmatic grounds as "our sonofabitch," but he would never call him "the Abraham Lincoln of his people," as Jesse Jackson has praised Communist dictators like Fidel Castro and Daniel Ortega. Nor would the Right defend Chile as a brave new society pioneering the path to humanity's future, the way the Left has defended Soviet Russia, the People's Republic of China, Communist Cuba, Nicaragua, and all the other socialist despotisms. It is this religious confusion and moral corruption that defines the utopianism of the Left. It insists on imposing the idea of salvation on a temporal reality that is by its nature flawed; in so doing, it exploits mankind's faith, as well as its hope and charity.

If self-righteousness is the moral oxygen of the radical creed, self-deception is the marrow of its immune system. *Credo quia impossibile*: because what he believes is impossible, the radical believes because it is *necessary* to believe.

Malcolm Muggeridge observed the prototypes of the radical faithful on a tour of Russia in the 1930s:

> Their delight in all they saw and were told, and the expression they gave to this delight, constitute unquestionably one of the wonders of our age. There were earnest advocates of the humane killing of cattle who looked up at the massive headquarters of the OGPU with tears of gratitude in their eyes, earnest advocates of proportional representation who eagerly assented when the necessity for a Dictatorship of the Proletariat was explained to them, earnest

clergymen who walked reverently through anti-God museums and reverently turned the pages of atheistic literature, earnest pacifists who watched delightedly tanks rattle
across the Red Square and bombing planes darken the
sky, earnest town-planning specialists who stood outside
overcrowded ramshackle tenements and muttered: "If
only we had something like this in England!" The almost
unbelievable credulity of these mostly university-edu-
cated tourists astonished even Soviet officials used to handling foreign visitors.

After Stalin's death, when the Soviet rulers were forced
to admit a considerable part of the terrible truth, many of their
progressive supporters also had confessions to make: In fact,
they had not really been so credulous as they appeared. Their
seeming innocence, as Nobel novelist Halldór Laxness explained, actually had an element of guile: "We feared that the
final victory of Socialism would be hampered and hindered if
the truth about Stalin's paradise were revealed to the public."
    It is easy for today's Leftists to dismiss such revelations,
saying that "that was then and this is now"—that Stalin is long
dead, his memory having been exhumed and then desecrated
by Gorbachev as well as Khrushchev. But as new Marxist par-
adises have sprouted in China, Cuba, Vietnam, Nicaragua,
and elsewhere, new generations of revolutionary tourists have
made their visits and come away reporting that they had seen
a future that *really* worked. Back home they have spread the
new gospel, their voices filled with what Milan Kundera has
called the "totalitarian poetry" of the socialist cause: the lyrical
promises that lead directly to the gulag—waiting room of the
socialist paradise.
    But while utopian fantasies provide socialism with a
shield against external criticism, within its own borders a brutal
pragmatism rules the state. The millions who have been "liberated" by revolutionaries *know* the dirty little secret of their
liberation: that they are more oppressed by the revolution itself
than they ever had been by the regime it replaced.
    It is the need to bridge the chasm between the socialist
dream and the socialist reality that produces the totalitarian
state. The essence of that state and its difference from the

democracies with which it will always be at war was foreseen with crystal clarity by Machiavelli. Because people are susceptible, he wrote, "it is easy to persuade them, [but] difficult to fix them in that persuasion. Thus it is necessary to take such measures that, when they believe no longer, it may be possible to make them believe by force." In the year zero of the revolution, Lenin showed himself to be Machiavelli's disciple: "If the workers and peasants do not wish to accept socialism, our reply will be: Why waste words when we can apply force? . . . If we do not apply terror and immediate executions, we will get nowhere. It is better that a hundred innocent are killed than that one guilty person escapes." It is this bleak landscape that the totalitarian poetry is meant to beautify.

Faith and terror are the twin pillars of the revolution's defense. But there is argument as well—an architectonic system of casuistry that keeps faith on course. In addition to the secret police who will apply its terror, the socialist state requires a Ministry of Truth—that deep bunker of expedience in which history is forever being rewritten and images of the present are perpetually retouched. Here the contradictions that might discomfit faith ("it couldn't happen") are removed to keep faith intact ("you're right, it didn't happen"). Thus Trotsky is airbrushed out of his photos with Lenin, Potemkin villages are constructed for revolutionary pilgrims, and the contents of encyclopedias are always in flux because of changes required by new political realities. ("For Beria, substitute Bering Strait.") Nor is the Ministry of Truth simply a Stalinist relic or an Orwellian construct. In Nicaragua today, for instance, real institutions—the church, the media, labor unions, human rights organizations—are parodied by agitprop institutions in their mirror image created by the Sandinistas. Meanwhile, Interior Minister Tomas Borge piously meets church groups in a pseudo office filled with rosaries and crucifixes, then leaves to go to his *real* headquarters, the one decorated by the icons of Marx and Lenin, where he renders only to the FSLN Caesar.

Truth is the first casualty of revolution. The paradigm for all the black holes in the socialist universe is the Ukrainian famine of 1930–33—an episode in Stalin's war on the peasantry

—in which thirteen million Ukrainians were deliberately starved and systematically slaughtered. In those years, more people were murdered by socialist reformers than were killed by the armies on all sides in World War I. The Ukrainian atrocity has never been investigated or acknowledged by Soviet authorities (not even under *glasnost*) and was "discovered" only when an overly punctilious bureaucrat noticed an inexplicable deficit in the 1937 census. The census taker's reward was the firing squad.

Progressives in the West, deprived of the right to stage executions, came to the aid of the socialist utopia with what would become the first line of defense—the argument that *it never happened*. They denied the reports that had trickled out of the U.S.S.R. about people being starved and murdered in the People's State; they defended the socialist policy that had caused the Ukrainian famine as a plan designed to feed the hungry and create a better world; they defamed Stalin's critics and skeptics as enemies of humanitarian progress and reactionary opponents of social change. With the help of such progressives, Stalin was able not only to get away with his crimes but also to go on to create a society in which mass executions became part of daily existence and serfdom was reinstituted— among those lucky enough to survive.

Eventually it became fashionable to say that the Ukrainian tragedy, like all the others in Stalin's reign, was the consequence of a bad man rather than a bad theory and a bad system. At the exact moment in the Sixties that this claim was first being pushed by the New Left, however, China was in the middle of its Great Leap Forward, whose utopian ends and means radicals universally applauded. When the death toll in the People's Republic later became too obvious to deny—an estimated twenty million casualties during Mao Tse-tung's social experiment—Leftists again said that a cult of personality was to blame. The Soviet Union, the People's Republic of China, Castro's Cuba, Mengistu's Ethiopia: the scale of these socialist tragedies may differ, but their outcome is always the same—*déjà vu* all over again, as Yogi Berra might say.

In fact, the tragedies of socialist revolutions are tragedies not of unintended consequence but of malign intention. War against the peasant—be it the Ukrainian *kulak* or the Nicaraguan *campesino*—is an integral part of the Marxist program.

The heroic figure of the post-Stalin revolutionary era, Ernesto "Che" Guevara, conceded as much in a speech on July 11, 1964, five years after he and Castro took power—a speech that shows the lethal cynicism of the socialist faith.

> We continue to speak of the small farmer, the poor, small farmer, and we never say that the farmer, no matter how poor and small he is, manifestly generates capitalism. . . .
> It is very true that the *campesino* has been a pillar of the Revolution, that he was always in favor of it, that he fought in the Sierra, that he was one of the first to join the Rebel Army. In spite of all this, he must be eliminated.

Today, the claim that "it never happened"—crucial to the success of the radical reclamation project—is far more difficult to sustain, but in some ways it is almost as effective as in the days of Stalin himself. Even when it doesn't work, it works. By the time the truth trickles out, no longer deniable genocides have become admissible "errors"; previously hidden atrocities are grudgingly acknowledged as "mistakes." By the time the facts of the socialist experiments are generally acknowledged, they have been nibbled to death by partial explanations and incomplete admissions, until they have become emotionally, morally, and politically distanced—mere curiosities of the historical past. Did Stalin kill twenty or thirty or sixty million of his own countrymen to create the socialist future in the U.S.S.R.? Did Mao kill twenty or thirty or fifty million during his Great Leaps and Cultural Revolutions? How many millions of dead people can dance on the head of the socialist pin?

Even in the era of *glasnost*, this impenetrable fog of uncertainty churned out by the Ministry of Truth befuddles the minds of those who don't live within it, as well as those who do. Thus, on a recent congressional junket to Moscow to promote détente, House Speaker Jim Wright scolded those Americans still fearful of Soviet militarism by telling them that they must try to "understand" Soviet anxieties arising from the loss of twenty million dead in World War II. These twenty million are the most famous Soviet statistic of all. In fact, according to Nicholai Tolstoy and others an estimated thirteen million of the twenty died as a result of the actions, direct and indirect, of the Soviet regime itself. But because these corpses lie in a memory hole, Communism not only gets to triumph over its victims but accumulates sympathy credits for them in the credulous West as well.

The obfuscations of "progressives" always make it impossible to know with certainty how great (or even whether) a socialist atrocity has been committed. The doubt they generate creates a sort of moral amnesia. It allows one of the large ironies of modern history to go unrecognized: Even though Marxist socialism is a doctrine that has exploited, impoverished, and murdered more people than any other creed in our time, the Communist (and neo-Communist) Left remains part of respectable society in a way, for example, that the heirs of Nazism never could.

Today, only diehards of the Communist Party buy the myths of the utopian Soviet workers' state; even they have become reluctant Gorbachevites and believers in *glasnost*, willing to acknowledge some "errors." The partial admission of guilt, of course, is strategic rather than sincere. It is not part of an honest inventory of the past but rather a step in the manufacture of innocence, on which the Left depends. While the partial admission concedes that the old styles of Marxist revolution may have been inadequate and perhaps at times even counterproductive, it insists with equal zeal that the new styles are pure and promising.

For these counterfeiters of the old radical currencies, the invention of the "Third World" has been of crucial importance. The Soviet Union, for years the First World of Leftism, ultimately could not bear the burden of belief. Thus the discovery of the third world was critical to the continuance of radicalism's utopian project. In this sense, it is actually not the Third World at all, but the New World, a virgin land where the seed corn of radical fantasy can grow in new and magic strains —*Fidelismo* and *Sandinismo* in Latin America and a uniquely gentle brand of Confucian Marxism in North Vietnam: strains allegedly immune to the diseases infecting Stalin's malicious agriculture. Here, the shopworn panaceas—finally putting an end to inequality and want, creating communities of the New Man and Woman, building a New Jerusalem of social justice

—that were so bloodily discredited in the Soviet Union could be resurrected with intellectual impudence and moral impunity. Here a generation of Americans unable to maintain a vision of the class struggle at home because of the liberal nature of their society could nonetheless project that vision onto a world stage.

In the intellectual cartology of the Left, the Third World is the oppressed world, the world where the weak are perpetually at war with the strong—the world of domineering Prosperos and put-upon Calibans, of noble blacks and predatory whites, of permanent victims and perennial innocents. Embarrassed by their defense of totalitarian superstates like Stalinist Russia and Maoist China, the progressives have found in the Third World an arena in which the banners of the Red Internationals can be taken out of mothballs and again held high. On the Third World battlefields, the equations of moral superiority work once again. Marxist revolutionaries always appear as guileless Davids, while America and its allies are always guilty Goliaths.

Third World peoples are the "victims" not only of present predations by imperialism but victims, too, of the long half-life of its past offenses. Thus even when Third World revolutionaries are guilty they are innocent, because of the "imperialist legacies" they inherit. If they embrace terror as a weapon in their struggle, this terror is justified by their accumulated "rage"; if they join the Soviet empire, this alliance is justified by the implacable hostility of the American foe. In all cases, they are morally exculpated in advance by a single explanation: *the devil made them do it.*

This devil theory of history is the fallback position of the radical argument when it is impossible to claim that it didn't happen, and lies at the heart of the current revival of Leftism. It is an inverted cold war paranoia, where the only evil empire is the U.S.A. In this radical demonology, America not only controls the Third World's economy and culture but, even worse, forces its revolutionary leaders to act immorally. This claim—the devil made them do it—protects the patina of idealism which is the Teflon element of the radical's identity; it produces the alchemy by which the Left transforms the enduring guilt of its bloodstained past into the golden innocence of its redemptive future.

The intellectual most associated with the view that America is the great Satan is MIT linguistics professor Noam Chomsky. Once a prestigious specialist in his field, Chomsky turned his pen in the Sixties to political themes, which since then have increasingly obsessed him. In "The Responsibility of the Intellectuals," a famous broadside issued during the Vietnam War, Chomsky writes deprecatingly, "It is an article of faith [among intellectuals] that American motives are pure and not subject to analysis." Since then, in a seemingly endless series of tracts on U.S. policies in the Third World, he has argued compulsively that the evil of American motives is so transparent that it ought to be assumed as an article of faith. Freighted with footnotes and scholarly apparatus, Chomsky's volumes express an impassioned hatred of America's institutions and national identity. Often reaching paranoid extremes, his animus would serve to stigmatize anyone of less imposing credentials as a political crank. And to some extent Chomsky has earned precisely that reputation, despite his achievements as a linguist, through such episodes as his defense of Robert Faurisson, a leading intellectual proponent of the claim that the Nazi Holocaust is a "Zionist hoax." No longer published in *The New York Review of Books* and other prestigious liberal magazines that once clamored for his essays, Chomsky has become the Dr. Demento of American political commentary.

But within the Left itself, Chomsky's reputation has prospered. He is now easily the most influential figure in the radical movement, speaking regularly to large campus audiences, providing the argument for most left-wing texts on contemporary politics, and inspiring a coterie of disciples such as radical journalist Christopher Hitchens, who unctuously lauds Chomsky as "a man I greatly revere." The heroic dimensions of Chomsky's status derive from his performance of an absolutely critical service to the contemporary Left—developing the devil theory that holds America and the West responsible for all the world's evil.

This work began in the mid-Seventies. In a series of articles and then in voluminous books, Chomsky laid out an argument designed not only to rescue the Left from the bloody *cul-de-sac* into which its extremism had led it in the Vietnam years, but also to frame a moral indictment of U.S. policy that would allow the Left to resume the offensive against the "Amerika" its fantasies had created in the Sixties. *After the Cataclysm*, for instance, the second of two volumes Chomsky published under the portentous title *The Political Economy of Human Rights*, is a systematic effort to erase the catastrophic results of the Communist victory in Southeast Asia and to pin the blame for the tragedies that occurred there on the malevolence of the defeated combatant, the United States. Chomsky sets out to argue in this work that the Communist genocide in Cambodia was the big lie Washington created to reconstruct its own rationale for world domination.

As the Communist rebel armies approached Phnom Penh, Chomsky and other radicals were not alone in celebrating the U.S. defeat they believed would initiate the dawn of a new era of "social justice" in Indochina. The last U.S. official was being helicoptered out of Saigon when the liberal *New York Times* reporter Sydney Schanberg filed a story under the suggestive headline "Indochina Without Americans: For Most, a Better Life?" One month earlier, the liberal columnist Anthony Lewis had asked: "What future could possibly be more terrible than the reality of what is happening to Cambodia now?"

As the bodies began to pile up, however, the Lewises got their answers. Sadder if not wiser, they finally deserted the cause of the Khmer Rouge. But not Chomsky. He was still busily working on an intellectual edifice designed to conceal the atrocities of the Communist liberators. This cover-up, in the words of David Hawk, former antiwar activist and later director of the Cambodia Documentation Commission, included "confident assertions that the reports of atrocities were exaggerated propaganda; letters of protest to human rights groups that sought to mobilize opinion against the atrocities . . . [attacks on] the reliability of the refugee accounts and the honesty and credibility of the journalists and publications that gathered, reported and printed the terrible atrocities recounted by the refugees lucky enough to survive escape attempts from the Khmer Rouge."

The disinformation campaign had a significant impact. In Hawk's words, "The alacrity and persistence of Pol Pot's defenders diverted attention and refocused discussion from 'how should Khmer Rouge bloodlust best be exposed and protested' to 'whether or not the refugee accounts were exaggerated and were the accounts of largely politically motivated propaganda.' " Hawk believes that Chomsky's grotesque thesis had "a chilling effect on the mobilization of opinion against the Cambodian genocide."

Chomsky's goal in denying the atrocities was less to defend the Khmer Rouge than to prevent the gruesome facts of their genocide from deflecting guilt from the United States. Thus he tricked out his cover-up as an "analysis" of how the American media were "brainwashing" the public with concocted reports of Communist misdeeds in order to reconstruct the "imperial ideology" of the pre-Vietnam era.

In the Thirties, protected by the Stalinist monolith, Chomsky's argument might have remained convincing, at least for a while, as were the impassioned assertions of American progressives of that era that reports of a famine and genocide in the Ukraine were not only false but malicious. But there was no Stalinist Ministry of Truth to protect Chomsky when he was betrayed by Pol Pot, author of atrocities that were finally too horrible to be hidden and head of a revolution so mad that his North Vietnamese sponsors finally invaded and conquered Cambodia, adding another 350,000 deaths to the already enormous toll.

Chomsky was just completing his 160-page, footnoted assault on the Western media for fabricating the genocide that Hanoi was now ready to confirm. He responded not by throwing out the pages of his perverse text but by hedging its claims. "When the facts are in," Chomsky now speculated, "it may turn out that the more extreme condemnations were in fact correct." Moreover, he added:

> If a serious study of the impact of Western imperialism on Cambodian peasant life is someday undertaken, it may well be discovered that the violence lurking behind the Khmer smile . . . is not a reflection of obscure traits in peasant culture and psychology, but is the direct and *understandable response* to the *violence of the imperial system,* and that its current manifestations are a no less direct and understandable response to the still more concentrated and extreme savagery of a *U.S. assault that may*

in part have been designed to evoke this very response . . .
[Emphasis added.]

In other words, the Khmer Rouge were really innocent of the atrocities Chomsky was now forced to concede they might have committed. Why? Because *the U.S. devil made them do it.* Why would the U.S. make them commit such crimes? Chomsky had a ready answer: *In order to discredit the socialist future.* In making these arguments, Chomsky had discovered the Archimedean principle of the Leftist revival.

However tendentious in fact, the devil theory was always far more palatable to Western liberals than the flat claim that the bad had never happened. Several books appeared after Chomsky's work that attacked his cynical attempt to dismiss the *facts* of the Cambodian genocide but nonetheless echoed his thesis that the United States was ultimately responsible for the tragedy. Chief among them was *Sideshow* by William Shawcross, subtitled "Kissinger, Nixon and the Destruction of Cambodia," whose contents suggested that the Americans who tried to prevent a Communist victory were ultimately responsible for the atrocities the Communists had committed once they were in power. In its most popular version, this indictment appeared in the award-winning film *The Killing Fields*, which was based on a story by Sydney Schanberg, the reporter who had in 1975 suggested that a Communist victory might be better for the Cambodians than the continued influence of America. At a climactic moment in the film, the actor playing Schanberg accepts a journalism award for his reporting from Cambodia. He does not use the occasion to acknowledge his mistaken prediction but to point a finger at his own country once again. Citing the money America spent on bombs for Cambodian targets, the film's Schanberg says: "Often politicians create what they fear. . . . Unfortunately our country made a spectacular contribution to this tragedy." Dith Pran, Schanberg's Cambodian friend who was left behind to suffer under the Khmer Rouge, would not be guilty of such simplistic and sanctimonious thinking.

The atrocities committed by the Khmer Rouge were clearly the outgrowth of Marxist ideas, although there was a half-baked Third Worldism in such exotic additions to dogma as the assumption that anyone with eyeglasses must be eradicated because of presumed bourgeois intellectual tendencies. Most of the deaths occurred during the forced evacuations the Paris-educated Communist leaders had ordered as part of their un-remitting assault on the cities as centers of bourgeois culture for three years before taking Phnom Penh. Their savagery was thus not an impulsively irrational response to the U.S. bomb-ing but a systematic strategy dictated by their Marxist political program, which required the destruction of traditional institu-tions like religion and family, and which required as well forced collectivization, liquidation of the "parasitic" classes, and po-lice terror. All these techniques had been part of the standard Marxist-Leninist repertory since 1917.

But then the myth that the United States is guilty for the Cambodian tragedy is a subsidiary part of the myth that makes the United States wholly guilty for the war in Vietnam itself. During the Sixties, the proponents of this myth argued that America was in Vietnam not to stop aggression but to suppress an indigenous peasant rebellion in the South, headed by the National Liberation Front. This is why an apparently small issue like whether or not North Vietnamese regulars were fighting in the South could evoke such passionate and menda-cious denials on the part of the Left in the early stages of the war. This is why the Tet offensive was hailed at the time by opponents of the war as a victory for the NLF and proof that America could not defeat a popular revolution.

But when the war was over, of course, the NLF did not emerge as a triumphant victor, and that popular revolution never came to pass. Instead Hanoi's armies marched into Sai-gon and installed their own cadre in power. The NLF and the other leaders of the South's "indigenous rebellion" (in reality subservient to Hanoi from the beginning) vanished from the political scene. Publicly the North now conceded that Tet had been a military defeat—misinterpreted at the time by the American media and exploited by the American Left; and that the NLF, carrying out what amounted to a massive suicide mission on orders from Hanoi, had been virtually extermi-nated. But instead of recognizing what the newly admitted facts revealed—that the NLF had been a mere front for Hanoi, that the war was really an aggression from the North—the Left invoked the devil theory to blame the entire catastrophe on the United States.

Forced to acknowledge that U.S. forces had actually defeated the puppet NLF, the Left still denied the aggression of Hanoi by claiming that the United States had *caused* the North to conquer the South. "The battering of the peasant society," Chomsky wrote, "particularly the murderous post-Tet accelerated pacification campaigns, virtually destroyed the indigenous resistance by eliminating its social base, setting the stage for the northern domination now deplored by Western hypocrites." Thus America was doubly guilty—of eliminating the NLF, which allegedly would have led the South on a gentler course, and of the barbarism the North ultimately inflicted on this conquered land. In Chomsky's world, it is hell if you do and hell if you don't.

What Chomsky suppresses, of course, is the fact that it still required a bloodbath *after* Hanoi's victory—an estimated one hundred thousand summary executions, a million and a half boat people driven to exile and death, and a like number consigned to tiger cages and Marxist "reeducation" camps—to complete North Vietnam's subjection of the South. Nor should such an outcome have been a surprise for someone aware that tens of thousands of domestic opponents were killed by Uncle Ho Chi Minh after 1954, or that thousands of civilians were clubbed to death in Hue during Hanoi's brief occupation of that city in 1968.

In the Stalin era, it would have been unthinkable for most Leftists to admit such possibilities as socialist concentration camps and summary executions, or socialist imperial conquests. Today, such things can at last be admitted, but only so long as it can also be claimed that in the final analysis the United States is responsible. Chomsky is far from being alone in this kind of thinking. Is there a gulag in the Soviet Union whose thaw defies *glasnost?* America's cold warriors are to blame. Did Soviet legions invade Afghanistan and slaughter a million guiltless inhabitants? It was only because the CIA destabilized a neighboring regime. Did Fidel Castro subvert a democratic revolution and turn Cuba into a Communist gulag? The United States drove him into the arms of the Soviet Union. And so on.

And that is why, finally, Nicaragua is not another Cuba, as far as Leftists and their sympathizers are concerned. Because Cuba is not even Cuba—not really. It is a paradise lost as a result of American hostility. In the eyes of the Left, Cuba is a noble revolution tragically (and probably temporarily) diverted from the shining path by the malignity of its capitalist foe. Forget the fact that Soviets administer the still one-crop Cuban economy; and that Soviet subsidies amounting to one quarter of Cuba's GNP keep Castro's island afloat. Forget, finally, that Cuba today is a more abject and deformed colony of the Soviet empire than it ever was of America in the days before the revolution. America made it happen. Similarly, it is Washington, not the Sandinista directorate, that has stunted the growth of a new society in Nicaragua, twisting the revolution there into odd and malignant shapes as a result of its animosity toward utopia.

In the intellectual laboratory where Chomsky works, America's alleged ability to render the sane mad becomes a kind of ineluctable law of capitalist depravity. Suppose, he says, that revolutionaries in a Third World country anywhere on earth were to try to put their utopian agenda into action:

> Any such development, whether libertarian or authoritarian in tendency, . . . would lead to unremitting hostility on the part of the great powers—in the domains of our influence, to an attack by the United States. The primary goal would be to prevent any infringement on private privilege linked to U.S. power, to abort these efforts by subversion or direct attack or economic pressures that no weak and underdeveloped country can withstand. Or, second best, to drive the perpetrators of this iniquity into the hands of the Soviet Union; then further attacks can be justified in terms of "defense" and the revolutionary leadership will be compelled to institute harsh and authoritarian measures under duress, so that popular discontent will mount and the endeavor will fail for that reason. Nicaragua today is a case in point.

Marxist-Leninists can engage in *no* behavior so base that the United States did not first *imagine* it for them. Forget that Fidel Castro by his own admission was a Marxist-Leninist long before he landed in the Sierra Maestre* or that Daniel Ortega and his comrades were devotees of the Eastern bloc long before they rode a democratic revolution to power in Nicaragua. The U.S. devil made them subvert their utopias. Forget that Castro and Ortega in their respective ways, rather than looking to the U.S.S.R. as a last desperate resort, assiduously wooed the Soviets from the beginning. The United States set out craftily to discredit their revolutions by *forcing* them to become lackeys of the Soviet state.

The circle of American guilt and radical innocence is complete, the knot drawn tight by the great *what if?* What if Castro and the Sandinista *comandantes* had not been pro-Soviet Leninists from the beginning; what if they had been determined liberal nationalists instead? Demon America, in Chomsky's choplogic, would nonetheless have forced them to become left-wing fascists and America's enemies anyhow. Thus do the distinctions that make history different from fantasy disappear.

It would be comforting to believe that this malevolent argument is quarantined on the radical fringe, that land of the blind where a one-eyed thinker like Chomsky can be king. But it is not. The same logic surfaces in liberal texts like Peter Davis's *Where Is Nicaragua?* which opens with the identical theme:

> Is Nicaragua the enemy of the United States? The anthem of the Sandinistas, who won the war in 1979 against the Somoza succession, contains the words "We fight against the Yankee, enemy of humanity." There are two ways . . . to look at that line. The first is that if they call us their enemy, they are our enemy, and we should act accordingly. This is simple, straightforward, without reference to context. The second is that the Somozas made that anthem inevitable, and every Nicaraguan knows who made the Somozas.

---

* "Fidel Castro in 1968 explained to me that he had become a Marxist from the very time that he read the *Communist Manifesto* in his student days, and a Leninist from the period when he read Lenin while in prison on the Isle of Pines in 1954."—Saul Landau, "Cuba and Its Critics," *Monthly Review*, May 1987. Carlos Franqui (*Family Portrait with Fidel*) and Tad Szulc (*Castro*) have also exposed the duplicity of Castro's pretensions at the time of being a democrat and a nationalist whose politics were "beyond" the cold war conflict.

The devil made them do it. It is irrelevant to such a view of the world that Washington had joined the political opposition to the Somoza dictatorship in 1978, that without America's support the Sandinista revolution would not have succeeded, or that U.S. aid to the very regime that denounced the Yankee as the enemy of humanity amounted to more than that of any other nation.* The Yankee devil, not their own commitments, made the *comandantes'* hostility inevitable.

Why should America want to make enemies of the Sandinistas in the first place? Chomsky has a ready answer. "The primary concern of US foreign policy," he explains in his *Managua Lectures*, "is to guarantee the freedom to rob and exploit. Elsewhere, I have referred to this as 'the Fifth Freedom,' one that was not enunciated by President Franklin Delano Roosevelt." According to Chomsky, it was actually the *good* deeds of the Sandinistas that provoked "virtual hysteria among US elites," prompting them to take measures in defense of the "Fifth Freedom." The Communist threat, therefore, is nothing more than the "threat of a good example":

* Cf. the testimony of former Sandinista official Arturo Cruz, Jr.: "From 1979 to 1981 I was the Sandinistas' man in Washington in charge of handling Congress. It was my task to negotiate the $75 million assistance package the Carter Administration was arranging for the Sandinista regime. It provided crucial balance of payments support on very generous terms. The money came from the Special Support Funds which were reserved only for very close allies of the United States like Israel or Egypt. Not only was the U.S. government giving us economic aid, but quality aid. And not only Special Support Funds, but also PL 480—food for peace funds—and loans for development projects from AID. The U.S. government was also supporting us in our requests to renegotiate our national debts with the private New York banks. Finally, the Carter Administration was using its good offices with the World Bank, the Inter-American Development Bank and other multinational organizations to be very generous with the revolutionary regime. With enemies like this, one doesn't need friends. The line I took as the Sandinista representative in Washington was that if the U.S. was generous with us we would not go to the Soviets for aid. But in reality, even while the U.S. was providing us this generous financial support, we were signing every possible agreement under the table with the U.S.S.R. and the other Communist governments for military support and to establish Party to Party relations. What we Sandinistas wanted was to establish a division of labor: the west would provide the money for socialist economic development, while the Communist states would provide us with the weapons and technical support in setting up the institutions of power— the army, the police, the 'block committees' charged with spying on the population. So while America and the other western democracies supplied advisers to our economic ministers, the internal and external security ministers and the ministries responsible for the new ideological apparatus—communications, education—were reserved for foreign advisors from the Soviet Union, Cuba, East Germany, Bulgaria, North Vietnam and North Korea." In Peter Collier and David Horowitz, eds., *Second Thoughts* (Madison Books, 1989).

> If peasants starving to death in Honduras can look across the borders and see health clinics, land reform, literacy programs, improvement in subsistence agriculture and the like in a country no better endowed than their own, the rot may spread; and it may spread still farther, perhaps even to the United States, where the many people suffering from malnutrition or the homeless in the streets in the world's richest country may begin to ask some questions. It is necessary to destroy the rotten apple before the rot spreads through the barrel.

This calumny has become a kind of conventional wisdom, appearing as the basic explanation of cold war conflict in "feed the hungry" pamphlets distributed by Oxfam and "disarmament" speeches delivered by SANE director William Sloane Coffin. It is an argument that appeals particularly to pampered American Leftists—not even Gorbachev could believe in a fairy tale like this. Especially not Gorbachev, for if *glasnost* reveals anything for certain, it is the bankruptcy of Marxist solutions for poverty and hunger. The socialist "good example" doesn't exist in the U.S.S.R. or anywhere else in the world, not as a fact, let alone as a threat. Socialism has provided the world with nothing more than famine, fear, and chronic backwardness. Is there an industrial power as economically pathetic as the Soviet Union, which is a first world power only in the military sphere? Or a Third World country poorer than Vietnam, where as late as May of 1988 there was an outbreak of famine near Hanoi even though its army is the fourth largest in the world?

If revolutionaries actually improved the lot of the people they ruled, they would not have to close their borders behind a barrier of secret police to maintain their control. But for seventy years this is precisely how they have dealt with the competition from the capitalist world. It is socialism that is fearful of the contagion of the good example of the economic prosperity and social justice of the West. The socialist states are closed societies and military despotisms precisely because they are unable to fulfill their promises even at the admittedly nonutopian levels of the despised capitalist nations.

And so the Leftist hard core of the Eighties no longer really argues the virtues of socialism but instead argues the vices of America. More cynically still, it *evokes* socialist totalitarianism as a way of condemning the institutions of democracy. Thus Chomsky's texts are sprinkled with sentences like "we have over here the 'mirror image' of the Soviet Union," and descriptive phrases like "state terrorism," "state propaganda," and "disinformation" (a coinage of the KGB) to describe the normal functions of American government. Radicals attempting to overthrow American democracy are pointedly referred to as "dissidents"—as though they were the prisoners of a police state. Chomsky's *Political Economy of Human Rights*, in which not a single chapter is addressed to the socialist bloc, features a long section devoted to what he calls "The Pentagon-CIA Archipelago," by which he means "the spread of neo-fascist torture-and-corruption states in the Third World under U.S. sponsorship." Taken from Solzhenitsyn's tragic chronicle of the many millions murdered in the name of socialism in the U.S.S.R., "archipelago" used in this fashion transforms a corrupt argument into an obscenity.

During the latter part of the Eighties, Chomsky's malicious fantasies have attained truly heroic proportions. In *The Culture of Terrorism* (by which Chomsky means America's culture), he draws an exceptionally crude parallel between the United States under Ronald Reagan and Nazi Germany under Adolf Hitler:

History teaches terrible lessons about how easy it is to descend to unimaginable horror. Germany was the pinnacle of civilization, science, and high culture in the years when Hitler came to power. Famous as a "great communicator," he became perhaps the most popular political figure in the history of Germany as long as he was winning cheap victories abroad and carrying out the "Hitler revolution" at home: reinstating "traditional values" of family and devotion, revitalizing the economy through military production, stimulating pride in the nation's glory and faith in its mission.

This passage reveals the deep structure of Chomsky's political grammar. Chomsky does not use words like "Nazi" and "terrorist" as mere political epithets. Instead he uses them to construct an intellectual universe in which the United States functions as the center of evil itself. And this has become the political theology of the American Left. An extraordinary encomium to Chomsky in *The Nation* (May 1988), written by an editor of Irving Howe's *Dissent*, testifies to Chomsky's preeminent status on the Left. *The Nation* article does not shrink at comparing Chomsky to Karl Marx and eulogizes him as "the most valuable critic of American power that we have." A recent collection of his writings is said to exemplify "the remarkable moral and intellectual consistency that he's maintained for more than twenty years. . . . No one has given himself more deeply to the struggle against the horrors of our time."

Chomsky's first service to the Left may have been in providing a *Weltanschauung* in which socialist totalitarians are always innocent and American democrats are always guilty. But his ultimate contribution is to construct an ethical defense of totalitarian falsehood, while elevating intellectual malfeasance into moral principle.

> American dissidents . . . have to face the fact that they are living in a state with enormous power, used for murderous and destructive ends. Honest people will have to face the fact that they are morally responsible for the predictable human consequences of their acts. One of these acts is accurate criticism, accurate critical analysis of authoritarian state socialism in North Vietnam or in Cuba or in other countries that the United States is trying to subvert. The consequences of accurate critical analysis will be to buttress these efforts, thus contributing to suffering and oppression.

In other words, lying about the crimes of totalitarian governments is a moral duty, since these governments are at war with the United States. Whatever else one might say about such ravings, however, it cannot be denied that Chomsky lives by his principles. At the end of the Seventies, in a conversation with radical historian Ronald Radosh, he confided:

You notice I never said anything about what I saw in Vietnam when I went there during the war. My responsibility was to address myself only to the U.S. war against Vietnam. That's why I never went to Cuba. I knew Cuba would be horrible—a real Stalinist nightmare—but because there was no war like in Vietnam I wouldn't have the excuse not to say what I thought.*

If Chomsky is the intellectual godfather of the post-Vietnam Left, he now has many children, all of whom have adopted the devil theory of contemporary history that he has carried to such extremes. As the Left began its political resurgence in the latter part of the Reagan era, some of these former radicals published memoirs of the Sixties. It was an opportunity for them to recapture lost innocence by asserting that whatever excesses they had committed had resulted from America's madness, a social insanity that had temporarily diminished their capacity. "Explaining" the past was thus a means both of self-revisionism and of self-rehabilitation.

"Our values were decent ones, even if we could not always live up to them," proclaims Sixties urban guerrilla and eighties Democrat Tom Hayden at the start of his autobiographical memoir, *Reunion:* "We of the Sixties accomplished more than most generations in American history."

But if one puts aside the civil rights struggles of the early part of the decade (which Hayden and his peers may have participated in but did not inspire), what did this generation accomplish to merit such smugness? Is Hayden thinking of the defeat of America and the resultant genocide in Southeast Asia? Or perhaps the disintegration of civil order and the eruption of violence in American cities? Perhaps he has in mind the explosion of the social epidemics of the Eighties—"feminized" poverty, AIDS, drugs, and drug-related crime—which

---

* Actually Chomsky was only being half-truthful in claiming that he had never said anything about what he saw in Vietnam while he was there. On April 14, 1970 he made a speech in Hanoi in which he declared: "The people of Vietnam will win, they must win, because your cause is the cause of humanity as it moves forward toward liberty and justice, toward the socialist society in which free, creative men control their own destiny." In the speech he described the United States as an "empire that has no place in the twentieth century, that has only the capacity to repress, murder, and destroy."

resulted from the heedless assault on The System that took place in the Sixties.

The real problem for Hayden and others who would rehabilitate the Sixties and themselves is explaining how a Movement that had begun supporting the American Dream of equal opportunity could end up worshiping American Mayhem, romanticizing murderers like George Jackson and Charles Manson, supporting totalitarian enemies, and sponsoring a race war against "Pig Amerika"? The radical alibi was served up recently at the twentieth anniversary of Columbia's student "uprising" by former Weatherman Mark Rudd. Now a teacher in Albuquerque, Rudd spoke in praise of two of his fallen comrades—one blown up by his own terrorist bomb and the other in jail for "political" bank robbery and first-degree murder. Rudd explained, with no apparent self-irony: "I now believe the Vietnam War drove us crazy."

The adolescent whine of this claim, filled with unspoken remorse for the lost excitement of those bygone days, shows that the years intervening between the deed and the thought have not been intellectually productive ones for people like Rudd. Yet we see in this plaint the basis for a reassertion of lost innocence. It is analogous to Chomsky's exculpation of Third World tyrants: The devil made them do it. This defense reopens the gates of Eden for Rudd, as well as for Hayden and his old SDS sidekicks, whose lives and books he has influenced. One of them is Todd Gitlin, a radical in the Sixties and a college professor in the Eighties.

The publication of Gitlin's partisan memoir, *The Sixties: Years of Hope, Days of Rage*, was accompanied by extravagant praise for its "honesty" from Hayden and other Movement alumni, showing that they viewed it as a credible apologia for those bygone times. Like Hayden's *Reunion*, Gitlin's book relies for its argument on the basic themes established by Chomsky—the bad for the most part didn't really happen; and where it did, America was responsible. Thus, striking a moral balance sheet at the end of the decade, Gitlin presents a "casualty roll call":

On August 24, 1970, a bomb planted by the Madison, Wisconsin, New Year's Gang blew up the army's mathematics research building, killing a graduate student who was working late: *the movement's first innocent casualty.* This headquarters of war research had been a focus of Madison's non-violent protest for years. The bombers were veteran activists—a tiny minority, true, but they played out a logic. In the illumination of that bomb the movement knew sin. [Emphasis added.]

Here we see the minimal veracity required for the Left to claim credit for intellectual honesty. Two weeks before Gitlin's first innocent fell, George Jackson's brother Jonathan —a New Left hero and an avatar of political terrorism never mentioned in Gitlin's five-hundred-page text—entered the Marin County courthouse with guns supplied by Communist leader Angela Davis. Jackson's purpose was to free his even more celebrated brother, George, who was awaiting trial for one of the several murders he had already committed. A judge, an assistant district attorney, and several jurors were taken hostage, and within minutes a shoot-out began, in which the judge's head was blown off by a shotgun that had been taped to his chin by Jonathan, and the assistant district attorney was paralyzed from the waist down, and Jackson and two prisoners were killed in the exchange. There is no mention of these innocent victims of Movement violence in Gitlin's book, nor of the guard whom George Jackson had heaved off the third tier of Soledad Prison (targeting him solely because he *was* a guard and white), nor of the three guards whose throats were slit during Jackson's subsequent attempt to escape, nor of the many others gone.

There was a Movement "logic" in these murders too: the same logic that celebrated the killers of policemen like Oakland officer John Frey, who, in an encounter with Black Panther Huey Newton, was shot in the back from twelve inches away; or the logic that defended the Black Panther torturers of Party member Alex Rackley, shutting down Yale University with protests that a black could not get a fair trial in racist America —which indeed was true if he happened, like Rackley, to have been murdered by the Left.

And this is but a small sampling of the sins against innocents omitted from Gitlin's account. Nor is he himself free of blame. He admits that he knew that thousands of Trotskyites were murdered by Hanoi in the Fifties, yet, like other radicals, he promoted the Left-wing cartoon of Uncle Ho as the George Washington of his people and the entire leadership of Hanoi (ready to fight to the last Vietnamese, we now know, to achieve their ends) as Confucian icons. This sort of thinking bears the same relationship to belief that sentimentality does to feeling.

But if Gitlin is soft on himself and his Movement comrades, he is hard on America. Dealing with the question of why "idealists" like Hayden and the Weathermen set out to destroy America from within at the end of the Sixties, he discovers that the devil made them do it. As he puts it, "murderous" America killed their hope by assassinating leaders who promised peaceful change and plunged the country into war and division.

Thus Gitlin "explains" the conversion to violence of Weather leader Bernadine Dohrn by invoking the slaying of Martin Luther King. However, Gitlin's source, an article by Dohrn's friend Lindsay Van Gelder, recalls the real mood of the radical hard core at the end of the decade, which, far from regarding King's murder as a political *tragedy*, saw it as a political *opportunity*:

> Bernadine was sincerely moved, and she began to cry. She said she hadn't always agreed with him, but she responded to him as a human being. . . . She said she was changing into her riot clothes: pants. We went up to Times Square, and there was a demonstration going on of pissed-off black kids and white radicals. We started ripping signs and getting really out of hand and then some kids trashed a jewelry store. Bernadine really dug it. She was still crying, but afterward we had a long talk about urban guerrilla warfare and what had to be done now by any means necessary.

This may be the swiftest transition from belief to disillusionment in recorded history. But Gitlin believes he has found the philosopher's stone in the notion that *any* excess of the era can be explained and justified by what America did to its young. He uses the same rationale to explain his friend Tom Hayden's plan to assault the Democratic convention in 1968: Hayden had been driven to a state of temporary insanity by homicidal America. According to Gitlin, Bobby Kennedy's assassination in June of that year had destroyed the last vestiges of Hayden's belief in the democratic process, making a riot in Chicago seem politically "necessary":

> Most New Left radicals were, in the end, reluctant revolutionaries. Hayden's reaction to Kennedy's assassination was comparable to Bernadine Dohrn's to the murder of Martin Luther King six weeks earlier; he redoubled his energy toward the impending showdown in Chicago. With King and Kennedy dead, a promise of redemption not only passed out of American politics, it passed out of ourselves.

In fact, of course, the Left—the radical Left of Hayden and Gitlin and Bernadine Dohrn—had long since turned its back on Martin Luther King, after Stokely Carmichael upped the ante by declaring the advent of "Black Power" in 1966, and had never supported a Kennedy or any other Democratic Party candidate after 1960. The Left wanted *revolution*; it hated "co-opting" liberal reform far more even than it hated reaction. Far from being the Left's inspiration, as Gitlin implies, the "hated liberals"—as he accurately remembers them elsewhere in his book—were the designated enemies of the Movement from the very beginning. Thus, while claiming that RFK's death robbed Hayden of hope on one page, Gitlin notes, in a kind of Freudian slip on another page: "A few days before Bobby Kennedy was killed Hayden had called him 'a little fascist' to my face."

Now that he is trying to further his political career by moving into the Kennedy aura, Hayden prefers to forget this remark. Because they involve his personal ambitions, his attempts to turn radical guilt into liberal innocence have an especially brazen quality. (Even as a radical, Hayden elicited a kind of scorn for his careerism, leading one Movement heavy to quip in 1970, "Tom gives opportunism a bad name.") In an acceptance speech on the night he was elected to the California state assembly, Hayden recalled the Sixties in these disingenuous words: "I grew up in my father's image but in a new and very different America from the Thirties. . . . There was little authority to respect. The few who could inspire us were assassinated, and with their deaths came the death of hope itself. . . . We arrived at a confrontational stance not out of political preference but only as a last resort."

Actually, Hayden—who omits from his memoirs his own efforts to incite paramilitary insurrections in Berkeley and other American cities—arrived at a confrontational stance quite eagerly and well in advance of a thorough exploration of nonviolent alternatives. According to James Miller's *Democracy Is in the Streets*, by 1961 he was a proponent of the view that the United States was more responsible for the cold war than the Soviet Union. And in a *Partisan Review* article written in 1966, Hayden outlined a future for the New Left that anticipated violence without apparent qualms: "Perhaps the only form of action appropriate to the angry people are violent. Perhaps a small minority, by setting ablaze New York and Washington, could damage this country forever in the court of world public opinion."

This is exactly the thinking with which Hayden set out —while Kennedy and King were still alive—to make an example of Chicago in 1968. Ever one to cover his bets, Hayden might show up at the RFK funeral to weep a few well-publicized tears, but he was more in his element a few months later back in Berkeley, urging the Black Panthers to spark the revolution and taking up rifle practice under the guiding eye of the "Minister of Defense" of the "Red Family" collective he had joined. Such experiences were, of course, airbrushed out of his autobiography. It is another sacrifice to the cause: he is so committed to the restoration of radical innocence that he is willing to subtract even from the sum of his own life.

A one-man cult of personality, Hayden has made his rehabilitation effort for himself alone. Todd Gitlin's hope is to reclaim the innocence of the Left in general. "Kennedy, King, Kennedy," he intones. "They sometimes felt like stations in one protracted murder of hope." The truth is just the opposite. Kennedy, King, Kennedy: Radicals ultimately despised all three. In the history of the Left, liberalism has always been the target. Lenin's Bolsheviks did not overthrow the Russian czar but the liberal Kerensky. It was by overthrowing Cuba's liberal President Urrutia that Castro defined his own revolution. And it was by crushing the liberal wing of the anti-Somoza coalition led by social democrats like Alfonso Robelo and Violetta

Chamorro that the Sandinistas unveiled their totalitarian agenda. And it was in their bitter war against the liberals—the "cold war liberals" who had fought Communism at home and abroad—that America's Sixties radicals found their reason for being.

Gitlin inadvertently reveals just how unreasoning and un-self-aware this hostility is in an anecdote he tells about a trip he took with an SDS delegation (including Hayden) to a Cultural Congress in Castro's Cuba in 1967. "Like any revolutionary tourist, I thought little about what I didn't get to see," he writes in the spirit of faint self-criticism. "I walked on the bright side, sampling some combination of reality and wishful thinking." Gitlin claims that at the time he was not unaware that Cuba was part of the Soviet bloc; that strikes were outlawed in the socialist state; that food was rationed and there were chronic shortages; that homosexuals and intellectuals had been rounded up by security police; and that Committees for the Defense of the Revolution spied on individuals at the neighborhood level. But while such things might have disturbed his unconscious, Gitlin was ready to make allowances and look the other way—until, that is, he saw a reminder of his own country again:

> What was palpable was the pain of reentry to my homeland, whose trade embargo and violence . . . were certainly not helping Cuba's chances for independence. At the Mexico City airport, having a drink with Dave Dellinger and Robert Scheer, I looked out the window and saw a billboard advertising Cutty Sark. I had to change seats: after twenty-three days where public space was turned to revolutionary use, capitalist propaganda disgusted me.

Having gladly "walked on the bright side" in totalitarian Cuba, he is now overcome with such nausea upon seeing an ordinary advertising billboard that he has to turn away. The visceral quality of Gitlin's reflex at the time and the fact that he recounts this moment with an utter absence of irony betrays the emotional taproot of the Leftist passion, which is a profound alienation from one's own community and culture.

This alienation, whether self-induced or acquired

through some "radicalizing" experience, precedes the embrace of the socialist fantasy, an observation that was made fifty years ago by Ludwig Von Mises: "Socialism is the grandiose rationalization of petty resentments." This is why the nihilism of the Left toward the liberal societies of the democratic West is always stronger than any secret doubts it might have about the socialist utopia it professes to believe in but whose opposite it creates. In *The Sixties*, Gitlin reprints a diary entry in which he analyzes the impressions of his 1967 trip:

> We look to Cuba not only because of what we sense Cuba to be but because of what the United States is not. For generations, the American Left has externalized good: we needed to tie our fates to someone, somewhere in the world, who was seizing the chances for a humane society. Perhaps we need an easy diversion from the hard business of cracking America. Now we dig Cuba. . . . We preserve our quick optimisms with fantasies of an assault on our barracks, a landing in our yacht, a fight in our mountains."

In the puerile fantasy whose dreamwork remains indelibly imprinted on the mind of the unreconstructed radical self, Gitlin arrives accidentally at a home truth: The source of radical innocence about the socialist future is radical hostility toward one's own community.

In the revolutionary year 1968, when the Vietnam War was still raging and Leszek Kolakowski still considered himself a Communist, the Polish philosopher put his finger on just what it was that would make him an ex-Communist a few years later. What he recognized was the fact that making a utopia is an act of destruction. "To construct a utopia," he wrote, "is always an act of negation toward an existing reality, a desire to transform it." But suppose this utopia were so remote as to be unrealizable? How would this affect the socialist movement attempting to realize it? Kolakowski's answer in 1968 was that if a utopia proved too remote from reality, "the wish to enforce it would be grotesque" and would lead instead to a "monstrous deformation" threatening the very freedom of mankind. If the Left persisted in its attempt to make such a utopia, it "would then turn into its opposite—the Right. But then, too, the utopia would cease to be a utopia and become a slogan justifying every current practice." *

This describes exactly what has happened since the era of Stalin. The socialist ideals of the Left have proved themselves ever more remote from reality. Socialism has become a slogan justifying every current practice of totalitarian power. In those countries where the revolutionaries have yet to succeed—in the West in particular—the negative goals of the utopian project have dominated its course. The Left has been consumed by its own energies of negation and nihilism, branding America—the most progressive democracy—as the devil incarnate, while embracing the destructive agendas of a global reaction. Where in the Soviet Union, China, and elsewhere in the Eastern bloc, liberal reforms have begun to move these desperate societies toward the more humane standards and more productive institutions of the capitalist West, the Left has taken this not as an indication of Western virtues but as indication that anti-Communism is mere ideological prejudice and western defense concerns mere military paranoia. Emotionally allied to anti-Western Islamic fundamentalists, anti-Semitic terrorists, and anti-American totalitarians in its hatred of the Great Satan, while instinctively linked to a bloc of Marxist dictatorships permanently at war with democratic societies, the Left has indeed "turned into its opposite," as Kolakowski worried that it might. The shells of broken eggs pile up, but there are no omelets. The chefs of the Revolution have never fed anyone yet.

Sophisticated cynics like Chomsky, sentimental revisionists like Gitlin, and opportunists like Tom Hayden would never put their own faith in "the final victory of Soviet Socialism," as the Ortegas and Castros and Oliver Tambos do. Their agenda is that of the destructive generation whose target was—and is—America. In singing their songs of innocence, they create a music that can only be heard by the deaf.

---

* Leszek Kolakowski, "The Concept of the Left," in *Towards a Marxist Humanism* (New York, 1968).

III

Self-Portraits

— • —

chapter 9 _____

Peter Collier

Something Happened to Me Yesterday

The longest way round is the shortest way home.
—Joyce, *Ulysses*

It is true that history did not provide our generation with a great issue, as Stalin and Soviet Communism was for the Thirties, which would force a decision either to continue knowingly the commitment to totalitarianism or to denounce past belief and thus risk being stigmatized for apostasy. There was no great Rubicon to cross, like the purge trials or the Hitler-Stalin pact. But there have been events over the past two decades—the fate of Vietnam, revelations about the Cuban gulag, the invasion of Afghanistan—that should have prompted a rethinking about who exactly we were in the Sixties, what we did, the way we viewed the world, and the heritage we left. The fact that there has been so little soul-searching reinforces the thought that many of us suppressed at the time—that the New Left, to put it charitably, was not a thinking movement. It was vaunt and braggadocio. Despite all the "struggle sessions," the intellectual nattering, and endless talk, the New Left always had an allergic reaction to ideas, and this is what has made it incapable, retrospectively, of grand disillusions.

In the Thirties, the era against which we always measured our own, the main actors were at least adults—embracing adult evil and, in some cases at least, making adult atonement. The Sixties was a decade of adolescence filled with lost boys and girls who never grew up politically and have thus ignored the promptings of history to take stock of the consequence of their acts. This is why none of the Movement heavies has written credibly, let alone eloquently, about such issues as belief and betrayal; or why none of them ever had a political dark night of the soul that would cast light on the common experience.

Nonetheless, it is obvious why there should be such retrospective affection for the Sixties. It was a time, perhaps the last time, when talk was cheap and life was fun. It was the last time when it was possible to be innocent. Yet even then it was innocence with a knowing smile. Most of the radicals I knew were, at least by the end of the decade, confirmed cynics and connoisseurs of chaos. What we called politics in the Sixties was exactly what Lewis Feuer and many of our other political elders tried to say it was before we shouted them down—an Oedipal revolt on a grand scale; a no-fault acting out. We liked to think of ourselves as characters out of Malraux. As I think back on it now, however, it seems to me that we were always political Katzenjammer kids whose American Mischief turned into American Mayhem without missing a beat.

The Sixties was a time that existed in the eye of history as few other times have, yet for all this its years were oddly ahistorical. There were great events—a cataclysmic war, assassination and fratricidal strife, the disaffection of an entire generation—yet the time itself has none of the perverse grandeur Arthur Koestler and others managed to salvage from the Thirties. This is why the decade plays less authentically in the chambers of memory as tragedy than as melodrama and farce.

• • •

Many of the people I came to know in the Movement were red-diaper babies who had been political all their lives. They seemed still to be living on a green card, intellectual expatriates in their own land. Their provisional status—they were citizens of the world rather than of the U.S.A.—made me envious of them. By comparison, I felt that I had spent most of my life in America's air-conditioned nightmare, and that my politics were not the outgrowth of some honorable adversarial tradition but rather homemade and ad hoc.

When these red-diaper friends of mine were growing up, I fantasized, they talked about Hegel and Marx at the dinner table. By contrast, my own parents, to the extent they discussed politics at all, focused on such mundane concerns as the ominous growth of taxes and bureaucracy in Washington. (FDR's capitulation at Yalta was as exotic as they got.) They had been New Dealers during the Depression, but they had become conservative Republicans after the war. It was a transition that had nothing to do with affluence—they never rose above the lower depths of the middle class—but rather with a sense of loss: loss of community, of freedom, of breathable air; loss of something it was impossible to define decisively and impossible not to feel every day of one's life. One of my strongest memories is of a family drive down Sunset Boulevard in Hollywood when I was ten or so. My father saw a newsboy, slammed on the brakes, jumped out of the car, and came back with a paper whose heavy black headlines said that the United States was sending troops to Korea. "The bastards have done it to us again," my father said, quickly scanning the story. It was *them* (Washington, big government, etc.) against *us*. The modern era was threatening and invasive.

I suppose my political "consciousness," as we radicals grandly called it, began when I left southern California in 1959 to go to UC Berkeley. The city has since become a self-parody. It is a place where the school system, once one of the best in the nation, has been crippled by radical schemes and schemers; where elected officials have concentrated on an anti-American "foreign policy" while allowing problems of crime, housing, and economic stagnation to go unchecked; where a merchant, in an elliptical comment on the miasmic bureaucracy that has sprung up over the years of radical rule, posted a sign in his shop that drew universal assent: "Everything that is not expressly forbidden is mandatory."

The last time I was there, a sewer had broken, spewing human excrement onto Telegraph Avenue. Some people walked out into the street to avoid it, or tiptoed in mincing little steps to expose as little shoe surface as possible. But most plowed stoically through the mess, pretending not to see or smell it. The scene was right out of Kundera and offered itself as a metaphor for Berkeley civic life.

It was different in the late Fifties. Berkeley was a clean, well-lighted place, a city with the feel of a town. Relatively small, it conveyed a sense of space. It was self-identified as a refuge for creative eccentricity and an arena for discovery. California as a whole had not yet discovered its identity as a place of cultural early warnings and had a certain coastal backwardness. Berkeley was a liberated zone of cosmopolitanism within the provincial squareness of the state. Everybody seemed to be writing a novel; everyone was an "existentialist." The city was implicated in the beatnik happening across the Bay, and indeed, an awed undergraduate might occasionally see Jack Kerouac himself strolling down Telegraph Avenue.

But for me, Berkeley's primary appeal was that it was not southern California, where I had grown up in the middle of what seemed the distilled essence of the Fifties, a time and place of ponderous boredom, "conformity," and Ike. Juvenile delinquency was a threat and an enticement. I drag-raced my 1947 Ford on city streets. I went to poetry readings staged by Ferlinghetti and Ginsberg with a sense that I was a truant from my preordained fate. I dreamed of getting away from "L.A.," which to me meant getting *into* the real world.

I spent the summer of 1958 attending the University of Mexico in Mexico City. Students there snake-danced through the campus chanting "Yankee Go Home," and I joined them. Someone pointed out the famous mural by Siqueiros and said that he had been implicated in the assassination of Trotsky; I said, "Who was Trotsky?" At one point during my stay, a Mexican friend said, "Let's go to help Castro." It seemed like something Brando or James Dean might do. Several of us tried lackadaisically to arrange for a private yacht like the *Granma* which would take us to Cuba. The deal, which had almost nothing to do with politics, fell through. Instead of going to Havana, I went to Berkeley.

Ann Arbor usually gets the credit for being the birthplace of the New Left because of the Port Huron Statement. But before Tom Hayden and the other founding SDSers made their manifesto, Berkeley was already feeling the first faint tremors of the eruption to come. There were vigils to protest the execution of the "red-light bandit," Caryl Chessman, and sit-ins against racial discrimination on San Francisco's Auto Row. There were demonstrations against HUAC, in which the police washed students and other protesters down the steps of City Hall with fire hoses, taking obscene pleasure in aiming the spray of water at women and moving it up and down their skirts between their legs. The film which purported to "expose" the demonstrators, *Operation Abolition*, played for years afterward. It might have been taken seriously in the hinterlands, but at Berkeley it was a joke, a little like *Reefer Madness* now. Joe McCarthy was dead, and we had insulted his corpse just as Khrushchev had Stalin's.

For me, it was all the political equivalent of a fashion statement; all this had to do with how I wanted to be *seen*. I thought of myself as a "liberal," which seemed fairly daring in a state still dominated by John Birchism. Yet there was something more to it than being a bad boy. A distant sound beckoned. It had to do with being better than one thought one might be; with having a more spontaneous fate. Nobody knew what to call it yet, but we talked about a new politics that would avoid the ideological ossification of the Soviet Union as well as America's long status quo; a politics that would be a *personal witness* and lead to *authenticity*.

I was working on a graduate degree in English when JFK was assassinated. The years after his inauguration had been our equivalent of the phony war. Everything was ready; we were geared up, although we weren't quite sure for what. As the news flashed from Dallas, I realized that there had been a seismic shift. In an instant, the political landscape had changed. It was more than a feeling of loss, or even the stunned comprehension that the era of the lone crazed gunman was at hand. It was more a realization that "the system" was perhaps incapable of protecting itself. I remember the ripple of fear and also the sense of anticipation: what if *they* ever took us seriously?

The Free Speech Movement of 1964 offered a first opportunity for an answer. As the protest ripened, the FSM proposed that the university was actually an allegory for society at large, where power worked secretly to crush personal freedom just as the chancellor crushed our student rights. Slowly we paralyzed the campus by our protest, feeling that we were coming of age in a glorious rush. We would seize our destiny while we were still in our prime. We had to, because you couldn't trust anyone over thirty.

As the conflict with the university administration reached a crisis, we had the heady feeling that history was not something one reads about but something one could actually make. Nor did one have to wait for one's middle years to have adult power. People were *watching* us; we were *on television*. There was also a sense that underneath all its talk about the importance of rules, the system was riddled with self-doubt. Wordsworth was never my favorite poet, but when the Alameda sheriffs began to gather on the edge of campus shortly before dawn for what would be the first mass arrest of students in decades, I kept thinking about his lines on the French Revolution: to be alive was bliss, and to be young was very heaven.

When the FSM began, I was well into a Ph.D. thesis on Jane Austen. When it ended, so had my career as a graduate student. I could no longer conceive of life as a methodical march through predictable stages. Now there were CORE marches against employment discrimination in restaurant row of Oakland's Jack London Square, pickets at William Knowland's dread Oakland *Tribune*. In the spring of 1965, Berkeley had its Vietnam Day, one of the first major teach-ins against the war in the country. Previously, Saigon had been a fantasy name like Katmandu or Sri Lanka. Listening to Isaac Deutscher, I. F. Stone, and other speakers, I integrated Vietnam into my developing political geography. It was a place, as one speaker said, occupied by American soldiers just as the Alameda County sheriffs had recently occupied our campus.

That summer I went to Birmingham to teach at Miles College. The president of the small black school, Elijah Pitts, reminded me powerfully of the cagey college president in

Ralph Ellison's *Invisible Man*. He had walked a tightrope that allowed the school to keep its autonomy while Miles students were heavily involved in the demonstrations that had caused Bull Connor to unleash his police dogs the previous summer. When I got there, President Pitts had hired a group of middle-aged black men in overalls to walk the perimeter of the campus with shotguns because of drive-by shootings by the Klan. I got to know one of them. His name was Raymond. He once gave me half of his lunch, a sandwich of rich, pungent meat he later told me was possum.

The experience was an intense one, which I remember less as a whole than as a series of images frozen in montage: The swooping figure of a commemorative black Christ in stained glass at the Baptist church where four little black girls had been blown up in a bombing the year before. Young whites with baseball bats following us when we tried to register voters as part of a SNCC project. A new bombing in Birmingham, with an elderly white-haired black man standing in front of his charred house, looking like a photographic negative.

I felt the example of Goodman, Chaney, and Schwerner constantly before me. I visualized my charred body being kicked desultorily by men with lank hair and recessed chins, men in overalls with a menacing look of inbred sameness. The Klan did chase us every once in a while, in rickety pickups, when we sallied forth from the Miles campus. It seemed like some sort of ritual, war games carried out within prescribed roles. Once the back window of the car we were in exploded and collapsed on our shoulders in squares of safety glass. That was as close as martyrdom came.

All the blacks I met that summer idolized Martin Luther King, except for a short, coffee-colored SNCC worker named John Jefferson. A director of the voter registration project, he ridiculed King as "Gee-zuz" and "de Lawd." During one of our discussions, he surprised me by saying, "It's not important who's got the Bible. It's important who's got the guns." He spoke with appealing cynicism about nonviolence, a philosophy whose days, he said, were numbered. It was the first time I had heard this kind of talk, and Jefferson was the first black I met in the South who regarded white civil rights workers with open ambivalence.

The summary moment of that Birmingham summer (although I didn't fully understand the lesson until later on) came from a girl named Hazel, who was a student in one of the English classes I taught at Miles. She was very dark, almost blue-black, tall and thin, with coltish legs and a perpetually startled look like that of a deer surprised at water. She never said much in class but turned in essays I felt were remarkable, better by far than most papers I had gotten as a graduate teaching assistant in the English department at Berkeley.

In my fantasies, Hazel became part of a parable of wasted potential—the one who, if she could be saved, would help redeem an evil situation. She became my project. I told her she should be thinking of going to a college in the North where she could develop her gifts. I said I wanted to talk to her parents so that we could figure out a way for this to happen. She begged me not to, but I insisted. I borrowed a car and drove to their house on Saturday afternoon, following a red dirt road to a yard filled with automobile carcasses and old bathroom fixtures with rust leaking down onto the porcelain. Hazel's mother came to the door of a tar-paper shack and invited me in. She was a large woman with a shiny face and large crescents of sweat staining the underarms of her dress. I talked; she smiled and fanned herself while sitting below a painting of JFK on velour, nodding in automatic agreement with whatever I said. I told her that I was going to get her daughter away from all this, that I was going to get her into a school in the North where she could *be* someone. Hazel's mother smiled and nodded and shooed the flies with her fan.

A week or so later, one of the other teachers at Miles, to whom I'd shown some of Hazel's work, brought me an anthology of literature from the Harlem Renaissance. He opened the book to a marked page, set it down on my desk, and left the room. I picked it up and began to read. It was the same thing that Hazel had written in one of her essays, almost word for word. As I read further in the anthology, I saw the sources for most of her other writing as well. I was devastated and told John Jefferson about the plagiarism. He laughed until tears came into his eyes. "You been punching the tar baby all along," he said.

• • •

By the time I got back to Berkeley, I had the feeling that Martin Luther King and white civil rights workers were about ready to become obsolete. But it didn't matter. I had already made a personal transition from civil rights to Vietnam. The question was not what to do. Like others, I passed through the early stages of the foreign policy debate painlessly: It was necessary to support the NLF and work against the U.S. The only question was how to do it. How to become an activist, or, as we called it then, an "organizer"? Whom to organize? How to get paid for it? These questions got a partial answer when I became one of the coordinators of Robert Scheer's bid for Congress.

A radical journalist who had become a minor Bay Area personality, Scheer had established himself as an early critic of the war. He was articulate and outspoken, and after interminable wrangling about whether or not to work within the electoral system, we decided to run him against incumbent Berkeley congressman Jeffrey Cohelan, one of LBJ's favorite liberals. We came close to winning the Democratic primary in a campaign that drew national attention. After the election, Scheer got me a job at *Ramparts*, where he was an editor.

The magazine was just then undergoing its transformation from a small quarterly published by liberal Catholics to a big-circulation monthly funneling radical politics into the mainstream. This metamorphosis came about as a result of two factors. One was the New Left, represented by several of us, notably Scheer, who was not a prolific writer himself but had the ability to make the radical gestalt yield a provocative journalistic point of view. The other factor in the success of *Ramparts* was the salesmanship of the editor in chief, Warren Hinckle, who was the same age as the rest of us but only faintly interested in the New Left. (He became a radical later on, in the mid-Seventies, starting to celebrate just as the party was over.)

Hinckle liked to think of himself as an old-fashioned newspaperman, a heavy-drinking, muckraking troublemaker in the tradition of Ambrose Bierce and Citizen Kane, his heroes when he edited the college paper at the University of San Francisco. Coming from a local Irish-Catholic family, he was almost comically anxious to acquire panache and cultivated a dandy's style that emphasized patent-leather dancing pumps and three-piece suits instead of the proletarian look the rest of us had adopted. His trademark was a patch covering a missing or mutilated eye, whose fate remained a mystery. My son Andrew, then three years old, couldn't keep from staring at the eyepatch when I brought him to the *Ramparts* office, and referred to Warren as "that pirate guy." This was closer to the truth than he could have known, as the investors Hinckle convinced to pour a king's ransom into *Ramparts* over the next few years could have ruefully affirmed.

Ramparts seized the country's attention in 1967 with the first big exposé on the CIA—in this case, the agency's infiltration of the National Student Association. Others followed. Soon the magazine was making news as well as reporting it. Featuring investigative reporting and splashy four-color art direction at a time when other political magazines were filled with interminable commentary and unrelieved blocks of type, *Ramparts* became a sort of synecdoche for the New Left itself —a triumph of aggressive self-dramatization, not particularly intelligent or at all introspective but very much on the scene, kicking the shins of the establishment and demanding to be taken seriously.

It was also a clearinghouse for people who eventually became part of the media establishment. Scheer eventually joined the staff of the Los Angeles *Times.* Hinckle now writes for the San Francisco *Examiner.* A variety of others who would make a mark had brief encounters with *Ramparts* over the years—people like Britt Hume of ABC and Daniel Zwerdling of National Public Radio. Jann Wenner was a sort of glorified copyboy who tried to write rock criticism for *Sunday Ramparts,* a newspaper we began during the San Francisco newspaper strike of 1967 and whose design he ultimately appropriated when he began *Rolling Stone.*

Hunter Thompson, then a little-known journalist, came through San Francisco to meet us because of a flattering review I had written about his first book, on the Hell's Angels. At the time of Thompson's visit, Warren had a monkey named Henry Luce he kept in the office. Hunter left his rucksack near Henry Luce's cage while we went to lunch. Somehow the monkey got out and opened the bag. When we got back we found the floor strewn with the pharmacopoeia of red and white pills Hunter carried with him. Henry Luce had to have his stomach pumped.

Ramparts got Eldridge Cleaver out of jail after it published the first essays of what became *Soul on Ice*. The first day Eldridge came into the office after being paroled, I could tell he was going to become an important figure. He walked with a cantilevered prison-yard strut; his hooded green eyes conveyed a sense of danger mitigated by an odd introspection and self-irony. Talking to him was like playing tennis against a wall: the ball always came back just as hard as you hit it. He seemed amused that his background as a rapist was an aphrodisiac for certain women of the Left, and he talked about "pussy" with the laconic humor of a stand-up comedian. I remember coming into the office one Saturday afternoon and hearing rustling noises in the only room with a sofa. Soon Eldridge opened the door and came out grinning, followed by a blond girl whose picture I had seen on the society page of the San Francisco *Chronicle*, and who was now rearranging herself in the manner of a hen that has just had an encounter with a rooster.

Eldridge gave us a certain authenticity we had lacked with radical blacks, as he brokered a coalition between *Ramparts* and the Black Panther Party, a group which became, for a time at least, something like a wholly owned subsidiary of the magazine. Yet we never really knew how to relate to him other than as an odd asset we had accidentally acquired. I heard that he had approached James Baldwin at a San Francisco party and greeted him with a deep kiss, a noteworthy event primarily because he had earlier tried to establish himself as a black writer by attacking Baldwin (just as Baldwin himself had done by attacking Richard Wright). I know Eldridge liked to mock white radicals' solemn left-wing pieties. Once he caused a sudden silence in one of our editorial meetings, which had digressed into an encomium on Trotsky, by interrupting with the statement, "Trotsky was a white bourgeois intellectual like you all. Stalin, now, he was a brother off the block. More people were killed trying to see that brother's corpse than ever followed any Trotsky." We were horrified by the heresy but dared not contradict him.

People occasionally ask about the strange twists in Eldridge's subsequent career—how, after his return from exile in Algiers and Paris (where he is rumored to have shared a mistress with Giscard d'Estaing), he got involved with the Moonies and other odd organizations. My only answer is that he is now what he always was—a hustler.

In truth, *Ramparts* did not produce much good journalism. The pressure to shoehorn the facts into our view of reality was too great. As the violence of the Movement escalated, so did the violence of our journalism. We did not just assign stories; we assigned writers to *do in* certain American personalities, to *destroy* certain American "myths," to *attack* certain American organizations and institutions. Aside from its disregard for the truth, such an editorial policy, if it could be called that, obviously did not give most writers enough intellectual legroom to discover their subject and themselves. But it did demand a tough adversarial stance; a perception that there were moral and political issues embedded even in seemingly "value-free" phenomena; and a commitment to comfort the oppressed, as Mencken had described the journalist's task, and to oppress the comfortable. And so for someone like myself, whose views on life had been formed according to Jamesian laws of moral ambiguity, the atmosphere of *Ramparts* was tonic.

Our journalistic politics, like the politics of the New Left as a whole, invariably involved liberal-bashing. The Republicans and conservatives were not our enemy; they were irrelevant. It was the liberals we were after—the ones most identified with what Henry Luce (the man, not the monkey) had prematurely called the American Century. The liberals were the ones who had been present at the creation; the ones who had, in the revisionist clichés that became the foundation for New Left thought, begun the cold war; the ones who had taken the anti-Communism of the Truman Doctrine (not the buffoonery of McCarthy) as an excuse to extend American power into every crevice of the globe. Irving Kristol later said that a neoconservative was a liberal who had been mugged; we identified ourselves as the muggers long before the comment was made.

As the "literary" one of the magazine, I got to take on

some interesting targets. One was Eric Hoffer, the "longshore-man philosopher" of San Francisco, who had become a sort of poet laureate for the Johnson administration. Another was John Steinbeck, whom I attacked for forgetting his old sympathies with the Okies and other victims of power in his rush to embrace the President and his war. (After the piece appeared, I got a couple of fan letters from Steinbeck's disaffected son, then fighting in Vietnam, who applauded my attack against his father. During one of *Ramparts*'s times of financial hardship, I sold them for fifteen dollars apiece to a rare-book dealer.) I also wrote about some cultural organizations, writing the first investigative report on Synanon (an organization that was then a favorite of the liberal media) because of what even then were its clearly totalitarian tendencies.

As with the mainstream of the New Left at this time, *Ramparts* was "political" as opposed to "cultural," regarding the shotgun marriage Jerry Rubin had tried to perform between these two opposites during the 1967 Summer of Love as a deviation that would pollute radicalism. For this reason we missed the significance of the Haight-Ashbury scene, for instance. And we not only missed but actually *dismissed* the significance of women's liberation, publishing an early article in which we attacked Betty Friedan and also convinced the Leftist women we proposed as her betters to model for the cover of the magazine in elegant maxiskirts).

We didn't check facts very energetically, and paranoia and ideology always overcame professional skepticism. It is hard not to wince when leafing through *Ramparts* back issues (some of which, I am told, now sell for a considerable sum). Yet it is also true that the magazine will probably get at least an agate-type footnote in the histories of journalism to come. It midwifed the rebirth of investigative journalism taken up by the *New York Times* and the Washington *Post* with greater resources in the 1970s, and it accurately—if often somewhat unintentionally—chronicled the temper of the times.

1968 was a turning point. Tet, Johnson's withdrawal, the assassinations of Martin Luther King and Bobby Kennedy, the riot in Chicago: the year is a metaphor that contains the whole story of the great unraveling of the Sixties. As it unfolded, we sensed—although we didn't admit it—that the New Left had decided to go crazy. The slogans were afflicted by moral scurvy. ("Bring the troops home" had become "Bring the war home.") A chic hatred of America had long since replaced any intention to make America better. Even the most quotidian moments took on the coloration of significant political experiences. We were exhilarated by the disasters that befell U.S. athletes at the Mexico City Olympics; Tommie Smith and John Carlos were heroes for giving the clenched-fist salute on the victory stand, and George Foreman was a "Tom" for waving an American flag after winning the Games' heavyweight boxing championship. The only Christmas card I remember getting that year was one whose cover showed a silhouette of a Vietnamese peasant woman with a rifle, under the words "Peace on Earth"; inside the card were the words "By Any Means Necessary."

The war lowered our resistance to the intellectual toxins in the air. We had a weekly ritual of sitting in front of the television set and cheering as Walter Cronkite announced the ever-rising body count on CBS. I carried a comb Tom Hayden brought back from Hanoi, where he had gone to pledge our solidarity with the Vietnamese war effort. It is made out of the fuselage of a downed F-105 and shaped like that plane, and is stamped with the words "The American Pirates 1700th plane shot down in North Vietnam."

We hated the war, but we loved it too. Vietnam made us special, a generation with a mission. Vietnam gave the semblance of moral shape to what was actually a formless hatred of "the system." The war justified every excess, every violent thought and deed. Heaving a rock at some corporation's window, we banished guilt by the thought: This is for the Vietnamese. Trying to set fire to a university library, we said to ourselves: This is for the Vietnamese. If the war gave us license, it also gave us an addictive sense of moral superiority: we were better than the circumstances in which we were forced to live. If we committed small misdemeanors of indecency, they were in the long run justified by the much larger and more obscene crime in Southeast Asia.

Vietnam was in our marrow. It was *our* war, the experience that defined us. I remember one day in 1968 having a chilling thought after hearing rumors of negotiations: What if it ends? What will we do then? But I quickly put the thought aside. It was impossible that the war should ever end; it was the time of our life, a fiery fountain of youth.

Chicago became the *Kristallnacht* of the New Left. Jerry Rubin was there, talking about putting LSD in the water supply. Hayden had the shrewd intention of provoking the cops, knowing that Mayor Richard Daley had already threatened to shoot looters. If one intention was to inspire a police riot while the whole world was watching, the other was to deliver a final deathblow to the centrists of the Democratic Party, the "cold war liberals" we so hated. The New Left went to Chicago to have some fun, trash the liberals, and elect Nixon. We believed that what transpired there would "maximize the contradictions" and drive the country more swiftly and effectively toward "fascism," where we believed it was ineluctably headed in any case.

Reform was not enough; there had to be revolution. We weren't sure what this meant exactly. But we were sure it had to be. Before we had called ourselves "radicals"; now we were "revolutionaries." We awaited the apocalypse like huddled millenarians scanning the skies for a sign. The 1969 People's Park riots in Berkeley, a combination of crackpot utopians and hard-core politicos, was one such portent. It involved the trashing of Berkeley: plate-glass windows heaving and falling like icebergs; city cops looking frightened as they found themselves isolated within our circle. The "blue meanies" of the Alameda County sheriff's department arrived once again. At one point during the riots, I threw a piece of slag through the tear gas and hit one of them in the shoulder. His partner pointed his shotgun at me. I held up my press card and screamed, "Journalist!"

There was a sudden fad for Frantz Fanon's notion of "revolutionary violence." We were the Americong, and it didn't seem implausible at the time to talk about "taking" Berkeley and making it a model for the "liberated zones" we wanted to create in strategic locales across the country. During the chaos on the streets, Tom Hayden was holed up in a garret somewhere, drafting what he called the Berkeley Liberation

Program. He was also talking about the need to strike back against the sheriffs, an "occupying army" that could be defeated by guerrilla action. (Vietnam was a template that fit over every experience.) White radicals and counterculturalists couldn't do it, he said; they weren't ready. The only ones who could bring off "armed resistance" were the Panthers, whom Hayden called "our" NLF. Cleaver, Huey Newton, and Bobby Seale were all either in jail or on the run at the time of People's Park, and I heard that he went to David Hilliard, the Panthers' interim leader, to talk about the possibility of trying to shoot down an Alameda sheriff's helicopter. Hilliard is said to have looked at Hayden in disgust and responded: "Just like you, Tom. Get a nigger to pull the trigger."

It was a time of breathless waiting, a time whose spirit was captured by the Doors' song about breaking through to the other side. My friend David Horowitz and I had taken over *Ramparts*, removing Robert Scheer and some others in one of those rites of radical purification that affected most Left organizations during the latter part of the decade. (Scheer responded by trying to outflank us on the Left; he organized a radical junket to North Korea and returned to Berkeley saying that he had seen a future that worked and praising the brain-dwarfing "thoughts" of Kim Il Sung.) But running the magazine didn't seem like a sufficient political act. Everyone else seemed to be stockpiling weapons and breaking into "affinity groups" that would, when the revolution came, turn into street-fighting collectives. They were *getting ready*.

It was a time when those of us whose sensibilities had been formed in the Fifties felt in danger of being upstaged by a younger group who'd come of age in the Sixties and seemed to have few qualms about anything. It was the era of the "gut check": those who questioned revolutionary violence were themselves questioned. "The heavier the better" was the new slogan. A symbol of this second wave of the New Left was Bernadine Dohrn, who came through Berkeley with a tiny miniskirt and a sweet, heavy-chinned face—a radical pinup with a moue. "It's time to stop talking," she said. "We've got to *do it!*" She was about to go to Cuba as part of the SDS faction calling itself Weatherman, which met the Cubans and Vietnamese in Havana and came home with a commitment to begin acts of terrorism in the heart of the mother country.

Although we had begun a few years earlier as a movement opposed to dogma, we now began to talk of ourselves as "Marxist-Leninists." We all claimed to be reading *Kapital*; there were soporific discussions about parallels between 1970 and 1917. In this regard, the main attraction in Berkeley was the Red Family, a collective whose principal personalities were Scheer and Tom Hayden. Controlled by sexual politics (there were said to be interminable struggle sessions over such topics as whether or not it was "bourgeois privatism" to go into the bathroom alone and shut the door), the Red Family waited for the revolution by taking target practice and positioning itself as a vanguard that could provide the spark. One day not long after Kent State, David Horowitz and I were sitting with Hayden on the porch of one of the houses the Red Family rented for its "cadre." "Well," Hayden said without any apparent regret, "there will be civil war soon." He said that fascism was inevitable under Nixon. On his advice, I bought a gun so I could be armed when the revolution arrived. I hid the loaded clip in one place and the gun itself in another, so that my children could not find them. I always forgot where the hiding places were and went for months unable to put the whole gun together if the FBI storm troopers had barged into my house to take me to one of the concentration camps we believed they maintained.

At the very moment that the New Left was beginning to degenerate, it was also becoming chic. I realized this early in 1970 when I got a call from a man in Hollywood who said he represented Jane Fonda. He said that Fonda had broken with her former husband, Roger Vadim, and had just completed a session of transcendental meditation with the Maharishi in India. While there, she had read a piece I had written in *Ramparts* about the Indian occupation of Alcatraz. Because of it, she had decided she wanted to come home and "get involved." Would I introduce her to the New Left? Naturally I said yes.

A few days later, she herself phoned and said that she wanted to go to Alcatraz. She arrived one foggy morning in San Francisco, fresh-looking and self-confident, still in her shag-cut *Klute* phase. As we stood at the dock waiting for the boat that would take us to the island, she said she'd been in exile in France for too long, that she wanted to be back in America because this was where it was "happening." I joked that perhaps she had waited too long; the Sixties were over. A look of horror crossed her face, and she said, "Oh, I hope not."

As we landed on the rock, she moved among the Indians with charming self-abasement. She was an incredibly quick study, understanding intuitively what the power arrangements were on the island. She saw, for instance, that there was a factional fight between the Sioux and the other tribes for control of Alcatraz and that the Sioux were more "radical." By the time I left, she was over in the Sioux corner of the old prison exercise yard, smoking dope with them.

Later on, as Jane went off on a tour of the reservations that I had helped arrange for her, she wrote me a note in a backhanded scrawl, expressing her hope that she could be of use in the struggle. It ended with the slogan "Power to the people!" Instead of a dot under the exclamation point, there was a little circle. (My wife looked at it later on and said, "I'm surprised she didn't make it into a little smily face.") The next thing I knew, Fonda was involved in the G.I. Coffee House movement and making appearances such as one on the Dick Cavett TV show with Mark Lane, arguing a vulgar Marxist line about Southeast Asia. We were there because our imperialism required the natural resources of the area, she said, especially the "tung and tinsten."

I watched Jane's rapid progress through the Movement over the next couple of years (culminating in her propaganda appearances in Hanoi) with an appreciation of the spectacle. I always remembered two things: that cute little circle under the exclamation point in the letter she sent me, and the classic spoonerism on the Dick Cavett show.

By the early Seventies, a subtle panic had overtaken the Movement. The revolution that we had awaited so breathlessly was nearing the end of what we now realized would be a dry labor. The monstrous offspring of our fantasies would never be born. People who had gathered for the apocalypse were dropping off into environmentalism and consumerism and fatalism, and (to the ultimate detriment of communities like Berkeley) into local politics. I watched many of my old comrades apply to graduate school in the universities they had failed to burn down so that they could get advanced degrees and spread the ideas that had been discredited in the streets under an academic cover. What German New Leftist Rudi Dutschke called "the long march through the institutions" had begun.

Among the odd developments of the mid-Seventies, we noticed a new tolerance for members of the Communist Party. For nearly a decade, they had hung around our meetings and institutions, trying to find an organization, any organization, they could infiltrate. We hated them for the wrong reasons: not because they supinely supported the Soviet Union but because they were always so *moderate*, always trying to find a way to vote Democratic while we were looking for things to blow up. Now the Communist Party was being reevaluated, if not rehabilitated, as an organization that might provide a model for the suddenly more complex future of the Left. The Party had endurance; its members, whatever their politics, had been in the struggle for the long haul.

About this time, David Horowitz and I became interested in the Panthers, for some of the same reasons that caused others to take a kindly second look at the CP. Huey Newton had disavowed the violence of the previous few years, changing the focus of the group from shoot-outs with the police to community organizing. He emphasized that revolution was not an overnight thing but rather a patient process involving methodical political action and evolutionary change. "Put away the gun," he said. "Concentrate on survival; put together a real community program." To one who had been in the New Left theater of the absurd for so long, such a message seemed refreshing; it was reminiscent of the early days of the civil rights movement, when we had worked to create concrete change rather than theatrical events.

But if there was something attractive in Huey's message, there was something deeply disturbing about the man himself. When I went with David to see him at his Lakeshore apartment, it was like attending a performance that played well enough at the time but left the viewer with doubts that couldn't be answered. There was always a cheering section of whites at his apartment (led by Hollywood producer Bert Schneider), along with black lackeys from the Panther Party. Huey always found some excuse, even on cold days, to take off his shirt and prance around his living room, vamping everyone by flexing the huge pectoral muscles developed by prison push-ups. He would slap palms with his black bodyguards and grab whites around the shoulders in sudden embraces of solidarity. He would occasionally interrupt his nonstop monologues to peer out of a telescope he kept trained on the holding cell in the Alameda County courthouse, where he'd first done time for killing Oakland policeman John Frey, back in 1967. He always carried a water tumbler with him, but it was filled with vodka, not water. He had the face and body of a model, but there was a liverish look in his eyes and a fanged quality in his smile.

Our interest in the Panthers (David's always far greater than mine) continued even when Huey fled to Cuba after being charged with the murder of an Oakland prostitute. In the weeks that followed, David convinced the *Ramparts* book-keeper, a woman named Betty Van Patter, to help the Party get its books in order. Apparently she stumbled onto information showing that they were dealing in drugs and protection rackets. Wanting them to live up to her radical high hopes, she must have confronted them with what she had learned. The next thing we heard, she had been found floating in the Bay, her head caved in by a blow from a heavy object.

There had been rumors on the Left for a long time that the Panthers had used the Santa Cruz Mountains as a sort of killing grounds, where they got rid of members who had been accused, in councils of pandemonium, of being "police agents." We not only ignored these rumors; we said that it was *good* for a revolutionary organization to purge its ranks of informers. But now one of our friends was the victim, and the fact that those who knew about it refused to say anything gave the situation a different coloration. I went to a Berkeley police lieutenant and told him that they had to do something. He said he thought he knew who was responsible for Betty's death and smiled bitterly: "Yeah, well, how can we? You guys have been cutting our balls off for the last ten years. You destroy the police and then you expect them to solve the murders of your friends."

The Black Panther Party, which had begun as a street gang, had never really changed. They had just allowed us white radicals to project our violent fantasies about "vanguards" onto them. They had remained a gang. The gang, it occured to me, might be an appropriate metaphor for the Left as a whole.

As experiences such as this one made me draw back from the radical brink, I took refuge in my family. Because I had a "nuclear" family (some of my comrades used the term with an undertone that suggested that old-fashioned arrangements such as my own were politically radioactive), I had often felt like an impostor, someone whose Movement life was undone by his private life. I had seen others try to heal this dichotomy by forcing their intimate relationships to conform to their politics. They rearranged their marriages to eliminate "bourgeois sexual privatism"; they made their relationships obey the laws of the new feminism and raised their children to become the new men and new women of the coming socialist paradise.

Like others, I paid lip service to all this, but I kept it out of my own life, knowing instinctively that it would first trivialize and then destroy everything that was important to me. This conviction did not come in a rush but in small *aperçus*. I remember one of them quite clearly. Two of my Movement comrades decided to get married. After a ceremony filled with gibberish about liberation and the Third World, there was a reception, featuring a large wedding cake frosted with the slogan "Smash Monogamy!" It occurred to me at the time that the newlyweds were like cannibals as they ate their cake, consuming their own future. Needless to say, their marriage didn't last long, leaving in its rubble a pair of pathetic children, whom I still occasionally see walking around Berkeley looking like the survivors of an airplane disaster.

At about this time, my daughter Caitlin was born. Soon after, my father was diagnosed as having terminal cancer. Being sandwiched between birth and death not only took politics further out of focus for me but also told me something about life, about the fact that it was a game played for keeps. It was a message that I resisted; it meant that we could not continue forever as we had been, that time itself must have an end.

My father and I had fought over politics for years. I

would occasionally tell him some of the things I was doing; he would flinch as if I had slapped him. He couldn't master all the facts about Vietnam ("I don't know Bao Dai from Bo Diddley," he once grumbled during one of my harangues about the French colonial experience). Giving up arguing with me about the war, he had talked inarticulately about his life, what this country meant to him—how he had come to California during the Depression, so poor that he and his mother and father had survived by eating the "road meat" of domestic and wild animals killed by passing cars; how he had worked two jobs during the war and gotten a citation signed by FDR for an improvement he'd designed on a certain power lathe; how he had made a life in California after a youth of dust bowl poverty in the Midwest. I had responded by ridiculing him for seeing himself as a stick figure in the national melodrama, and after a while he stopped talking about anything significant. For years, our visits began by quickly exhausting the noninflammatory subjects and then progressed schematically to wild confrontations and then long silences.

But once I found out he was sick, all our past troubles seemed irrelevant. He was dying, and I suddenly realized that history was dying with him. Not the Hegelian claptrap radicals had in mind when they talked of History, but *lived life*, the human record of an individual trying to make his way through real obstacles and finding victories and losses along the way. My father had created a world that would vanish when he died; this was something for which I was not prepared.

My father's last summer, we decided to go to South Dakota, where he had been born. We drove in his old Chevrolet, reversing the trip he had made fifty years earlier with his parents, to find a new life in the West. I watched him poke around in the crumbled foundations of the sod house near Pierre where he'd lived as a boy. We went to the Black Hills, where he'd hiked as a young man, and to the Pine Ridge Sioux reservation, where he had watched clandestine performances of the sun dance. We didn't talk much while we were there, but it was the best time we had ever spent together. As we were returning home, and his sickness was growing in him, my father began to reminisce about his life. During a long blank stretch of highway in Nevada, he said: "You know, I'm glad I was born a South Dakotan and an American. I'm glad I saw the beginning of the twentieth century. I'm glad I lived through the Depression and the war. I think these things made me a stronger man. I'm glad I came to California, because I met your mother there. I'm glad we had you for a son."

It was the longest speech I'd ever heard him make. It was stagy in the sense that he had obviously thought about the words before he spoke them and was trying to make me feel the power of his emotions. Yet what he said was not maudlin or smarmy. It was a moment of acceptance and affirmation by someone whose life had often been disfigured by unremitting hard work and responsibility, someone to whom words had never come easily. He knew these sentiments were the only estate he would be able to leave me.

What he said and how he said it were so different from the bitterness and anger I had lived with for fifteen years that I was taken aback. My generation had been given a more comfortable fate than my father's, but we hated our lives, despite all the talk of "love." We had projected that hatred onto everything around us. The excuses we gave—that America had alienated us with its post-scarcity plenty—were shallow and puerile.

As I sat beside my father in the hospital a few months later, watching as the last breaths were snatched out of his body, I had a feeling that part of my life was ending too. It was like those artists' conceptions of stages of rockets separating: I could see my past decoupling from my future and falling away into deep space.

My father's death came at about the same time as the U.S. defeat in Vietnam. This was what we had worked for all those years, but it was an outcome that gave no pleasure. We said that we believed Ho Chi Minh City would be a paradise compared to Saigon, but this was a perfunctory expectation. I felt cast adrift, and so did many of my Movement friends. On a deeper level, I wondered what we had really accomplished. Feeling a vague sense of nausea, I remembered something Orwell wrote after returning from Spain: "This war, in which I played so ineffectual a part, has left me with memories that are mostly evil."

As the consequences of the Communist takeover in Vietnam began to be clear, Joan Baez and a few others tried to protest against the reeducation camps and the revolutionary tribunals, the boat people and the new imperialism of Hanoi. But what was left of the Left attacked the attempt to apply the standards of political morality we had claimed to believe in to the Hanoi regime. Tom and Jane, who were on their way to becoming the Mork and Mindy of California politics, were opposed to Baez. So, back east, was the coalition of old-line Communists, neo–fellow travelers, and unreconstructed Sixties radicals, which was slowly (and, it must be said, covertly) forming into the present "Solidarity" Left. No matter that our old allies in the National Liberation Front were among the first to be crushed; no matter that the Khmer Rouge, which we had supported with such great enthusiasm, had embarked on a policy of genocide. There were no enemies on the Left.

To come to terms with what was happening in Southeast Asia would have been a cleansing experience for the Movement. But the Left wasn't capable of this reckoning. It was readying itself to move to the next cause—in South Africa, Central America, or wherever—ignoring the body count that began to pile up in the long totalitarian night it had left behind. The Left had become a revolutionary cargo cult.

It was one thing secretly to think such things, of course, and quite another to say them aloud. That would have meant stepping purposefully away from what I had been most of my adult life and leaving the community of the Left with its powerful vision of humanity as a mass of victims requiring the ministrations of a few select caretakers. It was less the ideas of the Left, such as they were, that I found it hard to disentangle myself from, than the community of the Left, with its seductive postulate that members of its church are on the side not only of decency but of History as well. I could see saying goodbye to most of that, but not all. Most of all, I couldn't visualize the circumstances of the break—how it would feel to be regarded as one full of grace on one day and as someone irreparably damned on the next. I entered a period of dormancy and hibernation, hoping events would take a turn that would reconfirm my old faith and help me to be born again. Deep down, of course, I knew it was over. After the first doubt, to paraphrase Dylan Thomas, there is no other.

Writing finessed the exit. During the time that I had first been feeling traumatized by my left-wing commitments, David Horowitz and I had begun a book on the Rockefeller family. The project was actually an outgrowth of our successful efforts to fund-raise the guilt-ridden fourth Rockefeller generation, our contemporaries, as a way of keeping *Ramparts* alive so that it could publish further attacks on Nelson, David, and the other Rockefeller family elders. We had started the book with the hand-me-down Marxist notion that the Rockefellers were a sort of executive committee of the ruling class, a Rosetta stone by which we could understand American imperialism and power. The truth turned out to be quite different. Far from controlling the world, they were a family not even able to control their own children, who were running away from the Rockefeller name, money, and influence. We started out to write about American power. We wound up writing about American lives.

After the Rockefeller book, I began writing fiction— short stories for little magazines and a novel, *Downriver*, which explored, under a sort of artistic grant of immunity, the issues I couldn't yet bring myself to confront in my daily life: the way people got caught up in movements and in history; the effects of political belief on the affective life; the tension between political and personal commitment, between love of those close to you and love of an Idea.

After receiving a National Endowment of the Arts fellowship in 1979, I was asked by the United States Information Agency to lecture in Europe. The Soviets were already in Africa, along with their Cuban lackeys, and had just invaded Afghanistan; the Iranians were holding U.S. citizens hostage. The Europeans I spoke to assumed I would join the parade of U.S. writers who, like some traveling freak show, attacked America for their amusement. Earlier I would have done it gladly. But now I found the double standard Europeans used in judging the U.S. and the U.S.S.R. revolting, especially since our defeat in Vietnam had so changed what we used to call the "objective conditions" and created a vacuum into which the Soviets had moved with such brutality. Not really relishing the role, I nonetheless found myself defending America in my talks. It wasn't what was expected or desired.

When I got back home, David Horowitz and I began

another family-dynasty book, this time on the Kennedys. We had gone through a lot together—at *Ramparts* before it went under in 1973, and afterward. We still had a kind of political collaboration, but it was far different from what it had been when we were radicals cruising down the party line. We found ourselves in roughly the same mood—bruised by our past beliefs. We took turns playing devil's advocate, each of us creating arguments he knew would move the other forward in apostasy. There was the continuing wound of the murder of our friend Betty, a murder that had gone unsolved and unpunished. There was what we now saw as the selective morality of the Left, which might wax indignant about the Carter administration's rather moderate stand against Communist guerrillas in Central America but was yet unable to become aroused by the Soviet genocide in Afghanistan. (The *mujahideen* were not "progressive" enough, one of our ex-comrades told us during an argument; they countenanced clitorectomies, after all,·and believed in capital punishment.) We tried to bury ourselves in the Kennedy book, telling each other in long talks that we hadn't left the Left, but it had left us. But it was hard to accept the feeling of being in internal exile, and we began to explore our New Left experiences indirectly through a series of magazine articles. It was not just a coming out, we later realized, but a coming home as well.

Our first project was a piece on Fay Stender, the radical feminist lawyer who had been George Jackson's lover and attorney and who had been paralyzed years after his death when she was shot by one of his former prison followers. We had of course supported Jackson when we were at *Ramparts*, proposing him as an innocent victim of a conspiracy of the criminal justice system. But as we began to reconstruct Fay Stender's life and death (she had recently committed suicide), we discovered that Jackson had killed several people in prison, and that far from being a sensitive prisoner-poet, he had been a deranged con. The slogan inspired by the presumed passion of George Jackson—"All prisoners are political prisoners"—seemed absurd to us in light of what we had discovered. We saw now what authorities close to the Jackson case had known all along: There are individuals who, for whatever reason, are so flawed that they ought to be locked as deeply as possible into the prison system.

We concluded this article by pointing out that the Left had honored Fay Stender as a fallen heroine but ignored her quintessential truth: that she had been taken advantage of and debased by her Left convictions. We were immediately attacked by such individuals as Jessica Mitford, Queen Mother of the Bay Area's Left, and by former Washington *Post* editor Ben Bagdikian, who refused to accept a service award from a local media association because we were members. Previously, attacks against our standing as radicals would have been devastating. But these gave us a sense of confirmation. Clearly, it was not *what* we had said that was wrong, but the fact that we had said it all. We experienced the perverse pleasure of the fallen angel: *Non serviam.*

The next story we wrote was about what happened to the Weather Underground. Among other things we discovered in our chronicle of the rise and fall of this organization was the fact that the bomb that had blown up three of the soldiers of the Weather Army in the Manhattan town house had been intended for a dance hall full of U.S. Army enlisted men and their dates at Fort Dix. When our old friends attacked us for publishing the piece, we said that we were trying to revive the memory of the Left and to serve its real truth. Pushed to the wall, we finally said that we felt that if someone had to die, it was better that it was the Weatherpeople than the soldiers. It was not just an arguing point but one of those lines over which one steps knowing that there is no return.

We next became involved in a story about the juvenile justice system in California, showing how liberal pieties had created a system in which it was quite literally possible to get away with murder. Then came an article at the onset of the AIDS epidemic about how San Francisco's gay political establishment—anxious to protect their "liberated" life-style—had pressured the elected leaders of the city to forestall public health measures that would have stopped the spread of the disease and saved countless gay lives.

Writing these stories drew us into a deeper reevaluation of our past and a greater candor about where it had led. Before, we had been collaborators. Now David and I began to feel as if we were a party of two. We compensated for each other's defects and drew on each other's strengths. David's strength was an intellectual honesty of a kind I never saw elsewhere in the Movement. He had grown up in a Marxist family and set out to build a Marxist theory of his own in influential books such as *Free World Colossus*. (He was one of the few in the Movement intellectually capable of doing so.) During a stint at the Bertrand Russell Peace Foundation, he had worked for the socialism most of us merely talked about. When he embarked on an inventory of his life and broke with the Left, it was a jettisoning not merely of belief but of a life's work as well. It was a painful experience but also a courageous one.

In the spring of 1985, we published "Lefties for Reagan" for the *Washington Post Magazine*. It was a piece about the atrocities the Left had committed in the Sixties and defended in the Seventies. We said that we had voted for Ronald Reagan (whom we had attacked as a "fascist" when he was governor of California) because he acknowledged the fragility of American democracy and the degree to which it was on the defensive in the world. We were probably not the first New Leftists to cast a ballot for Reagan, but we may have been the first to admit it. There was a lot of press attention and a lot of criticism from our old friends, who attacked us as "turncoats" and "sellouts." After one such encounter, I told David that I felt like an American for the first time in twenty-five years. As someone born into the emotional and political ghetto of the Communist Party, with an alienation far greater than mine had ever been, he shook his head in agreement: "I feel like an American for the first time in my life."

The Sixties seem very far away now, a lifetime away. Since then we have moved on, trying to manage our passages and make our transitions. (For me, the first jolt came when I turned thirty and realized that I would someday die; the second came when I turned forty and realized that, yes, I would die, but until then I had to manage somehow to live.) Yet I know that this era is still very much with us—in our memories and also in our politics. That was a strange time, serious but also foolish, superficial but also destructive. The stones we threw into the waters of our world in those days caused ripples that continue to lap on our shores today—for better and more often for worse.

When thinking about the good old days, I sometimes

remember a story, perhaps apocryphal, about Bruce Franklin, then a Stanford University English professor who gained brief notoriety in the Bay Area as a red-hot Maoist. It was 1969, when the apocalypse seemed finally to be at hand. One of Bruce's colleagues, a junior professor at Stanford, had escaped to the Bolinas Lagoon and spent the summer in the guilty pleasure of the sunshine and ocean. When the fall term began, he ran into Franklin, who immediately asked him what he had been doing. It was a question freighted with a portentous sub-text: What have you been doing *for the revolution?* The junior professor, looking sheepish, said, "Well, Bruce, I have to tell you that I did a lot of swimming." Franklin glowered at him for a moment and then, in the manner of many abstruse revolutionaries of the day, stumbled onto something redeeming in this apparent waste of time: "Well, that's okay. We're going to need frogmen."

The revolution never got far enough to require wet suits and underwater demolitions, thank God. But people from the Sixties Left are still out there—the dark shapes under our political waters. After my years as a New Leftist, I could never join another movement or subscribe to another orthodoxy. But I feel there is still a small role to play—keeping an eye on these deep swimmers and, when I see one of them come near the surface, pointing out who he is, what he is doing, and what the consequences are likely to be. It may not be much to show for a fifteen-year indenture to radicalism, but it is the only way I know to put that perverse experience to use.

chapter 10 _____

David Horowitz

Letter to a Political Friend

Communism is the philosophy of losers.
—Doctorow, *The Book of Daniel*

Dear M——,

I'm sorry it has taken me so long to answer your letter. When I returned to California after my father's funeral, I spent a long time thinking about what happened during that weekend in New York. I thought about my phone call to you on Friday after I came back from the cemetery; how I had invited you to the memorial service we had planned for Sunday at my mother's house; how you had said you would come and how comforting that felt; how our conversation had turned to politics and changed into an argument, and our voices had become angry; how I had begun to feel invisible, and how the loneliness this caused in me became so intense I said we should stop; and how, when we could not stop, I hung up.

I thought about my feelings when you did not call back that day or the next; and when you did not come to my father's memorial on Sunday as you had said you would. I thought about the plane ride back home, when I began to realize how deep the wound in our friendship had become.

I thought about how our friendship had begun nearly half a century before at the Sunnyside Progressive Nursery School—so long in memory that I have no image of a life without it. In the community of the Left, it is perfectly normal to erase the intimacies of a lifetime over political differences. On the long plane ride home, it occurred to me that I might never hear from you again.

And then, a week after my return, your letter arrived in the mail. You were sorry, you said, about the way our phone call ended. *Because of our common heritage* [you said] *the personal and the political cannot really be separated.* Your words reminded me of the "Khrushchev divorces" of 1956—the twenty-year marriages in our parents' generation that ended in disputes between the partners over the "correct" political position to take toward his secret report on the crimes of Stalin. As though a political idea defined their reality.

But then, as though a political idea defined our reality too, your letter suddenly forgot about what had happened between us as friends and reopened the wound to resume the argument.

Dear David,

I was sorry that your call ended the way it did. It was not my idea to get into a political argument, but apparently you had a need to provoke it. I would have preferred to talk more about personal matters. But because of our common heritage, the personal and the political cannot really be separated. And that is why I can't help thinking that the views you now hold are psychological rather than intellectual in origin.

I want to add some things to clarify my position. I still consider myself part of the Left, but my views have changed significantly over the years. I haven't been a Stalinist since I visited the Soviet Union in 1957, when I was nineteen. After that, like you, I became part of the New Left. I no longer consider the Soviet Union a model for the socialist future. But after all the garbage has been left behind, I do hold certain basic tenets from my old Left background. The first is that there are classes, and the rich are not on the same side as the rest of us. They exploit. The second is that I am still a socialist. I still believe in theory socialism is better than capitalism. If it has not worked so far, it is because it has not really been tried.

What concerns me about you is that you have lost the compassion and humanism which motivated our parents to make their original choice. There can be no other explanation for your support of the vile policies of Ronald Reagan. Except that you are operating from an emotional position which surpasses rational thinking. Also, by assuming that because you are no longer "left" you must be "right," you appear to be lacking a capacity to tolerate ambiguity; and the real world is indeed ambiguous. Why do you feel the need to jump on establishment bandwagons? I assume they are paying you well for your efforts.

Your old (one of the oldest) friend,

M——

The wound in our friendship is really a mirror of the wound that a political faith has inflicted on our lives: the wounds that political lives like ours have inflicted on our times.

Let me begin with a concession. It is probably correct of you to blame me for our argument. *Apparently you had a need to provoke it.* I probably did. I had just buried a father, whose politics was the most important passion in his life. Political ideas provided the only truths he considered worth knowing, and the only patrimony he thought worth giving. When I was seventeen and had political ideas of my own for the first time, politics made us strangers. The year was 1956. My father and I were one of the Khrushchev divorces.

We never actually stopped speaking to each other. But the distance was there just the same. After I had my own children and understood him better, I learned to avoid the areas where our conflicts flourished. I was even able to make a "separate peace," accepting him as the father he was rather than fighting to make him the one I wanted him to be. But he never was able to make the same peace with me. In all those thirty years that were left to us after I left home, there was not a day I was not aware of the line that politics had drawn between us, not a day that I did not feel how *alien* my ideas made me to him.

Emotions of grief and mourning make a perverse chemistry. If I provoked you to attack me on my father's burial day, perhaps I had a need for it: to do battle with the ideas that in ways and at times seemed more important to him than I was; to resume the combat that was his strongest emotional connection to other human beings and to me. Perhaps I thought I could resurrect his ghost in you, one of my oldest and dearest friends, who despite "all the garbage" you have left behind remain true enough to the faith of our fathers to act as his stand-in.

I don't mean to excuse my provocation, but only to remind you of what you forgot in your political passion that evening and in the silence that followed. Me. David. An old friend in need. I had been obliterated by a political idea. I felt like those ideological enemies of the past whom Stalin had made into "unpersons" by erasing the memory of who they had been. Which is what happened to my father at his own memorial that Sunday you did not come.

For nearly fifty years our parents' little colony of "progressives" had lived in the same ten-block neighborhood of Sunnyside in Queens. And for fifty years their political faith had set them apart from everyone else. They inhabited Sunnyside like a race of aliens—in the community but never of it; in cultural and psychological exile. They lived in a state of permanent hostility not only to the Sunnyside community but to every other community that touched them, including America itself.

The only community to which they belonged was one that existed in their minds: the international community of the progressive Idea. Otherwise, they lived as internal exiles, waiting for the time when they would be able to go home. "Home," to them, was not a place somewhere other than Sunnyside and

America; "home" was a *time* in the future when the Sunnyside and America they knew would no longer exist. No compromise with their home ground could put an end to their exile; only a wave of destruction that would sweep away the institutions and traditions of the communities around them and allow the international community of the progressive Idea to rise up in their place.

To my father and his comrades, the fantasy of this future was more important than the reality around them. All the activities of the Sunnyside progressives—the political meetings they attended five and six nights a week, the organizations they formed, the causes they promoted—were solely to serve their revolutionary Idea. The result was that after five decades of social effort, there was not a single footprint to show that they had really lived in our little ten-block neighborhood. When my father's life came to its close, he was buried as a stranger in the community where he had spent his last fifty years.

My father lived the sinister irony that lies at the heart of our common heritage: The very humanity that is the alleged object of its "compassion" is a humanity it holds in contempt. This irony defined my father's attitude toward the people around him, beginning with those who were closest—the heirs of his Jewish heritage, whose community center he would never be part of and whose synagogue he would never enter. Every Friday night his own mother still lit the *Shabbat* candles, but as a progressive he had left such "superstitions" behind. To my father, the traditions his fellow Jews still cherished as the ark of their survival were but a final episode in the woeful history of human bondage, age-old chains of ignorance and oppression from which they would soon be set free. With the members of the real communities around him, my father was unable to enjoy the fraternity of equals based on mutual respect.

The only community my father respected was the community of people who shared his progressive Idea, people like your parents. To my father and his Sunnyside comrades this meant the orthodoxies that comprised the Stalinist faith. But when he was just past fifty, a Kremlin earthquake shattered the myth that held together the only community to which my father belonged. The year was 1956. It was the year my father's world collapsed.

By the time I reached Sunnyside from California, as you remember, my mother had already decided that his burial arrangements would be made by the Shea Funeral Home on Skillman Avenue. The Shea Funeral Home had been the last stop for the Catholics of the neighborhood for as long as I could remember. My father hated its very name. To him, the little storefront was a symbolic fortress of the enemy forces in his life—the Christian persecutors of the ghetto past he tried to forget, the anti-Communist crusaders of his ghettoized present. My father took his hate to the grave. But for his widow, the battles were already forgotten, the political passions dead with the past. What was alive was her new solitude and grief, and her terror in the knowledge that everything had changed. To my mother, the Shea Funeral Home was an ark of survival, as familiar and comforting as the neighborhood itself.

My father's burial was attended only by his immediate family. We were accompanied to the cemetery by a rabbi I had somewhat disloyally hired to speak at the graveside after confirming with my mother that she would find his presence comforting too. Having been primed with a few details of my father's life, the rabbi observed that death had come to him the week before Passover, whose rituals commemorated an exodus to freedom not unlike the one that had brought him as an infant from Russia eighty-one years before. Not unlike the dream of a promised future that had shaped his political life.

The place of burial was Beth Moses, a Jewish cemetery on Long Island fifty miles away from Sunnyside, the last of my father's exile homes. It seemed appropriate to me that my father, who had struggled so hard in life to escape from his past, should find peace in the end in a cemetery called "House of Moses." And that this final compromise should have been made for him by the international community of his political faith. The grave where my father was buried among strangers was in a section of the cemetery reserved for Jews who had once belonged to the International Workers Order, a long-defunct Communist front, which had sold the plots as fringe benefits to its members.

On Sunday, the last of my father's surviving comrades assembled in my mother's living room for the memorial. No ceremony had been planned, just a gathering of friends. Those present had known my father—some of them for more than fifty years—with the special intimacy of comrades who shared the scars of a common battleground, lifetime cohabitants in a community of exiles.

I could remember meetings when the same room had reverberated with their political arguments in the past. But now that the time had come to speak in my father's memory, they were strangely inarticulate, mute. As though they were unequal to the task before them: to remember my father as a man.

My father was a man of modest achievements. His only real marks were the ones he made in the lives of the individuals he touched. The ones who were there now. The memories of the people who had gathered in my mother's living room were practically the only traces of my father still left on this earth. But when they finally began to speak, what they said was this: *Your father was a man who tried his best to make the world a better place . . . your father was a man who was a teacher to others . . . your father was a man who was socially conscious; progressive . . . who made a contribution.*

And that was all they said. People who had known my father since before I was born, who had been his comrades and intimate friends, could not really remember him. All that was memorable to them in the life my father had lived—all that was real—were the elements that conformed to their progressive Idea. My father's life was invisible to the only people who had ever been close enough to see who he was.

The obliteration of my father's life at his own memorial is the real meaning of what you call "our common heritage."

Our common heritage. Such a precious evasion. Our common heritage was totalitarianism, was it not? Our parents and their comrades were members of the Communist Party, were they not? Your need for this Orwellian phrase is revealing. It can hardly be for the benefit of an old comrade like me. In fact, its camouflage is for you. "Our common heritage" betrays your need to be insulated from your own reality—the reality of your totalitarian faith.

I'm sure this charge upsets you. In your own mind, the only elements that survive of our heritage are the innocent ones: *I haven't been a Stalinist since I visited the Soviet Union in 1957, when I was nineteen. . . . I no longer consider the Soviet Union a model for the socialist future.* But what Leftists who are able to enjoy the privileges of *bourgeois* democracy in the West think of themselves as Stalinists anymore, or the Soviet Union as a socialist model? Such vulgar convictions are reserved for the revolutionary heroes of the Third World, who actually wield the power—the Vietnamese and Cuban and Nicaraguan comrades—to whom you and other left-wing sophisticates pledge your loyalties and faith. *They* are Stalinists even if you are not.

Not an intention, but a totalitarian *faith* is what creates the common bond between revolutionary cynics like Stalin and Fidel and the Sandinista *comandantes* and progressive believers like yourself.

Totalitarianism is the possession of reality by a political Idea—the Idea of the socialist kingdom of heaven on earth, the redemption of humanity by political force. To radical believers, this Idea is so beautiful it is like God Himself. It provides the meaning of a radical life. It is the solution that makes everything possible; it is the end that justifies every regrettable means. Belief in the kingdom of socialist heaven is the faith that transforms vice into virtue, lies into truth, evil into good. For in the revolutionary religion, the Way, the Truth, and the Life of salvation lie not with God above but with men below— ruthless, brutal, venal men—on whom the faith confers the power of gods. There is no mystery in the transformation of the socialist paradise into Communist hell: Liberation theology is a Satanic creed.

Totalitarianism is the crushing of ordinary, intractable, human reality by a political Idea.

Totalitarianism is what my father's funeral and your letter are about.

Your letter indicts me because my ideas have changed. But the biggest change in me is not in any new political convictions I may have. It is in a new way of looking at things. The biggest change is seeing that reality is more important than any Idea. Reality—the concreteness of events and of people. In the years since we were close, I have gained respect for the ordinary experience of others and of myself. It is not a change I wanted to make. It is something that happened to me despite my resistance. But it is a change that has allowed me to learn from what I know. To connect, for example, the little episodes of our progressive heritage (like my father's memorial) with the epic inhumanities that its revolutions inspire. It is because you have not changed that these connections remain invisible to you.

What concerns me about you is that you have lost the compassion and humanism which motivated our parents to make their original choice.

You say their *original choice*. Another Orwellian evasion. Their "original choice" was Communism, was it not? Our parents were idolators in the church of a mass murderer named Joseph Stalin. They were not moralists but Marxist-Leninists. For them, the Revolution *was* morality (and beauty and truth as well). For them, compassion outside the Revolution was mere *bourgeois* sentimentality. How could you forget this? Compassion is not what inspired our parents' political choices. Nor is compassion what inspired the Left to which you and I both belonged—the *New Left*, which forgot the people it liberated in Indochina once their murderers and oppressors were red, which never gave a thought to the Cubans it helped to bury alive in Castro's jails, which is still indifferent to the genocides of Marxist conquest: the fate of the Cambodias and Tibets and Afghanistans.

Compassion is not what motivates the Left, which is oblivious to the human suffering its generations have caused. What motivates the Left is the totalitarian Idea: the Idea that is more important than reality itself. What motivates the Left is the Idea of the future in which everything is changed, everything *transcended*. The future in which the present is already *annihilated*; in which its reality no longer exists.

What motivates the Left is an Idea whose true consciousness is this: *Everything human is alien.* Because everything that is flesh-and-blood humanity is only the disposable past. This is the consciousness that makes mass murderers of well-intentioned humanists and earnest progressives, the Hegelian liberators of the socialist cause.

In the minds of the liberators, it is not really *people* who are buried when they bury their victims. Because it is not really people who stand in their way. Only "agents of past oppressions"; only "enemies of the progressive Idea." Here is an official rationale, from a Cheka security official of the time of Lenin, for the disposal of thirty million human souls: "We are not carrying out war against individuals. We are exterminating the bourgeoisie as a class. We are not looking for evidence or witnesses to reveal deeds or words against the Soviet power. The first question we ask is: to what class does he belong, what are his origins, upbringing, education, or profession? These questions define the fate of the accused. This is the essence of the Red Terror."

The Red Terror is terror in the name of an Idea.

The Red Terror is the terror that "idealistic Communists (like our parents) and "anti-Stalinist" Leftists (like ourselves) have helped to spread around the world. You and I and our parents were totalitarians in democratic America. The democratic *fact* of America prevented us from committing the atrocities willed by our faith. Impotence was our only innocence. In struggles all over the world, we pledged our faith and gave our support to the perpetrators of the totalitarian deed. Our solidarity with them, like the crimes they committed, was justified in the name of the revolutionary Idea. Our capabilities were different. Our passion was the same.

And yours is still. You might not condone some of the crimes committed by the Kremlin or Castro or the Nicaraguan *comandantes*. But you would not condemn the criminals who are responsible for the deed. Or withhold from them your comradely support. Nor, despite all your enlightenment since the time of Stalin, are your thoughts really very different from theirs.

Does it occur to you that you condemn me in exactly the same terms that dissidents are condemned by the present-day guardians of the Soviet state? *There can be no other explanation for your support of the vile policies of Ronald Reagan. Except that you are operating from an emotional position which surpasses rational thinking.* In other words, the only explanation for my anti-Communist convictions is that I am "anti-social" (lacking compassion) or insane.

What kind of revolution do you think you and your radical comrades would bring to the lives of people—ordinary people who supported the "vile policies of Ronald Reagan" in such unprecedented numbers, people for whom you have so little real sympathy and such obvious contempt? The answer is self-evident: exactly the same kind of revolution that radicals of our "common heritage" have brought to the lives of ordinary people every time they seized power. For when the people refuse to believe as they should, it becomes necessary to make them believe by force. It is the unbelieving people who require the "Revolutionary Watch Committees" to keep tabs on their neighborhoods, the gulags to dispose of their intractable elements, the censors to keep them in ignorance, and the police to keep them afraid. It is the reality of ordinary humanity that necessitates the totalitarian measures; it is the people that requires its own suppression for the revolution that is made in its name. To revolutionaries, the Idea of "the people" is more important than the people themselves.

The compassionate ideas of our common heritage are really masks of hostility and contempt. We revolutionaries are the enemies of the very people we claim to defend. Our promise of liberation is only a warrant for a new and more terrible oppression.

These are the realizations that have changed my politics. They were not clever thoughts that one day popped into mind but, as you know (and choose to forget), conclusions I was able to reach only at the end of a long period of reconsideration and pain.

Until then I had shared your conviction that we all were radicals for compassionate reasons, to serve benevolent ends. However perverted those ends might have become in the past, however grotesque the tragedies that occurred, I believed in the revolutionary project itself. I believed in it as the cause of humanity's hope. And I was confident that we could learn from history and would be able to avoid its destructive paths. I believed we could create a *new* Left that would be guided by the principles of the revolutionary ideal, that would reject the claims of dictators like Stalin, who had perverted its goals in the past.

After 1956, I joined others who shared this dream in the first attempts to create a New Left in America, and for nearly twenty years I was part of the efforts to make it a reality. But eventually I realized that our efforts had failed. I gave up my political activities and embarked on a quest to understand why. When it was over, I saw that what we had dreamed in 1956 was not really possible. I saw that the problem of the Left did not lie in sociopathic leaders like Stalin or Castro, who had perverted the revolutionary Ideal. It was the revolutionary Ideal that perverted the Left.

Because you knew me from the beginning, you were aware of the road I had traveled, the connection between what I had lived through and what I had come to believe. No matter how different the traveler appeared at the end of the journey, you were a witness to his true identity. To the reality he had lived. But it is clear now that this reality—*my* reality—is something you no longer want to know. You prefer to erase me instead. It is not unlike the erasure of my father's truth that occurred at his memorial service.

Let me tell you some things—things you once knew but have tried to forget about the person you accuse now of being unable to cope with real-life complexity, of responding to the loss of one ideological certainty by reflexively embracing its opposite.

The formative experience of my politics was the shattering of the Old Left's illusions by the Khrushchev Report and the events of 1956. You and I were seventeen at the time, now suddenly suspended between a political past that was no longer possible and a future that was uncertain. Our parents' political faith had been exposed as a monstrous lie. It was impossible for us to be "Left" in the way they had been. But I did not assume therefore that I had to be "Right." I swore I would never be part of another nightmare like theirs. But I didn't want to give up their beautiful Idea. So I joined the others in our generation who were setting out to rescue the Idea from the taint of the past and create a Left that was new.

In the years that followed, I could always be seen in the ranks of the New Left, standing alongside my radical comrades. But in all those years, there was a part of me that was always alone. I was alone because I never stopped thinking about the ambiguous legacy we all had inherited. I was alone because it was a legacy that my New Left comrades had already decided to forget.

It was as though the radicals who came to politics in the

Sixties generation wanted to think of themselves as having
been born without parents. As though they wanted to erase
the bad memory of what had happened to their dream when it
had become reality in the Soviet past. To them, the Soviet
Union was "not a model" for the revolutionary future, but it
was also not a warning of a revolutionary fate. It was—in the
phrase of the time—"irrelevant."

All during the Sixties, I wrestled with the troubling legacies that my comrades ignored. While others invoked Marx as
a political weapon, I studied the four volumes of *Capital* to see
"how much of the theory remained viable after the Stalin debacle" (as I explained in the preface to a book I wrote, called
The Fate of Midas). For most New Left radicals who were
impatient to "bring the System down," Marxism provided the
convenient ax. Even if Marx was wrong, he was right. If Marxism promoted the desired result, what did it matter if the theory was false? But to me it mattered. All the nightmares of the
past cried out that it did.

In the mid-Sixties, I moved to London and came under
the influence of Isaac Deutscher, an older Marxist who had
written panoramic histories of the Russian Revolution and the
lives of its protagonists Stalin and Trotsky. For me, Deutscher
was the perfect mentor, fully aware of the dark realities of the
revolutionary past but believing still in the revolutionary Idea.

Inspired by my new teacher, I expanded my study of
revolutionary history and intensified my search for a solution
to the problems of our political inheritance. Before his un-
timely death in 1967, Deutscher encouraged me to expand one
of the essays I had written into a full-length literary effort.
When *Empire and Revolution* was completed in 1968, it represented my "solution" to the radical legacy. I had confronted
the revolutionary Idea with its failures, and I had established a
new basis for confidence in its truth. In Europe, my book
joined those of a handful of others that shared its concerns,
but in America, *Empire and Revolution* stood all by itself. I
don't think you will find another book like it written by an
American New Leftist during that entire radical decade. In
living with the ambiguities of the radical legacy, in my generation I was virtually unique.

When it was published in America, *Empire and Revolu-*

tion made no impression. The willful ignorance of New Left activists had by then become an unshakable faith that long since had ceased to be innocent. Alliances had been struck with totalitarian forces in the Communist bloc; Stalinist rhetoric and Leninist vanguards had become the prevailing radical fashions. Even a New Left founder like Tom Hayden, previously immune to Marxist dogmas, had announced plans to form a new "Communist Party." As though the human catastrophes that had been caused by such instruments had never occurred.

In the face of these developments, I had begun to have doubts as to whether a New Left was possible at all. Whether the very nature of the Left condemned it to endless repetitions of its past. But I deferred my doubts to what I saw at the time as a more pressing issue—the issue of America's anti-Communist war in Vietnam. Opposing the war was a moral obligation that in my mind took precedence over all other political tasks. The prospect of revolution, which was the focus of my doubts, was a reality remote by comparison. Even though I was uncomfortably allied with "Marxist-Leninists" I found politically dangerous and personally repellant, I didn't break ranks. As long as the Vietnam War continued, I accepted the ambiguity of my political position and remained committed to the radical cause.

But then the war came to an end, and my doubts could no longer be deferred. The revolutionaries we had supported in Indochina were revealed in victory as conquerors and oppressors: millions were summarily slaughtered; new wars of aggression were launched; the small freedoms that had existed before were quickly extinguished; the poverty of the peoples increased. In Asia, a new empire expanded as a result of our efforts and over the peoples of Laos and Cambodia and South Vietnam fell the familiar darkness of a totalitarian night.

The result of our deeds was devastating to all that we on the Left had said and believed. For some of us, this revelation was the beginning of a painful reassessment. But for others, there were no second thoughts. For them, the reality in Vietnam finally didn't matter. All that mattered was the revolutionary Idea. It was more important than the reality itself. When they resumed their positions on the field of battle, they recalled

"Vietnam" as a radical victory. The "Vietnam" they invoked in their new political slogans was a symbol of their revolutionary Idea: *Vietnam has won, El Salvador will win.* The next generation of the Left had begun. The only condition of its birth was forgetfulness, forgetting what really had happened in Vietnam; erasing the memory of its own past.

But even before history had run its course in Vietnam, the refuge I had reserved for myself all these years in the Left had already been cruelly destroyed. The murder of an innocent woman by people whom the New Left had celebrated as revolutionary heroes, and whom I had considered my political comrades, finally showed me how blind I had been made by my radical faith.

The murder was committed by the leaders of the Black Panther Party. Throughout the Sixties, I had kept my distance not only from the Panthers but from all the Leninists and their self-appointed vanguards. But at the same time, I shared the reasoning that made gangs like the Panthers part of the Left. According to this logic, the Panthers were "primitive rebels" who had become "politically aware" as a result of the "struggle" and had left their criminal past behind. By the same reasoning, their crimes were not something shameful but "pre-political" rebellions against their oppression as blacks. I accepted this logic for the same reason everyone else did, because it was the most basic tenet of our radical faith: Reality was defined by politics and could be changed by political ideas.

When the decade was over and the war that had fueled its radical passions had begun to draw to an end, the political apocalypse suddenly receded. Almost overnight, the "revolution" disintegrated. Its energies were exhausted, its organizations in varying stages of dissolution, its agendas quietly shelved. The Panthers survived to embrace the change with a new slogan, proclaiming: "It's time to put away the gun" and, as their actions showed, to put away the Leninist posturing too. It was a time for practical community efforts, a time for reality. For me, it seemed a time to end my long alienation in the Left. In 1973, I began a project with the Panthers to create a Community Learning Center in the heart of the East Oakland ghetto.

I allowed myself to be persuaded by the Panthers that they did not intend to use the Center as a Panther enclave but to turn it over to the ghetto community as a model of what good intentions could do. And I had persuaded myself that my intentions in working with the Panthers to accomplish this end were truly modest: to help the people in the community it would serve. But looking back afterward, I could see that my intentions were not modest at all. Every aspect of what I did was informed by the revolutionary Idea. That was the bond that connected me to the Panthers in the first place. That was what made what we were going to do resonate with the socialist future. That was what made me so ready to trust intentions I should not have trusted and to forget the violent realities of the Panthers' past. That was what inspired me to ignore the surface betrayals of character that provided warnings to others but were dismissed by me as the legacies of an oppression that radical politics would overcome.

So I raised the necessary funds and bought a church facility in East Oakland to house a school for 150 children. I organized technical support systems and teacher training programs and a variety of community services for the Center, and I found a bookkeeper named Betty Van Patter to keep its accounts. In the winter of 1974, the Panthers murdered Betty Van Patter and ended my career in the Left. I suspected, and was later told by the Panthers, that they had committed the crime. There were others in the Left who suspected them too, and knew that Betty was not the only person the Panthers had killed.

The Panthers were (as they had always been) a criminal gang extorting the ghetto. But as a vanguard of the Left, they were a far more dangerous gang than before, when they had simply been street toughs without any other pretense. Whenever the police accused the Panthers of criminal activity, the Left responded with cries of "racism" and "fascist repression," defending their innocence in the same way that the Left in our parents' generation had defended the innocence of Stalin. For the Left, the facts were not what mattered. What mattered was the revolutionary Idea.

It was a familiar pattern: the cynical exploiters of the revolutionary cause; the faithful defenders of the revolutionary name; the "political" silences that erased the truth; the blindness of believers like you and me. The legacy that I had tried so hard to leave by joining the New Left had now become the very center of my life.

The summer after Betty was murdered, you and I shared a tragedy of our own. Our friend Ellen R., who had grown up with us in that overrich Sunnyside political soil, was brutally raped and strangled by a black youth in her Englewood, New Jersey, home. We all had been members of the Sunnyside Young Progressives, which we founded when we were twelve years old under the covert auspices of the Communist Party. The premier issue of our *S.Y.P. Reporter* featured an editorial I wrote quoting a Negro Communist poet ("We, as a youth club, express our feelings best in the words of the great poetess Beulah Richardson, who said: 'let our wholehearted fight be: peace in a world where there is equality' ") and an original poem by Ellen about a Negro named Willie McGee, who had been executed in the South for raping a white woman:

> Did he have a fair trial?
> Did they have any Negroes in the jury?
> Did they have any proof of his guilt? NO!
> The only proof they had was that he was a Negro. A NEGRO!

In the years that followed, Ellen had been more faithful than either of us to the heritage we shared (joining the Communist Party *after* the invasion of Czechoslovakia). She was a missionary to the people she considered oppressed, naming her third child after Martin Luther King. As a high-school teacher, she was devoted beyond the call of professional duty to black youngsters whose problems others considered difficult if not intractable. ("She had the most intense rescue fantasies of anyone I have ever known," you wrote me after her death.) To Ellen, these were not individuals with problems, but victims of a racist system that she was determined to change. She would not let her own children play with toy guns or watch TV cartoons because they were violent, but she took real felons who had committed real crimes with real guns into the bosom of her family, "understanding" their actions and then disregarding the implications because the criminals were black.

She took them all on as a cause, and was willing to incur risks that others would not, making not only her talents and intellect available but her paycheck and her household as well. In your own words, "she was a sucker for a good sob story," losing over $1,000 by *twice* cosigning a loan for one of her students who conned her. On another occasion, she came close to losing her job when one of her outraged neighbors went to the school principal to complain that Ellen had abetted her daughter's flight from home.

On that fateful summer night, it was one of those troubled students whom Ellen had taken up as a cause and set out to redeem who returned to her house to murder her in her bed.

That summer you and I were able to share a grief over the friend we had lost, but we were never able to share an understanding of why she was dead. In your eyes, Ellen died a victim of circumstance; in mine she died the martyr of a political faith that had made her blind.

Because of this faith, Ellen's middle-class existence was constantly beset by unsuspected enemies and unseen perils. As a young instructor at Queens College, she helped militants take over a SEEK program she was employed in that they had targeted as racist. By publicly confirming the charge and personally betraying her professional colleagues, she was able to provide the radicals with the keys to their triumph. But, as you noted, "it also ultimately led to the loss of her job—because once the Black and Puerto-Rican Coalition came into power they did not want any troublemakers around to disturb *their* comfortable sinecures!"

Even though her three children were asleep, Ellen had left her house unguarded. In our dialogues, you managed to find a way around this fact, and everything else you knew about Ellen—including the battles you had had with her over locking her doors after her own house was broken into, and her unwillingness to keep her boyfriend's dog in the house when she was alone: "I guess the fact is that Ellen was not killed by her heroics, naivete, innocence, trust in human nature . . . or idealism. She had the bad luck to be alone that night . . . and had refused to keep Mel's very vicious German Shepherd at the house because neighborhoods kids were always in and out." Well, it was a psychotic neighborhood kid who had been "in and out" who killed her. And if Ellen had kept Mel's guard dog that night, she would be alive today.

To me, it is evident that Ellen's house was unguarded not by chance, and certainly not because the neighborhood was safe, but because of a political Idea. An Idea that to Ellen was more important than reality itself. The same Idea was expressed in the choice she had made of a place to live—one of the first integrated neighborhoods in America. To Ellen, Englewood was a social frontier that showed whites could live together with blacks. Over the years, experience had chastened Ellen enough for her to begin to lock her doors and to allow Mel's dog to stay when he stayed over. But, in her heart, locked doors and guard dogs were still symbols of racist fear, of a world divided. The night Ellen was killed, her home was unguarded because of her faith in the Progressive Idea. The Idea of the future that progressives like her were going to create: the future when human conflicts would vanish as part of the oppressive past; when there would be "peace in a world where there is equality."

In the months past, incidents of violence had been reported in the neighborhood and rumors had made its inhabitants afraid. As a good soldier of the faith, Ellen would not allow herself to surrender fully to this fear. Her house had been recently broken into and she was alone with her children, but she refused to keep the dog that would have saved her life. On the night she was killed, Ellen's house was left unguarded *because* it was unsafe.

Ellen had no more understanding of the black people who lived in her neighborhood than she did of the black militants whom she had helped to dismiss her or the troubled teenager who finally killed her. Ellen had made all of their causes her own; had befriended them and given them her trust until finally she gave them her life. But Ellen never once really understood who they were. How could she possibly have understood? It was not because of who they were that Ellen had reached out to the black people she had tried to help. It was not because of their *reality* as individuals. It was because of an Idea she had of them as people who were "oppressed."

The night Ellen was killed the black people in her neighborhood guarded their houses and locked their doors. While

Ellen was setting a progressive example, her black neighbors worried among themselves about the recent incidents and talked about them even more ominously than the whites. Ellen's black neighbors knew their fear was not symbolic and what threatened them was not an idea. They had a special reason to worry that a dangerous criminal was stalking their neighborhood, because all his previous victims were black.

In Ellen's fate I saw a mirror of mine. Our progressive mission had been destructive to others and, finally, destructive to us. It had imbued us with the greatest racism of all—a racism that was *universal*, never allowing us to see people as they really were but only as our political prejudices required. With Ellen's death I had come to the last step in my political journey, which was to give up the progressive Idea—the fantasy of a future that made us so blind.

Why was this Idea so hard to give up? Since 1917, perhaps one hundred million people had been killed by socialist revolutionaries in power; the socialisms they created had all resulted in new forms of despotism and social oppression, and an imperialism even more ruthless than those of the past. But the weight of this evidence had failed to convince us. We were able to hold on to our faith by rejecting this experience as a valid test. The ugly socialism of record, we explained to ourselves, was not "really" socialism. It was not our *Idea*. (*If it has not worked so far, it is because it has not really been tried . . . in theory socialism is better than capitalism . . . I still believe . . .*) If there was any validity to the Idea at all, to give up on it seemed an unthinkable betrayal, like turning one's back on humanity itself.

And so the last question I came to ask was whether there was any reality to the socialist Idea. In 1973, a conference was held at Oxford University with this very question as its main agenda. The organizer of the conference was a Marxist philosopher who was one of the founders of the European New Left and had traveled a road that ran parallel to my own.

When East Europe's satellites rebelled against their Soviet oppressors in 1956 in the aftershocks of the Khrushchev Report, Leszek Kolakowski was one of their New Left leaders. The rebellions were brutally crushed by the Soviet armies, but

Kolakowski remained a New Leftist until 1968. Then Soviet tanks again moved in to quell dissident Communists in Prague, and Leszek Kolakowski fought a last-ditch defense of his New Left faith. For his efforts, he was expelled from his party and driven into exile in the West. When Kolakowski organized the Oxford conference on the socialist Idea, nearly twenty years had passed since he had joined the struggle to create a New Left in the Communist world. For two decades, he had led the efforts to create a new "humanistic Marxism" and to liberate socialism from its totalitarian fate. But by the time of the conference, Kolakowski could no longer ignore what his experience had shown. He was ready to admit defeat and give up the attempt to resolve the ambiguities we all had inherited.

The paper Kolakowski read at the conference* examined the idea of a classless, unified human community—the progressive goal to which we had dedicated our lives. The catastrophic experience of Marxist societies, he showed, had not been an accident. It was implicit in the socialist Idea. The forces required to impose the radical equality that socialism promised inevitably led to a new *in*equality and a new privileged ruling elite. The socialist unity of mankind we all had dreamed of could only be realized in a totalitarian state.

Kolakowski's arguments had been made before, by critics of socialism in every generation since Marx himself. And in every generation since, the societies that Marxists had created had only served to prove them right. And now they had been proved right in mine. In the light of all I had come to experience and know, Kolakowski's arguments were utterly correct. But I was still not ready to embrace their conclusions, whose consequences seemed as unthinkable as before. I decided to suspend judgment and take Kolakowski's arguments to my comrades in the Left. I wanted to know how they would respond and whether they had the answers that I did not.

I initiated discussions in radical circles and even organized a seminar addressed to the question "Is Socialism a Viable Idea?" The reactions I encountered proved personally frustrating, but in the end they were finally instructive. Most radicals, I discovered, did not see the issue as one that was

* "The Myth of Human Self-Identity," in Leszek Kolakowski and Stuart Hampshire, eds. *The Socialist Idea* (New York: Basic Books, 1974).

important at all: People whose lives were absorbed in efforts to replace an "unjust" society with one that was better were not interested in whether their efforts might actually make things worse. The few who recognized the gravity of the issue reacted to my questions with suspicion and mistrust. To ask whether the socialist Idea was more than a fantasy was like asking believers about the existence of God.

My search finally ended when I was visited by a British New Leftist who had been one of my earliest mentors. In the days when we were all setting out on our journey, Ralph Miliband had guided me in my first encounters with the troubling legacies of the radical past. After Isaac Deutscher's death in 1967, Miliband was the Marxist whose intellect and integrity I respected most. I had not seen him for more than a decade, but I still read the socialist journal he edited. It was the only socialist publication that had printed Kolakowski's recent ideas.

After we caught up on the years that had passed, I told him about the crisis I had reached. I recalled the impact of Kolakowski's arguments and the resistance I had met when I confronted other Leftists with the issues he raised. I told Miliband it seemed irresponsible for radicals like us to call ourselves "democratic socialists" while Kolakowski's arguments remained unanswered and—even worse—when most of the Left didn't care if his arguments could be answered at all. I didn't see how I could justify a commitment to a political movement with a history like the Left's, which was dedicated to destroying society without a viable plan for what would come next. I was still ready, I said, to oppose injustices wherever I perceived them, but I could not be a part of a movement that would not examine its goals.

When I was finished, I waited for an answer. Not an answer to Kolakowski (which I knew by then did not exist) but the answer I had been looking for all along. The one that would say: *David, you are not as alone as you think. The experiences of these years since we all began have indeed shown that the crisis of the socialist Idea is the crisis of the Left itself. If this crisis can't be resolved, if socialism is not a viable future, then our radicalism is really nothing more than a nihilistic passion and the Left a totalitarian force. But there is another possibility. The possibility that answers can be found, that a viable conception of socialism will result: a new agenda for the radical forces and a renewal of the radical hope. Ours may be a small contingent in the radical ranks, but the consequences of failure are too great for us to give up without trying.*

If my old teacher had answered me like this, perhaps the illusion would have been given new life. But when I was finished, Ralph Miliband said: "David, if those are your priorities, you are no longer a man of the Left." What my old teacher had told me was that the Left was really a community of faith and that I was no longer part of it.

My conversation with Ralph Miliband occurred sometime in the summer of 1979. I did not then leap to the right side of the political spectrum but waited another five years before casting a vote for Ronald Reagan and the policies that you consider so "vile." During that time and for twenty-four years previous, I had lived in the teeth of political ambiguity—never free from doubts about the Left yet never feeling I had to resolve my doubts by embracing the views of the opposite side. Your image of me not only denies the meanings of my life but actually reverses them.

And finally misunderstands them. If I had to label the perspective my experience has given me, I would call it "conservative." And would mean by that respect for the accumulated wisdom of human traditions; regard for the ordinary realities of human lives; distrust of optimism based on human reason; caution in the face of tragedies past. Conservatism is not the other side of the coin of radicalism, any more than skepticism is the mirror of faith. I have not exchanged one ideology for another; I have freed myself from the chains of an Idea.

Why was my freedom so hard to win? Why is the Idea so difficult to give up? When I asked myself these questions afterward, I realized that to do so had seemed to me, at the time, like giving up something I could not do without—hope itself. Life without the Idea of the socialist future felt to me like life without meaning. It was then that I realized that the reason the Idea is so hard to give up is that a radical faith is like any other faith: It is a matter not of politics but of self.

The moment I gave up my radical beliefs was the moment I had to look at myself for the very first time. At *me*. As I really was—not suspended above everyone else as an avatar of their future salvation but standing beside them as an equal, as one of *them*. Not one whom History had chosen for its vanguard but a speck of ordinary human dust. I had to look at the life ahead of me no longer guided and buoyed by a redeeming purpose, no longer justified by a missionary faith. Just a drop in the flow to the common oblivion. Mortal, insignificant, inconceivably small.

Marx was a rabbi after all. The revolutionary Idea is a religious consolation for earthly defeat. For the Jews of our Sunnyside heritage, it is the consolation for internal exile; the comfort and support for marginal life. A passage home. Belief in the Idea is the deception of self that made people like my father and you and me feel real.

Self-deception is what links you to the "common heritage" that is so difficult for those who inhabit it to name. Communism was the center of my father's world, but the word never passed the lips of the comrades who rose to speak at his memorial. A political faith dominated both their lives and his, but in the end the faith could not be named. To name it would make their lives too uncomfortably real. In their silence was their truth: What my father and his comrades were finally seeking in their political faith was not a new reality for the world but an old illusion for themselves. What they found was comfort for their lives of pain.

For my father, it was the pain of a chosen son. My father was the only male child of poor immigrants who could not speak English and who were as fearful of the strange world they had come to as of the one they had fled. His own father had failed as a provider, and when my father was still only a child, he realized the family had already placed its fate in his hands. From that time until his death, he felt like a man treading in water, that was over his head with the shore forever out of sight.

At the age of nineteen, my father found a means to support his parents and a life raft for himself in a job teaching English to other immigrant youngsters at Seward Park High School on the Lower East Side. But until he was thirty, he continued to live in his parents' apartment, and his own life remained dangerously adrift. Clarity entered my father's life through the Communist Party and the socialist Idea. The moment he joined the Party, he felt himself touch the shore of a landmass that circled the globe and extended into the future itself. As a soldier in the Party's vanguard and a prophet of its truth, my father gained wisdom and power beyond his faculty, and finally achieved what his own father had not, his self-esteem as a man. But in the memorials of his comrades there was no mention at all of the Party that had given my father so great a gift. It was like a secret they all were keeping from themselves. And my father would have wanted them to keep their secret. Because he had a secret too. *My father had left the Communist Party more than thirty years before.*

It was only toward the end of his life that my father felt able to tell me his secret, and then in a voice full of emotion and pain, as if it had all not happened so many years past. The events had taken place in 1953, when I was fourteen and my father was approaching fifty (which is my age now). The anti-Communist crusade of the early cold war was reaching its height, and my father was about to lose the first life raft that had kept him afloat. For twenty-nine years he had remained a teacher of English at the same high school on the Lower East Side, but now a new law had been passed that barred Communists from his lifetime vocation.

In the ordinary business of his life outside politics, my father had remained timid like his father before him, clinging all that time to his very first job. But in the drama of history that he now entered, my father was the tall man his faith had made him. He was ready to stand up to his inquisitors and bear the blows they were about to give him. To defend his Party and its cause, my father was even ready to give up his raft of survival and to swim for the first time in uncharted seas. It should have been my father's moment of glory, but instead it became his hour of shame.

For "political reasons," the Party had decided that my father would not be allowed to make his stand as a man on trial for his political beliefs. Instead he would have to defend himself as the victim of an "anti-Semitic" campaign. All my father's pride as a man lay in the cause he had joined, in the fact that he had reached the shores of progressive light and had left his

Jewish ghetto behind. Even in the best circumstances, the lie that the Party now required would have been excruciating for a man of my father's temper. But when the court of history called him to account, there was no place for my father to hide.

When his moment came, my father followed the Party line, as he always had done. In his moment of glory, my father colluded in his own public humiliation and was fired as a Communist from his only profession, protesting his rights as a Jew.

When my father was betrayed by the Party he loved, he was forced to look at the truth. The Party was everything to him, but to the Party he was nothing at all. His faith in the Party had not really given him power; it had only made him a political pawn. The secret my father could only reveal to me late in his life was the terrible truth he had seen.

The truth made it impossible for my father ever to go back, but he did not have the strength to go forward. He could not leave (any more than you can leave) the faith that was the center of his life. It was a dilemma my father resolved (as you do) with a strategic retreat. He quietly left the Party that had betrayed him, but he kept his political faith. He was never again active in a political way, but every day of the thirty years he had left, he loyally read the Communist press and defended the Party line. All those years, my father kept his secret as though he were protecting a political cause. But in fact, as anyone else could see, all those years my father was keeping his secret in order to protect himself.

My father's deceit was small. The hurt it caused was only to him. But my father's deceit is a metaphor for all the lies of the political faithful, the self-deceit and the deceit of others that have made their cause a blight on our time. The immediate intent of my father's deceit was to conceal the reality of his political cause—its casual inhumanities and devious methods, its betrayal even of its own. But the real purpose of my father's deception was to avoid the reality that made his faith necessary in the first place, that makes the Idea so hard to give up. The reality my father could not confront was his own.

It is the same with you. When you deny my reality for a political Idea, what you really don't want to confront is your own. *I assume they are paying you well for your efforts.* Can you really think I sold out my faith for money? How can you, who know the price I had to pay for what I have learned, point such an accusing finger at me? Only if you feel so deprived in your own life that your words really mean this: *I am not being paid well for mine.*

The rich are not on the same side as.the rest of us. They exploit. The radical truth (which is your truth still) is the *class war* of the social apocalypse, the war that divides humanity into the "Haves" who exploit and the "Have Nots" who are oppressed, into those who are paid well for their efforts and those who are denied, into the Unjust and the Just, into *their* side and *ours.* The radical truth is the permanent war that observes no truce and respects no law, whose aim is to destroy the only world we know.

This is the "compassionate" cause that makes radicals superior to ordinary humanity and transforms the rest of us into "class enemies" and unpersons and objects of contempt.

Take a careful look at what you still believe, because it is a mirror of the dark center of the radical heart: not compassion but resentment—the envious whine of *have not* and *want*; not the longing for justice but the desire for revenge; not a quest for peace but a call to arms. It is war that feeds the true radical passions, which are not altruism and love but nihilism and hate.

The farcical surfaces of the political divorces over the Khrushchev Report masked a deeper reality of human pain. Consider what terrors of loneliness inhabit the hearts of people whose humanity must express itself as a political construction. Consider what passions accumulate in such unsatisfied souls.

This is the poisoned well of the radical heart: the displacement of real emotions into political fantasies; the rejection of present communities for a future illusion; the denial of flesh-and-blood human beings for an Idea of humanity that is more important than humanity itself. This is the problem of "our common heritage," as you so delicately name it, and it is our problem as well.

Your old friend and ex-comrade,
David

chapter 11 ——————————

The Middle of the Journey

Coming into Managua from the airport was like entering a zone of heavy air. It was the fall of 1987, and the *apertura*—the "opening" the Arias Plan was supposed to make in Nicaragua's civic life—had just begun. But the city itself seemed not to have heard the good news; it was still enveloped in a sleepy menace that made it seem year zero of the revolution. Slogans and bad folk art defaced every wall. Teenagers in khaki cradling AK-47s stood guard on every street corner. There was a hard edge to the squalor. Managua had the feel of a run-down, tropical East Berlin.

But the most striking thing about the city, as we drove in from the airport, was that there was no "there" there. It had a bombed-out quality, the result not of the civil war but of the 1972 earthquake, whose damage had never been repaired—not in the last seven years of the Somoza regime, not in the first eight of the revolution. We observed to the driver that it was a city without a center. A few minutes later, as we drove by a building with large letters proclaiming "The Sentinel of the People's Happiness"—Tomas Borge's Ministry of the Interior —the driver said, *"That* is the center of Managua now."

We checked into the Intercontinental, feeling that we were in enemy territory—a feeling not unlike the one we had experienced when doing civil rights work in the American South almost twenty-five years earlier. Camera crews from various countries rushed in and out of the elevators, as flagrantly anonymous men who looked as if they had stepped from the pages of a Graham Greene novel sat in the lobby peering over the rim of newspapers to keep track of things. As we registered at the desk, a couple of Americans wearing sandals and carrying colorful Central America *borsas* came up behind and peeked over our shoulders. "What are *you* doing here?" one of them asked, apparently having recognized our names. We began to answer that we were in Managua to speak to the groups that made up the civic opposition, but before we could finish, the other one broke in: "They're here to bash the revolution. This is the middle of their journey."

The allusion to a novel that is about, among many other things, Whittaker Chambers was meant as an indictment, and the young man who made it smiled smugly as he and his companion walked off. Yet in a metaphorical as well as a factual sense, the phrase seemed to fit. Twenty-five years earlier, we probably would have been among the American *internacionalistas* milling around in the lobby of the Intercontinental giving fraternal embraces to Sandinista cadres and greeting as though they were comrades the dour delegations from Bulgaria and North Korea. But the world around us had changed, and so had we. The immediate cause of our being in Managua was a call we had received a couple of weeks earlier from Elliott Abrams's office. "Are you willing to serve your country?" one of the Assistant Secretary's youthful aides had asked. (Later on, in comparing notes, we discovered that we had had almost identical reactions to this opening gambit: not knowing whether to smile or salute.) It turned out that the patriotic summons was for something we were willing to do: speak to the non-government-controlled labor unions, the opposition parties, and other groups trying to take advantage of the *apertura* to widen the space for political democracy. But we would have agreed even before the phrase was used against us that the real reason we had gone to Nicaragua was that we were in the middle of the journey.

In Managua, American Leftists were everywhere—in the streets with FSLN bureaucrats and soldiers, in the nearly empty restaurants, gorging on food made cheap (for them) by socialist hyper-inflation, having earnest talks that seemed to be conducted primarily in hand gestures with East bloc "specialists." We recognized the journey they were on; it was one that had only beginnings, no ends and certainly no middles. When one beginning failed, these radical travelers would always find another. For them, history was a giant station at which there was always another train about to leave.

The one place where we didn't see American Leftists was at the offices of *La Prensa*, the opposition newspaper, which was reopened on our first day in Nicaragua, after a long suppression by the Sandinistas. We recognized Stephen Kinzer of the *New York Times*. But most of the crush of media in the composing room were foreigners. We struck up a conversation with an El Salvadoran journalist and asked him if he thought, as many were saying, that there was a Nicaraguan *glasnost* in the offing. He smiled: "One must always be optimistic. But one must be a realist too. What happens after the *contra* is dead and Reagan is gone? The breath of fresh air you hear in Managua may actually be the whisper of an ax you can't see yet."

As the presses of *La Prensa* began to roll, Violetta Chamorro and her elegant daughter, Cristina, walked through the crowd, hugging their workers. We had seen the two women about a year earlier at a Washington lunch. At that time, the question of the death of Pedro Joaquin Chamorro, editor of *La Prensa* and leading opposition figure in the struggle against the Somoza regime during the 1970s, had come up, and Violetta, her daughter translating, had said she believed the Sandinistas were implicated in the murder of her husband,* afterward cynically making him into a martyr for their revolu-

---

* Violetta Chamorro's charges were made to us at a meeting of the editorial board of *The New Republic* in the fall of 1987. A few months later, on January 10, 1988, the Costa Rican paper *La Republica* published an article linking Bayardo Arce and other high Sandinista officials to the assassination of Pedro Joaquin Chamorro. The following week, Violetta Chamorro's own paper, *La Prensa*, ran a front page story based on the *La Republica* account. "Quién mató a Pedro . . . ? Una nueva versión." *La Prensa*, January 16, 1988.

tion. She had summarized the difference between pre- and post-revolutionary life in Nicaragua in this way: "Back in the old days, Somoza would lose patience with someone like Pedro and throw him in a brutal cell for a while, and then let him go. When they arrest someone today, they have the East German specialists"—here she made the gesture of someone shooting a syringe—"giving *las inyecciónes*. We have now scientific *Somozismo*."

But on this day in Managua, Violetta's face was flushed with victory. As the first issues of *La Prensa* came off the presses, she joined hands with her workers, some of them with tears streaming down their faces, and they sang the Nicaraguan national anthem. She held up the paper and gave a clenched fist salute.

After leaving *La Prensa*, we met with Alvin Guthrie. A Miskito Indian who grew up in Bluefields, Guthrie is the head of CUS, largest of the independent unions. Like many other Nicaraguans we were to meet during our days in Managua, he explained to us how the Sandinista inflation has made the country "poorer than it was in 1956" and talked about the organizing tasks ahead. Chief among his goals was forming agricultural co-ops. "We cannot do that now. that is reserved for the Sandinistas. They offer some *campesino* who is willing to join them a little bit of land and a gun. They tell him if he wants the land, he must become part of their military. This is their idea of land reform. To oppose this, we need to do social projects at the same time that we struggle against the Sandinistas. The Sandinistas have all the *structure*. The democratic opposition is not allowed to have any structure of its own. We need to be able to give people the organization and ideas with which to defend themselves."

Like others in the democratic opposition in Managua, Guthrie is amused but at the same time appalled by American *sandalistas* who come here to support the FSLN. "They harass and slander people like me for being affiliated with the AFL-CIO. They don't realize what good the American labor unions have done for Nicaraguans. They come down in their buses, these Americans, and chant, 'We are Sandinistas too!' They think the Nicaraguan people like them for this. They are wrong. The Nicaraguan people *hate* it. I recently saw one delegation of Americans go into a *barrio* early one morning. The

Sandinistas roused everybody: 'Come on, get up, the gringos are here for a little solidarity.' One of these young Americans goes over to an unhappy-looking Nicaraguan and says, 'What is the trouble with you, my friend?' The Nicaraguan looks at him and says, 'The trouble is that you are here and I am not in bed. The trouble is that you are more Sandinista than the Sandinistas.' "

Next we went to the Independent Commission of Human Rights. The derisive slogans—all of them having to do with the CIA—successive waves of *turbas* had spray painted over the entire building did not keep peasants from coming to the office. By eight in the morning, the lobby was filled with people, some carrying suitcases which were proof of long travel, waiting stolidly to tell someone their troubles.

The head of the commission, Lino Hernandez, was still bruised from a recent attempt to demonstrate on behalf of political prisoners, during which he had been beaten and cattle-prodded by Sandinista security men in a scene reminiscent of Bull Connor's Alabama. Hernandez, a round-faced man with implacable Indian features, pointed out that the number of political prisoners he believed were being held by the FSLN —as many as seven thousand—might seem small but is actually the per capita equivalent of about half a million in a country the size of the United States. He talked about the difficulty of getting to see these prisoners, of even documenting their existence, and he complained that human rights organizations like Amnesty International had not had a resident field representative in Nicaragua in three years. As Hernandez spoke about the problems of bringing democracy to his country, his thoughts inevitably moved, as Alvin Guthrie's had, to the Americans whose support, he believes, allows the *comandantes* to succeed.

"Just recently a U.S. congressman was here," he said, "a man whose name you would recognize as that of a sympathizer with the Sandinista cause. I told him about the huge number of political prisoners in Nicaraguan jails. He was not so very interested. He said, 'Yes, well, they are all former Guardsmen and therefore murderers anyhow.' I said, 'You are right that some of these political prisoners are former Guardsmen. But you are wrong that they are murderers. The Sandinistas killed the bad ones a long time ago. The ones that are left were at a low level in the Guard—the truckdrivers and gardeners and gatekeepers.' "

To go from Lino Hernandez's group to the official Sandinista Human Rights Office was to experience the cognitive dissonance that has become part of Sandinista political theory and one of the permanent features of Nicaraguan life. The waiting room was empty except for us. The head of the organization—an American nun with the improbable name Sister Mary Hartman, who has spent several years working for the FSLN—appeared for a reluctant interview, accompanied by a young woman named Mira Santiago. A gaunt woman with thick glasses and a forbidding overbite, Sister Mary responded to our question about political prisoners with a harangue about *contra* atrocities and American evil. We pressed her: Were there any political prisoners in Nicaragua? "No." Not a one? "None." At this, Santiago, one of those sharp young Sandinistas who, like Ortega's translator Alejandro Bendana, was educated at elite schools in the United States (B.A., Princeton, 1982), tried to smooth the wrinkled dialogue: "Of course there are a few prisoners. How could there not be? There is a war going on."

Oblivious of the fact that she was being corrected, Sister Mary waited impatiently for Santiago to finish and then went on, her Adam's apple bobbing convulsively and her words punctuated occasionally by a smacking sound like a glottal click. "Your problem is you don't understand the poor. I think the United States is evil. I am afraid to go back home very often because I fear the outbreak of fascism in the streets. It could happen, you know."

Over the next few days, we spoke to most of Managua's political parties, squabbling among themselves in the Nicaraguan fashion, but also trying to make common cause because of what they agreed was the likely evanescence of the "opening." ("It is good times and also bad times," a member of the Popular Socialist Party told us. "Good times now when the Sandinistas are on their best behavior for the TV and bad times because later on, when the TV leaves, the noose will tighten around our necks.") The words and opinions we heard rushed out torrentially, with the pent-up force of something that has long been suppressed and may, the speakers fear, soon be dammed up again.

In between meetings, we drove around Managua. We stopped at a huge statue of the Heroic Guerrilla, which Managuans irreverently call the Incredible Hulk and where American Leftists come to have their pictures taken with hands raised in a clenched-fist salute of solidarity. We saw two places where capitalism has reared its ugly head. One of them might be called the center of people's capitalism. It is the *mercado orientale*, the Eastern Market, not so much a market as a ghetto-sized garage sale, several squalid acres of people trying desperately to acquire worthless *cordobas* by displaying the odd ends of machines and whatever other junk they have begged, borrowed, or stolen on card tables or blankets, in hopes of selling it or bartering it for something else. Contrasted to this bustling penury is the "dollar store," located in an air-conditioned supermarket, where the *comandantes* and their Eastern bloc allies can use American money to purchase everything from Pampers and *Playboy* to diamond jewelry and quadraphonic stereos. We saw a pair of Soviets surreptitiously open and dip their fingers into a jar of Skippy peanut butter and then screw the lid back on.

Our driver took us through endless *barrios* of shanties made of corrugated tin. "Sandinista housing projects," he said, cynically nodding in their direction. Off in the distance, there were what appeared to be some newly constructed stucco houses. We asked them what they were. "New housing, the only new housing in Managua, as a matter of fact." We noted that this at least seemed promising. "Only until you find out who lives there," he said. Who? we asked. "The Cuban soldiers," he replied.

We drove up a rise leading to the American ambassador's residence. Some of the homes looked like estates that had been transplanted from Beverly Hills, the more striking because of the hovels everywhere else. "Somoza's relatives and cronies used to live up here," our driver said. "Today it is home for the *comandantes*." He pointed out the estates confiscated by Tomas Borge, and the sprawling *hacienda* claimed by Bayardo Arce.

The revolutionary double standard exists in matters

other than housing. One of our stops was the U.S. Embassy, a one-story compound fortified to prevent car bomb attacks. Acting U.S. ambassador John Moderno told us that the same *comandantes* who denounce the United States with such great vigor often approach him surreptitiously to ask for visas for friends and relatives. Borge wanted one for a niece in school in Arizona. The firebrand Arce wanted one for his wife so she could visit her sister. Ramon Solis wanted one for his pregnant wife so she could go to New Orleans and have her child in an American hospital, thus giving it the right to American citizenship in the future if the Sandinistas' brave new world didn't work out.

Moderno told amusing stories about official U.S. delegations traveling in Sandinistaland, and one that was not so amusing—how Iowa Senator Thomas Harkin, known to be one of the members of Congress most sympathetic to the FSLN, had come through Managua recently and, as a favor to the government, tried to coerce Violetta Chamorro to reopen *La Prensa* under Sandinista censorship.

Historian Ronald Radosh, who was traveling with us, gave another example of the American Left's activity in behalf of the FSLN. During a previous visit to Managua, Radosh said, he had been in the bar of the Intercontinental when Alejandro Bendana, chief of the foreign ministry, came in with several Sandinistas, accompanied by American University professor William Leogrande (an "expert commentator" for CBS on matters relating to Central America) and Robert Borosage, president of the radical Institute for Policy Studies (and subsequently Jesse Jackson's issues coordinator). Thinking they were unobserved, Leogrande and Borosage had laid out on the table a series of liberal U.S. publications and systematically described how they should be "played" for maximum advantage by the FSLN; they then went over the "reliability" of figures of the American Left such as Michael Harrington, responding to Bendana's request to know who was "with us" and who was "against us" and assuring him that all the Sandinistas had to do to survive in whatever form they chose was to outlast the Reagan administration.*

* This exchange was also witnessed by Nina Shea of the Puebla Institute and Devon Gaffney of the Smith-Richardson Foundation, who were accompanying Radosh.

• • •

Later in the week, we visited members of the July 22 Movement, named to commemorate the killing of demonstrators by Somoza on that day in 1967. Also known as the Mothers' Movement, it is made up of women who have banded together to get sons (and husbands and brothers) out of prison and who demonstrate for human rights even though they have been set upon and beaten by the *turbas*.

Everyone in Managua seems to have a story, and when the women who compose the Mothers' Movement found out that we were coming, they lined up to tell theirs, mistakenly (and pathetically) believing that because we were Americans we had some official connections that would allow us to get their loved ones out of prison. At first, we tried to explain that we had no such power; after a while, however, we just took out pads of paper and began writing down what they told us.

Their stories were different from the tales of atrocity heard on both sides of the civil war, narratives of rape and torture and murder that are all caught up in polemics. These stories were homier and more matter-of-fact, and disturbing for those reasons. A thin woman named Lupe, who was suffering from such a bad case of conjunctivitis that her eyes appeared to be bleeding, described how she had walked hundreds of miles from her village to complain to the authorities about the way her husband had been brutally arrested, transported to Managua, and falsely imprisoned as a *contra* sympathizer. The Sandinista response was to jail her, too, for several weeks, placing her in *El Chipote* prison, in one of the tiger-cage cells, called *la chiquita*, that the Cubans had introduced into Nicaragua.

"They put me in *la chiquita*, this narrow place," the woman said, using her hands to define a space the exact width of her body. "It was completely dark, and I stayed there, standing upright and suffocating in the heat. I could not lie down; I had to stand. I could not move. I was not let out even to relieve myself and had to do so in the box itself. I was in there for several days, my waste going onto my legs and remaining on the floor directly beneath me. Finally, I was released, but my husband was not. I must have help in getting him out. Can you help me?"

There were more stories at our next stop—a youth or-

ganization run by the Social Christian Party. The leader of the
young people gathered there was Fanor Avendano, in his early
twenties, a young man whose brief life summarizes recent Nicaraguan history. At fourteen, he began to fight against Somoza. At sixteen, he was arrested and jailed, one of the
prisoners whose freedom Éden Pastora demanded in his daring
raid on the National Palace in 1978. A supporter of the FSLN
until the revolution succeeded, Avendano now leads an anti-
draft movement of young people who try to evade and frustrate
the press gangs the Sandinistas send out into the night to find
teenagers for their army. "If we were protecting our country I
would gladly serve," Avendano says. "But young people in Nicaragua are being drafted to protect a party, not a country. We
will not fight just to keep the Sandinistas in power."

One of the young women in Avendano's youth movement asked us what we would do if we were in their place.
What aspect of our experience as people who once had protested against our own government could be useful to them?
We tried to explain the difference between America in the
Sixties, when protest was a no-fault exercise, and Nicaragua
today, where the possible consequences were so serious. Then
we told her that one of the things American radicals had
learned was that a movement weak in power but strong in
resourcefulness could create symbolic situations, which would
epitomize the struggle at hand and would cause the whole
world to watch. What would be such a situation in Managua
of the *apertura*? she asked. We said that one thing the young
people in her movement might do was tell the television crews
swarming all over town that they were going to demonstrate
against U.S. imperialism and then, once they had their attention, picket the American *internacionalistas* who gathered
in front of the U.S. Embassy every Tuesday to voice their support for the Communist regime. The young woman and her
friends looked delighted by the idea but fearful of the likely
outcome.

The damage wrought by U.S. Leftists was still on our
minds when we were checking out of the Intercontinental the
next day and ran into an old friend. It was Loni Hancock,
Leftist mayor of Berkeley, whom we had known from our days
there. She was in town with her husband, Tom Bates, a Cali-

fornia state assemblyman, and others in a Berkeley delegation visiting their sister city León and showing solidarity with the Sandinistas. We had seen Hancock at the buffet table that morning and started to make conversation. At first, she was pleasant, but then a look of horror crossed her face. We had seen this look before; it occurred when someone we had known in the past began to relate to us in the old terms and then remembered that we had not kept the faith.

Now the delegation was back in the hotel after a fraternal meeting with Rosario Murillo, wife of Daniel Ortega. Tom Bates came over to where we were standing with a truculent look on his face. He asked why we were there. We told him that we were speaking to the civic opposition of Managua, the people yearning for democracy, whom his delegation had ignored, and that later on we would probably write about what we had experienced. "You're really objective observers!" he sputtered. "No, we're like you," we replied, "not objective at all. But then we're not here supporting a bunch of corrupt *comandantes* who are oppressing their own people, either."

We were still thinking about this encounter a few days after we returned home, when we went to Boulder to give a speech at the University of Colorado. On our way to the auditorium, we had to pass through a small picket line handing out xeroxes of an article about us that Bates and Hancock had already fed to the *People's World*. The article described us as paid government agents, no doubt because of the one-hundred-dollar honorarium we each received from the USIA. The picket line was headed by an ancient man in a baggy suit. We asked who he was. Someone said he was Sender Garlin. The name caused a tiny ripple of memory: Garlin was the man who Whittaker Chambers says recruited him into the Communist Party in 1925. In *Witness*, Garlin is described as having red hair and a sense of humor; now he is gaunt and dour, a Communist version of Father Time.

In our speech, we talked about what we had seen in Managua. Each time we reached a point that seemed to condemn the Sandinistas or their American supporters, Garlin yelled out, in a baritone heckler's voice obviously developed in the Thirties, "What about Letelier?" Finally, we yelled back, "He was killed by Chilean secret agents. What about him?"

Garlin turned his back and gave a significant look to one of the handful of young people for whom he was apparently a guru: "Chileans? He was killed by *American fascism.*"

As we were leaving the auditorium, Garlin came up to us and said, "Why did you *really* go to Nicaragua?" We looked at him and smiled because of the opportunity he had given us: "We went there because it was the middle of the journey."

II.

Lionel Trilling's novel is, of course, only incidentally about the real Whittaker Chambers, who remains—ironically enough—Sender Garlin's only claim on the History he has spent a lifetime chasing. Trilling's achievement in *The Middle of the Journey* was to write about breaking with the radical Left, about ex- and anti-Communists in a context that is primarily about far more important issues—confronting one's passages; learning and relearning how to live a life.

Trilling presented his Chambers character, Gifford Maxim, as the quintessential Leftist, a man defined by "his commitment to the future"—the future in which "reason and virtue will prevail." A supporting context for this commitment, wrote Trilling, was provided by the liberal culture, which was characterized by "an ever more imperious and bitter refusal to consent to the conditioned nature of human existence." The function of the Maxim character in the novel, as a man who had broken with the Communist Party, was to confront the radical illusion "with what he knew, from his experience, of the reality which lay behind the luminous words of the great promise."*

Trilling's own persona in *The Middle of the Journey* is represented by John Laskell, a man of liberal sympathies whose near-fatal illness causes him to see that "there was really no future," that its promise might be useful "as a way of seducing the child to maturity, but maturity itself meant that the future and the present were brought together." Laskell's insight was connected with a new feeling: "that he had the full measure of existence—now, at this very moment, now or never, not at some other and better time that lay ahead."

Put another way, the lesson of mortality that had brought

---

* Lionel Trilling, *The Middle of the Journey*, (New York, 1975).

Laskell to maturity lay in this perception: we are always in the middle of the journey; we just don't always accept it as such.

As with many of our old friends, the idea that the journey would have a middle and an end was not something that occurred to us back in the Sixties, when we were still wholly young and halfway innocent. Then, there were only beginnings—an infinity of them. If one beginning didn't work out, there would always be others that might. This, we eventually came to realize, is the pathology at the heart of Leftism, the desire that makes it truly an infantile disorder. It is why Managua has become a new laboratory for the same old experiments that failed before; why sixty years after Lincoln Steffens hailed the dawn of a new world in Stalin's Russia, the revolutionary tourists in Nicaragua still believe they have seen the future and that it works. Abbie Hoffman's recent lament to the *New York Times* about the trials of being an activist in the 1980s—"It is hard to have an anti-war movement without a war"—is really a wish for yet another beginning by a fifty-four-year-old who ought to know better.

In the Sixties, we were radicals, but radicals who stopped short of the most radical behavior. In part, this hesitation was the result of a generation gap within our leftist generation. Most of us who had come of age in the Fifties could never quite accept the admonition that so appealed to the second wave of activists, who appeared a few years later amidst assassination, war, and racial strife: *"Do it!"* We were more comfortable thinking or talking about it. We might store weapons for groups like the Black Panthers or hide their armed fugitives but "Pick up the gun" never became more for us than a slogan. In an anti-intellectual movement we were closet intellectuals who always held a piece of ourselves apart from what was going on. Some "bourgeois values," such as responsibility for one's acts and respect for the truth—not revolutionary truth but truth beyond considerations of ideology—were hard to get rid of. We never succeeded. That, in brief, is probably why we weren't Leftists anymore when we found ourselves in the middle of the journey.

When we first began to be disillusioned, we tried to cope with what we would eventually see as the intrinsic dishonesty of the Left by sidestepping the issue altogether. Like others who had been on the front lines in the Sixties, we tried to find surcease in the Seventies by shifting attention from History to the intimate self. As writers, we turned from the clotted analyses of Left polemics to narrative; from what should be to what was; from broadsides to biography. For our subjects, we picked dynastic families like the Rockefellers and Kennedys, because they had been part of the fantasy life of our radical generation —the Rockefellers because they controlled the world (or so we thought at the time) and the Kennedys because they had seized the American dream in a way no other group of people had. As we wrote their stories, however, we felt the mythology peel away. We had the feeling of discovering America *de novo*; not the deathscape bodied forth by radical paranoia but a land of dreams that had beckoned to modest families as much as to rich and powerful ones. We saw ourselves too, and we saw the wisdom in Thoreau's witty and perceptive emendation of Emerson's statement that there is no history, only biography: there is really not even biography, the author of *Walden* said, just autobiography.

As the Sixties receded, we also began—tentatively at first —to write about the lives of people we had known at the beginning of the journey: Huey Newton and the Black Panthers, Fay Stender and George Jackson, the Weatherpeople, and others. At this point, we still considered ourselves part of the Left community, even if we had moved away from Left orthodoxy. We didn't realize at this time that once the slide away from an indefensible commitment begins, it is impossible to stop until the momentum of reevaluation has been exhausted and an angle of repose has been reached. Each point at which we did attempt to draw a line that would allow us to "keep the faith" was soon erased. The problem was less the undermining view of Left "politics" we had acquired than the private truths that this new perspective taught.

Like Trilling's John Laskell, we realized that one cannot live the "life of promises" without remaining a child. Life is about imperfection. It is about limits—imposed by time and opportunity and the inherited materials of genetics. We understood that it was simply impossible to live any longer like figures in a socialist romance, buoyed by the Grand March of History and its progressive *finale*. And once we had this realization, we were out of the Left, even if the Left was not entirely out of us.

In part, our leaving was motivated by what we no longer wanted to be. Hatred of America, which for us had coincided with the war in Vietnam, ended with America's defeat in Vietnam. For many of our old friends, it did not. For them, this hatred had become a sort of addiction. They could not do without the rush of seeing themselves as a moral vanguard leading the way to the utopia that America was presumed to block. No matter that in Vietnam (and everywhere else) this utopia had turned out to be an oppressive nightmare, a terror state. The old postures were too comforting to give up; there were always new beginnings—in South Africa, Central America, the Middle East. When we challenged our old friends, they said they were keeping the faith. We saw it as something else, a pathology Arthur Koestler had identified when he wrote, "Clinging to the last shred of the torn illusion, is typical of the cowardice that prevails on the Left."

The hostility directed at us as we moved into the middle of the journey occasioned an equal and opposite reaction on our part: a determination to continue to probe and question, to contest the disputed ground. Perhaps if it had been a new generation embracing Leftism out of its own youthful idealism and ignorance, we would have stood aside and abandoned the field to others. But the revival of the Left at the beginning of the Eighties was led by the same old group—older now and somewhat drearier—who hadn't learned very much over the years except the art of averting their eyes from the consequences of those new beginnings they continued to embrace.

Shortly after the 1984 election, an editor from the *Washington Post Magazine* called to ask us some questions for an article he was writing on young Joe Kennedy. Because we expressed doubts about the Kennedy legacy young Joe had inherited—one of homogenized charisma and cynical liberalism—the conversation turned to our own politics. We mentioned that we supported Reagan and had in fact voted for him. The editor said that he felt "Lefties for Reagan" (as he put it) was a good story, so why didn't we write an article giving our reasons?

In the article we did in fact write, we explained that "casting our ballots for Ronald Reagan was a way of finally saying good-bye to all that—to the self-aggrandizing romance with corrupt Third Worldism; to the casual indulgence of Soviet totalitarianism; to the hypocritical and self-dramatizing anti-Americanism which is the New Left's bequest to mainstream politics." We noted that our vote for the Reagan Doctrine—however inconsistently and ineptly this doctrine may have been applied—was a vote for the containment policy announced by Harry Truman at the beginning of the cold war, a policy that has now paid off with *glasnost* and a possible mellowing of the Soviet dictatorship of Gorbachev, who has declared that "socialism must change or die."

The *Washington Post Magazine* piece was reprinted in dozens of papers, at home and abroad. In a way, it was a man-bites-dog story—the first New Leftists to repudiate the Movement in favor of Ronald Reagan—and could have ended there. But there was a ferocious reaction from our old friends on the Left. Relationships of twenty years were severed overnight. One woman we had both known since 1960 said, "I can see how you might have done something like voting for Reagan, but why didn't you have the decency to keep it to yourselves?" Others went further, as in the case of an old comrade who refused to shake hands with us when we met, walking away with the terse comment, "I don't shake hands with traitors." We were reminded of the obloquy into which radicals of the Thirties like Whittaker Chambers had fallen once they had broken with the Communist Party, their defections regarded not as political acts but as moral transgressions. We were reminded, too, of the waning days of the Sixties Movement— the rococo moment of its embrace of totalitarian styles—when it became fashionable to call those with whom you disagreed "enemies of the people."

There was interest in us on the part of the Right—curiosity, primarily, but also a desire to make us allies. The Right has its religious enthusiasts and its political paranoias. But the surprising thing for us was to discover the paradox Irving Kristol described, that in contemporary America, political labels are out of joint—the liberals have more or less assimilated the ideas of the socialist Left, while the conservatives are really yesterday's liberals:

> . . . the institutions which conservatives wish to preserve
> are, and for two centuries were called, *liberal* institutions,
> i.e., institutions which maximize personal liberty vis-à-vis

a state, a church, or an official ideology. On the other hand, the severest critics of these institutions—those who wish to enlarge the scope of governmental authority indefinitely, so as to achieve ever greater equality at the expense of liberty—are today commonly called "liberals." *

Most conservatives were generous in their attitudes toward us, especially in comparison to our old friends on the Left, who all had a bit of the Torquemada in them. We realized this when we were introduced to Senator Jeremiah Denton by his son Jim, who had offered us his support. Like the rest of the Left, we had ridiculed the elder Denton when we were editors at *Ramparts*, portraying the former Navy pilot on his release from seven years of imprisonment and torture in North Vietnam as a contemptible pawn of Nixon's propaganda. Now, talking to him in his Senate office one afternoon, we were struck by the fact that he was a witty and courteous man whose survival in the Hanoi Hilton was a story of true courage and self-discovery. It also seemed perverse that such an individual should be regularly condemned for a patriotism that was by no means extreme, while our former comrades on the Left, who hated America and wanted to see its global defeat, were extolled for "morally principled" stands.

But if the conservatives we met were far from the "fascists" of the radical psychodrama, we found ourselves unable to become part of their movement. Our own experience was simply too different. The differences surfaced in a clear way one afternoon when we were talking to a pair of speechwriters who worked in the Reagan White House. The conversation turned to presidential phrasemakers. They claimed that "It's morning in America" was a great line. We said that even though we had doubts about the rhetorical partnership between JFK and his amanuensis Theodore Sorensen, we felt that Sorensen's phrase "the long twilight struggle" from the Kennedy inaugural was a far better one. It became obvious after a lengthy discussion that we were really talking about something more than speechwriting rhetoric; it was really a difference in cultural experience and outlook. Conservatives

* Irving Kristol, *Two Cheers for Capitalism* (New York, 1978).

such as these two individuals seemed to need a dose of optimism, whereas we had become fatalists of a sort and were able to see the prospect ahead only as an existential struggle with a dubious outcome.

We decided to try to make contact with others like ourselves who had come out of the New Left. As we talked around, we saw that most of them had paid a high price for their apostasy. The experience of Robert Leiken was typical. A radical at Harvard during the Sixties, he had carried a number of his Leftist assumptions into his work in the Seventies as a Latin American expert. He had been, in fact, a supporter of the Sandinista revolution in its early stages. Repeated visits to Nicaragua convinced him, however, that the country threatened not only its own people but the rest of Central America as well. It was a conclusion honestly arrived at, based on values that he felt were consistent with his socialist commitment, and backed by evidence that was publicly documented in his writings. Nonetheless, Leiken became the object of a vicious hate campaign orchestrated by the Left. He was vilified as a CIA agent and a State Department stooge; attempts were made to get him fired from the Carnegie Endowment and to keep Harvard from offering him an appointment. (The latter campaign was spearheaded by Leiken's one time thesis adviser, a self-identified Communist and former chairman of the Harvard History Department, John Womack.) When Leiken became ill with a persistent virus, the same people who whispered that he was a fascist now spread the rumor that he had AIDS.

After talking to a number of people who'd had experiences like Leiken's, we decided to bring them together publicly for an event that we decided to call the Second Thoughts Conference. It took place in Washington at the Grand Hyatt, in the fall of 1987, shortly after we got back from Nicaragua.

III.

It turned out to be quite an extraordinary event, this two-day gathering. Present were activists who had worked to reform the system in the Sixties, people like Reverend Richard Neuhaus of Clergymen and Laity Concerned About the War and David Hawk of the Cambodia Documentation Commission, who had come back to tell of the Khmer Rouge genocide, only to be attacked for his efforts by the Left; Washington attorney David Ifshin, as president of the National Student Association, had gone to Hanoi and made propaganda broadcasts for the North Vietnamese. Other participants had been part of the heavy infantry of the Movement, who had spelled America with a *k*. Ronald Radosh, a onetime member of the Young Communist League, as a Marxist historian had helped develop the assault on "corporate liberalism." Jeff Herf had been a member of the Revolutionary Youth Movement faction of SDS at the time the Weatherman sect went underground to begin a campaign of terrorism. Now a professor at the Naval War College, he had become an "enemy of the people" in the early Eighties when he published an insightful series of articles in the socialist journal *Telos*, arguing the case in behalf of the placement of U.S. Pershing and Cruise missiles in Europe to counter the Soviet military threat.

Each had come, in the manner of Trilling's Gifford Maxim, to confront the radical tendencies of the time "with what he knew, from his experience, of the reality which lay behind the luminous words of the great promise." But they had not, like Whittaker Chambers, necessarily embraced a religious alternative or the right-wing agenda. Their political backgrounds had been varied, spanning the full range of the radical spectrum, and their destinations were similarly diverse. But in one respect the conclusions they had drawn were identical: The Left had failed them personally, and, worse, it had failed the very people whom it claimed to liberate—the poor and downtrodden, the powerless and oppressed.

Some of the Second Thoughters (as the press called them) had become conservative; some thought of themselves as liberal and some still styled themselves, even, men of the Left. But—and this was another political conclusion they shared—all were now anti-Communist and saw America's democracy as something worth defending. This rediscovery of patriotism was perhaps the most telling common ground of all. It was not a patriotism of the naive flag-waving kind but one dramatized by the memory of how they had abused America during their years of radicalism and of the remarkable tolerance they had discovered during the years of their reunion. Retrospectively, they saw that they had not been powerless—

as their theory had once predicted—but had been able to accomplish tremendous damage (much of it still unrepaired) to America's values and institutions. And it was this insight that motivated them now.

Almost all of those who participated in the conference had experienced some dramatic moment that crystallized the new and disturbing insight they had gotten into the nature of the Left as a destructive agency, a moment that would ultimately cause them to reject what Orwell termed its smelly little orthodoxies. All had been shaken by one tragedy at least—the one that followed the U.S. withdrawal from Southeast Asia and the Left's casual reaction to the catastrophe in which it had been so deeply implicated. This turned out to be something like an archetypal trauma.

But there were more personal reasons as well for their political changes—the slow, glacial action of doubt and self-recognition. For film critic Michael Medved, for instance, a onetime student radical at Yale, it was a growing sense of his identity as a Jew and the realization that Israel might well have been defeated during the Yom Kippur War if not for the backing of U.S. arms. For Michael Novak, a self-identified "Left-wing Catholic" in the Sixties, it was the realization that the attempt of the Left to make politics a religious experience trivialized the spiritual realm and implanted toxic materials in the political one.

The experience black civil rights worker and writer Julius Lester recounted at the conference was one that we all understood. It had come in 1969 during the New Haven trial of seven Black Panther Party members accused of murdering another Party member, Alex Rackley, a time when Lester was writing for the radical magazine *Liberation*. He told other Second Thoughters:

Three Party members admitted their active participation. Yet black and white radicals were demonstrating in the New Haven Green and many articles were published in the radical press demanding that the New Haven Seven be freed. The rationale? It was impossible for blacks to receive justice in America. White sycophancy toward the black movement had set a new standard for madness. I sat down to the typewriter. . . . The editors of *Liberation* held the article for three months. Finally I had a tense meeting with them in which they argued that the prosecution could use my article against the Panthers. Did I want that? How many times during my years in the Movement had someone tried to control my thoughts, my words, or my deeds by saying that such-and-such would not be in the interest of The People; that such-and-such would merely play into the hands of The Enemy; that I was being "individualistic" and that people in the Movement had to "submit to discipline."

There were similarly dramatic moments at the conference. Doan Van Toai, a student in Saigon in the Sixties, told how he had fought against and then been imprisoned by the Thieu regime. A proponent of the "third way" (between Communist totalitarianism and U.S. "imperialism"), he had been imprisoned once again, this time much more harshly and with no chance for appeal, after the Hanoi takeover. Fanor Avendano, the young anti-Somoza socialist we had met in Nicaragua, had come to tell others his story of the persecution of young people under the Sandinista dictatorship. Perhaps the most moving speech came from Fausto Amador Fonseca, stepbrother of the founder of the Sandinista movement, Carlos Fonseca. Fausto had been involved in the founding of the FSLN, but he had become aware that its bloody-mindedness and Soviet loyalties were insurmountable obstacles to its success. As a teenager, he had hitchhiked from Managua to Selma, Alabama, to bear witness with Martin Luther King, at the same time that his stepbrother Carlos was stopping off at the Cuban embassy in Mexico City to make his way to Castro's Havana. The road Fausto chose led him away from the Sandinistas but not away from social conscience. He now leads a nonviolent self-help movement of some thirty thousand poor people in Costa Rica.

In the perhaps exaggerated words of one Washington political observer, the Second Thoughts Conference was "one of the most important events of the Eighties." A number of newspapers in the United States and across the world reported it. Yet the members of the left-wing press, which we had made a special point of inviting, in a remarkable display of mendacity and malice, attempted to prevent their readers from learning what had been said. These writers simply ignored the profound challenge that veteran activists like Doan Van Toai, Fanor Avendano, and Fausto Amador Fonseca—representatives of the principles the New Left had begun by supporting—posed to Leftism. These three remarkable individuals, in fact, were scarcely mentioned in accounts of the Second Thoughts Conference that appeared in the radical press. The Left journalists had come not to report the testimony of the witnesses but to form a verbal firing squad in an effort to destroy their credibility and silence them for good.

The tone was set by Sidney Blumenthal, a reporter for the life-style section of the Washington *Post*. The day after the conference was over, he came out with his attack. Under a banner headline, "Thunder on the New Right," he portrayed the conference as exactly what it was not: a planned conversion rite from one extremist creed to another. Blumenthal then invented an incident to provide his story with a "factual" basis. "In the midst of the choreographed conversions," he wrote, "there was a spontaneous conversion—the wrong way."

Blumenthal's reference was to Bruce Cameron, a panelist, who, as a former congressional lobbyist, had been important in getting the House to vote for *contra* aid in 1986 but had since decided that the *contras* couldn't win. Blumenthal wrote that Cameron's announcement of his change of heart was unexpected and a major embarrassment to us. But Cameron had told him in an earlier interview that we had known about the change weeks before the conference took place. Because his position had integrity (and because support for the *contras* was not a political litmus test for us), we insisted that Cameron participate. When Blumenthal's falsification appeared in print, Cameron said, "I told him the truth, and I don't know why he didn't report it."

Blumenthal set the tone, although past writing such as a puff piece he had done on the left-wing Institute for Policy Studies had somewhat undermined his credibility. This was not the case with Todd Gitlin, onetime SDS president and onetime friend of ours, who had cachet because of a book of his that had just appeared, *The Sixties: Years of Hope, Days of Rage*. Writing in *Tikkun* magazine, he said of those who attended the conference, "Some [came] to confess, some simply to describe and deplore their thought crimes." By calling the radical actions discussed that weekend "thought crimes," Gitlin implied that they were imaginary. He did go on to concede that to some extent things *had* gone wrong during the Sixties:

> Much of the American Left *did* go dreadfully silent about Southeast Asian abominations after 1975, and has *still* failed to work out a principled and practical position on Afghanistan, Ethiopia and the other revolutionary omelets that litter the ground with eggs that stink to high heaven. . . . But it is one thing to come clean about stupidities and quite another to hasten after a new theology of Third World Revolution led, this time, by the anti-communists.

But the concession Gitlin makes is a political gesture rather than a moral one—an attempt to save appearances for the Left rather than to examine its acts. He is basically a mortician for the Movement, and has taken it upon himself to compose the features of its corpse. In fact, it was more than silence that characterized the New Left's response to the genocide its comrades committed in Southeast Asia after 1975, and it was less than an ability to work out principled and practical positions that has shaped its complicity in the atrocities in other revolutionary zones.

For Gitlin, as for most of the Left, acts of complicity in Communist mass slaughter constitute a "stupidity"; but the anti-Communism of people who have second thoughts about this slaughter—now, this is something that is truly dangerous. The litter of eggshells left over from the Sixties may be malodorous, but any attempt honestly to come to grips with the philosophy of the omelet-makers must be righteously resisted. This rhetorical formula—a modest admission of left-wing misdemeanor in order to secure an exoneration for the felony—is the language of moral hypocrisy.

Gitlin's posture in his attack on Second Thoughts is the traditional one of the fellow traveler—*anti-anti-Communism*.

That "meeching phrase," as Lionel Trilling characterized it in his introduction to *The Middle of the Journey*, is the basis for the Left's abiding authority over those liberal intellectuals who hide behind it.

The strongest attacks on the conference, however, came not from former American New Leftists suffused with nostalgia for the old days but from a pair of English expatriates, Christopher Hitchens and Alexander Cockburn, who write for *The Nation*. In their attitudes toward America, these two embody a kind of political anti-matter with respect to those who had discussed their second thoughts that weekend in Washington.

For Hitchens and Cockburn, America is a sort of lost colony—a place where they have come, like deracinated Englishmen of the past, to forge a new identity. Both would say that they are here because America is the "belly of the beast." In fact, however, on arrival they both quickly exchanged their green cards for gold ones. America is the place of choice for them because it *is* an opportunity society, a place where they can practice the art of making it, while pretending not to. All that is necessary are two faces and two sets of clothes: a tux for power cocktails at the Washington *Post* and some tattered Levi's for the campus speaking circuit.

Remembered by Oxford classmates as part of a coterie of self-styled revolutionaries who joked about compiling a list of social democrats to be killed after the revolution, Hitchens is perhaps best known in America for an article in *Harper's* attacking the idea that there is such a phenomenon as terrorism, or that American power ought to resist it. According to Hitchens, terrorism cannot be defined except polemically. American "state terrorism" is thus said to exist coequally with Shiite terrorism, although it is called something different by the brainwashed American media and thus escapes the verbal and political onus that Third World bomb throwers and kidnappers must bear. Because terrorism cannot be taxonomically defined, it does not exist. This is one of those Oxonian debating points that give ivory towers a bad name. The sufficient response was provided by the wit who read Hitchens's article and then shrugged: "I can't define 'red' either, but I know it when I see it."

Hitchens is one of those post-Khrushchev Marxists who is always "critical" of last year's revolution in theory and always in solidarity with next year's in practice. It is a posture that makes for a sort of moral epilepsy. Hitchens watches the Eastern bloc like an enraptured yogi looking for the slightest spasm of the sort of bourgeois democracy and capitalist efficiency he loathes in the West. At the Second Thoughts Conference, *New Republic* editor Martin Peretz, spying Hitchens in the back of the room, observed that some anti-American Englishmen didn't have the decency to report America as foreign correspondents but preferred to settle here and take advantage of this country's generosity while slandering it in their writing. It was a speech that left Hitchens muttering petulantly about "petty xenophobia." But the hit was palpable. Hitchens, like Cockburn, does indeed practice the journalistic equivalent of bulimia: having eaten gluttonously at our table, he then puts a finger down his throat to call up abuse.

Hitchens's attack on the Conference focused on the claims that there was something "implicitly smug" about the name Second Thoughts (because it implied that "revisionism . . . is more thoughtful") and "something unmistakeably sinister about its deliberations." This sinister element turned out to be the participants' determination to raise the issue of loyalties and to stress the importance of commitments to one's country.

In this reaction, as in other things, Hitchens plays second fiddle to Alexander Cockburn, who writes flatteringly of the life-styles of the rich and famous in *Architectural Digest* and *House and Garden*, and scathingly on money and power in *The Nation*. In an obsequious article in the *Tatler*, Hitchens tried to exonerate his friend from charges of hypocritical enrichment and from the notion that he came to America on a trust fund, as his seigneurial manner in dealing with our politics suggests. Alexander's only inheritance was his father, Claud—says Hitchens—whose "memories of the Spanish Civil War taught him to know what side he was on."

Cockburn has indeed modeled his style on that of his father, who was the other side of his generation's coin to Whittaker Chambers. Not long after the Second Thoughts Conference, both father and son came under attack by another

Englishman, Henry Fairlie, in a *New Republic* article archly titled "Fifth Columnist." In a letter of protest to the editor, Alex made a great show of defending his father's "honor," because Fairlie, who had known Claud back in the mother country, wrote that the elder Cockburn had sent back falsified accounts from America when he worked as the London *Times* correspondent here in the Thirties. Although he himself uses evidence as a ductile material, Alex (seconded with spaniel-like fidelity by Hitchens) demanded to know how Fairlie came to this conclusion. Fairlie said that he had it from the horse's mouth: Claud had bragged to him about it himself.

It was a sign of declining times that there should have to be a symposium on Claud Cockburn's journalistic ethics. Lying for the higher purpose was an admitted part of the old chap's idea of journalism. Whatever his attitude toward his days in America, the elder Cockburn certainly did brag about having gone to Barcelona to serve the Soviet cause during the Spanish Civil War. Having long concealed that he was a Communist so that he could write simultaneously for *Time* and *Pravda*, Claud adopted the *nom de guerre* "Frank Pitcairn" to file his war reports for the *Daily Worker*. Acting under the inspiration of Stalin's personal NKVD agent in Republican Spain, he sent back dispatches attacking the anti-Stalinist POUM, which he accused of being run by "agents of Trotsky and Hitler." By smearing the POUM leaders, Cockburn-Pitcairn could be said to have set them up for liquidation by Stalin's agents. It is little wonder that Orwell portrayed him in *Homage to Catalonia* as the very model of the party-lining literary thug.

Later, Cockburn founded *The Week*, a homemade "liberal" gossip sheet that flourished briefly in England as the world was sliding into war. Once again he used his talent to give journalistic aid to Stalin and Hitler. After the Nazi-Soviet Pact in 1939, he trumpeted the "improvement in relations between the German government and the great neutral to the east of it." In issue after issue, he relentlessly portrayed English democracy as no different from Hitler Germany.

> Although there are a great many people in Britain who find it quite reasonable to expect British working people

to put up with any amount of sacrifice rather than to "have Hitler over here," there are many who do not grasp the complementary fact that there are also a large number of people in Germany who think any sacrifice . . . quite reasonable rather than "have Churchill over here" . . . or the allies of the British Government such as Polish generals and landlords.

In 1939, the British government finally closed *The Week* for promoting Nazi war propaganda in the midst of the Blitz. But a year or so later, the publication was allowed to open again; Hitler had invaded the Soviet fatherland, which caused Cockburn to stop equating England and Germany. Now he saw the difference between Hitler and Churchill with sudden clarity and was all for the war. As a journalist, he was exactly the sort of figure Orwell might have had in mind when he wrote: "Don't imagine that for years on end you can make yourself the bootlicker of the Soviet regime or any other regime and then suddenly return to mental decency."

Claud's politics are reflected in those of his son like an inherited genetic defect. Alex postures as an ideologue hacking at the sinews of empire, but he is really a sort of *merdiste* whose heart belongs to dada. As one of his enemies once remarked, "You can tell what the KGB line will be if *Pravda* doesn't arrive on time by looking at Alex's column in *The Nation*."

This is only a slight exaggeration. It was Cockburn who began the drumbeat about how the shooting down of KAL 007 was a U.S. plot, never sympathizing with the victims or condemning the Soviet air command. When *Against All Hope*, Armando Valladares's eloquent prison memoir about his twenty-two years in Castro's gulag, first appeared in America, Cockburn again led the charge, casually repeating the slanders of Cuba's secret police against their former prisoner. He found ways to defend the hijackers of the *Achille Lauro* and the murderers of Leon Klinghoffer, who was pushed over the side of the ship strapped in his wheelchair; he gave moral support to the KGB claim that Anatoly Shcharansky was a CIA agent. Indeed, the only KGB calumny that Alex has not repeated, at least not yet, is that AIDS was caused by germ warfare experiments at Fort Dietrick. Comrades like Edward Said have praised Cockburn rather disingenuously for what they see as his *savage indignatio*, but in fact the pen of the satirist is wielded by the hand of the hack, whose distinctive signature could be seen in his reaction to the Soviet invasion of Afghanistan: "If ever a country deserved rape it's Afghanistan. Nothing but mountains filled with barbarous ethnics with views as medieval as their muskets, and unspeakably cruel too."

In his father's day, Stalinists killed the messenger; today, their moral equivalents have to be content with killing the message. Thus, in his column on the Second Thoughts Conference (which was largely cribbed from Sidney Blumenthal's article in the *Post*), Cockburn informed his *Nation* readers: "The Saturday session had been a sort of masque of the Second Thinkers, an ideological Halloween. . . . But plans had gone awry with the swerve toward Third Thoughts by Bruce Cameron." Next, Cockburn plagiarized the *People's World* charges about our trip to Nicaragua as paid government agents, along with the fantasy that we had traveled through Managua in a "white limousine" provided by the embassy. (It was an aging Ford Ranch Wagon). But his ultimate charge was wholly original. Second Thoughters would, he declared, ultimately "face the dilemma of all renegades living on their memories"—our stories would grow old. "Renegades": one of those words with a fine antique ring to it. In fact, we would have gone out of business already if memories of the Sixties were all we had to talk about. But the subversive duplicities of people like Alex himself, who are engaged in a permanent "class war" against the Western democracies, will provide people like us with steady work for years to come. The final struggle in this generation will not be between the Communists and ex-Communists, as Silone said of his time, but between those who have had second thoughts about their experiences in the Sixties, and those who have not.

IV.

What have we learned by the middle of the journey? In brief, that the radical future is an illusion and that the American present is worth defending; and that we were part of a destructive generation whose work is not over yet.

In the middle of the journey, we feel none of the reassuring certitude we felt at the beginning. Then, defeats were merely momentary setbacks, preludes to the final victory; then, time seemed clearly to be on our side. It is difficult now not to feel almost the exact opposite—that the losses America suffers in the world may be permanent; that the victories democracy achieves may be reversed. In this mood, we find ourselves remembering Whittaker Chambers's remark to his wife when he decided to defect from the Communist cause: "You know, we are leaving the winning world for the losing world." Later, he explained: "I meant that, in the revolutionary conflict of the 20th century, I knowingly chose the side of probable defeat."

Why was this so then, and why should it still seem so now? Why, despite its monstrous record of criminality and failure, should the revolutionary cause continue to prosper? Chambers's answer was that the Left, whose real enemy was liberal society, had nonetheless succeeded in the industrial democracies in making itself appear to be the ally of liberal progress. This was partly because the secular society the Enlightenment created could not satisfy the human longing for belief, which had previously been satisfied by established religion. The Left had stepped in with a creed that could.

The resilience of the Left is primarily a result of the fact that it has built its political religion on liberal precepts; its luminous promise—equality, fraternity, and social justice—is in fact preeminently the promise of the progressive Idea. If the bloodstained reality of the Left is indefensible within the framework provided by liberal principle, its ideals nonetheless seem beyond challenge. This is the basis for the left-wing intellectuals' attack on anti-Communism, as Lionel Trilling pointed out: While they were not actually *for* Communism, they were convinced that "one was morally compromised, turned toward evil and away from good, if one was against it." The impasse was dramatized by the fictional archetypes Trilling created for his novel, the liberal John Laskell and the revolutionary Gifford Maxim:

> Certain things were clear between Laskell and Maxim. It was established that Laskell accepted Maxim's extreme commitment to the future. It was understood between them that Laskell did not accept all of Maxim's ideas. At the same time, Laskell did not oppose Maxim's ideas. One could not oppose them without being illiberal, even reactionary. One would have to have something better to offer and Laskell had nothing better. He could not even imagine what the better ideas would be.

In the years since Trilling's novel and Whittaker Chambers's witness, the relationship between the culture of liberalism and the revolutionary vanguard has not fundamentally changed. The radical Left still cloaks itself in the liberal promise, and liberalism, as it has come to be defined, still accepts the Left as a political ally. This is what makes second thoughts so important. Second thoughts show the malice of ideas that so often masquerade as "progressive." Second thoughts speak to the reality behind the veil. Second thoughts are a reaffirmation of the old liberalism that has become "conservative."

For our own part, philosophically, we are ready to take on third, fourth, and fifth thoughts; but practically, we are more in tune with Chambers's response to the dilemma posed by having chosen the side of probable defeat. "Nothing," he added, "has changed my determination to act as if I were wrong—if only because, in the last instance, men must act on what they believe right, not on what they believe probable."

Shortly after the Second Thoughts Conference, we were in Florida to speak about a book we had written on the Ford dynasty at the Miami Book Fair. The usual suspects had been rounded up for this event, among them Susan Sontag, whose advice "On the Right Way (for Us) to Love the Cuban Revolution" we had once printed in *Ramparts*. She gave her talk before we gave ours. It was a big to-do. She was introduced by her son David Rieff, a book editor, with whom we had chatted briefly before her appearance and who talked possessively about *his* author Mario Vargas Llosa, while at the same time ridiculing the conservative Peruvian novelist's attempts to rally his country against a bloody guerrilla movement.

Rieff presented his mother to the overflow crowd as one of the few living writers marked for immortality. His hyperbolic introduction expanded to tout her "pioneering" use of language and technique—the sort of warm-up that made it seem as if Jacques Derrida were about to step onto the stage. The short story Sontag actually read, in lieu of a lecture, was a rather unexceptional and straightforward account of her own coming of age in Los Angeles during the war, when she and a high school friend had screwed up their courage to go and call on Thomas Mann, then in southern California as an exile from Nazism. The teenaged "I" put down America as vulgar and crass and not having a high culture; an America that let her down because it did not ascend above the middlebrow. It was a good posture for an adolescent but not so good for an adult, and as Sontag answered questions from the audience after her reading, there was not a hint of irony about that former self or its precocious opinions, or any suggestion that those opinions had been modified by age.

We queued up to talk to her afterward while she was signing copies of *The Sontag Reader*. Her son was there too, and as we stood in line he made a thrust at our current politics. "Well, I guess you guys are upset that the *contras* are finished now," he chuckled. Before we could respond, it was our turn with his mother. Thinking that there still might be common ground between us, we told her how courageous her Town Hall speech, "Communism Is Fascism with a Human Face," had been and how much it had meant to us. She gave us a look that was first friendly and then became clouded. We asked why she hadn't followed it by further challenges to the adversary culture's conventional wisdom about America and democracy. "Because I'm really not political," she said curtly. Warming to the occasion, we asked why she had allowed her euphoric 1969 account of Communist North Vietnam to be reprinted without caveat. She shrugged and looked away.

Changing the subject to the story she had just read, we noted that the European high culture she prized so greatly as a teenager and an adult had produced Hitler as well as Mann, while the American culture she so scorned had sustained a democracy that had come to the rescue of Europe, saving it from the barbarisms of the East. She glared at us in exasperation and said, "Look, European culture is just a *better* culture. But I'm not really interested in having this discussion. You're just projecting your own Manichaean politics onto the world. I don't want to enter your world, where you push everything to extremes."

A young woman dressed in black who had been hovering around Sontag even before we appeared hissed, "You guys are really pissing a lot of people off." At this point, David Rieff stepped in and said, "Susan has to go now." As mother and son walked off arm in arm, we realized she was right—we did push things to extremes. But the judgment on us was also a judgment on her and others who understood the political stakes but didn't push things far enough.

Looking Backward

After our experiences in the sixties, we had always said—in the words of the old Phil Ochs song—that we weren't marching anymore. But on May 1, 1989, we found ourselves in the streets of Krakow, massing with the members of Solidarity for an anti-May Day march against the Jaruzelski regime and its Soviet backers, who for once wisely decided to maintain a discreet distance.

It was a chill spring day unfolding under a heavy gray sky that even *felt* leaden—a term chemically as well as climatically accurate, since the Communist industrial enterprise of the past forty-five years had spewed so many pollutants into the air of Poland that the U.S. embassy advised its personnel there to spend as much time as possible indoors.

We were in Krakow with a handful of other former Sixties radicals we had brought to Poland in order to hold a conference, titled Second Thoughts on Communism, at Jagiellonian University. The idea was to get in the face of a still repressive

but teetering government, and to perform what would hope-
fully become a post-mortem before the actual death. We could
sense that the regime which the Soviets had imposed on the
people of Poland (long since rendered illegitimate by the civil
society they had erected around it like the cell wall that encap-
sulates a virus) was beginning to fall with that time-lapse
inevitability of an under-demolition building collapsing from
its foundation up.

We had brought copies of *Destructive Generation* with
us, and the industrious underground press of Krakow immediately began to translate it for publication. The book had just
come out in the United States, to a reception that was both
more and less that we had hoped for. As the first significant dissent about the Sixties from people who had helped define the
decade in action (and were now making sure, by writing histories of the era, that this definition stuck), *Destructive Generation* enjoyed a much wider general readership than we had
anticipated. It was well reviewed, the *Washington Post* going so
far as to call it the most important anti-Communist polemic
since Whittaker Chambers' *Witness*. But our hope, perhaps a
naive one, that the book would help begin a serious self-exami-
nation, on the part of the American Left, of the damage it had
done the country—both during *and* after the Sixties—was
doomed. Magazines of the Left, like *The Nation*, *The New
Republic*, and *Dissent* had trashed the book, attempting to stigmatize us as "renegades" and worse.

The most symptomatic attacks were by *New Republic*
editor Hendrick Hertzberg, and a writer for the magazine, Paul
Berman, who had attacked us previously in New York's *Village
Voice*. In our book, we discussed how we New Leftists had used
the war in Vietnam as an excuse to project our violent fantasies
onto America. Hertzberg took the *we* and made it into a *they*,
suggesting that *Destructive Generation* was sort of a large-scale
Freudian slip by the two of us, whose *we* was narrowly autobiographical, applying only to us, and not at all generic. In his
view, the two of us—apparently acting alone—not only had
held these destructive ideas, but also had participated in the
destructive acts that they inspired. These ideas and acts all were
motivated not by altruism and love, but by nihilism and hate,
Hertzberg wrote—across-the-board hatred of God, country, par-

ents, selves, and all the rest of humanity. Finally, we were guilty of being accessories to murder both before *and* after the fact— not only the faraway murders of nameless Vietnamese and Cambodians after the Communist victory we ardently supported, but also (and much more chillingly) the murders of Bay Area neighbors and co-workers killed by members of the Black Panther Party.

Parroting these ideas, Berman wrote that we were part of a small criminal-intellectual subculture of outlaw Leftism presumably confined to the Bay Area. (In point of fact, Weatherman, America's terrorist underground, originated in the midwest and blew itself up in a New York town house.)

The fact is, of course, that *we* were at the time of *Destructive Generation*'s 1989 publication (and still are, many years later) the *only* individuals deeply involved in the events of the Sixties described in this book to admit how profoundly the God of Leftism had failed us and our country alike. That fateful pronoun "we" refers not just to ourselves, but also to the entire New Left, through whose dark recesses we had walked and whose guilty secrets we knew. Among many whom Hertzberg and Berman—and others of their ilk—continue to admire for having also maintained their silence, and thus protected the sanctity of the Sixties Left, we were the only ones to admit having committed treason of the heart and deed.

The Left's attack on *Destructive Generation* was part of an intellectual offensive on behalf of the myth of the innocence and idealism of the Sixties generation, a myth that would outlast their actual political commitments and take on some of the characteristics of a cover-up as its members attained positions of power and influence. The hypocritical silence of self-proclaimed responsible critics of the Sixties, such as Hertzberg and Berman, about its wretched excesses would become an indictment of them as these excesses continued to have a destructive impact on American life. An appalling instance of this hypocrisy could be seen in a private exchange we had with Hertzberg's friend Todd Gitlin, about our portrayal of the Black Panthers as a murderous gang and symptom of the era. "I don't doubt [the Black Panthers'] vicious, murderous record," Gitlin wrote us in a letter some time after the appearance of *Destructive Generation*, "nor do I attribute it to the depredations of the

FBI." Yet in Gitlin's book *The Sixties,* an account which Hertzberg and others praised for its honesty, and recommended as an antidote to ours, Gitlin's chapter on the Panthers (unchanged, incidentally, in 1992's revised edition) is called "The Bogey of Race" and claims that the Panther threat was merely an invention of the police and other establishment racists.

The attacks from the Left that appeared after *Destructive Generation* was published accused us of racism and xenophobia, and, perhaps worst of all, of being "anti-Sixties." This last term is a giveaway. Our real sin, in the eyes of our former comrades, was to leave the Church of the Left—and those who continue to be part of the congregation (although their worship increasingly takes place more secretly in the form of ever more empty ritual) will never, it appears, forgive us. It is one thing to have doubts; it is another thing to express them in a way that strengthens the enemy. And the enemy, of course, is made up of all those who fail to see themselves as alienated from America.

"You were apologists for Communism," Hendrick Hertzberg told us when *Destructive Generation* had just come out, "and you are apologists for anti-Communism now." Only a stealth radical drawing a handsome salary (of late from *The New Yorker*) could make this statement, which is based on the assumptions that there is no difference between these two commitments, and that the change from professing the one to the other is not potentially meaningful. He certainly would not have dared utter such foolishness if he had been with us in 1989, a few months before the first hammer blows sent shivers through the Berlin Wall. As the anti-May Day march began in Krakow, a member of Solidarity came by our small contingent of Second Thoughters and said, head wagging and hands gesturing in an attempt to aid the speaking of a foreign language, "We want to be like American. Live free or die."

That was the sort of statement, we told each other at the time, that would strike Leftists at home as amusing *kitsch.* And this is exactly why Leftists here in the United States were blindsided by the fall of Communism. The American Left was wrong about the mystique of Communism. They were wrong too about its economic power, its intellectual force, and its responsibility for the Cold War. Cynical about and implacably hostile toward Ronald Reagan, they nonetheless believed that Gorbachev could say "It is morning in the U.S.S.R.," and thus reanimate the spirit of a broken people. At least since 1956, Leftists had always been quick to say that they didn't "believe in" the Soviet Union. Yet most wouldn't have disagreed with a Communist like Angela Davis when she noted that the U.S.S.R. was almost always on the right side of international conflicts. Moreover, they elevated the Soviets indirectly with their theories of moral equivalence which made the U.S.S.R. no worse than the U.S.

As the Cold War came to an end, the American Left found itself afflicted not only with an identity crisis but with a crisis of explanation: What had happened? The Left had no clue, because the idea that the U.S. would be victorious in the Cold War was inconceivable. As Gorbachev practiced *perestroika*, the American Left said he was taking the Revolution back to a position of legitimacy it had before Stalin (and could have again) in figures like Bukharin and Lenin. But in reality, of course, these were only stops on the elevator Gorbachev had boarded that was taking Communist history down to the bottom floor. The Left refused to understand that *de*volution under Gorbachev was not a voluntary attempt to cleanse Communism of its sins, but part of a desperate unraveling which had its own momentum and indeed would not stop until the system itself had disappeared.

With the U.S.S.R. dead, the American Left was reduced to trying to deny America its victory. One claim held that America hadn't won the Cold War; the Soviet Union had lost it—the latter an outcome that would in fact have materialized earlier if cold warriors in the U.S. hadn't given the Stalinists status by means of their hysterical opposition. The other explanation was equally tortured. In defeat, the U.S.S.R. had actually won, the American Left said, because by depriving America of its enemy, it was throwing the U.S. (whose sense of self depended on external enemies) into a possibly fatal identity crisis.

The fall of Communism should have occasioned blushes by those who in the 1970s had proposed theories of convergence, which held that the only way democracy could survive was by shedding its preoccupation with procedural rights and moving toward socialism, with its promise of economic rights, as well. It should have occasioned blushes on the part of those who said that the problem was "actually existing Marxism," and not the theory behind the practice. (This was like Heidegger, hero of the post–Cold War academic Left, saying that the failings of actually existing Nazism did not mitigate the theory of Nazism.)

Most of all, the fall of Communism should have caused all those who had attacked anti-Communism from the late Forties through the late Eighties to hang their heads in shame. As the events in the former U.S.S.R. showed, and the opening of Soviet archives confirmed, most of what the much-vilified anti-Communists had said about a conspiracy of domestic Leftists on behalf of a foreign power was right, and almost everything the progressives had said in defending the conspirators as homegrown idealists was wrong.

The fifty years of war between the West and the U.S.S.R. *had indeed* been precipitated by Stalin's desire to conquer Eastern (and, if possible, Western) Europe. The states that the Soviets had "liberated," to use the language of the Left, *actually were* captive nations, in the more honorable and just phrase of the Right. Moreover, there *was* a pro-Soviet Fifth Column in America, just as Elizabeth Bentley, Whittaker Chambers, and all the other informers reviled by the intellectual elite of the Fifties had said. Robert Oppenheimer *did* allow himself to be used by Soviet spies. Julius Rosenberg *did* pass information about the atomic bomb to his Soviet contact. Treason *was* committed by the American Left in the Forties and Fifties for Moscow, and in the Sixties and Seventies for Havana and Hanoi. And the New Left's continuing alienation from the side of the West in the Cold War *did* resurface in the Eighties when what was left of the New Left appeared for an encore by pushing for a nuclear freeze, and other demands of the so-called peace movement. Had they succeeded, they more than likely would have consolidated Soviet nuclear hegemony in Europe, and provided its dictators with a respite.

Progressives should blush most of all for their treatment of Ronald Reagan, the very symbol of their political animus. They said that he was starting World War III by pushing the

U.S.S.R. into a corner from which it would have no alternative but to lash out in an attempt to protect itself. They said that he was destroying the possibility of détente by using terms such as "Evil Empire." But Reagan was right and they were wrong. With the help of a counter-establishment of policy-makers from the Scoop Jackson wing of the Democratic Party, he picked up the fallen standard of the Truman Doctrine, which had been trampled in Vietnam. But Reagan did not seek merely to contain Communism. Through the Reagan Doctrine, he supported wars of liberation in the outposts of the expanding Soviet Empire. And, despite the attempts of the Left to hamstring his policies, Reagan fought the Cold War to a successful conclusion. In the end, Communism wound up exactly where he said it would—on the ash heap of history.

Reagan was right. Harry Truman was right. Whittaker Chambers was right. The Left and its liberal allies were *wrong*. What we said earlier in *Destructive Generation* is, if anything, even truer six years (and counting) later, after the fall of Communism: The Left is malign because it never draws up a balance sheet of its commitments, let alone a profit-and-loss statement. It just moves on to the next target of opportunity. Leftists perversely turn Santayana's famous warning inside out: They refuse to learn from their history precisely because they *want* to repeat it.

So it was that the Left made a swift transition from the Cold War to the culture wars, from Marxism to multiculturalism. Having failed to burn down the universities in the Sixties, radicals went back to graduate school in the Seventies in response to German New Leftist Rudi Dutschke's call for a long march through the institutions—and now they sit on tenure committees, making sure that only those who think as they do are hired.

The universities have become the last refuge of the anti-Americanism that is one of the enduring legacies of the Sixties. In the controlled environment of the academy, weird intellectual growths have been cultured. One dominant motif of the contemporary university is a deconstructionism that casts doubt on the notion of truth; it has its origins in Paul DeMan's attempt to rub out the empiricism of his Nazi associations.

Another motif is a race–class–gender theory that tries to create a post-Stalin version of the proletariat made up of victim groups in a situation where power is the only reality, and the idea of American nationhood is an act of violence achieved on the backs of the poor and oppressed. These two tendencies—a skeptical nihilism on the one hand and a vulgar Marxist-identity politics on the other—collaborate in the intellectual equivalent of the Hitler–Stalin pact to produce an intellectual wasteland and a politics of grievance which combine to both covertly and overtly attack democratic values and institutions.

Under the new dispensation, the contemporary university has become a maze of double standards and special preferences. With its contempt for individualism, and its insistence that the *group* is the basic unit of society, the tenured Left has infused the university with a kind of apartheid secessionism. It has become a mad laboratory for the creation of racism, with more talk about blood quantum and ethnic membership on the campus today than at any time since the Nuremberg Laws.

But (as the history of Marxism attests) ideas have consequences. Even false and crackpot ideas do. Professor Leonard Jeffries' racist notions about the role of melanin in human affairs, and about the inferiority of Ice People to Sun People, may be perverse inversions of KKK white-supremacy theory, but—legitimized by the university and transmitted to a new generation of black leaders—they factor nevertheless into the increasing social lunacy of black rage. If the black community did not have its own race-conscious Studies centers in elite institutions across the nation, would hundreds of thousands of college-educated black men have marched behind a racial demagogue like Louis Farrakhan? Having lost its class war, the Left, through its *kulturkampf,* is dangerously close to endorsing race war.

We did, in fact, get some things wrong in *Destructive Generation.* For instance, having been part of the Left and seen its obdurate hostility and implacable will, we assumed that we were facing a long twilight struggle on the international scene that would continue to define domestic politics. We should have had more faith in the staying power of democracy and democratic values. We also underestimated the ability of the Left to wage a culture war after its international commitments had been revealed to be bankrupt. The Sixties created the victim groups that now tear at the fabric of American enterprise. That they could have so quickly acquired a legitimacy in locales such as the university, and that their assault on the notion of *e pluribus unum* could continue to be so successful, are ominous developments requiring close surveillance at the very least.

Our "wrongs" notwithstanding, we were right about the mendacity of the Left, and its hatred of America. We saw Pandora's box being opened in the Sixties. We are still committed to describing the bizarre and dangerous contents as they escape confinement, and to helping close the lid once again. True, this commitment puts us in the trenches of the culture war—but it has given us one thing that we never expected when we began our first involvement in the New Left some thirty-five years ago: steady work.

NOTES
AND
ACKNOWLEDGMENTS

"Requiem for a Radical" is based on taped interviews with principals, including Marvin and Oriane Stender, Charles Garry, Greg Armstrong, Betty Ann Bruno, Rose Linsky, Sanne DeWitt, Ying Lee Kelley, Ezra Hendon, John Irwin, Eve Pell, Doron Weinberg, Patti Roberts, Barbara Price, Roberta Brooks, Lee Halterman, "Katherine," Linda Castro, Howard Janssen, Mary Millman, and Thomas Broome. Other sources include George Jackson, *Soledad Brother* and *Blood in My Eye*; Joseph Durden-Smith, *Who Killed George Jackson?*; Gregory Armstrong, *The Dragon Has Come*; and Min Yee, *The Melancholy History of Soledad Prison*. "Doing It" is based on taped interviews with members of the Weather Bureau and the Underground, including Billy Ayers, Mark Rudd, James Mellen, Jeff Jones, Eleanor Stein, Gerry Long, Rick Ayers, Melody Ayers, Steve Tappis, Martin Kenner, "Laurie Meisner," Sue LeGrand, and Jane Alpert. Printed sources include Harold Jacobs, *Weatherman*; Thomas Powers, *Diana*; Jane Alpert, *Growing Up Underground*; and Kirkpatrick Sale, *SDS*. "Post-Vietnam Syndrome" is based on interviews with Luther and Mona Lisa Brock, Steve Bosshard, and members of the San Francisco Police Department.

We wish to express our appreciation to the Lynde and Harry Bradley Foundation, and the John M. Olin Foundation for their support. Thanks, too, to Jim Denton of the National Forum Foundation for offering friendship and sanctuary, and to Jim Silberman of Summit Books, who believed that *Destructive Generation* should be published although he personally took exception to some of its conclusions.

"Baddest" is based on extensive firsthand observation, confidential taped interviews with former Black Panthers, and interviews with Professors Gary Lease, Bob Trivers, and Page Smith of the University of California, Santa Cruz. Printed sources include Huey P. Newton, *Revolutionary Suicide*; Bobby Seale, *Seize the Time* and *A Lonely Rage*; Kenneth O'Reilly, *Racial Matters*; Edward J. Epstein, "The Panthers and the Police," *The New Yorker*, February 13, 1971; Kate Coleman with Paul Avery, "The Party's Over," *New Times*, July 10, 1978; Lowell Bergman and David Weir, "Revolution on Ice," *Rolling Stone*, September 9, 1976; Kate Coleman, "Souled Out," *New West*, May 19, 1980; Ken Kelley, "Huey," East Bay *Express*, September 15, 1989.

Index